interchange

FIFTH EDITION

3

Student's Book

Jack C. Richards
with Jonathan Hull and Susan Proctor

WITH ONLINE SELF-STUDY

CAMBRIDGE
UNIVERSITY PRESS

CAMBRIDGE
UNIVERSITY PRESS

University Printing House, Cambridge CB2 8BS, United Kingdom

One Liberty Plaza, 20th Floor, New York, NY 10006, USA

477 Williamstown Road, Port Melbourne, VIC 3207, Australia

4843/24, 2nd Floor, Ansari Road, Daryaganj, Delhi – 110002, India

79 Anson Road, #06–04/06, Singapore 079906

Cambridge University Press is part of the University of Cambridge.

It furthers the University's mission by disseminating knowledge in the pursuit of education, learning and research at the highest international levels of excellence.

www.cambridge.org
Information on this title: www.cambridge.org/9781316624050

First published 2005
Second edition 2013
20 19 18 17 16 15 14 13 12 11 10 9 8 7 6 5 4 3 2 1

Printed in Malaysia by Vivar Printing

A catalogue record for this publication is available from the British Library

ISBN 9781316620519 Student's Book 3 with Online Self-Study
ISBN 9781316620533 Student's Book 3A with Online Self-Study
ISBN 9781316620540 Student's Book 3B with Online Self-Study
ISBN 9781316620557 Student's Book 3 with Online Self-Study and Online Workbook
ISBN 9781316620564 Student's Book 3A with Online Self-Study and Online Workbook
ISBN 9781316620588 Student's Book 3B with Online Self-Study and Online Workbook
ISBN 9781316622766 Workbook 3
ISBN 9781316622773 Workbook 3A
ISBN 9781316622797 Workbook 3B
ISBN 9781316622803 Teacher's Edition 3 with Complete Assessment Program
ISBN 9781316622308 Class Audio CDs 3
ISBN 9781316624050 Full Contact 3 with Online Self-Study
ISBN 9781316624074 Full Contact 3A with Online Self-Study
ISBN 9781316624098 Full Contact 3B with Online Self-Study
ISBN 9781316622322 Presentation Plus 3

Additional resources for this publication at www.cambridge.org/interchange

Informed by teachers

Teachers from all over the world helped develop *Interchange Fifth Edition*. They looked at everything – from the color of the designs to the topics in the conversations – in order to make sure that this course will work in the classroom.
We heard from 1,500 teachers in:

- Surveys
- Focus Groups
- In-Depth Reviews

We appreciate the help and input from everyone. In particular, we'd like to give the following people our special thanks:

Jader Franceschi, **Actúa Idiomas,** Bento Gonçalves, Rio Grande do Sul, Brazil

Juliana Dos Santos Voltan Costa, **Actus Idiomas,** São Paulo, Brazil

Ella Osorio, **Angelo State University,** San Angelo, TX, US

Mary Hunter, **Angelo State University,** San Angelo, TX, US

Mario César González, **Angloamericano de Monterrey, SC,** Monterrey, Mexico

Samantha Shipman, **Auburn High School,** Auburn, AL, US

Linda, **Bernick Language School,** Radford, VA, US

Dave Lowrance, **Bethesda University of California,** Yorba Linda, CA, US

Tajbakhsh Hosseini, **Bezmialem Vakif University,** Istanbul, Turkey

Dilek Gercek, **Bil English,** Izmir, Turkey

Erkan Kolat, **Biruni University, ELT,** Istanbul, Turkey

Nika Gutkowska, **Bluedata International,** New York, NY, US

Daniel Alcocer Gómez, **Cecati 92,** Guadalupe, Nuevo León, Mexico

Samantha Webb, **Central Middle School,** Milton-Freewater, OR, US

Verónica Salgado, **Centro Anglo Americano,** Cuernavaca, Mexico

Ana Rivadeneira Martínez and Georgia P. de Machuca, **Centro de Educación Continua – Universidad Politécnica del Ecuador,** Quito, Ecuador

Anderson Francisco Guimerães Maia, **Centro Cultural Brasil Estados Unidos,** Belém, Brazil

Rosana Mariano, **Centro Paula Souza,** São Paulo, Brazil

Carlos de la Paz Arroyo, Teresa Noemí Parra Alarcón, Gilberto

Bastida Gaytan, Manuel Esquivel Román, and Rosa Cepeda Tapia, **Centro Universitario Angloamericano,** Cuernavaca, Morelos, Mexico

Antonio Almeida, **CETEC,** Morelos, Mexico

Cinthia Ferreira, **Cinthia Ferreira Languages Services,** Toronto, ON, Canada

Phil Thomas and Sérgio Sanchez, **CLS Canadian Language School,** São Paulo, Brazil

Celia Concannon, **Cochise College,** Nogales, AZ, US

Maria do Carmo Rocha and CAOP English team, **Colégio Arquidiocesano Ouro Preto – Unidade Cônego Paulo Dilascio,** Ouro Preto, Brazil

Kim Rodriguez, **College of Charleston North,** Charleston, SC, US

Jesús Leza Alvarado, **Coparmex English Institute,** Monterrey, Mexico

John Partain, **Cortazar,** Guanajuato, Mexico

Alexander Palencia Navas, **Cursos de Lenguas, Universidad del Atlántico,** Barranquilla, Colombia

Kenneth Johan Gerardo Steenhuisen Cera, Melfi Osvaldo Guzman Triana, and Carlos Alberto Algarín Jiminez, **Cursos de Lenguas Extranjeras Universidad del Atlantico,** Barranquilla, Colombia

Jane P Kerford, **East Los Angeles College,** Pasadena, CA, US

Daniela, **East Village,** Campinas, São Paulo, Brazil

Rosalva Camacho Orduño, **Easy English for Groups S.A. de C.V.,** Monterrey, Nuevo León, Mexico

Adonis Gimenez Fusetti, **Easy Way Idiomas,** Ibiúna, Brazil

Eileen Thompson, **Edison Community College,** Piqua, OH, US

Ahminne Handeri O.L Froede, **Englishouse escola de idiomas,** Teófilo Otoni, Brazil

Ana Luz Delgado-Izazola, **Escuela Nacional Preparatoria 5, UNAM,** Mexico City, Mexico

Nancy Alarcón Mendoza, **Facultad de Estudios Superiores Zaragoza, UNAM,** Mexico City, Mexico

Marcilio N. Barros, **Fast English USA,** Campinas, São Paulo, Brazil

Greta Douthat, **FCI Ashland,** Ashland, KY, US

Carlos Lizárraga González, **Grupo Educativo Anglo Americano, S.C.,** Mexico City, Mexico

Hugo Fernando Alcántar Valle, **Instituto Politécnico Nacional, Escuela Superior de Comercio y Administración-Unidad Santotomás, Celex Esca Santo Tomás,** Mexico City, Mexico

Sueli Nascimento, **Instituto Superior de Educação do Rio de Janeiro,** Rio de Janeiro, Brazil

Elsa F Monteverde, **International Academic Services,** Miami, FL, US

Laura Anand, **Irvine Adult School,** Irvine, CA, US

Prof. Marli T. Fernandes (principal) and Prof. Dr. Jefferson J. Fernandes (pedagogue), **Jefferson Idiomas,** São Paulo, Brazil

Herman Bartelen, **Kanda Gaigo Gakuin,** Tokyo, Japan

Cassia Silva, **Key Languages,** Key Biscayne, FL, US

Sister Mary Hope, **Kyoto Notre Dame Joshi Gakuin,** Kyoto, Japan

Nate Freedman, **LAL Language Centres,** Boston, MA, US

Richard Janzen, **Langley Secondary School,** Abbotsford, BC, Canada

Christina Abel Gabardo, **Language House,** Campo Largo, Brazil
Ivonne Castro, **Learn English International,** Cali, Colombia
Julio Cesar Maciel Rodrigues, **Liberty Centro de Línguas,** São Paulo, Brazil
Ann Gibson, **Maynard High School,** Maynard, MA, US
Martin Darling, **Meiji Gakuin Daigaku,** Tokyo, Japan
Dax Thomas, **Meiji Gakuin Daigaku,** Yokohama, Kanagawa, Japan
Derya Budak, **Mevlana University,** Konya, Turkey
B Sullivan, **Miami Valley Career Technical Center International Program,** Dayton, OH, US
Julio Velazquez, **Milo Language Center,** Weston, FL, US
Daiane Siqueira da Silva, Luiz Carlos Buontempo, Marlete Avelina de Oliveira Cunha, Marcos Paulo Segatti, Morgana Eveline de Oliveira, Nadia Lia Gino Alo, and Paul Hyde Budgen, **New Interchange-Escola de Idiomas,** São Paulo, Brazil
Patrícia França Furtado da Costa, Juiz de Fora, Brazil
Patricia Servín
Chris Pollard, **North West Regional College SK,** North Battleford, SK, Canada
Olga Amy, **Notre Dame High School,** Red Deer, Canada
Amy Garrett, **Ouachita Baptist University,** Arkadelphia, AR, US
Mervin Curry, **Palm Beach State College,** Boca Raton, FL, US
Julie Barros, **Quality English Studio,** Guarulhos, São Paulo, Brazil
Teodoro González Saldaña and Jesús Monserrta Mata Franco, **Race Idiomas,** Mexico City, Mexico
Autumn Westphal and Noga La`or, **Rennert International,** New York, NY, US
Antonio Gallo and Javy Palau, **Rigby Idiomas,** Monterrey, Mexico Tatiane Gabriela Sperb do Nascimento, **Right Way,** Igrejinha, Brazil
Mustafa Akgül, **Selahaddin Eyyubi Universitesi,** Diyarbakır, Turkey
James Drury M. Fonseca, **Senac Idiomas Fortaleza,** Fortaleza, Ceara, Brazil
Manoel Fialho S Neto, **Senac – PE,** Recife, Brazil
Jane Imber, **Small World,** Lawrence, KS, US
Tony Torres, **South Texas College,** McAllen, TX, US
Janet Rose, **Tennessee Foreign Language Institute,** College Grove, TN, US
Todd Enslen, **Tohoku University,** Sendai, Miyagi, Japan
Daniel Murray, **Torrance Adult School,** Torrance, CA, US
Juan Manuel Pulido Mendoza, **Universidad del Atlántico,** Barranquilla, Colombia
Juan Carlos Vargas Millán, **Universidad Libre Seccional Cali,** Cali (Valle del Cauca), Colombia
Carmen Cecilia Llanos Ospina, **Universidad Libre Seccional Cali,** Cali, Colombia
Jorge Noriega Zenteno, **Universidad Politécnica del Valle de México,** Estado de México, Mexico
Aimee Natasha Holguin S., **Universidad Politécnica del Valle de México UPVM,** Tultitlàn Estado de México, Mexico
Christian Selene Bernal Barraza, **UPVM Universidad Politécnica del Valle de México,** Ecatepec, Mexico
Lizeth Ramos Acosta, **Universidad Santiago de Cali,** Cali, Colombia
Silvana Dushku, **University of Illinois Champaign,** IL, US
Deirdre McMurtry, **University of Nebraska – Omaha,** Omaha, NE, US
Jason E Mower, **University of Utah,** Salt Lake City, UT, US
Paul Chugg, **Vanguard Taylor Language Institute,** Edmonton, Alberta, Canada
Henry Mulak, **Varsity Tutors,** Los Angeles, CA, US
Shirlei Strucker Calgaro and Hugo Guilherme Karrer, **VIP Centro de Idiomas,** Panambi, Rio Grande do Sul, Brazil
Eleanor Kelly, **Waseda Daigaku Extension Centre,** Tokyo, Japan
Sherry Ashworth, **Wichita State University,** Wichita, KS, US
Laine Bourdene, **William Carey University,** Hattiesburg, MS, US
Serap Aydın, Istanbul, Turkey
Liliana Covino, Guarulhos, Brazil
Yannuarys Jiménez, Barranquilla, Colombia
Juliana Morais Pazzini, Toronto, ON, Canada
Marlon Sanches, Montreal, Canada

Additional content contributed by Kenna Bourke, Inara Couto, Nic Harris, Greg Manin, Ashleigh Martinez, Laura McKenzie, Paul McIntyre, Clara Prado, Lynne Robertson, Mari Vargo, Theo Walker, and Maria Lucia Zaorob.

Classroom Language Student questions

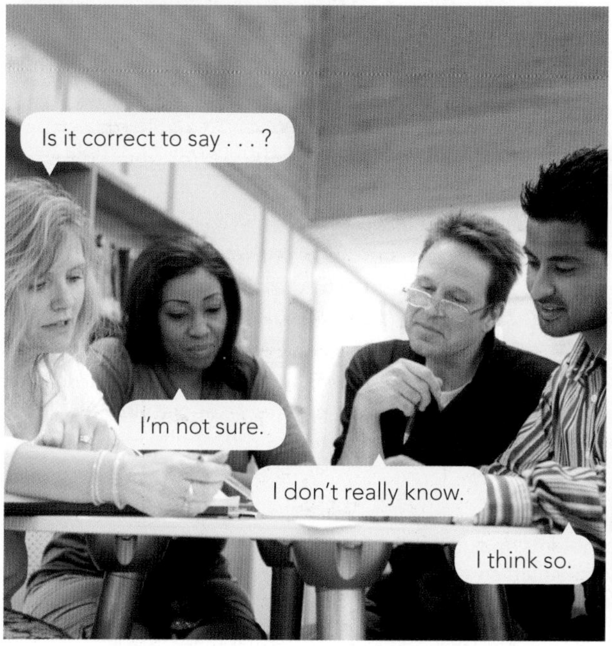

Plan of Book 3

Titles/Topics	Speaking	Grammar
UNIT 1 PAGES 2–7 **That's my kind of friend!** Personality types and qualities; relationships; likes and dislikes	Describing personalities; expressing likes and dislikes; agreeing and disagreeing; complaining	Relative pronouns as subjects and objects; *it* clauses + adverbial clauses with *when*
UNIT 2 PAGES 8–13 **Working 9 to 5** Jobs; career benefits; job skills; summer jobs	Talking about possible careers; describing jobs; deciding between two jobs	Gerund phrases as subjects and objects; comparisons with adjectives, nouns, verbs, and past participles
PROGRESS CHECK PAGES 14–15		
UNIT 3 PAGES 16–21 **Lend a hand.** Favors; formal and informal requests; messages	Making direct and indirect requests; accepting and declining requests	Requests with modals, *if* clauses, and gerunds; indirect requests
UNIT 4 PAGES 22–27 **What happened?** The media; news stories; exceptional events	Narrating a story; describing events and experiences in the past	Past continuous vs. simple past; past perfect
PROGRESS CHECK PAGES 28–29		
UNIT 5 PAGES 30–35 **Expanding your horizons** Cultural comparisons and culture shock; moving abroad; emotions; customs; tourism and travel abroad	Talking about moving abroad; expressing emotions; describing cultural expectations; giving advice	Noun phrases containing relative clauses; expectations: *the custom to,* (*not*) *supposed to, expected to,* (*not*) *acceptable to*
UNIT 6 PAGES 36–41 **That needs fixing.** Consumer complaints; everyday problems; problems with electronics; repairs	Describing problems; making complaints; explaining something that needs to be done	Describing problems with past participles as adjectives and with nouns; describing problems with *need* + gerund, *need* + passive infinitive, and *keep* + gerund
PROGRESS CHECK PAGES 42–43		
UNIT 7 PAGES 44–49 **What can we do?** The environment; global challenges; current issues	Identifying and describing problems; coming up with solutions	Passive in the present continuous and present perfect; prepositions of cause; infinitive clauses and phrases
UNIT 8 PAGES 50–55 **Never stop learning.** Education; learner choices; strategies for learning; life skills	Asking about preferences; discussing different skills to be learned; talking about learning methods; talking about life skills	*Would rather* and *would prefer*; *by* + gerund to describe how to do things
PROGRESS CHECK PAGES 56–57		

Pronunciation/Listening	Writing/Reading	Interchange Activity
Linked sounds Listening for descriptions of people; listening for opinions	Writing a description of a good friend "Social Networks That Aren't for Everyone": Reading about unusual social networking sites	"Personality quiz": Interviewing a classmate to find out about personality characteristics PAGE 114
Stress with compound nouns Listening to the good and bad parts of a job; listening for complaints	Writing about two career choices "The Perfect Workplace?": Reading about different types of workplaces	"Networking": Comparing people's careers and personalities to make a seating chart for a dinner party PAGE 115
Unreleased consonants Listening to people making, accepting, and declining requests	Writing a message with requests "Can You Tell It Like It Is?": Reading about talking to friends about difficult topics	"Beg and borrow": Asking classmates to borrow items; lending or refusing to lend items PAGE 116
Intonation in complex sentences Listening to news stories; listening to messages and a podcast	Writing a personal account "Believing More Than We Should": Reading about the reliability of online content	"Spin a yarn": Inventing a story from three random elements PAGE 117
Word stress in sentences Listening for information about living abroad; listening to opinions about customs	Writing a pamphlet for tourists "Culture Shock": Reading about moving to another country	"Cultural dos and taboos": Comparing customs in different countries PAGE 118
Contrastive stress Listening to complaints; listening to people exchange things in a store; listening to a conversation about a "throwaway culture"	Writing a critical online review "Ask the Fixer!": Reading about a problem with a ride-sharing service	"Home makeover": Comparing problems in two pictures of an apartment PAGES 119, 120
Reduction of auxiliary verbs Listening to environmental problems; listening for solutions	Writing a post on a community website "Turning an Invasion Into an Advantage": Reading about a creative solution to lionfish on St. Lucia	"Take action!": Choosing an issue and deciding on an effective method of protest; devising a strategy PAGE 121
Intonation in questions of choice Listening to a conversation with a guidance counselor; listening for additional information	Writing about a skill "Are You Studying the 'Right' Way?": Reading about different studying styles	"Making choices": Choosing between different things you want to learn PAGE 122

Titles/Topics	Speaking	Grammar
UNIT 9 PAGES 58–63		
Getting things done Everyday services; recommendations; self-improvement	Talking about things you need to have done; asking for and giving advice or suggestions	Get or have something done; making suggestions with modals + verbs, gerunds, negative questions, and infinitives
UNIT 10 PAGES 64–69		
A matter of time Historic events and people; biography; the future	Talking about historic events; talking about things to be accomplished in the future	Referring to time in the past with adverbs and prepositions: *during, in, ago, from…to, for, since*; predicting the future with *will*, future continuous, and future perfect
PROGRESS CHECK PAGES 70–71		
UNIT 11 PAGES 72–77		
Rites of passage Milestones and turning points; behavior and personality; regrets	Describing milestones; describing turning points; describing regrets and hypothetical situations	Time clauses: *before, after, once, the moment, as soon as, until, by the time*; expressing regret with *should (not) have* + past participle; describing hypothetical situations with *if* clauses + past perfect and *would/could have* + past participle
UNIT 12 PAGES 78–83		
Keys to success Qualities for success; successful businesses; advertising	Describing qualities for success; giving reasons for success; interviewing for a job; talking about ads and slogans	Describing purpose with infinitive clauses and infinitive clauses with *for*; giving reasons with *because, since, because of, for, due to*, and *the reason*
PROGRESS CHECK PAGES 84–85		
UNIT 13 PAGES 86–91		
What might have been Pet peeves; unexplained events; reactions; complicated situations and advice	Drawing conclusions; offering explanations; describing hypothetical events; giving advice for complicated situations	Past modals for degrees of certainty: *must (not) have, may (not) have, might (not) have, could (not) have*; past modals for judgments and suggestions: *should (not) have, could (not) have, would (not) have*
UNIT 14 PAGES 92–97		
Creative careers Movies; media and entertainment professions; processes	Describing how something is done or made; describing careers in film, TV, publishing, gaming, and music	The passive to describe process with *is/are* + past participle and modal + *be* + past participle; defining and non-defining relative clauses
PROGRESS CHECK PAGES 98–99		
UNIT 15 PAGES 100–105		
A law must be passed! Recommendations; opinions; community issues; controversial topics	Giving opinions for and against controversial topics; offering a different opinion; agreeing and disagreeing	Giving recommendations and opinions with passive modals: *should be, ought to be, must be, has to be, has got to be*; tag questions for opinions
UNIT 16 PAGES 106–111		
Reaching your goals Challenges; accomplishments; goals; inspirational sayings	Giving opinions about inspirational sayings; talking about the past and the future	Accomplishments with the simple past and present perfect; goals with the future perfect and *would like to have* + past participle
PROGRESS CHECK PAGES 112–113		
GRAMMAR PLUS PAGES 132–150		

Pronunciation/Listening	Writing/Reading	Interchange Activity
Sentence stress Listening to New Year's resolutions	Writing a message of advice "Improving the World – One Idea at a Time": Reading about young scientist Jack Andraka	"Absolutely not!": Discussing different points of view of parents and their children PAGE 123
Syllable stress Listening for dates and time periods; listening to predictions	Writing a biography "Looking Into the Future": Reading about futurists and their predictions for the year 2050	"History buff": Taking a history quiz PAGE 124, 126
Reduction of *have* and *been* Listening to descriptions of important events; listening to regrets and explanations	Writing a message of apology "Stella's Answers": Reading about a conflict with a friend and advice on how to fix it	"Good choices, bad choices": Playing a board game to talk about how you were and could have been PAGE 125
Reduced words Listening for features and slogans	Writing a TV or web commercial "Brain Invasion: Why We Can't Forget Some Ads": Reading about what makes some advertisements memorable	"Advertising taglines": Creating a slogan and logo for a product PAGE 127
Reduction in past modals Listening to explanations; listening for the best solution	Writing about a complicated situation "Messages from Outer Space, or a Leaking Pipe?": Reading about unexplained events	"Think of the possibilities!": Drawing possible conclusions about situations PAGE 128
Review of stress in compound nouns Listening for parts of a movie	Writing about a process "The Truth About Being a Film Extra": Reading about what the job of film extra is like	"Celebrities": Guessing famous people from clues PAGE 129
Intonation in tag questions Listening for solutions to everyday annoyances; listening to issues and opinions	Writing a persuasive essay "That's Plagiarism?": Reading about plagiarism in the digital age	"On the wrong side of the law": Deciding on punishments for common offenses PAGE 130
Stress and rhythm Listening to past obstacles and how they were overcome; listening for people's goals for the future	Writing a personal statement for an application "Soaring Like an Eagle": Reading about the athlete Michael Edwards	"A digital nomad": Taking a quiz about working remotely PAGES 131

1 That's my kind of friend!

- Discuss personalities and qualities
- Discuss likes and dislikes

1 SNAPSHOT

ROMANCE AND MARRIAGE IN THE UNITED STATES

When choosing a spouse or partner, single Americans want to find someone with . . .

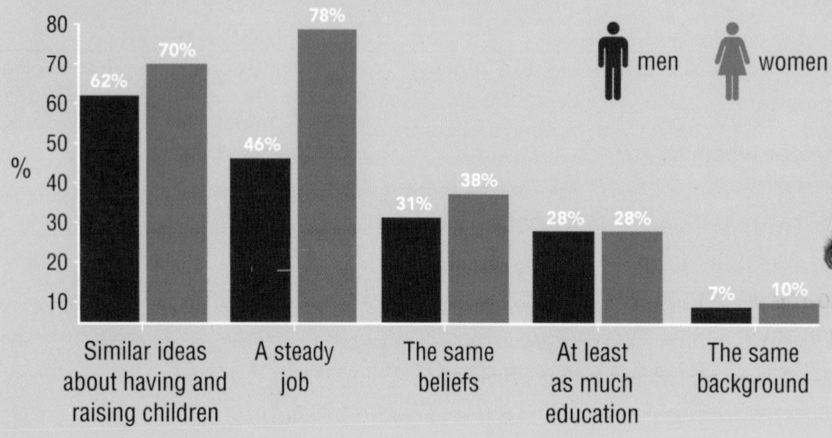

In your opinion, which of the things above are most important to look for in a partner? Did any of the items surprise you? Which? Why? Are there other important qualities missing from the list?

2 CONVERSATION What *are* you looking for?

A Listen and practice.

Joe: What are you doing?
Roy: I'm setting up my profile for this online dating site. I have to describe the kind of person I'm looking for.
Joe: I see. And what are you looking for?
Roy: Oh, I like people who aren't too serious and who have a good sense of humor. You know, someone I can have fun with.
Joe: OK. Uh, what else?
Roy: Well, I'd like someone I have something in common with – who I can talk to easily.
Joe: I think I know just the girl for you: my cousin Lisa. She's a lot of fun and she loves sports, just like you.
Roy: Well, why not? I'll give it a try.
Joe: OK, I'll invite her over for dinner, and you can tell me what you think.

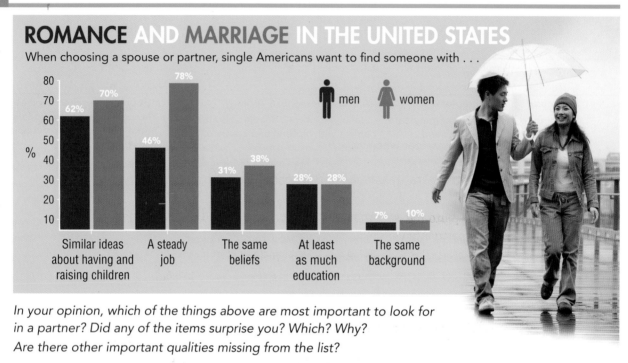

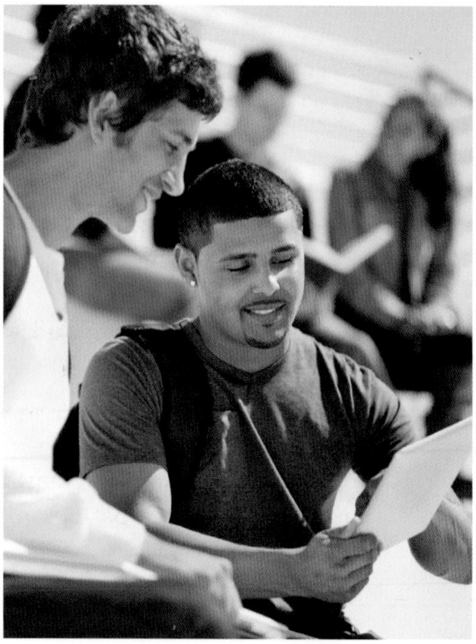

B Listen to Joe and Roy discuss Lisa after they had dinner together. What did Roy think of her?

3 GRAMMAR FOCUS

▶ Relative pronouns

As the subject of a clause	As the object of a clause
I like people **who/that** aren't too serious.	I want someone **(who/that)** I can have fun with.
I like people **who/that** have a good sense of humor.	I'd like someone **(who/that)** I can talk to easily.

GRAMMAR PLUS *see page 132*

A Match the information in columns A and B. Then compare with a partner.

A
1. I don't like to work with people who/that ___c___
2. I have some good, old friends who/that ___e___
3. I discuss my problems with people who/that _____
4. I don't want to have a roommate who/that _____
5. I'd like to have a boss who/that _____
6. I enjoy teachers who/that ___a___
7. I'm looking for a partner who/that ___f___

B
a. help me understand things easily.
b. is messy.
c. are too competitive.
d. I can respect as a leader.
e. I met in middle school.
f. I have a lot in common with.
g. can give me good advice.

B Put a line through *who/that* in part A if it's optional. Then compare with a partner.

C PAIR WORK Complete the sentences in column A with your own information.
Do you and your partner have similar opinions?

A: I don't like to work with people who are too competitive.
B: Neither do I. I like to work with people who are friendly and helpful.

4 WORD POWER Personality traits

A Match the words with the definitions. Then decide whether the words
are positive (**P**) or negative (**N**). Write **P** or **N** after each word.

___h___ 1. easygoing ___P___
___c___ 2. egotistical _____
___a___ 3. inflexible _____
___i___ 4. modest ___P___
_____ 5. outgoing ___P___
___b___ 6. stingy ___N___
_____ 7. supportive ___P___
_____ 8. temperamental ___N___
_____ 9. unreliable ___N___

a. a person who doesn't change easily and is stubborn (*testarudo*)
b. someone who doesn't like giving or spending money
c. someone who has a very high opinion of him- or herself
d. someone who is helpful and encouraging
e. a person who doesn't do what he or she promised
f. a person who enjoys being with other people
g. a person who has unpredictable or irregular moods
h. a person who doesn't worry much or get angry easily
i. someone who doesn't brag about his or her accomplishments

Jactarse

B PAIR WORK Cover the definitions. Take turns talking about the adjectives
in your own words.

"An easygoing person is someone who . . ."

C PAIR WORK Think of at least two adjectives to describe your favorite
relative. Then tell a partner.

5 LISTENING What's new?

A Listen to conversations that describe three people. Are the descriptions positive (**P**) or negative (**N**)? Check (✓) the box.

		P	N		
1.	Emma	☐ P	☒ N	inflexible	unreliable
2.	Mrs. Leblanc	☑ P	☐ N	supportive	
3.	Pablo	☑ P	☐ N	going	social

B Listen again. Write two adjectives that describe each person in the chart.

6 DISCUSSION The right qualities

A What is the ideal friend, parent, or partner like? Add your own type of person under **People**. Then write one quality each ideal person should have, and one each should *not* have.

People	This person is . . .	This person is not . . .
The ideal friend	supportive	arrogant inflexible
The ideal parent	modest	unreliable
The ideal partner	outgoing	tamental
The ideal ___dog___		messy

B **GROUP WORK** Take turns describing your ideal people. Try to agree on the two most important qualities for each person.

A: I think the ideal friend is someone who is supportive and who is a good listener.

B: I agree. The ideal friend is someone who isn't critical . . .

C: Oh, I'm not sure I agree. . . .

7 WRITING A good friend

A Think about a good friend. Answer the questions. Then write a paragraph.

What is this person like?
How long have you known each other?
How did you meet?
How are you similar?
How are you different?
What makes your relationship special?

> My friend Nolan is easygoing and doesn't take life too seriously. He's someone who loves to have fun, and he makes sure everyone else has a good time, too. We met about six years ago . . .

B **PAIR WORK** Exchange paragraphs. How are your friends similar? How are they different?

8 PERSPECTIVES Are you difficult to please?

A Listen to some common complaints. Check (✓) the ones you agree with.

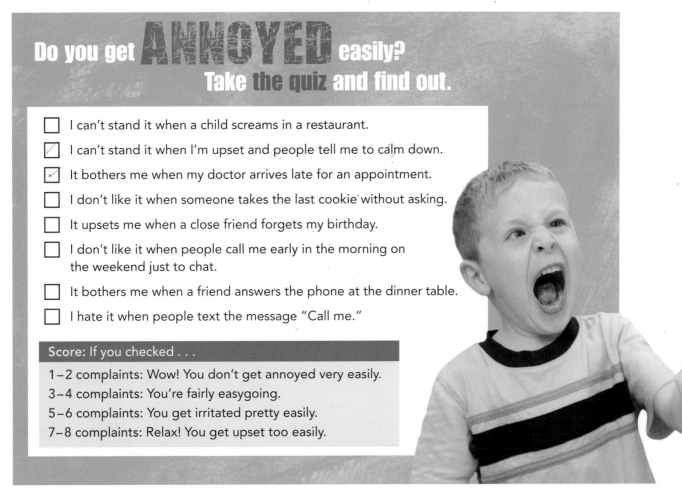

Do you get ANNOYED easily? Take the quiz and find out.

- [ ] I can't stand it when a child screams in a restaurant.
- [x] I can't stand it when I'm upset and people tell me to calm down.
- [x] It bothers me when my doctor arrives late for an appointment.
- [ ] I don't like it when someone takes the last cookie without asking.
- [ ] It upsets me when a close friend forgets my birthday.
- [ ] I don't like it when people call me early in the morning on the weekend just to chat.
- [ ] It bothers me when a friend answers the phone at the dinner table.
- [ ] I hate it when people text the message "Call me."

Score: If you checked . . .

1–2 complaints: Wow! You don't get annoyed very easily.
3–4 complaints: You're fairly easygoing.
5–6 complaints: You get irritated pretty easily.
7–8 complaints: Relax! You get upset too easily.

B Calculate your score. Do you get annoyed easily? Tell the class what bothers you the most.

9 PRONUNCIATION Linked sounds

A Listen and practice. Final consonant sounds are often linked to the vowel sounds that follow them.

It upsets me when a friend is late for an appointment.
I love it when a friend is supportive and kind.

B Mark the linked sounds in the sentences below. Listen and check. Then practice saying the sentences.

1. I hate it when a cell phone goes off at the movies.
2. I can't stand it when a person is inflexible.
3. Does it bother you when a friend is unreliable?

C PAIR WORK Take turns saying the sentences in Exercise 8. Pay attention to linked sounds.

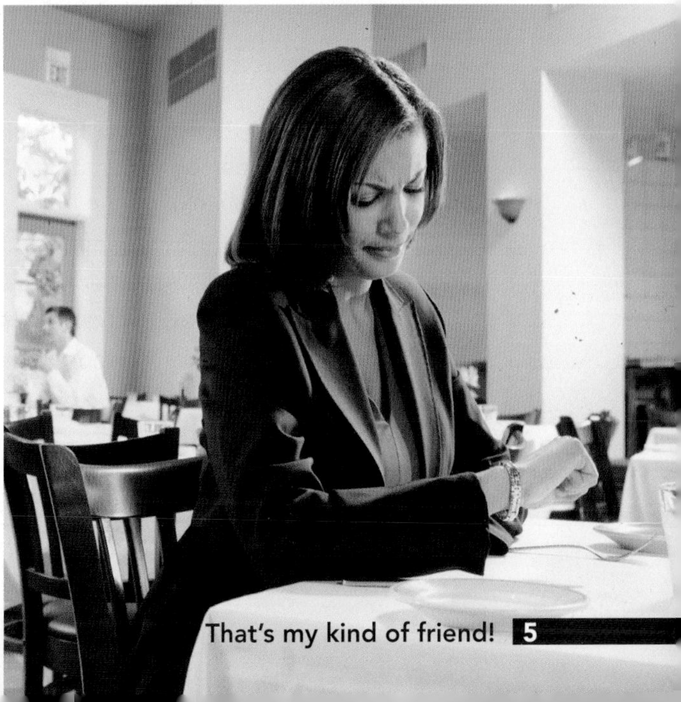

10 GRAMMAR FOCUS

It clauses + adverbial clauses with *when*

I like **it**	**when** my roommate cleans the apartment.
I don't mind **it**	**when** a friend answers the phone at the dinner table.
I can't stand **it**	**when** I'm upset and people tell me to calm down.
It makes me happy	**when** people do nice things for no reason.
It bothers me	**when** my doctor arrives late for an appointment.
It upsets me	**when** a close friend forgets my birthday.

GRAMMAR PLUS *see page 132*

A How do you feel about these situations? Complete the sentences with *it* clauses from the list. Then compare your sentences with a partner.

I love it	**I don't mind it**	**It annoys me**	**It really upsets me**
I like it	**It doesn't bother me**	**I don't like it**	**I can't stand it**
It makes me happy	**I hate it**		

1. ______________ when a friend gives me a present for no special reason.
2. ______________ when someone criticizes a friend of mine.
3. ______________ when friends start arguing in front of me.
4. ______________ when people call me late at night.
5. ______________ when salesclerks are temperamental.
6. ______________ when people are direct and say what's on their mind.
7. ______________ when someone corrects my grammar in front of others.
8. ______________ when a friend is sensitive and supportive.
9. ______________ when people throw trash on the ground.
10. ______________ when a friend treats me to dinner.

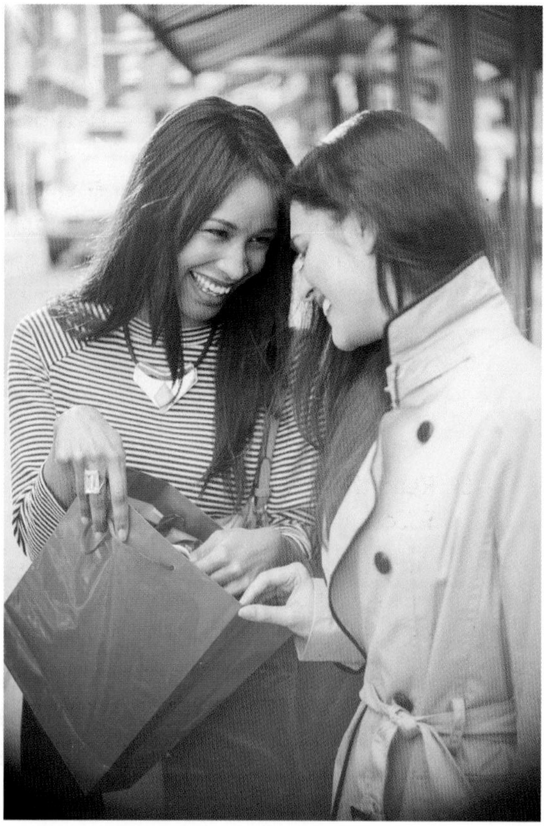

B GROUP WORK Do you ever get annoyed by a certain type of person or situation? Write down five things that annoy you the most. Then compare in groups.

A: I can't stand it when someone takes food off my plate.
B: I feel the same way. Especially when the person didn't order his or her own food!
C: Yeah, but it bothers me more when . . .

11 INTERCHANGE 1 Personality quiz

Interview a classmate to find out about his or her personality.
Go to Interchange 1 on page 114.

12 READING

A Are you a frequent social media user? What kinds of things get your attention on social media?

●●● ‹› ⌕ ⌂

HOME NEWS ABOUT CULTURE [] ⌕

SOCIAL NETWORKS THAT AREN'T FOR EVERYONE

Since social networking websites first appeared, many have come and some have gone. However, their purpose has generally been the same: keeping up with old friends, making new friends, and sharing pictures, videos, and bits of interesting news. In addition, some sites make it possible to pursue new relationships, either online or in the real world.

For some people who have very specific interests, generic sites like Facebook or Twitter are not sufficient. They want to be part of a supportive online community that shares their particular passions.

A good example is Stache Passions, a social site for people who wear, admire, or have an interest in moustaches. It features photos of men with all sizes and styles of moustaches, forums

for discussing the history, growing, and styling of the 'stache, and even a meet-up page to help you meet other moustache-lovers.

Purrsonals is a specialized site for those who love cats. Here you can meet and chat with cat-loving friends, set up feline play-dates with local people and their pets, and even find a home for a cat in need. And if your friends don't like it when you share endless cute cat videos on your regular social site, Purrsonals is where people are sure to appreciate them!

On a more serious note, Horyou is a website for people that want to do good in the world. On the site, you can connect with other social activists and entrepreneurs, plan meetings, share fund-raising strategies, and keep up with thousands of people who are working hard to make the world a better place. There are no funny videos here, but Horyou offers its own web-based video channel that features programs and documentaries about efforts to improve people's lives around the globe.

B Read the article. Which website is good for the people below? Write
S (Stache Passions), **P** (Purrsonals), or **H** (Horyou).

This site would be good for someone who . . .

1. has a strong interest in personal appearance. _____
2. is hoping to adopt a new pet. _P_
3. wants to watch a bit of light entertainment. _P_
4. wants ideas for improving others' lives. _H_
5. is interested in styles from the past. _S_
6. wants to raise money for a charity. _H_

C Find the words in the article that mean the following.

1. enough for a purpose _____
2. places where a discussion can take place _forums_____
3. to like and be grateful for something _appreciate_____
4. people who want to accomplish political or social change _____
5. plans of action _____

D **PAIR WORK** Do you belong to any specialized social networking sites? If yes, what is the focus? If not, what type of specialized site might you join?

2 Working 9 to 5

- ▸ Discuss opinions, advantages, and disadvantages of jobs
- ▸ Compare various jobs

1 SNAPSHOT

What do you want from your career?

 Security
If you want to have stability, choose a job that you can keep for your whole life. You could be a federal judge, a public school teacher, or a university professor.

 Adventure
Perhaps you can't picture yourself doing the same thing, at the same place, for years and years. In that case, be something that will allow you to explore other places and other cultures, like an environmentalist or a tour guide.

 Money
Do you want to have a high-paying job? You may want to look into being a financial analyst, a doctor, or a stockbroker.

Rank the factors from 1 (most important) to 3 (least important). Compare with a partner.
Which factors did you consider when you chose your present job or your future career? Why?

2 PERSPECTIVES Career choices

A Listen to students discuss career choices. Do you agree or disagree?
Check (✓) the speaker you agree with more.

 I'd like to work in the video game industry. Playing games all day would be lots of fun. ✓

 I disagree! Playing the same game every day for months would be boring.

 Designing clothes is not a man's job. Women are much more fascinated by fashion.

 Being a flight attendant sounds very exciting. Traveling all the time would be really interesting.

 But flight attendants get tired of traveling. They spend most of their time in airports! ✓

That's not true! Many great fashion designers are men. Just look at Michael Kors! ✓

B Compare your responses with your classmates. Give more reasons to support your opinions.

 I'd enjoy working with animals. I think working as a veterinarian could be rewarding.

 I'm not so sure. Animals can be very unpredictable. Getting a dog bite would be scary! ✓

3 GRAMMAR FOCUS

Gerund phrases

Gerund phrases as subjects	Gerund phrases as objects
Playing games all day would be lots of fun.	She'd be good at **testing games**.
Being a flight attendant sounds exciting.	He'd love **being a flight attendant**.
Designing clothes is not a man's job.	He wouldn't like **being a fashion designer**.
Working as a veterinarian could be rewarding.	She'd enjoy **working with animals**.

GRAMMAR PLUS *see page 133*

A Look at the gerund phrases in column A. Write your opinion of each job by choosing information from columns B and C. Then add two more gerund phrases and write similar sentences.

A	B	C
1. working from home	seems	awful
2. doing volunteer work	could be	stressful
3. having your own business	would be	fantastic
4. working on a movie set	must be	fascinating
5. being a teacher	wouldn't be	pretty difficult
6. making a living as a tour guide	doesn't sound	kind of boring
7. taking care of sick people		really rewarding
8. retiring at age 40		very challenging
9. ______________		
10. ______________		

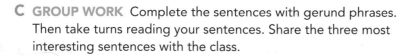

1. *Working from home could be very challenging.*

B **PAIR WORK** Give reasons for your opinions about the jobs in part A.

A: In my opinion, working from home could be very challenging.
B: Really? Why is that?
A: Because you have to learn to manage your time. It's easy to get distracted.
B: I'm not sure that's true. For me, working from home would be . . .

C **GROUP WORK** Complete the sentences with gerund phrases. Then take turns reading your sentences. Share the three most interesting sentences with the class.

1. I'd get tired of . . .
2. I'd be interested in . . .
3. I'd be very excited about . . .
4. I'd enjoy . . .
5. I think I'd be good at . . .
6. I wouldn't be very good at . . .

"I'd get tired of doing the same thing every day."

4 WORD POWER Suffixes

A Add the suffixes -er, -or, -ist, or -ian to form the names of these jobs. Write the words in the chart and add one more example to each column.

software develop er	freelance journal ist	marketing direct or	politic ian
computer technic ian	guidance counsel or	project manag er	psychiatr ist

-er	-or	-ist	-ian
software developer			

B PAIR WORK Can you give a definition for each job?

"A software developer is someone who creates apps for computers and other devices."

5 SPEAKING Career paths

GROUP WORK Talk about a career you would like to have. Use information from Exercises 1–4 or your own ideas. Other students ask follow-up questions.

A: I'd enjoy working as a guidance counselor.
B: Why is that?
A: Helping kids must be really rewarding.
C: Where would you work?
A: Well, I think I'd like to work at a high school. I enjoy working with teens.

6 WRITING What's more satisfying?

A GROUP WORK What would you choose: a job that you love that doesn't pay well, or a high-paying job that you don't like? Discuss and list the consequences of the two alternatives.

B Use the list to write a paragraph justifying your choice.

> Having a high-paying job that you don't like could be very frustrating. First of all, you'd have to do something you don't like every day. You would have a lot of money. However, it's not worth it if . . .

useful expressions

First of all, . . .
In addition, . . .
Furthermore, . . .
For example, . . .
However, . . .
On the other hand, . . .
In conclusion, . . .

C PAIR WORK Read your partner's paragraph. Do you agree or disagree? Why or why not?

7 CONVERSATION It doesn't pay as much.

A Listen and practice.

Tyler: Guess what? . . . I've found a summer job!
Emma: That's great! Anything interesting?
Tyler: Yes, working at a beach resort.
Emma: Wow, that sounds fantastic!
Tyler: So, have *you* found anything?
Emma: Nothing yet, but I have a couple of leads. One is working as an intern for a news website – mostly answering emails and posts from readers. Or I can get a job as a camp counselor again.
Tyler: Being an intern sounds more challenging than working at a summer camp. You could earn college credits, and it's probably not as much work.
Emma: Yeah, but the internship doesn't pay as much as the summer camp job. Do they have another opening at the beach resort? That's the kind of job I'd really enjoy.

B Listen to the rest of the conversation. What is Tyler going to do at the resort?

8 GRAMMAR FOCUS

Comparisons

with adjectives	with verbs
. . . sounds **more/less** challenging **than** . . .	. . . earns **more/less than** . . .
. . . is hard**er than** . . .	. . . earns **as much as** . . .
. . . is **not as** hard **as** . . .	. . . does**n't** pay **as much as** . . .
with nouns	**with past participles**
. . . has **better/worse** hours **than** . . .	. . . is **better** paid **than** . . .
. . . has **more** education **than** . . .	. . . is **as** well paid **as** . . .
. . . is**n't as much** work **as** . . .	. . . is**n't as** well paid **as** . . .

GRAMMAR PLUS see page 133

A Complete the sentences using the words in parentheses. Compare with a partner. (More than one answer is possible.)

1. In my opinion, being a firefighter is __________ (stressful) being a sales associate. In addition, sales associates have __________ (hours) firefighters.
2. In general, doctors need __________ (training) nutritionists. However, they usually __________ (earn) nutritionists.
3. Game testers don't need __________ (experience) software developers. As a result, they __________ (earn) software developers.
4. A career in banking is often __________ (demanding) a career in sales, but it is also __________ (paid).

B PAIR WORK Compare the jobs in part A. Which would you choose? Why?

9 PRONUNCIATION Stress with compound nouns

A Listen and practice. Notice that the first word in these compound nouns has more stress. Then add two more compound nouns to the chart.

●	●	●	●
firefighter	game tester	guidance counselor	
hairstylist	flight attendant	project manager	

B **GROUP WORK** Which job in each column would be more challenging? Why? Tell the group. Pay attention to stress.

10 LISTENING It's not what I thought.

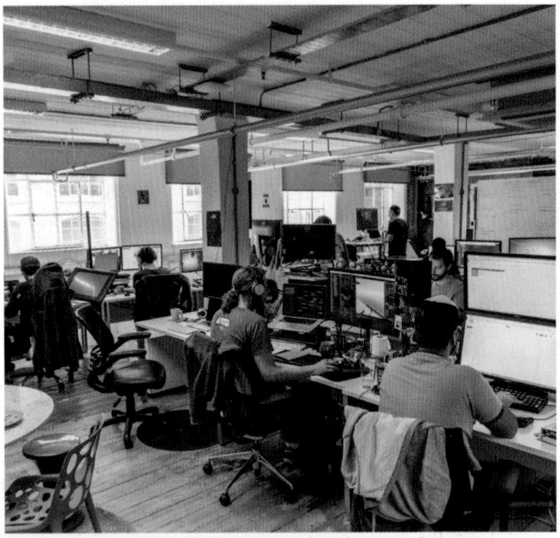

A Listen to Caden talk to Janelle about his job as a video game tester. Which parts of the job does he like and dislike? Check (✓) Like or Dislike.

		Like	Dislike
1.	The pay	☐	☐
2.	The hours	☐	☐
3.	Testing games	☐	☐
4.	Playing video games at home	☐	☐
5.	Thinking of new ideas for games	☐	☐

B Listen again. What does Caden decide to do?

C **PAIR WORK** What other advice would you give Caden?

11 DISCUSSION Which job would you take?

A What is a job you would like to have? What is a job you wouldn't like to have? Write each one on a separate slip of paper.

kindergarten teacher

tour guide

B **GROUP WORK** Mix all the slips from your group. One student picks two slips and the group helps him or her decide between the two jobs.

A: You should take the job as a kindergarten teacher because you enjoy working with kids.
B: But being a tour guide sounds more exciting. I could travel more and earn more money.
C: But you'd work longer hours and . . .

12 INTERCHANGE 2 Networking

Would you be a good party planner? Go to Interchange 2 on page 115.

READING

A Skim the web posts. Which person works in the most traditional workplace? the least traditional?

THE PERFECT WORKPLACE?

What is your workplace like? Tell us and see how other places compare!

My workplace is cooler than any office I've ever seen. Working here is really stimulating. I share a table with my co-workers, and the workplace is flooded with light. Getting free meals is great, and there are relaxing activities like billiards and board games. Plus we get a membership to a local gym! It isn't all play, of course – we work very hard – but the perks make it better than any other job I can imagine.

Lauren L., ***Palo Alto, California***

When I got my job as a project manager for a finance company in London, I imagined a modern building with views of the city and open workspaces. When I arrived for my first day, I was pretty surprised. I found a typical cubicle farm, with desks as far as the eye could see. It works for me, though. I can concentrate in my own space and then talk with colleagues in the meeting rooms. We do have a great gym on the ground floor, so that's a bonus!

Catherine D., ***London, UK***

I work in a research laboratory at a botanical garden. Working in a lab isn't as tedious as it sounds. That's because a lot of my work takes place in the greenhouses or outdoors. I love spending time among plants, and I enjoy working with other scientists who share my interests. True, the workplace isn't very luxurious. We have a tiny break room that some people complain about, and there isn't a place to work out or anything, but being outdoors so much makes up for the disadvantages.

Mark T., ***Bronx, New York***

B Read the web posts. Who would have written these sentences about their workplace? Write the names.

1. Working in different environments keeps me from getting bored. ______________
2. It's a perfect environment for sharing new ideas with co-workers. ______________
3. There's nothing unique about it, but it's fine for the kind of work we do. ______________
4. Visitors might get the idea that we don't take our work seriously. ______________
5. Some employees are dissatisfied with the workplace, but I don't mind it. ______________
6. I love being able to exercise without leaving the building. ______________

C Find the words below in the web posts. Then complete the sentences with the words.

stimulating	**perk**	**cubicle**	**tedious**	**luxurious**

1. One ___perk___ of my job is that we get free tickets to cultural and sporting events.
2. Working with creative people is very ______________ because we can share lots of great ideas!
3. The disadvantage of working in a ______________ is that you can hear everything that's going on around you.
4. The marketing director's office is very ______________, with beautiful furniture and valuable paintings.
5. Working with numbers all day seems ______________ to some people, but I enjoy it.

D **PAIR WORK** Which of the workplaces would you like the best? What features of a workplace matter most to you?

Units 1–2 Progress check

SELF-ASSESSMENT

How well can you do these things? Check (✓) the boxes.

I can . . .	Very well	OK	A little
Describe personalities (Ex. 1)	☐	☐	☐
Ask about and express preferences (Ex. 1)	☐	☐	☐
Understand and express complaints (Ex. 2)	☐	☐	☐
Give opinions about jobs (Ex. 3)	☐	☐	☐
Describe and compare different jobs (Ex. 4)	☐	☐	☐

1 SPEAKING Doing things together

A What two qualities would you like someone to have for these situations?

A person to . . .

1. be your business partner ________ ________
2. share an apartment with ________ ________
3. go on vacation with ________ ________
4. work on a class project with ________ ________

B CLASS ACTIVITY Find someone you could do each thing with.

A: What kind of person would you like to be your business partner?
B: I'd choose someone who has initiative and is hardworking.
A: Me, too! And I'd like someone who I can . . .

2 LISTENING I know what you mean!

A Listen to Suki and Andy discuss these topics. Complete the chart.

	Andy's biggest complaint	Suki's biggest complaint
1. websites		
2. children		
3. taxi drivers		
4. restaurant servers		

B PAIR WORK What is your biggest complaint about any of the topics in part A?

"I hate it when you can't find the products you want on a company's website."

3 SURVEY Job evaluation

A GROUP WORK What job would you like to have? Ask and answer questions in groups to complete the chart.

	Name	Job	Good points	Bad points
1.				
2.				
3.				
4.				

A: What job would you like to have?
B: I'd like to be a flight attendant.
C: What would be the good points?
B: Well, traveling around the world would be exciting.
D: Would there be any bad points?
B: Oh, sure. I'd dislike packing and unpacking all the time. . . .

useful expressions

I would(n't) be good at . . .
I would enjoy/dislike . . .
I would(n't) be interested in . . .
I would(n't) be excited about . . .

B GROUP WORK Who thought of the most unusual job? the best job? the worst job?

4 ROLE PLAY Choosing a job

Student A: Your partner, Student B, is looking for a job. Based on his or her opinions about jobs in Exercise 3, suggest two other jobs that Student B might enjoy.

Student B: You are looking for a job. Student A suggests two jobs for you. Discuss the questions below. Then choose one of the jobs.

Which one is more interesting? harder?
Which one has better hours? better pay?
Which job would you rather have?

A: I thought of two other jobs for you. You could be a hairstylist or a truck driver.
B: Hmm. Which job has better hours?
A: Well, a hairstylist has better hours, but it's not as . . .

Change roles and try the role play again.

WHAT'S NEXT?

Look at your Self-assessment again. Do you need to review anything?

3 Lend a hand.

- Discuss favors, borrowing, and lending
- Leave messages with requests

1 SNAPSHOT

ANNOYING FAVORS PEOPLE ASK

Could you . . .

1. babysit my kids on the weekend?
2. watch my stuff for a few minutes?
3. let me use your credit card?
4. drive me to the airport?
5. let me use your passcode to download a movie?
6. help me move to my new apartment?
7. come with me to my niece's school concert?
8. let me stay at your place for a couple of weeks?
9. donate to my favorite charity?
10. co-sign a bank loan for me?

Imagine that a close friend asked you each of these favors. Which would you agree to do? What are three other favors that you dislike being asked?

2 CONVERSATION Thanks a million.

A Listen and practice.

Carlos: Hey, Keiko. What's up?

Keiko: Hi, Carlos. I was wondering if you could help me. I'm moving to my new apartment this weekend, and my car is pretty small. Can I borrow your truck, please?

Carlos: Um, I need it on Saturday, but you can borrow it on Sunday.

Keiko: Thanks so much.

Carlos: Sure. So, have you packed already?

Keiko: Uh-huh. I mean, I'll have everything packed by Sunday. You know, I think some of my boxes are going to be kind of heavy. Would you mind helping me put them in your truck on Sunday?

Carlos: I guess not. I suppose you want my help taking them out of the truck, too?

Keiko: Oh, that'd be great. Thanks a million, Carlos!

B Listen to two more calls Keiko makes. What else does she need help with? Do her friends agree to help?

3 GRAMMAR FOCUS

Requests with modals, *if* clauses, and gerunds

Less formal
- **Can I** borrow your truck, please?
- **Could** you lend me your truck, please?
- **Is it OK if** I use your credit card?
- **Do you mind if** I use your credit card?
- **Would it be all right if** I used your credit card?
- **Would you mind if** I borrowed your truck?
- **Would you mind** helping me on Sunday?
- **I was wondering if** you could help me move.

More formal

GRAMMAR PLUS *see page 134*

A Circle the correct answers. Then practice with a partner.

1. **A:** **Is it OK if** / **Would** / **Do you mind** I use your cell phone? Mine just died.
   B: No problem, but can you keep it short? I'm expecting an important phone call.
2. **A:** Would you mind if I **stay** / **staying** / **stayed** at your place for the weekend?
   B: Not at all. It'll be fun to have you stay with us.
3. **A:** I was wondering **I could** / **if I could** / **if I would** borrow your car tomorrow.
   B: Sure, that's fine. Just be careful. I've only had it for a couple of months.
4. **A:** Could you **lend** / **lending** / **lent** me $20?
   B: I'm sorry. I don't have any money to spare right now.
5. **A:** Would you mind **help** / **helped** / **helping** me pack my stuff this weekend?
   B: No, I don't mind. I'm not doing anything then.
6. **A:** **Would you mind** / **Can** / **Is it OK if** you feed my cats while I'm on vacation, please?
   B: Sorry, I don't get along with cats.

B Rewrite these sentences to make them more formal requests. Then practice making your requests with a partner. Accept or decline each request.

1. Come to my cousin's wedding with me.
2. Can I borrow your notes to study for the test?
3. Can you lend me your camera to take with me on my vacation?
4. Drive me to the airport.
5. Help me paint my apartment.
6. I'd like to borrow your cell phone to call a friend in London.

1. *Would you mind coming to my cousin's wedding with me?*

4 PRONUNCIATION Unreleased consonants

A Listen and practice. Notice that when /t/, /d/, /k/, /g/, /p/, and /b/ are followed by other consonant sounds, they are unreleased.

Coul**d** Crai**g** ta**ke** care of my pe**t** skunk?
Can you as**k** Bo**b** to hel**p** me?

B Circle the unreleased consonants in the conversations. Listen and check. Then practice the conversations with a partner.

1. **A:** I was wondering if I could borrow that book.
 B: Yes, but can you take it back to Doug tomorrow?
2. **A:** Would you mind giving Albert some help moving that big bed?
 B: Sorry, but my doctor said my back needs rest.

5 LISTENING I was wondering . . .

A Listen to three telephone conversations. Write down what each caller requests. Does the other person agree to the request? Check (✓) Yes or No.

	Request	Yes	No
1. Jesse		☐	☑
2. Liz		☑	☐
3. Min-jun		☑	☐

B PAIR WORK Use the chart to act out each conversation in your own words.

6 WRITING A message with requests

A Write a message to a classmate asking for several favors. Explain why you need help.

B PAIR WORK Exchange messages. Write a reply accepting or declining the requests.

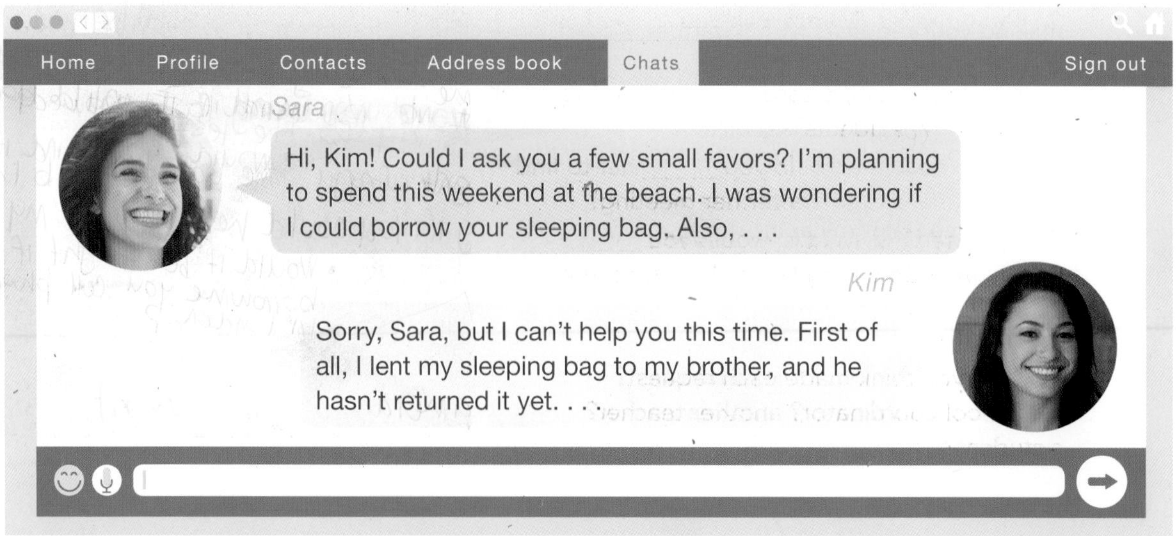

7 INTERCHANGE 3 Beg and borrow

Find out how generous you are. Go to Interchange 3 on page 116.

8 WORD POWER Verb-noun collocations

A Which verb is not usually paired with each noun? Put a line through the verb. Then compare with a partner.

1. return / do / ask for / make	a favor
2. owe / offer / do / accept	an apology
3. receive / accept / turn down / offer	an invitation
4. do / receive / give / accept	a gift
5. do / return / make / receive	a phone call
6. accept / make / decline / offer	a request
7. receive / return / do / give	a compliment

B PAIR WORK Add two questions to the list using the collocations in part A. Then take turns asking and answering the questions.

1. What are nice ways to return a favor? How do you usually return favors?
2. Have you ever invented an excuse to turn down an invitation? What excuse did you give?
3. When was the last time you declined a request? What was the request?
4. ____________________
5. ____________________

9 PERSPECTIVES Can you tell her . . . ?

A Listen to the requests people make at the school where Mary Martin teaches. Complete each request with *ask* or *tell*.

1. If you see Mary, can you ______ her that she left her phone in my car?
2. If you see Mary, could you ______ her whether or not she is coming to the teachers' meeting?
3. If you see Ms. Martin, can you ______ her if she's graded our tests yet?
4. If you see Mary, please ______ her not to forget the students' reports.
5. If you see Mary, could you ______ her to find me in the cafeteria after her meeting?
6. If you see Ms. Martin, would you ______ her what time I can talk to her about my homework?

B Who do you think made each request? the school coordinator? another teacher? a student?

10 GRAMMAR FOCUS

▶ Indirect requests

Statements	**Indirect requests introduced by** *that*
Mary, you left your phone in my car. →	★ Could you tell Mary (**that**) **she left her phone in my car**?
Imperatives	**Indirect requests using infinitives**
Mary, don't forget the students' reports. →	Can you tell Mary **not to forget the students' reports**?
Yes/No questions	**Indirect requests introduced by** *if* **or** *whether*
Ms. Martin, have you graded our tests? →	Can you ask her **if she's graded our tests yet**?
Mary, are you coming to the meeting? →	Could you ask her **whether or not she is coming to the meeting**?
Wh-questions	**Indirect requests introduced by a question word**
Mary, where are you having lunch? →	Can you ask Mary **where she's having lunch**?
Ms. Martin, what time can I talk to you about my homework? →	Would you ask her **what time I can talk to her about my homework**?

GRAMMAR PLUS *see page 134*

Read the things people want to say to Mary. Rewrite the sentences as indirect requests.
Then compare with a partner.

1. Mary, did you get my message about your phone?
2. Mary, will you give me a ride to school tomorrow?
3. Ms. Martin, when is our assignment due?
4. Mary, why didn't you meet us at the cafeteria for lunch?
5. Ms. Martin, I won't be in class tomorrow night.
6. Mary, are you going to the school party on Saturday?
7. Mary, please return my call when you get your phone back.
8. Mary, have you received my wedding invitation?

> 1. *Could you ask Mary if she got my message about her phone?*

11 SPEAKING No problem.

A Write five requests for your partner to pass on to classmates.

> *Would you ask Keith if he can turn off his phone in class?*

B **CLASS ACTIVITY** Ask your partner to pass on your requests.
Go around the class and make your partner's requests. Then
tell your partner how people responded.

A: Would you ask Keith if he can turn off his phone in class?
B: No problem. . . . Keith, could you turn off your cell phone in class?
C: I'm sorry, but I can't! I'm expecting an important phone call.
B: Lee, Keith says he's expecting an important phone call.

12 READING

A Scan the article. What are the three problems?

HOME NEWS ARTICLES COMMUNITY

CAN YOU TELL IT LIKE IT IS?

There are some things that are almost impossible to say to our close friends – especially if we want them to be our friends for life. Are you wondering what problems others have with bringing up difficult subjects? Read on.

1. "I can't stand your other friends."

My best friend sometimes hangs out with some people that I really don't like. I think they have a bad influence on her, and she only spends time with them because they are "cool." Could you tell me if I should bring the matter up with her, or if it would be better for me to keep quiet? I don't want to lose her as a friend. – Carly

2. "I won't help you cheat."

My closest friend has lost interest in school and studying. He says he's bored with the whole thing, so he often asks me whether I'll do him a favor and let him copy my homework. So far I've said no, but he keeps asking me. I told him that I think we'll get in trouble, but he just laughed and told me not to worry. I don't want to put my grades at risk, but I'm afraid to confront my friend about this, so I just keep avoiding the topic. How can I get him to stop asking? I was wondering if you could give me some tips for handling my problem. – Matt

3. "No, I CAN'T do that for you!"

My best friend and I get along really well, but she is constantly asking me to do things for her. "Could you help me pick out some new clothes? Would you mind if I borrowed your car? Can you look after my apartment while I'm away?" And these are just a few examples. I've said yes so many times that now I'm afraid I'll hurt her feelings if I say no. Any ideas? – Dana

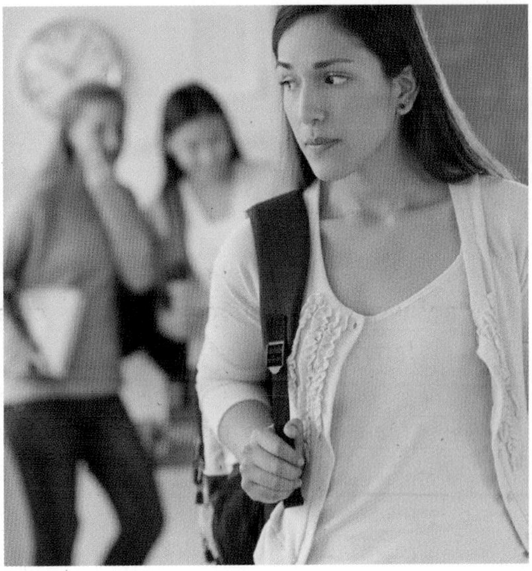

B Read the article. Then answer the questions.

1. Why is Carly concerned about her friend? ______
2. What is Matt most worried about? ______
3. Why is Dana afraid to say no to her friend? ______
4. Who is this advice best for?
   - **a.** Say that you know your friend can handle the work himself. ______
   - **b.** Agree to some requests, but only if your friend does something in return. ______
   - **c.** Tell your friend there are more important things than being popular. ______

C What do the underlined words in the article refer to? Write the correct word(s).

1. them ______
2. the matter ______
3. the whole thing ______
4. this ______
5. these ______

D **PAIR WORK** Have you ever had similar problems with friends? How were the problems resolved? What advice would you give to Carly, Matt, and Dana?

4 What happened?

- Describe past events
- Tell stories

1 SNAPSHOT

NEWS
Several Streets Closed After "Suspicious Package" Was Found

HEALTH
Why Weight Loss Isn't the Same as Being Healthy

TRENDING TOPICS
The Earth Is Getting Warmer and the Signs Are Everywhere

ARTS
The Top-Rated TV Shows You Need to Be Watching Right Now

SCIENCE
Women Need More Sleep Than Men Because They Use More of Their Brains

TECH
Here Are the Five Must-Have Apps for Runners

Which story would you like to read? Why?
What types of stories do you usually read online?
Where do you get your news? What's happening in the news today?

2 PERSPECTIVES Listen up.

A Listen to what people are listening to on their way to work. Which stories from Exercise 1 are they related to?

> Hey, I just downloaded this incredible app. I used it this morning and I think you're going to love it. While I was working out, it calculated exactly how many calories I burned. The bad thing is, it tells me I still need to run about 4 miles to burn off last night's dinner.

> As scientists were doing some research on the effects of sleep deprivation, they discovered that women need about 20 more minutes of sleep a night than men do. They think the reason is that women tend to do several tasks at once, which makes their brains work harder.

> Hi, Jeff. We're canceling our meeting in the downtown office this morning. We just learned that the police have closed all the streets in the area. It seems that a man was looking for his lost cat when he found a suspicious package inside a trash can. In the end, it was just an old box of chocolates.

B Which is a message from a co-worker? a message from a friend? a podcast?

3 GRAMMAR FOCUS

▶ **Past continuous vs. simple past**

Use the ~~past continuous~~ for an ~~ongoing action in the past.~~
Use the ~~simple past~~ for an ~~event that interrupts that action.~~

Past continuous	Simple past
While I **was working** out,	it **calculated** how many calories I burned.
As scientists **were doing** research,	they **discovered** that women need more sleep than men.
A man **was looking** for his cat	when he **found** a suspicious package inside a trash can.

GRAMMAR PLUS *see page 135*

A Complete the stories using the past continuous or simple past forms
of the verbs. Then compare with a partner.

Donations

1. **Bad memory, bad luck:** Marcia Murphy
 _____ (donate) her old pants to
 a thrift shop. As she _____ (walk)
 home, she _____ (remember) she
 _____ (leave) $20 in her pants pocket.

2. **Good intentions, bad interpretation:** Jason Clark
 _____ (walk) home one day, when he
 _____ (see) a little puppy crying on the
 sidewalk, so he _____ (stop) to help.
 As he _____ (pick) him up, a woman
 _____ (come) from nowhere screaming:
 "Stop that guy. He's trying to steal my puppy." Jason
 _____ (end) up spending three hours at the
 police station.

3. **A bad ride, a bad fall:** On her birthday last year,
 Diane Larson _____ (drive) to work
 when she _____ (have) a bad accident.
 This year, just to be safe, she decided to stay home
 on her birthday. Unfortunately, that night while she
 _____ (sleep) in her apartment, the floor
 of her living room _____ (collapse) and she
 _____ (fall) into her neighbor's apartment.

B GROUP WORK Take turns retelling the stories in part A. Add your own
ideas and details to make the stories more interesting!

4 PRONUNCIATION Intonation in complex sentences

▶ **A** Listen and practice. Notice how each clause in a complex sentence has
its own intonation pattern.

As Marcia was walking home, she remembered she left $20 in her pants pocket.

A man was looking for his cat when he found a package.

B PAIR WORK Use your imagination to make complex sentences. Take turns
starting and finishing the sentences. Pay attention to intonation.

A: As Lee was coming to school today . . .
B: . . . he saw a parade coming down the street.

5 LISTENING Crazy but true!

A Listen to three news stories. Number the pictures from 1 to 3. (There is one extra picture.)

B Listen again. Take notes on each story.

	Where did it happen?	When did it happen?	What happened?
1.			
2.			
3.			

6 WRITING A personal account

A Think of a story that happened to you or to someone you know. Choose one of the titles below, or create your own.

A Scary Experience
I Was Really Lucky
I'll Never Forget That Day
I Can't Believe It Happened

B Write your story. First, answer these questions.

Who was involved?
When did it happen?
Where did it happen?
What happened?

> <u>I Was Really Lucky</u>
>
> Last year, I took a trip to see my grandparents. I was waiting in the airport for my flight when a storm hit, and all the flights were cancelled. Luckily, I . . .

C GROUP WORK Take turns telling your stories. Other students ask questions. Who has the best story?

7 CONVERSATION That's terrible!

A Listen and practice.

CAROL Guess what? Someone stole my new bike yesterday!

MILO Oh, no! What happened?

CAROL Well, I was having lunch with a friend, and I had parked it on the street, just like I always do. When I came back, someone had stolen it. I guess I'd forgotten to lock it up.

MILO That's terrible! Did you report the theft to the police?

CAROL Yes, I did. And I also listed it on that site for stolen and lost bikes. But I doubt I'll ever get it back.

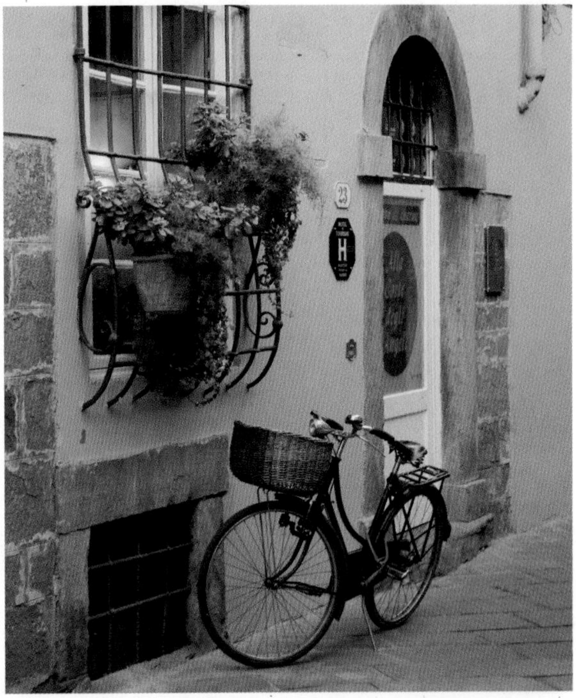

B Listen to the rest of the conversation. What did Milo have stolen once? Where was he?

8 GRAMMAR FOCUS

Past perfect

Use the past perfect for an event that occurred before another event in the past.

Past event	Past perfect event
I **was having** lunch with a friend,	and I **had parked** my bike on the street.
When I **came back,**	someone **had stolen** it.
They **were able** to steal it	because I **had forgotten** to lock it up.

GRAMMAR PLUS *see page 135*

A Write the correct verbs to complete the sentences. Then compare with a partner.

1. I ____________ (took/had taken) a trip to London last year. I was a bit scared because I ____________ (didn't travel/hadn't traveled) abroad before, but everything was perfect.
2. I ____________ (visited/was visiting) the British Museum one afternoon when I ____________ (ran/had run) into an old school friend who I ____________ (didn't see/hadn't seen) for over 10 years.
3. One weekend, we ____________ (were driving/had driven) to Liverpool when we ____________ (ran/were running) out of gas on the highway because we ____________ (forgot/had forgotten) to fill up the tank before leaving. Fortunately, a truck driver ____________ (stopped/had stopped) and ____________ (helped/had helped) us.
4. On the last day, as I ____________ (was going/had gone) up to my hotel room, I ____________ (got/had gotten) stuck in the elevator. After I ____________ (was/had been) stuck for an hour, someone ____________ (started/had started) it again.

B **PAIR WORK** Complete the sentences with your own ideas.

Until last year, I had never . . .

One day, as I was . . .

9 WORD POWER Exceptional events

A Match the words in column A with the definitions in column B.

A	B
1. coincidence ______	**a.** an unexpected event that brings good fortune
2. dilemma ______	**b.** a situation that involves a difficult choice
3. disaster ______	**c.** something puzzling or unexplained
4. emergency ______	**d.** an event that causes suffering or destruction
5. lucky break ______	**e.** a great success or achievement
6. mishap ______	**f.** an accident, mistake, or unlucky event
7. mystery ______	**g.** a sudden, dangerous situation that requires quick action
8. triumph ______	**h.** a situation when two similar things happen at the same time for no reason

B **PAIR WORK** Choose one kind of event from part A. Write a situation for it.

A man bought an old house for $10,000. As he was cleaning the attic of his new home, he found an old painting by a famous painter. He had never collected art, but when he took it to a museum, he found out it was worth almost one million dollars. (lucky break)

C **GROUP WORK** Read your situation. Can others guess which kind of event it describes?

10 SPEAKING It's a story about . . .

GROUP WORK Have you ever experienced the events in Exercise 9, part A? Tell your group about it. Answer any questions.

A: It's a story about a coincidence.
B: What happened?
A: My sister bought a new dress for her graduation party. She had saved for months to buy it. When she got to the party, another girl was wearing the exact same dress!
C: Wow! That's more than a coincidence. It's a disaster! And what did she do?

11 INTERCHANGE 4 Spin a yarn

Tell a story. Go to Interchange 4 on page 117.

12 READING

A Skim the article. Was the story about lice true or false?

Menu | Articles | Community | Search | Sign in / Sign up

Believing More Than We Should

Is everything you read on the Internet true? If your answer is "no," you are absolutely right. Many stories and even photos are not to be trusted. And don't believe that because a good friend or a well-known news source has posted something that it is necessarily trustworthy.

There are many reasons for the spread of inaccurate content on the Internet. One reason is that satirical websites can create very believable stories, which they invent in order to make a point or to make people laugh. Other reasons might be an attempt to gain more readers, a desire to damage someone's reputation, or simple curiosity about how far a fake story can spread.

One story that spread throughout the media before anyone had checked the facts involved teenagers, selfies, and head lice. The article claimed that when teenagers were posing together for selfies, their heads often touched and the tiny insects were jumping from head to head. The article went on to say that this was causing a massive outbreak of lice. Some major websites and news outlets picked up the story, not even bothering to consult the experts. It turned out that some entrepreneurs who were marketing a new treatment for head lice had made up the story and posted it. Their motivation was to get attention and more business.

The spread of this story is understandable. It involved one epidemic (selfies) causing another (lice), and the "ick" factor was irresistible. Because there is so much false information online, there are now websites, such as *Snopes* and *Factcheck*, which exist specifically to find out if stories are true or not. So the next time you see a story that sounds too good to be true, at least you have somewhere to turn for verification before you spread false information to all your friends.

B Read the article. Find the words in italics in the article. Then check (✓) the meaning of each word.

1. *inaccurate*	☐ not exact or true	☐ shocking or disgusting
2. *satirical*	☐ humorously critical	☐ completely factual
3. *reputation*	☐ hurtful news about someone	☐ public opinion of someone
4. *massive*	☐ small	☐ very large
5. *irresistible*	☐ hard to prove	☐ hard to fight against
6. *verification*	☐ proof of truth	☐ another opinion

C PAIR WORK Discuss these questions.

Do you think you would have believed the story about selfies and head lice?
Do you think the creation of the story was justified or not?
Who do you think is most responsible for the story being so popular?
Do you think there should be a penalty for spreading false information? If so, what should it be?

D GROUP WORK Have you ever read a story that turned out to be false? How did you find out the truth?

Units 3–4 Progress check

SELF-ASSESSMENT

How well can you do these things? Check (✓) the boxes.

I can . . .	Very well	OK	A little
Discuss favors (Ex. 1)	☐	☐	☐
Leave messages with requests (Ex. 2)	☐	☐	☐
Tell a story, making clear the sequence of events (Ex. 3, 5)	☐	☐	☐
Understand the sequence of events in a story (Ex. 4)	☐	☐	☐

1 ROLE PLAY Save the date!

Student A: You are planning a class party at your house. Think of three things you need help with. Then call a classmate and ask for help.

Student B: Student A is planning a party. Agree to help with some things, but not everything.

"Hi, Martina. I'm calling about the party. Would you mind . . . ?"

Change roles and try the role play again.

2 DISCUSSION Who said it?

A GROUP WORK Take turns reading each request. Then discuss the questions and come up with possible answers.

> Tell Rita that I'm going to be a half hour late for our meeting. Ask her to wait for me in her office.

> Tell your officers that he's white and wears a blue collar with his name on it – Rex. Please call if you find him.

> I'm sorry to bother you, but I really need it back for the office party on Friday. Please ask Sue to bring it over before that.

1. What is the situation?
2. Who is the request for? Who do you think received the request and passed it on?
3. Give an indirect request for each situation.

"Could you tell Rita . . . ?"

B CLASS ACTIVITY Compare your answers. Which group has the most interesting answers for each message?

3 SPEAKING And then . . . ?

A PAIR WORK Choose a type of event from the box. Then make up a title for a story about it. Write the title on a piece of paper.

disaster **emergency** **lucky break** **mystery** **triumph**

B PAIR WORK Exchange titles with another pair. Discuss the questions *who, what, where, when, why,* and *how* about the other pair's title. Then make up a story.

C Share your story with the pair who wrote the title.

The Mystery of the Message in a Bottle

I was walking on the beach when I saw a bottle with a message inside. The bottle looked very old, and it was hard to open it. Inside there was a message: "My beloved Catherine, I hope you . . ."

4 LISTENING What happened first?

Listen to each situation. Number the events from 1 to 3.

1.	☐ She got sick.	☐ She went on vacation.	☐ She went back to work.
2.	☐ John called me.	☐ I didn't get the message.	☐ I changed phone numbers.
3.	☐ I was very nervous.	☐ I left the office.	☐ I felt relieved.
4.	☐ We went out.	☐ My cousin stopped by.	☐ I was watching a movie.

5 DISCUSSION Beginning, middle, and end

GROUP WORK Choose the beginning of a story from column A and an ending from column B. Discuss interesting or unusual events that could link A to B. Then make up a story.

A

Once, I . . .
accepted an interesting invitation.
was asked to do an unusual favor.
received an unexpected phone call.
owed someone a big apology.

B

Believe it or not, . . .
I got home, and there were 30 people in my living room!
I had no idea where I was.
when I got there, everyone had left.
it was the star of my favorite TV show!

A: Once, I accepted an interesting invitation.
B: Let's see. . . . I was biking home when I got a text from an old friend.
C: I hadn't seen him in over five years.
D: I was really surprised, but . . .

WHAT'S NEXT?

Look at your Self-assessment again. Do you need to review anything?

5 Expanding your horizons

- Discuss living in a foreign country
- Describe cultural expectations and differences

1 PERSPECTIVES Challenges of living abroad

A Listen to people talk about moving to a foreign country. Check (✓) the concerns you think you would share.

- ☐ "One thing that I'd really miss is hanging out with my friends." ______
- ☐ "Something that I'd be worried about is the local food. I'm a picky eater." ______
- ☐ "Getting used to a different culture might be difficult at first." ______
- ☐ "I'd be worried about not knowing how to get around in a new city." ______
- ☐ "The people that I'd miss the most are my parents. We're very close." ______
- ☐ "Not knowing the local customs is something I'd be concerned about." ______
- ☐ "I'd be nervous about getting sick and not knowing how to explain my symptoms." ______
- ☐ "Communicating in a foreign language could be a challenge." ______

B Rate each concern from 1 (not worried at all) to 5 (really worried). What would be your biggest concern? Why?

2 WORD POWER Mixed feelings

A These words are used to describe how people sometimes feel when they live in a foreign country. Which are positive (**P**)? Which are negative (**N**)? Write P or N.

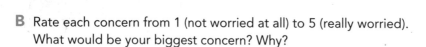

anxious	______	embarrassed	______	insecure	______
comfortable	______	enthusiastic	______	nervous	______
confident	______	excited	______	uncertain	______
curious	______	fascinated	______	uncomfortable	______
depressed	______	homesick	______	worried	______

B GROUP WORK Tell your group about other situations in which you experienced the feelings in part A. What made you feel that way? How do you feel about the situations now?

A: I felt very embarrassed yesterday. I fell down the stairs in a restaurant.
B: How did it happen?
A: I think I slipped on something.
C: Did you get hurt?
A: Just a couple of bruises, but the restaurant manager was worried, so he convinced me to go to the hospital.

confident

3 GRAMMAR FOCUS

Noun phrases containing relative clauses

Something (that) I'd be worried about is the local food.
One thing (that) I'd really miss is hanging out with my friends.
The people (who/that) I'd miss the most are my parents.

The local food **is something (that) I'd be worried about.**
Hanging out with my friends is **one thing (that) I'd really miss.**
My parents are **the people (who/that) I'd miss the most.**

GRAMMAR PLUS *see page 136*

A Complete the sentences about living in a foreign country. Use the phrases below. Then compare with a partner.

my friends	**trying new foods**	**being away from home**	**getting lost in a new city**
my family	**feeling like an outsider**	**my grandmother's cooking**	**not understanding people**
getting sick	**making new friends**	**speaking a foreign language**	**learning about a different culture**

1. . . . is something I'd be very enthusiastic about.
2. The thing I'd probably be most excited about is . . .
3. . . . is something I'd really miss.
4. Two things I'd be homesick for are . . .
5. Something I'd get depressed about is . . .
6. . . . is one thing that I might be embarrassed about.
7. The thing I'd feel most uncomfortable about would be . . .
8. . . . are the people who I'd miss the most.
9. One thing I'd be insecure about is . . .
10. . . . are two things I'd be anxious about.

B Now complete three sentences in part A with your own information.

1. *Going to different festivals is something I'd be very enthusiastic about.*

C **GROUP WORK** Rewrite your sentences from part B in another way. Then compare. Do others feel the same way?

1. *I'd be very enthusiastic about going to different festivals.*

4 PRONUNCIATION Word stress in sentences

A Listen and practice. Notice that the important words in a sentence have more stress.

Uruguay is a country that I'd like to live in.

Speaking a foreign language is something I'd be anxious about.

Trying new foods is something I'd be curious about.

B **PAIR WORK** Mark the stress in the sentences you wrote in Exercise 3, part A. Then practice the sentences. Pay attention to word stress.

5 DISCUSSION Moving to a foreign country

GROUP WORK Read the questions. Think of two more questions to add to the list. Then take turns asking and answering the questions in groups.

What country would you like to live in? Why?
What country wouldn't you like to live in? Why?
Who is the person you would most like to go abroad with?
What is something you would never travel without?
Who is the person you would email first after arriving somewhere new?
What would be your two greatest concerns about living abroad?
What is the thing you would enjoy the most about living abroad?

A: What country would you like to live in?
B: The country I'd most like to live in is Zimbabwe.
C: Why is that?
B: Well, I've always wanted to work with wild animals. Besides, . . .

6 SNAPSHOT

ETIQUETTE TIPS FOR INTERNATIONAL TRAVELERS
CANADA: Always bring a small gift for the host when invited to a meal at a Canadian home.
RUSSIA: Do not turn down offers of food or drink.
JAPAN: Take off your shoes before entering a house.
FRANCE: When eating, don't rest your elbows on the table.
CHINA: Never point your chopsticks at another person.
BRAZIL: You can arrive between 15 to 30 minutes late for a party at a Brazilian friend´s home.
THAILAND: Never touch a person's head.
MOROCCO: Don't eat anything with your left hand.

Does your culture follow any of these customs?
Do any of these customs seem unusual to you? Explain.
What other interesting customs do you know?

7 CONVERSATION Bring a small gift.

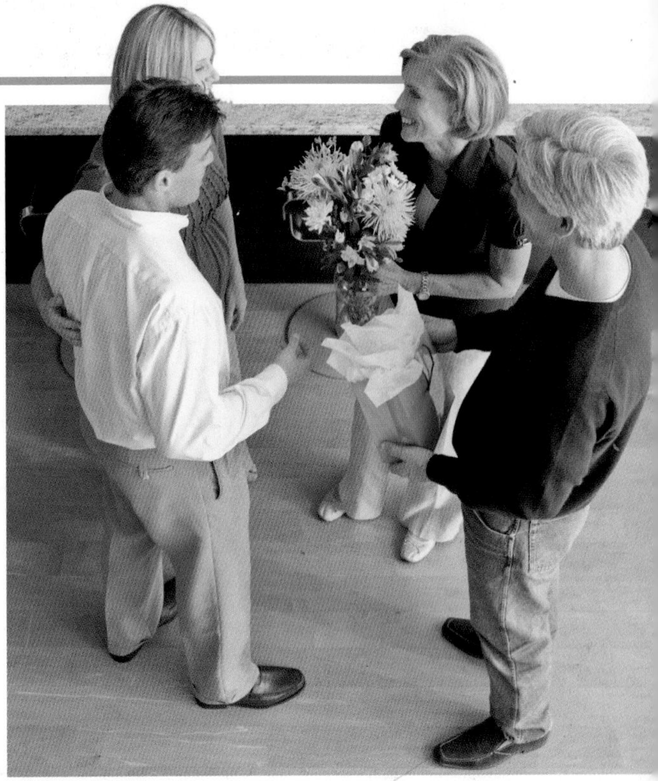

A Listen and practice.

Klaus: My boss invited my wife and me to dinner at his house.

Olivia: Oh, how nice!

Klaus: Yes, but what do you do here when you're invited to someone's house?

Olivia: Well, here in the U.S., it's the custom to bring a small gift.

Klaus: Like what?

Olivia: Oh, maybe some flowers or chocolates.

Klaus: And is it all right to bring our kids along?

Olivia: Well, if you want to bring them, you're expected to ask if it's OK first.

B Listen to the rest of the conversation. If you are invited to someone's house in Germany, when are you expected to arrive? What can you bring as a gift?

8 GRAMMAR FOCUS

Expectations

When you visit someone,	it**'s the custom to** bring a small gift.
	you **aren't supposed to** arrive early.
If you want to bring others,	you**'re expected to** ask if it's OK first.
	you**'re supposed to** check with the host.
	it**'s not acceptable to** bring them without asking.

GRAMMAR PLUS *see page 136*

A Match information in columns A and B to make sentences about customs in the United States and Canada. Then compare with a partner.

A

1. If someone sends you a gift, ______
2. If you plan to visit someone at home, ______
3. When you go out with friends for dinner, ______
4. If the service in a restaurant is acceptable, ______
5. When you meet someone for the first time, ______
6. When you receive an invitation, ______

B

a. you're supposed to call first.
b. it's the custom to leave a tip.
c. you aren't supposed to kiss him or her.
d. you're expected to respond to it quickly.
e. you're expected to thank the person.
f. it's acceptable to share the expenses.

B **GROUP WORK** How are the customs in part A different in your country?

C Complete these sentences with information about your country or a country you know well. Then compare with a partner.

1. In . . . , if people invite you to their home, . . .
2. When you go out on a date, . . .
3. If a friend is in the hospital, . . .
4. When you receive a gift, . . .
5. If you're staying at someone's home, . . .
6. When someone has a baby, . . .

9 LISTENING Different cultures

A Listen to people describe customs they observed abroad. Complete the chart.

	Where was the person?	What was the custom?	How did the person react?
1. Carla			
2. Nate			
3. Shauna			

B PAIR WORK Which custom would you have the most trouble adapting to? Why?

10 SPEAKING Local customs

A PAIR WORK What should a visitor to your country know about local customs? Make a list. Include these points.

greeting and addressing someone
eating or drinking in public
taking photographs
giving gifts
dressing appropriately
visiting someone's home
using public transportation
tipping

When you ride in a cab, you're supposed to tip the driver.

B GROUP WORK Compare your lists with another pair. Then share experiences in which you (or someone you know) *didn't* follow the appropriate cultural behavior. What happened?

A: Once, when traveling abroad, I took a cab, and I didn't give the driver a tip.
B: What happened?
A: Well, he looked kind of angry. Then my friend gave the guy a tip, and I realized my mistake. It was a little embarrassing. . . .

11 WRITING A tourist pamphlet

A GROUP WORK Choose five points from the list you made in Exercise 10. Use them to write and design a pamphlet for tourists visiting your country or city.

WE HOPE YOU ENJOY YOUR STAY.
When you visit Italy, there are some important things you should know. For example, you can't buy a bus ticket on the bus in most big cities. Actually, you are supposed to . . .

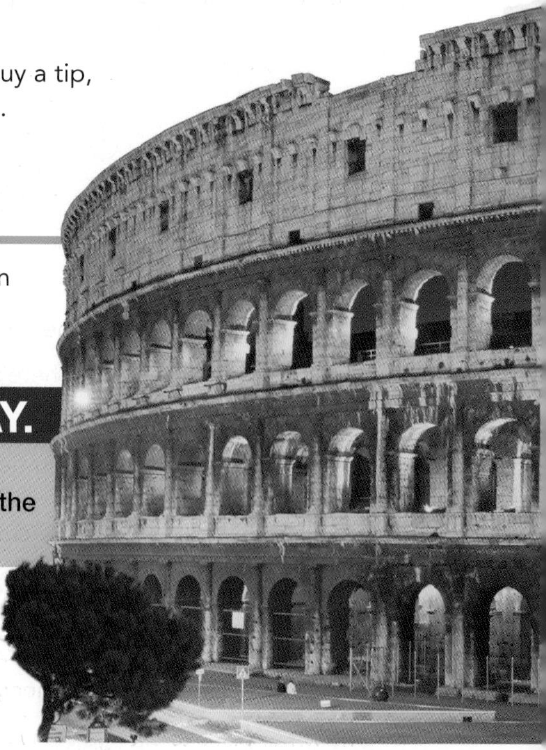

B CLASS ACTIVITY Present your pamphlets. Which of the points were the most useful? What other information would a tourist need to know?

12 INTERCHANGE 5 Cultural dos and taboos

Compare customs in different countries. Go to Interchange 5 on page 118.

13 READING

A Scan the blog. What kinds of culture shock did the writer experience?

CULTURE SHOCK

PROFILE | PHOTOS | BLOG | COMMUNITY

I'm an exchange student from Spain navigating life in the United States. *Lucia M.*

JANUARY 15 ____________

My hometown of Seville, Spain is a city with active, passionate people and a lively nightlife, so coming to Seattle, in the United States, has been quite an eye-opener. Americans think of Seattle as an exciting city, but the first time I went out with friends on a Saturday night, there was hardly anybody out in the streets. I actually thought something was wrong! Then my friend explained that most of their social life takes place indoors. In Seville, people fill the streets year-round, and Saturday nights are like a big celebration.

JANUARY 22 ____________

After a couple of weeks of classes, I've begun to notice some differences between Spanish students and American students. In Spain, students talk a lot during class, and it's not always related to the lesson. On the other hand, when Spanish students are enthusiastic about a lesson, they often ask unusual questions, and it's common to stay after class to talk to the teacher. American students are expected to talk less and listen more, and many of them take detailed notes. Most of them leave the room as soon as the class ends, though, and are already focused on the next lesson.

FEBRUARY 8 ____________

Before I came to the United States, a friend who had studied here told me that American friends don't greet each other like we do in Spain, where we touch cheeks and make kissing sounds. Americans often hug each other, but kissing is not common, and I've gotten used to that. So imagine my surprise when I was introduced to a new girl, and she immediately gave me the Spanish-style double kiss. When I asked my friend about this later, she explained that the girl was from a family of actors, and that "air-kissing" was a usual greeting for artistic people. My friend also said that some outgoing people greet their friends or family this way, but that it would make other people feel uncomfortable. I think I'll stick to handshakes and hugs while I'm here!

B Read the blog. Then add the correct title to each entry.

Meeting and greeting   Where's the party?   Class contrasts

C Check (✓) True or False for each statement. Then correct the false statements.

	True	False	
1. The writer was nervous because the Seattle streets were crowded at night.	☐	☐	
2. Spanish students often stay after class to ask questions.	☐	☐	
3. Hugging is a usual greeting among friends in Spain.	☐	☐	
4. The writer plans to change the way she greets American friends.	☐	☐	

D PAIR WORK How do things in your city compare with Seville? with Seattle?

6 That needs fixing.

- Describe problems and make complaints
- Discuss what needs fixing

1 SNAPSHOT

Some common complaints

Banking
The credit card company bills you for something you didn't buy.

Online shopping
The store sends you an incorrect size.

Internet providers
The Internet connection is not reliable, and you hardly ever get the speed you pay for.

Restaurants
The server rushes you to leave as soon as you finish your meal.

Vehicles
Your new car consumes too much gas.

Repair services
Your TV breaks again, a week after it was repaired.

Parking garage
Someone damages your car.

Have you ever had any of these problems? Which ones?
What would you do in each of these situations?
What other complaints have you had?

2 PERSPECTIVES That's not right!

A Listen to people describe complaints. Check (✓) what you think each person should do.

1. "I got a new suitcase, but when I arrived home, I noticed the lining was torn."
   - ☐ take it back to the store
   - ☐ ask the store to send you a new one
2. "My father sent me a coffee mug with my favorite team's logo, but when it arrived, it was chipped."
   - ☐ tell your father about it
   - ☐ contact the seller yourself
3. "I lent my ski pants to a friend, but when he returned them, there was a big stain on them."
   - ☐ clean them yourself
   - ☐ ask him to have them cleaned
4. "My boss borrowed my camera for a company event, and now the lens is scratched."
   - ☐ talk to him or her about it
   - ☐ say nothing and repair it yourself
5. "I bought a new washing machine just a month ago, and it's leaking already."
   - ☐ ask for a refund
   - ☐ send it back and get a new one

B Have you ever had similar complaints? What happened? What did you do?

3 GRAMMAR FOCUS

Describing problems 1

With past participles as adjectives	With nouns
The suitcase lining is **torn**.	It has **a tear** in it./There's **a hole** in it.
The car is **damaged**.	There is **some damage** on the bumper.
The coffee mug is **chipped**.	There is **a chip** in it.
My pants are **stained**.	They have **a stain** on them.
The camera lens is **scratched**.	There are **a few scratches** on it.
The washing machine **is leaking**.*	It has **a leak**.

Exception: is leaking is a present continuous form.

GRAMMAR PLUS *see page 137*

A Read the comments from customers in a restaurant. Write sentences in two different ways using forms of the word in parentheses. Then compare with a partner.

1. Could we have another water pitcher? This one . . . (crack)
2. That valet was so careless. My car . . . (dent)
3. The toilet is dirty. And the sink . . . (leak)
4. This tablecloth isn't very clean. It . . . (stain)
5. Would you bring me another glass? This glass . . . (chip)
6. The table looks pretty dirty. The wood . . . , too. (scratch)
7. The server needs a new shirt. The one he's wearing . . . (tear)
8. The walls really need paint. And the ceiling . . . (damage)

1. *This one is cracked.*
   It has a crack.

B **PAIR WORK** Describe two problems with each thing below. Use forms of the words in the box. You may use the same word more than once.

break	crack	damage	dent	leak	scratch	stain	tear

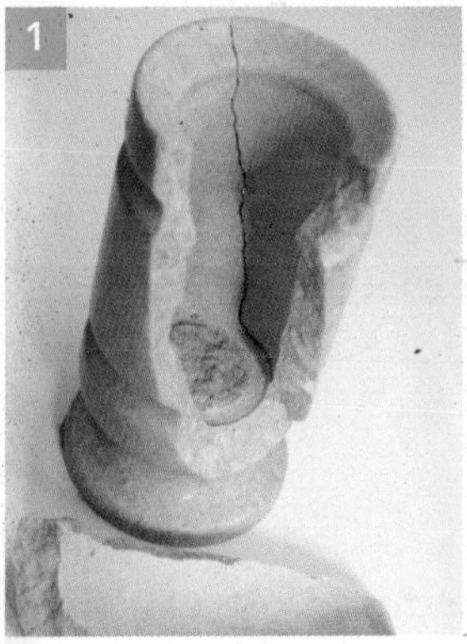

A: The vase is broken.
B: Yes. And it has a crack, too.

C **GROUP WORK** Look around your classroom. How many problems can you describe?

"The floor is scratched, and the window is cracked. The desks are . . ."

4 LISTENING I'd like a refund.

A Listen to three customers return items they purchased. Complete the chart.

	Did the store give a refund?	Why or why not?
1. Evie		
2. Darren		
3. Gisela		

B GROUP WORK How is your culture similar or different in terms of refunds and customer service?

5 ROLE PLAY How can I help you?

Student A: You are returning an item to a store. Decide what the item is and explain why you are returning it.

Student B: You are a salesperson. A customer is returning an item to the store. Ask these questions:

What exactly is the problem?
Can you show it to me?
Was it like this when you bought it?
When did you buy it?
Do you have the receipt?
Would you like a refund or a store credit?

Change roles and try the role play again.

6 CONVERSATION It needs to be adjusted.

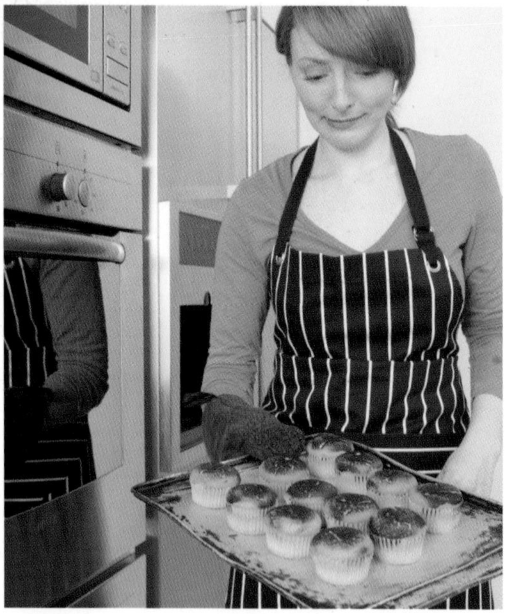

A Listen and practice.

MR. LEROY Hello?

HEATHER Hello, Mr. Leroy. This is Heather Forman.

MR. LEROY Uh, Ms. Forman . . .

HEATHER In Apartment 12C.

MR. LEROY Oh, yes. What can I do for you? Does your refrigerator need fixing again?

HEATHER No, it's the oven this time.

MR. LEROY Oh. So, what's wrong with it?

HEATHER Well, I think the temperature control needs to be adjusted. The oven keeps burning everything I try to cook.

MR. LEROY Really? OK, I'll have someone look at it right away.

HEATHER Thanks a lot, Mr. Leroy.

MR. LEROY Uh, by the way, Ms. Forman, are you sure it's the oven and not your cooking?

B Listen to another tenant's call with Mr. Leroy. What's the tenant's problem?

7 GRAMMAR FOCUS

Describing problems 2

Need + gerund	*Need* + passive infinitive	*Keep* + gerund
The oven **needs adjusting**.	It **needs to be adjusted**.	Everything **keeps burning**.
The alarm **needs fixing**.	It **needs to be fixed**.	The alarm **keeps going off**.

GRAMMAR PLUS *see page 137*

A What needs to be done in this apartment? Write sentences about these items using *need* with gerunds or passive infinitives.

1. the cupboards (clean)
2. the fire alarm (adjust)
3. the lights (replace)
4. the plants (water)
5. the oven (fix)
6. the ceiling (paint)
7. the window (wash)
8. the light switch (change)

1. The cupboards need cleaning.
OR
1. The cupboards need to be cleaned.

B PAIR WORK Think of five improvements you would like to make in your home. Which improvements will you most likely make? Which won't you make?

"First, the bedroom walls need painting. There are some small cracks. . . ."

8 WORD POWER Problems with electronics

A Circle the correct gerund to complete the sentences. Then compare with a partner.

1. My TV screen goes on and off all the time. It keeps **flickering** / **sticking**.
2. The music player app jumps to the next song every 20 seconds. It keeps **crashing** / **skipping**.
3. The battery in my new camera doesn't last long. It keeps **freezing** / **dying**.
4. Something is wrong with my computer! It keeps **crashing** / **jamming**.
5. I can't talk for long on my new phone. It keeps **dying** / **dropping** calls.
6. This printer isn't making all the copies I want. It keeps **jamming** / **flickering**.
7. My computer needs to be replaced. It keeps **dropping** / **freezing**.
8. The buttons on the remote control don't work well. They keep **skipping** / **sticking**.

B GROUP WORK Describe a problem with an electronic item you own. Don't identify it! Others will try to guess the item.

"Some keys on my device keep sticking, and some are loose. . . ."

9 PRONUNCIATION Contrastive stress

A Listen and practice. Notice how a change in stress changes the meaning of each question and elicits a different response.

Is the bedroom window cracked? (No, the kitchen window is cracked.)

Is the bedroom window cracked? (No, the bedroom door is cracked.)

Is the bedroom window cracked? (No, it's stuck.)

B Listen to the questions. Check (✓) the correct response.

1. a. Are my jeans torn?
- [✓] No, they're stained.
- [✓] No, your shirt is torn.

b. Are my jeans torn?
- [✓] No, they're stained.
- [] No, your shirt is torn.

2. a. Is the computer screen flickering?
- [✓] No, it's freezing.
- [] No, the TV screen is flickering.

b. Is the computer screen flickering?
- [] No, it's freezing.
- [✓] No, the TV screen is flickering.

10 LISTENING A throwaway culture

A Listen to a conversation between two friends. Answer the questions.

1. What is wrong with Hayley's phone? _____
2. What is Hayley's solution? _____
3. What is Aaron's solution? _____
4. Why doesn't Hayley like Aaron's solution? _____

B Listen again. What is a "throwaway culture"?

C GROUP WORK Do you agree that electronics aren't made as well as they used to be? Give an example to support your opinion.

11 WRITING A critical online review

A Imagine that you ordered a product online, but when you received it, you were unhappy with it. Write a critical online review. Explain all of the problems with the product and why you think others shouldn't buy it.

> ### Best 4U promises a lot, delivers nothing.
>
> I ordered a phone from Best 4U's website for my son's birthday. First, it took six weeks for the company to send it, and it arrived two weeks after his birthday. Now, the battery keeps dying very fast when he's just watching a movie or . . . READ MORE

B GROUP WORK Read your classmates' reviews. What would you do if you read this critical online review and worked for the company that sold the product?

12 INTERCHANGE 6 Home makeover

Do you have an eye for detail? Student A, go to Interchange 6A on page 119; Student B, go to Interchange 6B on page 120.

13 READING

A Skim the advice column. What problem did the reader have? How does the writer suggest solving the problem?

Home | Local | World | Entertainment | Advice column

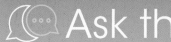

Ask the Fixer!

Our problem-solver Marci Davis addresses a common problem with ride-sharing services.

After a meeting downtown, I used my phone to book a ride with a private car service in order to get home. As soon as the pick-up was confirmed, a friend came out of the building, spotted me, and offered me a ride home. I immediately canceled the car. But the next day I got an alert on my phone – the car service had charged my credit card $10! I contacted the service, and they said it was for a late cancellation. I didn't realize they were going to charge me for that! Can you fix this? – Lawrence, New York City

The fact is, Lawrence, that you need to read the terms of your ride-sharing app. It states clearly – somewhere in all those thousands of words – that when you cancel your ride less than ten minutes before your car is scheduled to arrive, you have to pay a fee. After all, the driver has already refused other possible passengers and is driving in your direction, so it's a loss when you cancel.

On the other hand, I do think something needs to be fixed. Do you know anyone who reads all the way through the terms of use for any app? There isn't enough time in the day! I talked to a representative at your ride-sharing company and made two suggestions. First, they need to highlight their cancellation policy at the beginning of the terms, where people will see it. Then, when you cancel a ride, a notification needs to be sent that tells you about the cancellation charge. That way, riders won't keep getting this annoying surprise. Let's hope the company pays attention.

What do you think? Post your comments, suggestions, complaints, and anecdotes.

B Read the advice column. Find the words in italics in the article. Then check (✓) the meaning of each word.

1. *confirm*	☐ make something available	☑ state that something will happen
2. *cancellation*	☑ act of stopping something	☐ act of delaying something
3. *representative*	☑ person who speaks for a company	☐ person who owns a company
4. *terms*	☑ rules of an agreement	☐ features of an app
5. *notification*	☑ act of giving information	☐ act of asking a question

C For each statement, check (✓) True, False, or Not given.

	True	False	Not given
1. Lawrence booked a ride by mistake.	☐	☑	☐
2. Lawrence did not expect to be charged for his ride.	☑	☐	☐
3. The cancellation rule is available to read on the app.	☑	☐	☐
4. Marci Davis thinks the cancellation fee is too expensive.	☐	☐	☑
5. The company representative apologized for what happened.	☐	☐	☑
6. Marci says ride-sharing agreements should be more clear.	☑	☐	☐

D Have you ever used a ride-sharing service? What do you think of this type of service?

Units 5–6 Progress check

SELF-ASSESSMENT

How well can you do these things? Check (✓) the boxes.

I can . . .	Very well	OK	A little
Talk about feelings and expectations (Ex. 1)	☐	☐	☐
Discuss cultural differences (Ex. 2)	☐	☐	☐
Understand problems and complaints (Ex. 3)	☐	☐	☐
Describe problems (Ex. 4)	☐	☐	☐
Discuss what needs to be improved (Ex. 5)	☐	☐	☐

1 SPEAKING Facing new challenges

PAIR WORK Choose a situation. Then ask your partner questions about it using the words in the box. Take turns.

moving to another city
going to a new school
starting a new job
getting married

anxious	**excited**
curious	**insecure**
embarrassed	**nervous**
enthusiastic	**worried**

A: If you were moving to another city, what would you be nervous about?
B: One thing I'd be nervous about is not having any friends around. I'd be worried about feeling lonely!

2 SURVEY Cultural behavior

A What do you think of these behaviors? Complete the survey.

Is it acceptable to . . . ?	Yes	No	It depends
give money as a gift	☐	☐	☐
call older people by their first names	☐	☐	☐
greet friends with a kiss on the cheek	☐	☐	☐
ask how old someone is	☐	☐	☐
put your feet on the furniture	☐	☐	☐

B GROUP WORK Compare your opinions. When are these behaviors acceptable? When are they unacceptable? What behaviors are never acceptable?

A: It's not acceptable to give money as a gift.
B: Oh, I think it depends. I think it's OK to give money to kids and teens, and as a wedding gift, but . . .

3 LISTENING I have a problem.

A Listen to three tenants complain to their building manager. Complete the chart.

	Tenant's complaint	How the problem is solved
1.		
2.		
3.		

B **GROUP WORK** Do you agree with the solutions? How would you solve the problems?

4 ROLE PLAY Haggling

Student A: You want to buy this car from Student B, but it's too expensive. Describe the problems you see to get a better price.

Student B: You are trying to sell this car, but it has some problems. Make excuses for the problems to get the most money.

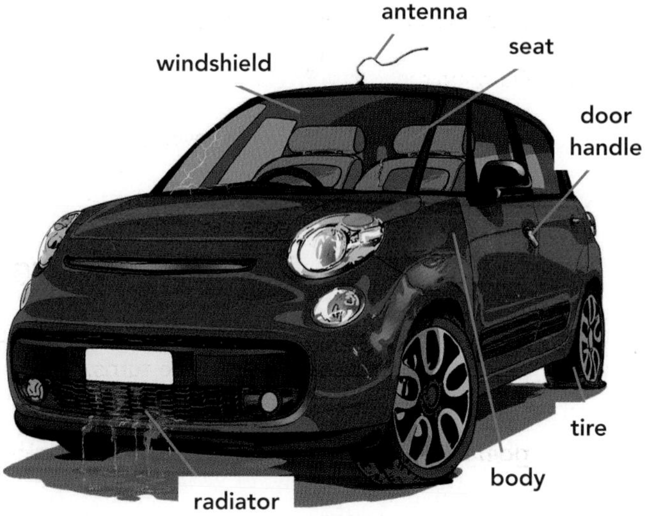

A: I'm interested in this car, but the door handle is broken. I'll give you $ . . . for it.

B: That's no big deal. You can fix that easily. How about $ . . . ?

A: Well, what about the windshield? It's . . .

B: You can't really see that. . . .

Change roles and try the role play again.

5 DISCUSSION School improvements

A **GROUP WORK** Imagine you are on a school improvement committee. You are discussing changes to your school. Decide on the five biggest issues.

A: The Wi-Fi connection needs to be improved. It keeps disconnecting, and it's not fast enough.

B: Yes, but it's more important to replace the couch in the student lounge. It has a big hole and stains.

B **CLASS ACTIVITY** Share your list with the class. What are the three most needed improvements? Can you think of how to accomplish them?

WHAT'S NEXT?

Look at your Self-assessment again. Do you need to review anything?

7 What can we do?

- ▸ Discuss environmental problems
- ▸ Compare solutions to social problems

1 SNAPSHOT

WHAT A WASTE!

The United States generates **254 million** tons of waste a year.
The average American produces almost **2** kilograms of waste a day.

Americans throw away around **130 million** cell phones a year.
Much of this e-waste ends up in landfills.

Fifteen hundred plastic bottles are consumed every second in the United States.
It takes at least **500** years for a plastic bottle to decompose.

In the U.S., **30–40%** of the food supply is wasted.
That could feed **millions** of hungry people.

How could we reduce the waste of each of these items?
What do you throw away? What do you tend to recycle?
What are two other environmental problems that concern you?

2 PERSPECTIVES Vote for a better city!

A Listen to an announcement from an election campaign. What kinds of problems does Grace Medina want to fix?

VOTE FOR GRACE MEDINA FOR CITY COUNCIL

Grace Medina's ideas for Riverside!

Have you noticed these problems in our city?

- Our fresh water supply is being contaminated by toxic chemicals.
- The roads aren't being repaired due to a lack of funding.
- Our community center has been closed because of high maintenance costs.
- Our city streets are being damaged as a result of heavy traffic.
- Many public parks have been lost through overbuilding.
- Low-income families are being displaced from their homes due to high rental prices.

GRACE MEDINA – THE CHANGE WE NEED

B Which of these problems affect your city? Can you give specific examples?

3 GRAMMAR FOCUS

Passive with prepositions

Present continuous passive

Our water supply **is being contaminated**	**by** toxic chemicals.
Our city streets **are being damaged**	**as a result of** heavy traffic.
The roads **aren't being repaired**	**due to** a lack of funding.

Present perfect passive

Our community center **has been closed**	**because of** high costs.
Many public parks **have been lost**	**through** overbuilding.

GRAMMAR PLUS *see page 138*

A PAIR WORK Match the photos of environmental problems with the sentences below.

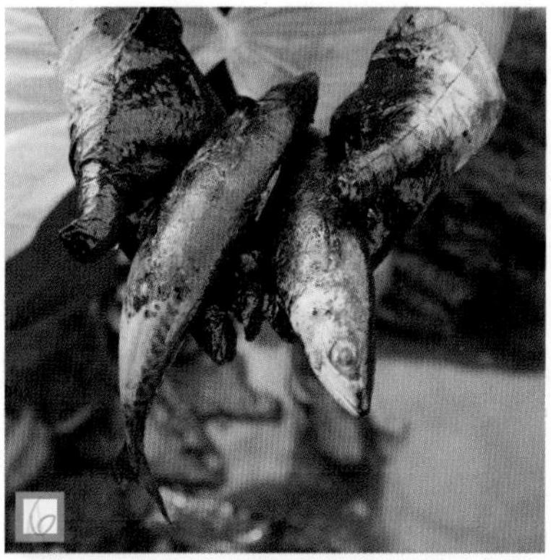

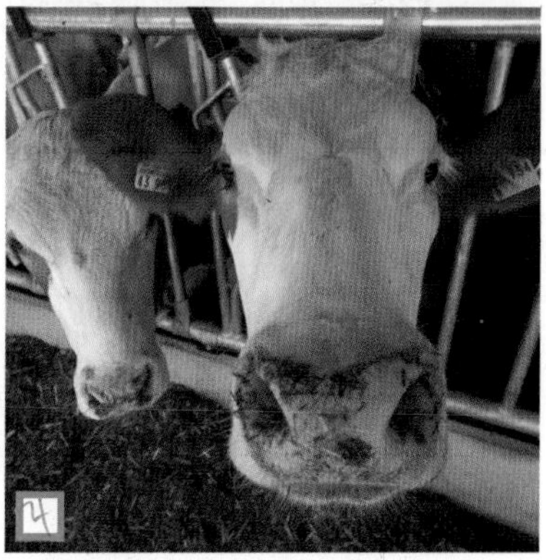

1. High emissions of carbon dioxide are causing climate changes. (by)
2. Rapid urbanization is depleting our natural resources. (through)
3. Water pollution has threatened the health of people all over the world. (due to)
4. Livestock farms have contaminated the soil and underground water. (because of)
5. The destruction of rain forests is accelerating the extinction of plants and wildlife. (as a result of)
6. Oil spills are harming birds, fish, and other marine life. (through)

B Rewrite the sentences in part A using the passive and the prepositions given. Then compare with a partner.

1. *Climate changes are being caused by high emissions of carbon dioxide.*

C PAIR WORK Cover the sentences in part A above. Take turns describing the environmental problems in the pictures in your own words.

4 PRONUNCIATION Reduction of auxiliary verbs

A Listen and practice. Notice how the auxiliary verb forms **is**, **are**, **has**, and **have** are reduced in conversation.

Food **is** being wasted.	Our community center **has** been closed.
Streets **are** being damaged.	Parks **have** been lost.

B PAIR WORK Practice the sentences you wrote in Exercise 3, part B. Pay attention to the reduction of **is**, **are**, **has**, and **have**.

5 LISTENING Saving the environment

A Listen to three people describe some serious environmental problems. Check (✓) the problem each person talks about.

	Problem		What can be done about it?
1. Morgan	☐ landfills	☐ poor farmland	
2. Dalton	☐ electricity	☐ e-waste	
3. Kendall	☐ air pollution	☐ water pollution	

B Listen again. What can be done to solve each problem? Complete the chart.

C GROUP WORK Which problem above worries you the most? What is being done to fix it?

6 WORD POWER Global challenges

A PAIR WORK How concerned is your partner about these problems? Check (✓) his or her answers.

Problems	Very concerned	Fairly concerned	Not concerned
unemployment	☐	☐	☐
famine	☐	☐	☐
global warming	☐	☐	☐
government corruption	☐	☐	☐
infectious diseases	☐	☐	☐
political unrest	☐	☐	☐
poverty	☐	☐	☐
recession	☐	☐	☐
violence	☐	☐	☐

B GROUP WORK Share your partner's answers with another pair. Which problems concern your group the most? What will happen if the problem isn't solved?

A: Many people have been affected by the high rates of unemployment.
B: We need to create more jobs and invest in education.
C: I agree. If we don't, young people won't have any opportunities in the future.

7 CONVERSATION What if it doesn't work?

A Listen and practice.

Cindy: Did you hear about the dead fish that were found floating in the Bush River this morning?

Otis: Yeah, I read something about it. Do you know what happened?

Cindy: Well, there's a factory outside town that's pumping chemicals into the river.

Otis: How can they do that? Isn't that against the law?

Cindy: Yes, it is. But a lot of companies ignore those laws.

Otis: That's terrible! What can we do about it?

Cindy: Well, one way to change things is to talk to the company's management.

Otis: What if that doesn't work?

Cindy: Well, then another way to stop them is to get a news station to run a story on it.

Otis: Yes! Companies hate bad publicity. By the way, what's the name of this company?

Cindy: Believe it or not, it's called Green Mission Industries.

Otis: Really? My uncle is one of their top executives.

B CLASS ACTIVITY What else could Cindy and Otis do?

C Listen to the rest of the conversation. What do Cindy and Otis decide to do?

8 GRAMMAR FOCUS

Infinitive clauses and phrases

One way **to change** things is	**to talk** to the company's management.
Another way **to stop** them is	**to get** a news station to run a story.
The best ways **to fight** unemployment are	**to create** more jobs and invest in education.

GRAMMAR PLUS *see page 138*

A Find one or more solutions for each problem. Then compare with a partner.

Problems

1. The best way to fight poverty is ______
2. One way to reduce government corruption is ______
3. One way to reduce unemployment is ______
4. The best way to stop global warming is ______
5. One way to help the homeless is ______
6. One way to improve air quality is ______

Solutions

a. to provide more affordable housing.
b. to create more jobs.
c. to make politicians accountable for decisions.
d. to have more vocational training programs.
e. to increase the use of cleaner energy.
f. to provide education to all children.
g. to build more public shelters.
h. to reduce deforestation.

B GROUP WORK Can you think of two more solutions for each problem in part A? Agree on the best solution for each.

9 DISCUSSION What should be done?

A GROUP WORK Describe the problems shown in the photos. Then make suggestions about how to solve these problems.

What can be done . . . ?

1. to reduce crime

2. to keep our water supplies safe

3. to improve children's health

4. to improve traffic and mobility

A: Our cities are being taken over by criminals.
B: Well, one way to fight crime is to have more police on the streets.
C: That's not enough. The best way to stop it is . . .

B CLASS ACTIVITY Share your solutions. Which ones are the most innovative? Which ones are most likely to solve the problems?

10 INTERCHANGE 7 Take action!

Brainstorm solutions to some local problems. Go to Interchange 7 on page 121.

11 WRITING A post on a community website

A Choose one of the problems from the unit or use one of your own ideas. Write a message to post on a community website.

NO MORE **JUNK FOOD!**

Our schools are serving poor quality food to our children. School cafeterias offer mostly fast food and soda to students. This has to change. One way to change this is . . .

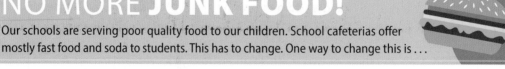

B PAIR WORK Exchange messages with a partner. Write a response suggesting another solution to his or her problem.

12 READING

A Skim the article. What problem did the island face? What solution did the inhabitants come up with?

Home | News | Feature stories | Sign in | Community

TURNING AN INVASION INTO AN ADVANTAGE

Lionfish are beautiful creatures. They are also one of the most invasive and destructive sea creatures on the planet, causing particularly serious problems in the Caribbean Sea. Their numbers have increased dramatically in a few years there, and they have already caused a great deal of damage to the ecosystem.

St. Lucia is a Caribbean island where action is being taken against the invasive species. The island is famous for its clear blue waters, and many tourists enjoy diving in order to explore the wonders of the extensive coral reefs. Unfortunately, lionfish eat the native fish that keep the reefs clean and healthy, putting the reefs at risk. It is estimated that lionfish can eat up to 80% of the small fish in a coral reef in five weeks, and because the invasive fish reproduce very quickly the problem could easily get worse in no time.

Instead of trying to trap or poison the destructive fish, islanders are turning the lionfish invasion to their advantage. They realized that one way to reduce the population of lionfish was to hunt them for sport and business, and then use them for food. Although the fish have a very poisonous sting, they can be prepared so they are safe to eat. And Caribbean cooks were sure to find a way to turn these unwelcome fish into an unforgettable treat.

Unfortunately, the lionfish population has not been reduced by much, but at least the fish have been kept from multiplying too quickly. Jobs have also been provided for unemployed fishermen, who were unable to fish for other types of sea life in the protected waters. The lionfish are still a problem, but the islanders are making the best of a bad situation – and they are making a living from it, too!

B Read the article. Answer the questions.

1. Why are the lionfish a concern?
2. Why is it important to protect the area around St. Lucia?
3. What characteristic makes the lionfish hard to control?
4. What solutions have the islanders come up with?
5. What have the results of the islanders' efforts been?

C GROUP WORK What environmental threats exist where you live? Can you think of any creative or unusual ways to deal with them?

8 Never stop learning.

- Discuss personal preferences
- Discuss ways of learning and life skills

1 SNAPSHOT

Learning: Anywhere, Anytime, for Any Reason

LEARNING PATHS

go to college
take online courses
take traditional training classes
study on your own
set up a study group
attend conferences
watch filmed lectures

LEARNING BENEFITS

get a degree
meet people and expand your network
change jobs or career path
get a raise or promotion at work
get a professional license or certification
learn something that makes your life easier
have fun

Which learning paths have you tried? How was your experience?
Which learning benefits do you consider the most important? Why?
Are you planning to learn anything new this year? What?

2 PERSPECTIVES A survey

A Listen to a survey that a school is conducting about student preferences. Check (✓) the student's answers.

Springfield Center for Continuing Education

New courses survey

1. Would you rather study on your own or join a study group?
   - ☐ a. I'd rather study on my own.
   - ☐ b. I'd rather join a study group.
   - ☐ c. I'd rather do both.
2. Would you rather take an art course or a professional course?
   - ☐ a. I'd rather take an art course.
   - ☐ b. I'd rather take a professional course.
   - ☐ c. I'd rather not take either. I'd rather take a language course.
3. Would you prefer to take an online course or a traditional course?
   - ☐ a. I'd prefer to take an online course.
   - ☐ b. I'd prefer to take a traditional course.
   - ☐ c. I'd prefer not to take either. I'd prefer to hire a private tutor.

B PAIR WORK Take the survey. You can change the underlined information. Discuss your answers with a partner.

3 PRONUNCIATION Intonation in questions of choice

Listen and practice. Notice the intonation in questions of choice.

Would you prefer to study online or at a school?

Would you rather learn something fun or useful?

4 GRAMMAR FOCUS

Would rather and would prefer

Would rather takes the base form of the verb. *Would prefer* usually takes an infinitive. Both are followed by *not* in the negative.

Would you **rather take** an art course or a professional course?
- **I'd rather take** an art course.
- **I'd rather not take either.**
- **I'd rather take** a language course than study art.

Let's join a study group.
- **I'd rather not join** a group.
- **I'd rather not.**
- **I'd prefer not to join** a group.
- **I'd prefer not to.**

Would you prefer to take an online course or a traditional course?

I'd prefer to take an online course. **I'd prefer not to take** either.

GRAMMAR PLUS *see page 139*

A Complete the conversations with *would* and the appropriate forms of the verbs in parentheses. Then practice with a partner.

1. **A:** ________ you rather ________ (take) a technical course or an art course?
   B: I would prefer ________ (take) an art course. I'd like to learn to paint.
2. **A:** ________ you prefer ________ (get) a promotion or a new job?
   B: Actually, I'm not very happy at my present job, so I'd rather ________ (get) a new job.
3. **A:** ________ you prefer ________ (learn) something fun or something practical?
   B: I guess I'd prefer ________ (study) something practical, like personal finance.
4. **A:** ________ you rather ________ (learn) English in England or Canada?
   B: To tell you the truth, I'd prefer ________ (not study) in either place. I'd rather ________ (go) to Australia because it's warmer there.
5. **A:** If you decided to learn to play an instrument, ________ you prefer ________ (attend) a class or ________ (have) a private tutor?
   B: I'd rather ________ (take) a class than ________ (hire) a tutor.
6. **A:** ________ you rather ________ (have) a job in an office or ________ (work) outdoors?
   B: I'd definitely rather ________ (have) a job where I'm outdoors.

B PAIR WORK Take turns asking the questions in part A. Pay attention to intonation. Give your own information when responding.

5 LISTENING Do what you love.

A Listen to a conversation between a student and his guidance counselor. Check (✓) the suggestions the guidance counselor gives.

- [ ] talking to professors
- [ ] job shadowing
- [ ] volunteer work
- [ ] informational interviews
- [ ] more classes
- [ ] internships

B **PAIR WORK** If you could learn more about a job, what job would it be? Why? Which options above would you use?

6 SPEAKING Learn something new

A **GROUP WORK** Think of a personal or professional skill you would like to learn or improve. Discuss how you are planning to learn it. Use the ideas from the Snapshot on page 50, or use your own ideas.

A: I want to speak Italian. I think I'm going to take an online course.
B: It's hard to learn a language online. I think you should go to a language school.
A: I don't know. I'm really shy. I'd rather not have classes with other people.
C: You could . . .

B **CLASS ACTIVITY** Share your ideas with your classmates. Who is going to learn something unusual? How are they going to learn it?

7 INTERCHANGE 8 Making choices

What would you most like to learn? Take a survey. Go to Interchange 8 on page 122.

8 CONVERSATION It works for me.

A Listen and practice.

Marta: So how's your Mandarin class going?
Kevin: Harder than I expected, actually. I'm finding the pronunciation very difficult.
Marta: Well, I imagine it takes a while to get it right. You know, you could improve your accent by watching movies.
Kevin: That's a good idea. But how do you learn new vocabulary? I always seem to forget new words.
Marta: I learn new English words best by writing them down and reviewing them many times. I've been using this vocabulary-building app. It really works for me. Look.
Kevin: Hmm. Maybe I should try something like that!

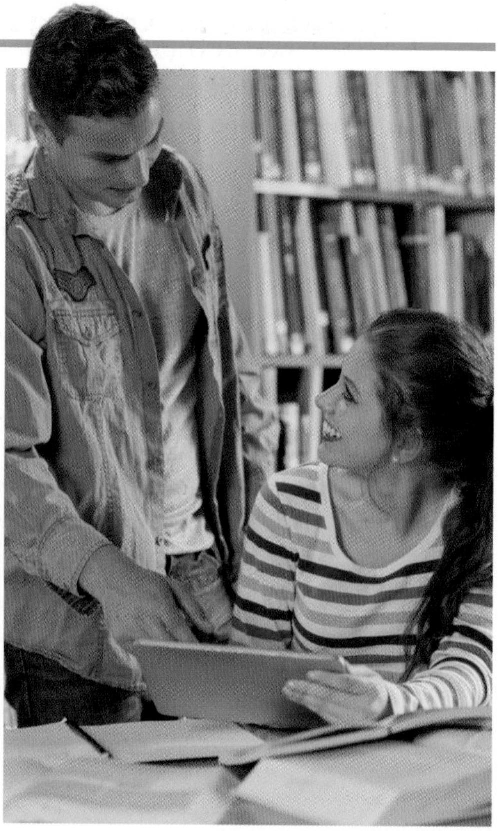

B Listen to two other students, Rick and Nia, explain how they learn new words. Who uses technology to study? Who organizes words by category?

C **CLASS ACTIVITY** How do you learn new words in a foreign language?

9 GRAMMAR FOCUS

By + gerund to describe how to do things

You could improve your accent **by watching** movies.
I learn new words best **by writing** them down and **reviewing** them many times.
The best way to learn slang is not **by watching** the news but **by watching** TV series.

GRAMMAR PLUS *see page 139*

A How can you improve your English? Complete the sentences with *by* and the gerund forms of the verbs. Then compare with a partner.

1. A good way to learn idioms is ________ (watch) American sitcoms.
2. The best way to practice what you have learned is ________ (use) it in messages or conversation.
3. Students can become better writers ________ (read) more.
4. You can learn to use grammar correctly ________ (do) grammar exercises online.
5. The best way to develop self-confidence in communication is ________ (talk) with native speakers.
6. You can improve your accent ________ (listen) to songs and singing along.
7. A good way to memorize new vocabulary is ________ (play) vocabulary games.
8. You could become a more fluent reader ________ (read) something you're interested in every day.

B **GROUP WORK** Complete the sentences in part A with your own ideas. What's the best suggestion for each item?

A: In my opinion, a good way to learn idioms is by talking to native speakers.
B: I think the best way is not by talking to native speakers but by watching TV shows.

10 DISCUSSION Learning styles

A Listen to James and Sophia describe how they developed two skills. How did they learn? Complete the chart.

	James	Sophia
1. become an effective public speaker		
2. learn to drive		

B **GROUP WORK** How would *you* learn to do the things in the chart?

C **GROUP WORK** Talk about different ways to learn to do each of these activities. Then agree on the most effective method.

take professional-looking photos
manage your time
cook
become a good conversationalist
break dance
swim
play a musical instrument

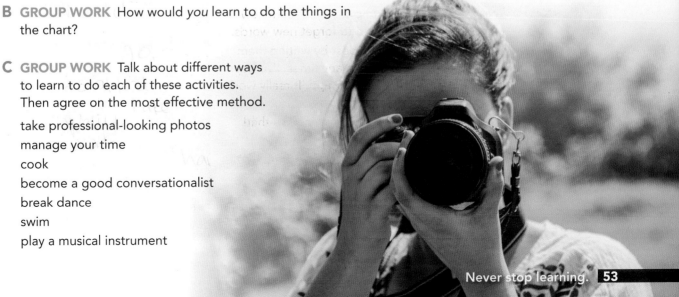

11 WORD POWER Life skills

A **PAIR WORK** How do we learn each of these things? Check (✓) your opinions.

	From parents	From school	On our own
communication skills	☐	☐	☐
competitiveness	☐	☐	☐
concern for others	☐	☐	☐
cooperation	☐	☐	☐
creativity	☐	☐	☐
money management	☐	☐	☐
perseverance	☐	☐	☐
problem solving	☐	☐	☐
self-confidence	☐	☐	☐
self-discipline	☐	☐	☐
time management	☐	☐	☐
tolerance	☐	☐	☐

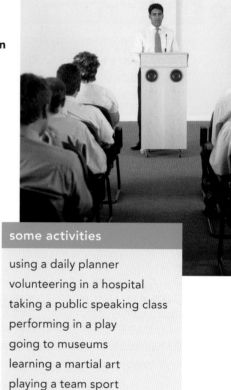

some activities

using a daily planner
volunteering in a hospital
taking a public speaking class
performing in a play
going to museums
learning a martial art
playing a team sport
making a budget

B **GROUP WORK** How can you develop the skills in part A? Use the activities in the box or your own ideas.

A: You can develop communication skills by taking a public speaking class.

B: You can also develop them by trying to be a better listener.

12 WRITING Something I learned

A Think of a skill you have learned. Read these questions and take notes. Then use your notes to write about what you learned.

What is required to be successful at it?
What are some ways people learn to do it?
How did you learn it?
What was difficult about learning it?

> I used to have serious problems managing my finances, and I never paid my bills on time. I have to admit I had very poor money management skills. Some people learn to manage their money at home or by taking courses at school, but I didn't.
>
> When a friend told me about a personal finance course, I decided to take it. I first learned to keep track of my expenses by recording every penny I spent. Then . . .

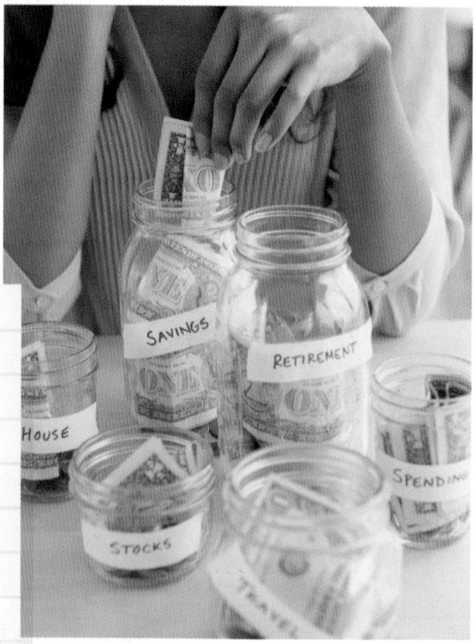

B **GROUP WORK** Share your writing. Have any of your classmates' experiences inspired you to learn a new skill?

13 READING

A Have you ever had trouble focusing when you're studying? What did you do about it?

Are you studying the "right" way?

Home | News | Articles | Sign in | Community   Search

You may study differently from your friends, but your study habits are probably not wrong!

Kelly and Maria are best friends with a lot in common. They love doing things together, such as going to movies and concerts, shopping, or just sitting at a local café. Since they take a lot of the same school subjects, they would love to study together, but they find this impossible. Their working styles are so completely different that they can't be in the same room while they are studying!

Kelly would rather study in a clean, open space, whereas Maria works best by surrounding herself with books, papers, and other clutter. Kelly prefers to study in a totally silent room, but Maria loves to play music or even have the TV on. Kelly can sit for hours without moving, and often gets all of her homework done in one sitting. Maria, on the other hand, is constantly getting up, and claims that she thinks best when she's on the move.

You might be asking yourself, which way of studying gets better results? Many people assume that a silent, uncluttered setting is the way to go, but it seems that is not necessarily the case. Some research has even shown that outside noise and clutter help some people concentrate because it makes them form a mental "wall" around what they are doing and improves their focus. So, if you're a student who chooses to study while sitting at a table in a busy shopping mall, don't worry about it. And if you work in total silence, that's OK, too. Judging from Kelly and Maria's study habits, the best way to study is the way that works for you. With their very different approaches, both of them do extremely well in school, and both finish their work in about the same amount of time as well.

One curious fact about the two friends: Despite their opposing studying styles, they have almost identical ambitions. Both are planning to go to law school – Kelly with the idea of becoming a human rights attorney and Maria hoping to become a public defender. But will they be study buddies? Not a chance!

B Read the article. Find the words in *italics* in the article. Then match each word with its meaning.

1. *clutter* ______
2. *sitting* ______
3. *concentrate* ______
4. *approach* ______
5. *identical* ______

a. focus attention on something
b. exactly the same
c. period of activity without a break
d. way of doing something
e. objects in a state of disorder

C Complete the summary with information from the article. Use one or two words in each blank.

Kelly and Maria are friends who have a lot ____________, but they can't study together because they have ____________. Kelly likes a ____________ that is very quiet, and she can ____________ for a long time. Maria prefers a space that is ____________, and she likes to ____________. Studies show that neither way of studying is ____________ than the other. Noise can help some people ____________, for example. Despite their different habits, Kelly and Maria are both ____________ students, and it is interesting that the friends have ____________ plans for the future.

D **GROUP WORK** Whose studying style is closest to yours, Kelly's or Maria's? Why?

Units 7–8 Progress check

SELF-ASSESSMENT

How well can you do these things? Check (✓) the boxes.

I can . . .	Very well	OK	A little
Describe environmental problems (Ex. 1)	☐	☐	☐
Discuss solutions to problems (Ex. 2)	☐	☐	☐
Understand examples of personal qualities (Ex. 3)	☐	☐	☐
Discuss personal preferences (Ex. 4)	☐	☐	☐

1 SPEAKING Environmental issues

PAIR WORK Choose a probable cause for each of the problems and discuss possible solutions.

PROBLEM

- Forests are being destroyed.
- The quality of the air is being lowered.
- Marine life is being affected.
- Water is being contaminated.
- Landfills are overflowing.
- City streets are being damaged.

CAUSE

- the lack of recycling
- heavy traffic
- rapid urbanization
- climate changes
- fumes from cars
- factory waste

A: Forests are being destroyed because of rapid urbanization.
B: We need plans for urban development that don't . . .

2 DISCUSSION Tricky social situations

A PAIR WORK Read these problems that friends sometimes have with each other. Suggest solutions for each problem.

Your friend is always criticizing you and your other friends.
Your best friend never pays for his or her share at group dinners.
A friend is having a party and you weren't invited.

B GROUP WORK Agree on the best solution for each problem.

"The best thing to do is to talk to your friend and say how you feel."

useful expressions

One thing to do is to . . .
Another way to help is to . . .
The best thing to do is . . .

3 LISTENING I got it!

A Listen to people talk about recent events and activities in their lives. What events and activities are they talking about? What two qualities does each person's behavior demonstrate? Complete the chart.

a. money management
b. competitiveness
c. creativity
d. concern for others
e. perseverance
f. self-confidence

	Event or activity	Qualities
1. Kate		*e,*
2. Mark		
3. Iris		

B PAIR WORK Describe a time when you demonstrated one of the qualities above. Can your partner guess the quality?

4 QUESTIONNAIRE Learning styles

A PAIR WORK Interview your partner. Circle the ways your partner prefers to improve his or her English.

1. When you don't understand a word, would you prefer to . . . ?
a. look it up in a dictionary or **b.** try to guess the meaning

2. If you don't understand what someone says, would you rather . . . ?
a. ask the person to repeat it or **b.** pretend you understand

3. When you hear a new word in English, would you rather . . . ?
a. write it down or **b.** try to remember it

4. When you make a mistake in English, would you prefer someone to . . . ?
a. correct it immediately or **b.** ignore it

5. When you meet a native English speaker, would you prefer to . . . ?
a. try to talk to the person or **b.** listen while he or she speaks

6. When you have to contact someone in English, would you rather . . . ?
a. call him or her on the phone or **b.** send him or her an email

"I'd prefer to try to guess the meaning of a new word."

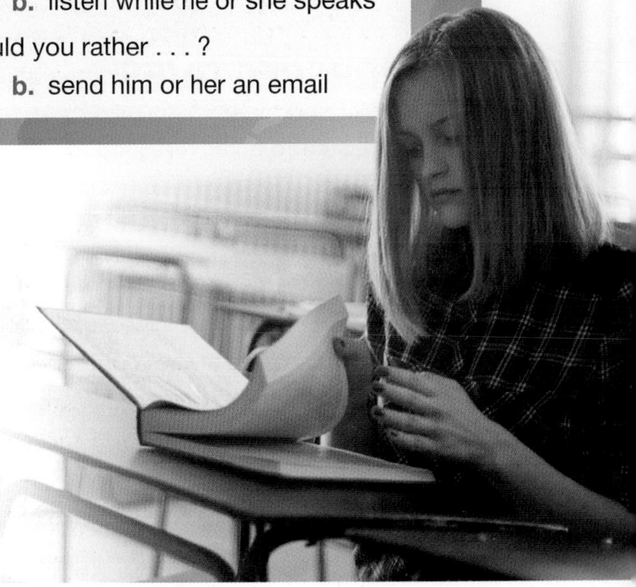

B GROUP WORK Discuss the advantages and disadvantages of each option in part A. Are there better options for each situation?

A: When I try to guess the meaning of a new word, it takes less time, so I can read faster.
B: Yes, but if you look it up, you learn a new word.
C: I think the best way to deal with a new word is to try and guess the meaning, and then check if it makes sense.

WHAT'S NEXT?

Look at your Self-assessment again. Do you need to review anything?

9 Getting things done

- Discuss professional services
- Make suggestions

1 SNAPSHOT

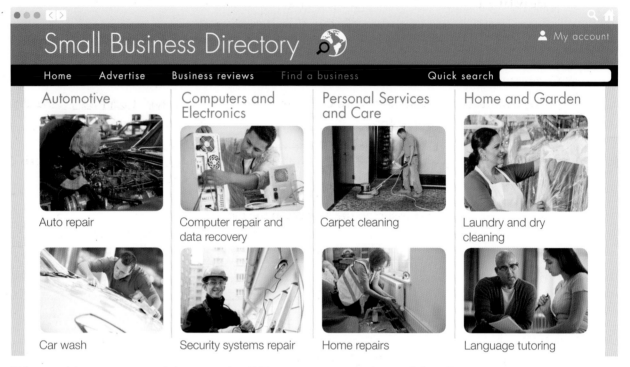

Small Business Directory

My account

Home | Advertise | Business reviews | Find a business | Quick search

Automotive	Computers and Electronics	Personal Services and Care	Home and Garden
 Auto repair	 Computer repair and data recovery	 Carpet cleaning	 Laundry and dry cleaning
 Car wash	 Security systems repair	 Home repairs	 Language tutoring

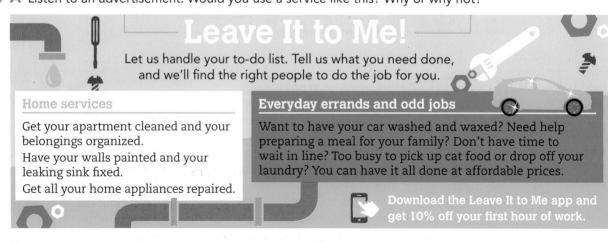

Why would someone need these services? Have you ever used any of them?
How do you choose a company or person to do any of these services?

2 PERSPECTIVES Get the job done!

A Listen to an advertisement. Would you use a service like this? Why or why not?

Leave It to Me!

Let us handle your to-do list. Tell us what you need done, and we'll find the right people to do the job for you.

Home services

Get your apartment cleaned and your belongings organized.
Have your walls painted and your leaking sink fixed.
Get all your home appliances repaired.

Everyday errands and odd jobs

Want to have your car washed and waxed? Need help preparing a meal for your family? Don't have time to wait in line? Too busy to pick up cat food or drop off your laundry? You can have it all done at affordable prices.

Download the Leave It to Me app and get 10% off your first hour of work.

B What services do you need or want? What questions would you ask before hiring a person to do these services for you?

3 GRAMMAR FOCUS

Get or have something done

Use get or have, the object, and the past participle of the verb to describe a service performed for you by someone else.

Do something yourself	*Get or have something done for you*
I **clean** my house every week.	I **get** my house **cleaned** (by a cleaner) every week.
He **is painting** his bedroom.	He **is having** his bedroom **painted**.
They **fixed** the sink.	They **got** the sink **fixed**.
Did you **paint** your bedroom?	Did you **have** your bedroom **painted**?
Where can I **wash** my car?	Where can I **have** my car **washed**?

GRAMMAR PLUS *see page 140*

A Complete the sentences to express that the services are performed by someone else.

1. My parents didn't paint their house before they moved in. They ____________. (have)
2. I didn't repair my own laptop. I ____________ at the electronics store. (get)
3. Many people don't wash their cars. They ____________. (have)
4. My bedroom carpet is very dirty, but I'm not cleaning it. I'm ____________ next week. (get)
5. My brother isn't repairing his bike. He ____________. (have)

B **PAIR WORK** Take turns describing the services in the pictures.

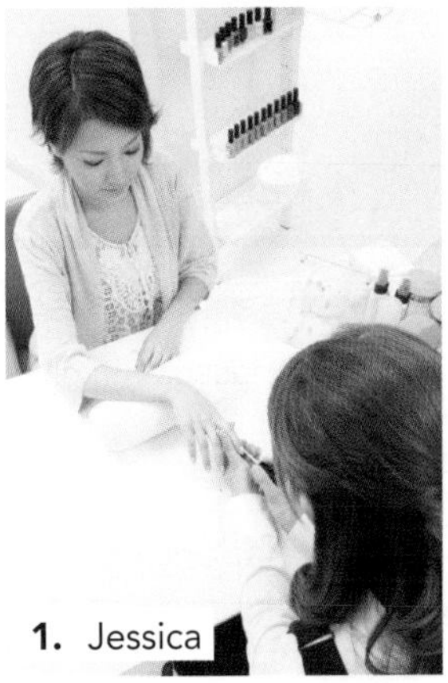
1. Jessica

2. Peter

3. Zoey

4. Tricia

"Jessica is having her nails done."

C **PAIR WORK** Tell your partner about three things you've had done for you recently. Ask and answer questions for more information.

4 PRONUNCIATION Sentence stress

A Listen and practice. Notice that when the object becomes a pronoun (sentence B), it is no longer stressed.

A: Where can I have my car washed?
B: You can have it washed at the auto shop.

A: Where can I get my nails done?
B: You can get them done at a salon.

B **GROUP WORK** Ask questions about three things you want to have done. Pay attention to sentence stress. Other students give answers.

5 DISCUSSION On demand

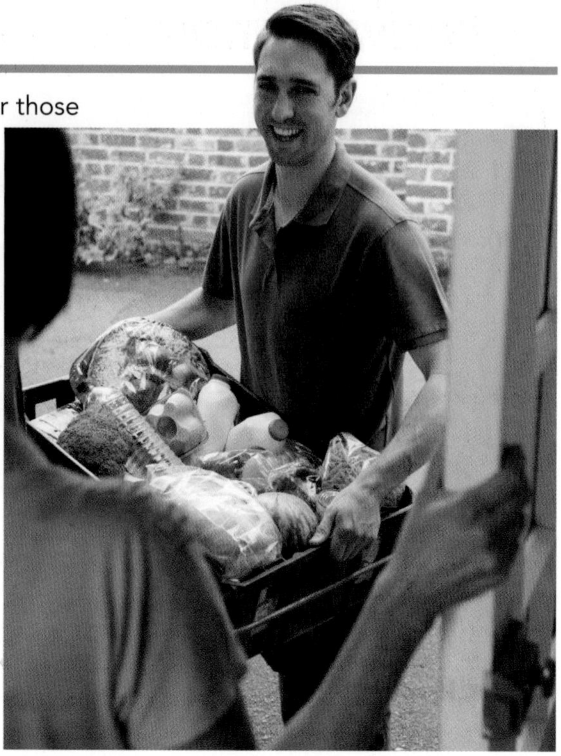

PAIR WORK Are these services available in your city? For those that aren't, do you think they would be a good idea?

Can you . . . ?

get groceries delivered to your door
have a five-star meal cooked at your home by a chef
have your home organized by a professional organizer
have your portrait drawn by a street artist
get your pet vaccinated at home
get your blood pressure checked at a pharmacy
have your shoes shined on the street
get your car washed for less than $15
have a suit made in under 24 hours
have pizza delivered after midnight

A: Can you get groceries delivered to your door?
B: Sure! You can have it done by . . .

6 INTERCHANGE 9 Absolutely not!

What do parents and teenagers usually argue about? Go to Interchange 9 on page 123.

7 WORD POWER Three-word phrasal verbs

A Match each phrasal verb in these sentences with its meaning. Then compare with a partner.

Phrasal verbs

1. Polly has **broken up with** her boyfriend. ______
2. Lin **came up with** a great idea for a new app for meeting people. ______
3. My brother is **looking forward to** getting married. He really loves his fiancée. ______
4. I can't **keep up with** all the new technology. It changes so fast. ______
5. Luisa doesn't **get along with** her roommate. They argue over every little thing. ______
6. My doctor says I'm overweight. I should **cut down on** sweets. ______
7. I can't **put up with** the noise on my street! I'll have to move. ______
8. I don't like to **take care of** my own finances. I have an accountant manage my money. ______

Meanings

a. reduce the quantity of
b. end a romantic relationship with
c. continue to learn about
d. tolerate
e. be excited for
f. have a good relationship with
g. be responsible for
h. think of; develop

B **PAIR WORK** Take turns making sentences with each phrasal verb in part A.

8 CONVERSATION I can't carry a tune.

A Listen and practice.

Emma: Are you going to Lina's party tonight?
Alice: No, I don't think so. I don't really feel up to it.
Emma: You haven't been going out much since you broke up with Carter.
Alice: I guess not. He's friends with all my friends, you know.
Emma: You need to meet new people. Have you thought about joining a running club? You love running.
Alice: I've thought about that, but they meet at 6 A.M. I'm not really a morning person.
Emma: Well . . . maybe you could take part in our singing group. I've made a lot of good friends there.
Alice: Um, I don't think so. Remember when we did karaoke? I can't carry a tune to save my life!
Emma: Yeah, I remember. . . . Well, I guess you'd better get used to waking up early. Just think of all the cute guys who go running in the park in the morning.

B CLASS ACTIVITY What are some other good ways to meet people?

9 GRAMMAR FOCUS

Making suggestions

With modals + verbs
Maybe you could take part in a singing group.

With gerunds
What about joining a running club?
Have you thought about asking your friends to introduce you around?

With negative questions
Why don't you do some volunteer work?

With infinitives
One option is to join a club.
It might be a good idea to check out the cultural events at the university.

GRAMMAR PLUS *see page 140*

A Circle the correct answers. Then practice with a partner.

1. **A:** What can I do to keep up with all my assignments in college?
   B: **Maybe / One option** you could stay in on weeknights.
2. **A:** What can I do to get in shape?
   B: **Why don't you / Have you thought about** working out at the gym?
3. **A:** How can I save money?
   B: **Why don't you / What about** come up with a budget?
4. **A:** How can I learn to dance?
   B: **Have you thought about / It might be a good idea** to take dance classes.
5. **A:** How can I build self-confidence?
   B: **What about / Why don't you** participating in more social activities?

B GROUP WORK Take turns asking and answering the questions in part A. Answer with your own suggestions.

10 LISTENING Resolutions

A Listen to a conversation between three friends on New Year's Eve. Check (✓) the resolution each person makes and write their friends' suggestions.

	New Year's resolutions		Suggestions
1. Edward	☐ get a better job	☐ start a project	
2. Selena	☐ have more energy	☐ go back to school	
3. Hannah	☐ fix her relationship problems	☐ spend more time on social media	

B GROUP WORK Decide on your own suggestion for each person. Then vote as a class on the best suggestions.

11 SPEAKING Breaking a habit

GROUP WORK Make three suggestions for how to break each of these bad habits. Then share your ideas with the class. Which ideas are the most creative?

How can I stop . . . ?

drinking too much soda

biting my nails

spending more money than I can afford

"One thing you could do is carry a bottle of water with you all the time. And why don't you . . . ?"

12 WRITING Sound advice

A Read the posts from a question and answer website. Choose one of the posts below and make a list of suggestions. Then write a reply.

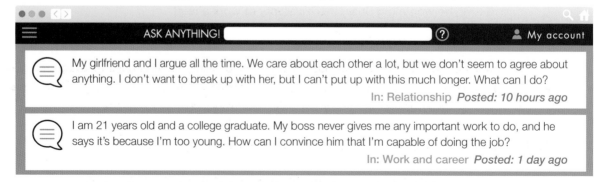

ASK ANYTHING! ? My account

My girlfriend and I argue all the time. We care about each other a lot, but we don't seem to agree about anything. I don't want to break up with her, but I can't put up with this much longer. What can I do?

In: Relationship *Posted: 10 hours ago*

I am 21 years old and a college graduate. My boss never gives me any important work to do, and he says it's because I'm too young. How can I convince him that I'm capable of doing the job?

In: Work and career *Posted: 1 day ago*

B GROUP WORK Take turns reading your advice. Whose advice do you think will work? Why?

13 READING

A Scan the article. Who is the article about? What idea did he have?

Improving the world – one idea at a time

[1] Jack Andraka was 15 when he came up with an idea for a new way to test for pancreatic cancer. When Andraka was 14, a family friend died of the disease, and this affected him deeply. This kind of cancer is particularly lethal because there is no test you can have done to find it in the early stages. By the time standard tests determine you have the disease, it is often too late. Realizing that this was the case, Andraka decided to try to develop a test that might catch problems at the earliest stages.

[2] The road ahead looked difficult for Andraka. He was still a high school student, and he wanted to create something that no one else had done. But Andraka read endlessly about the disease, wrote a proposal for his idea, and sent it out to 200 cancer researchers. Only one professor, Dr. Anirban Maitra, responded positively. Dr. Maitra agreed to work with Andraka on his idea, giving him guidance and access to a laboratory.

[3] The next big reward for Andraka's perseverance was winning the grand prize at the Intel International Science and Engineering Fair. This prestigious award is given to young innovators who have developed a world-changing idea. Developing the test is likely to take many years, but Andraka hopes the test will eventually improve people's lives – and maybe save them.

[4] Jack Andraka is not alone as a young innovator. After all, there were 1,499 other contestants for the Intel award, and all of them had ground-breaking ideas. For Andraka, having a family that loves science and encourages creative thinking gave him an advantage. But the key for Andraka is that reading, research, and discovery are just plain fun – and the chance to improve the world around him in the process makes it even better.

B Read the article. Write the number of each paragraph next to its summary sentence.

_____ One doctor's help makes the unlikely become possible.
_____ A personal experience creates a groundbreaking idea.
_____ Family support and a passion for discovery can lead to great things.
_____ Although he won a big prize, there's plenty of work ahead.

C Choose the correct answers.

1. Pancreatic cancer is so serious because **there is no treatment / it is hard to diagnose early**.
2. Andraka was inspired to find a solution by **an upsetting experience / reading about a disease**.
3. The response to Andraka's proposal was **fairly positive / largely negative**.
4. Andraka's test for pancreatic cancer is **in use now / being developed now**.
5. Andraka's family helped him by **encouraging him / working on his idea**.

D GROUP WORK If you could come up with an idea to help humanity, what would it be?

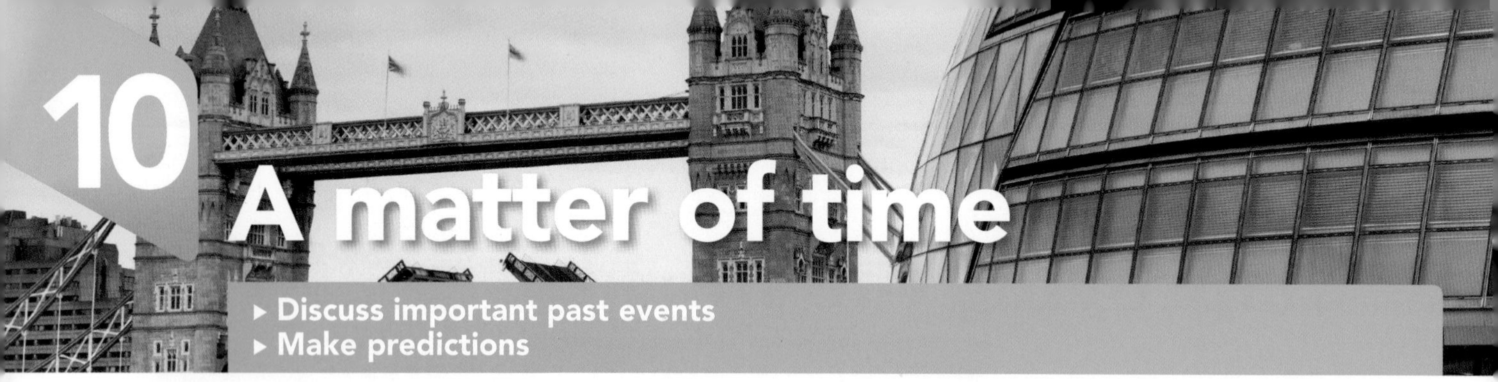

10 A matter of time

- Discuss important past events
- Make predictions

1 SNAPSHOT

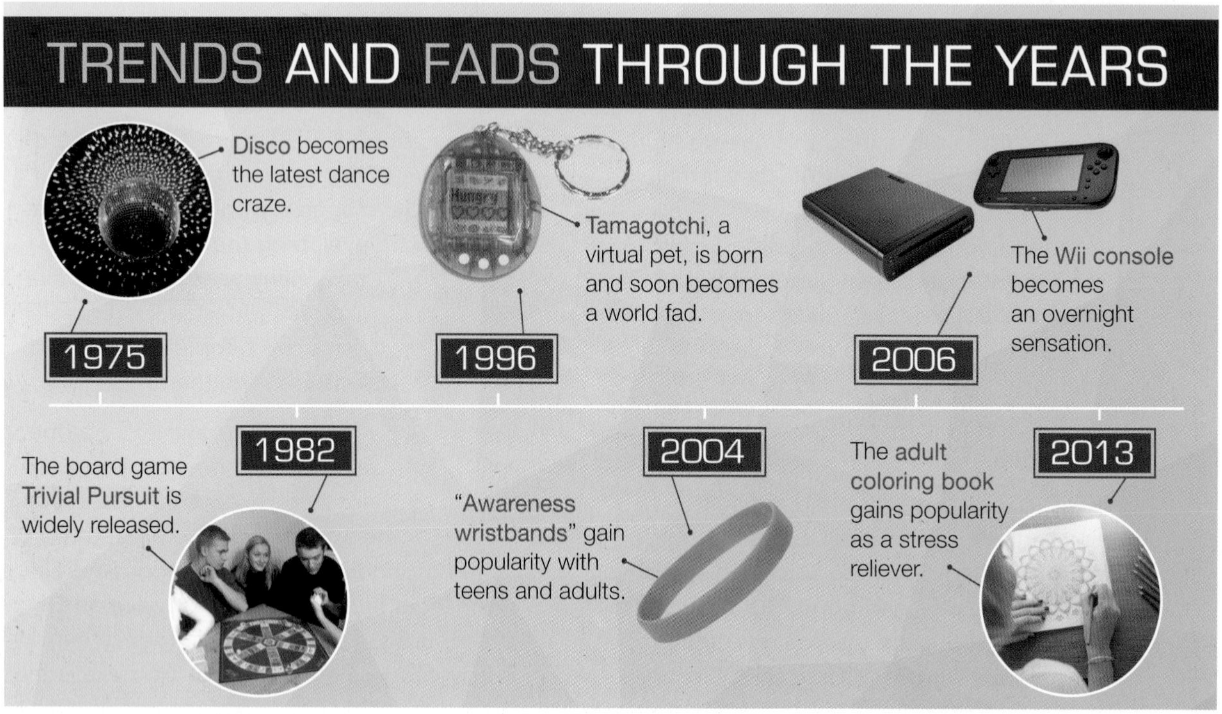

TRENDS AND FADS THROUGH THE YEARS
1975
Disco becomes the latest dance craze.
1982
The board game Trivial Pursuit is widely released.
1996
Tamagotchi, a virtual pet, is born and soon becomes a world fad.
2004
"Awareness wristbands" gain popularity with teens and adults.
2006
The Wii console becomes an overnight sensation.
2013
The adult coloring book gains popularity as a stress reliever.

Have any of these fads ever been popular in your country?
Can you think of other fads from the past or present?
Is there anything popular right now that you think is just a fad?

2 PERSPECTIVES Quiz show

A Read the questions from a quiz show. Do you know the answers? Check (✓) your guesses.

1. **When was the first home video game console released?**
   ☐ **a.** in 1967 ☐ **b.** in 1972 ☐ **c.** in 1981
2. **How long has Washington, D.C., been the capital of the United States?**
   ☐ **a.** since 1776 ☐ **b.** since 1783 ☐ **c.** since 1800
3. **How long were the Beatles together?**
   ☐ **a.** for 8 years ☐ **b.** for 10 years ☐ **c.** for 15 years
4. **When did World War I take place?**
   ☐ **a.** during the 1910s ☐ **b.** during the 1920s ☐ **c.** during the 1940s

B Now listen and check your answers. What information is the most surprising?

3 GRAMMAR FOCUS

> **Referring to time in the past**

A point or period of time in the past

When was the first video game console released?
During the 1970s. **In** the 1970s. Over 40 years **ago**.

How long were the Beatles together?
From 1960 **to** 1970. **For** 10 years.

A period of time that continues into the present

How long has Washington, D.C. been the capital of the United States?
Since 1800. **For** about 220 years.

GRAMMAR PLUS *see page 141*

A Complete the paragraphs with the **bold** words from the grammar box.
Then compare with a partner.

1. The Olympic Games originated in ancient
 Greece about 3,000 years _ago_. _During_ the
 eighth century BCE _to_ the fourth century CE,
 the games took place in Olympia. The first
 modern Olympics were held _in_ 1896 in Athens,
 with male participants from 14 nations. Women
 have only competed in the Olympics _in_ 1900.

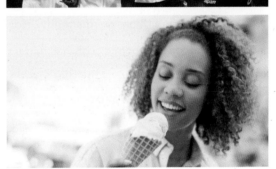

2. Although no one knows for sure, it's likely that the
 Chinese invented ice cream about 4,000 years
 ago. It was probably brought to Italy _in_
 the thirteenth century by Marco Polo, but the
 ice cream we enjoy today was probably created
 in Italy _from_ the seventeenth century and spread
 through Europe _to_ the eighteenth century.
 Since that time, different flavors have been
 created, but vanilla is still America's favorite.

B **GROUP WORK** Write two true and two false statements about world events.
Then take turns reading your statements. Others give correct information for
the false statements.

A: The United Nations was founded about 50 years ago.
B: That's false. It was founded in 1945, after the end of World War II.

4 PRONUNCIATION Syllable stress

A Listen and practice. Notice which syllable has the main stress in these four-
and five-syllable words. Notice the secondary stress.

● ●●●
identify

●● ● ●
disadvantage

● ● ●● ●
communication

| appreciate |
| assassination |
| catastrophe |
| consideration |
| conversation |
| revolution |

B Listen to the words in the box. Which syllable has the main stress?
Write the words in the correct column in part A.

5 WORD POWER Historic events

A Match each word with the best example. Then compare with a partner.

1. achievement ______
2. assassination ______
3. discovery ______
4. election ______
5. epidemic ______
6. natural disaster ______
7. revolution ______
8. terrorist act ______

a. In 2015, an earthquake hit Nepal and killed over 8,000 people.
b. Fidel Castro established a communist government in Cuba in 1959.
c. In 2015, scientists confirmed the existence of water on Mars.
d. Since the early 1980s, HIV has infected more than 70 million people.
e. Barack Obama became the first African American US president in 2009.
f. John Lennon was killed by a fan on December 8, 1980.
g. In 2003, scientists completed the Human Genome Project.
h. Two men invaded and killed the journalists of the *Charlie Hebdo* newspaper in Paris in 2015.

B PAIR WORK Give another example for each kind of event in part A.

"The invention of writing was a very important achievement for humankind."

6 DISCUSSION A major impact

GROUP WORK Choose two or three historic events (an election, an epidemic, an achievement, etc.) that had an impact on your country. Discuss the questions.

What happened (or what was achieved)? When did it happen?
What was the immediate effect on your country? the world? your family?
Did it change things permanently? How is life different now?

"The recent economic crisis has had a major impact on our lives . . ."

7 WRITING A biography

A Find information about a person who has had a major influence on the world or your country. Answer these questions. Then write a biography.

What is this person famous for?
How and when did he or she become famous?
What are his or her important achievements?

MALALA YOUSAFZAI
Activist for Women and Children's Rights

Malala was born in 1997 in Pakistan where she spoke out for girls' right to education. When she was 15, she suffered an attack on her life and almost died. She was flown to England, recovered from her injuries, and continued her fight. When she was 17, she became the youngest winner of the Nobel Peace Prize . . .

B PAIR WORK Exchange biographies. What additional details can your partner add?

8 INTERCHANGE 10 History buff

Find out how good you are at history.
Student A, go to Interchange 10A on page 124; Student B, go to Interchange 10B on page 126.

9 CONVERSATION I'll be their first guest!

A Listen and practice.

Hazel: Would you want to spend a vacation in space?
Oscar: No, thanks. I'd rather go to the beach. Would you?
Hazel: Of course I would! I'd stay longer, too. Do you think we'll have colonies on Mars in 20 or 30 years?
Oscar: I don't know. Considering how fast we're destroying Earth, we won't be living here for much longer.
Hazel: I'm serious! You know, international space agencies are investing a lot of money in research to develop more powerful rockets.
Oscar: Well, I guess that within 50 years, we'll have set up a research center on Mars, but not a colony.
Hazel: You're probably right. But I'm sure some company will have built a resort on the moon by then. And I'll be their first guest!

B CLASS ACTIVITY Do you think Hazel and Oscar's predictions are correct?

10 GRAMMAR FOCUS

Predicting the future with *will*

Use *will* to predict future events or situations.
We **will spend** vacations in space. We **won't have** colonies on Mars.
Use future continuous to predict ongoing actions.
Human beings **will be living** on another planet. We **won't be living** here.
Use future perfect to predict actions that will be completed by a certain time.
Within 50 years, we **will have set up** a research center on Mars.
By 2050, a company **will have built** a resort on the moon.

GRAMMAR PLUS *see page 141*

A Complete these predictions with the correct verb forms. (More than one answer is possible.) Then compare with a partner.

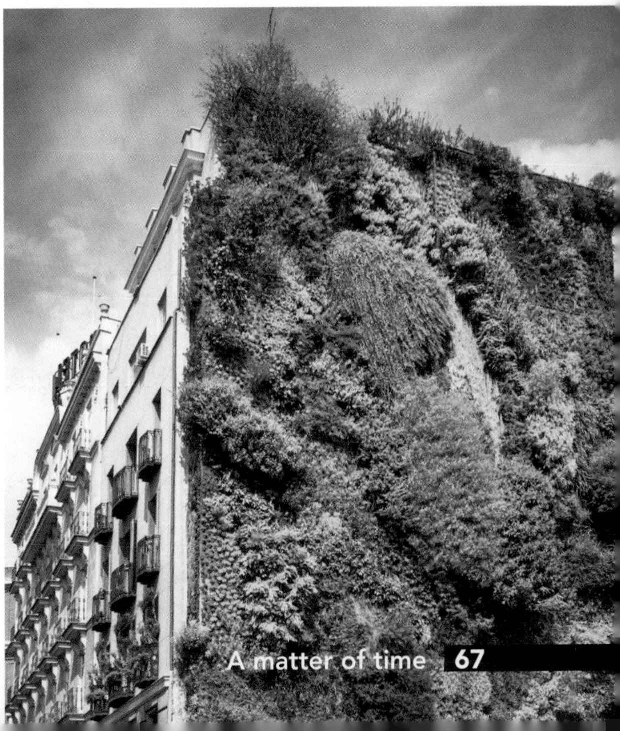

1. Sometime in the future, buildings ________________ (have) green walls and roof gardens to help retain carbon dioxide.
2. By the end of this century, half of the Amazon rain forest ________________ (be) deforested.
3. In 50 years, the world population ________________ (reach) 9 billion.
4. In the future, most of the population ________________ (live) in cities.
5. Soon, computers ________________ (become) more intelligent than humans.
6. In less than 20 years, scientists ________________ (discover) a cure for cancer, but we ________________ (suffer) from new diseases.

B GROUP WORK Discuss each prediction in part A. Do you agree or disagree?

A: Sometime in the future, buildings will have green walls and roof gardens to help retain carbon dioxide. What do you think?

B: Oh, I totally agree. That's also a good way to keep the temperature inside cooler in the summer.

C: I'm not so sure that will happen. Green walls are pretty expensive to maintain.

C CLASS ACTIVITY Discuss these questions.

1. What three recently developed technologies will have the greatest impact on our lives in the next 20 years?
2. What are the three most important changes that will have occurred on Earth by 2050?
3. Which three jobs will people *not* be doing in 50 years? Why?

11 LISTENING Not in our lifetime

A Listen to people discuss changes that will affect these topics in the future. Write down two changes for each topic.

	Future changes	
1. crime		
2. space travel		
3. environment		
4. energy		
5. money		

B PAIR WORK Which changes do you agree will happen? Which ones would most affect you? Why?

12 DISCUSSION Time will tell.

A Think about your dreams and goals for the future. Write down an idea for each category.

an activity you'd like to try
an experience you'd like to have
a skill you'd like to develop
a city where you would like to live
a job you'd like to have
a person you'd like to meet

B GROUP WORK Talk about these questions. Use your ideas from part A.

What do you think you'll be doing a year from now? five years from now?

Do you think you'll still be living in the same city? same country?

What are three things you think you'll have accomplished within the next 10 years?

What are three things you won't have done within the next 10 years?

In what ways do you think you'll have changed by the time you retire?

A: A year from now, I think I'll have a new hobby, like slacklining.

B: I'd like to try that, but I'm more interested in traveling.

C: Me too! I think in five years, I'll be living abroad.

13 READING

A Skim the article. Which sentence below could be another title for the article? Why?

Professionals Who Can Change the Future

An Unhappy View of the Future

Good Guesses About the Future

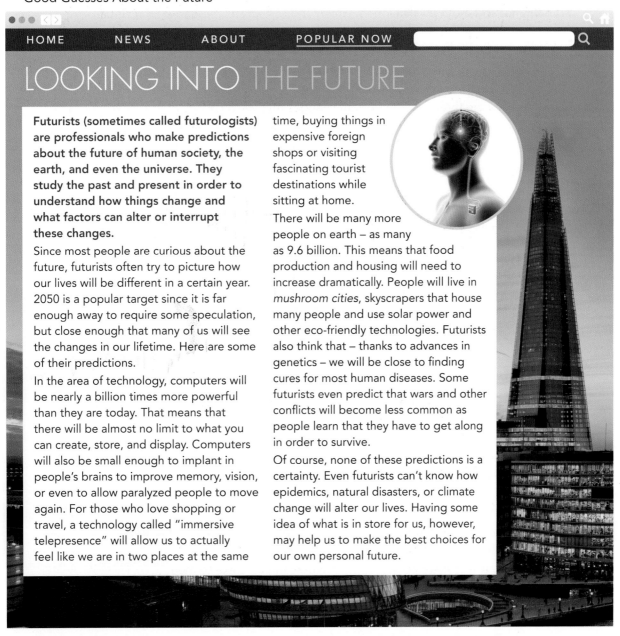

HOME NEWS ABOUT POPULAR NOW

LOOKING INTO THE FUTURE

Futurists (sometimes called futurologists) are professionals who make predictions about the future of human society, the earth, and even the universe. They study the past and present in order to understand how things change and what factors can alter or interrupt these changes.

Since most people are curious about the future, futurists often try to picture how our lives will be different in a certain year. 2050 is a popular target since it is far enough away to require some speculation, but close enough that many of us will see the changes in our lifetime. Here are some of their predictions.

In the area of technology, computers will be nearly a billion times more powerful than they are today. That means that there will be almost no limit to what you can create, store, and display. Computers will also be small enough to implant in people's brains to improve memory, vision, or even to allow paralyzed people to move again. For those who love shopping or travel, a technology called "immersive telepresence" will allow us to actually feel like we are in two places at the same time, buying things in expensive foreign shops or visiting fascinating tourist destinations while sitting at home.

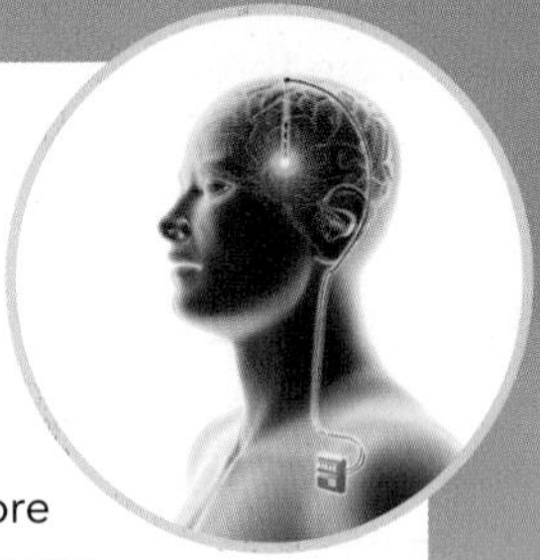

There will be many more people on earth – as many as 9.6 billion. This means that food production and housing will need to increase dramatically. People will live in *mushroom cities*, skyscrapers that house many people and use solar power and other eco-friendly technologies. Futurists also think that – thanks to advances in genetics – we will be close to finding cures for most human diseases. Some futurists even predict that wars and other conflicts will become less common as people learn that they have to get along in order to survive.

Of course, none of these predictions is a certainty. Even futurists can't know how epidemics, natural disasters, or climate change will alter our lives. Having some idea of what is in store for us, however, may help us to make the best choices for our own personal future.

B Read the article. Check (✓) the predictions futurists made about the year 2050.

1. ☐ Computers will be as powerful as they are today.
2. ☐ Tiny computers will help people with physical problems.
3. ☐ Travel will be faster than it is now.
4. ☐ People will be able to explore places without leaving home.
5. ☐ People will need less food.
6. ☐ Many people will live together in eco-friendly buildings.
7. ☐ People will not get sick anymore.
8. ☐ People will fight with each other over food and water.

C **GROUP WORK** Do you agree that the predictions in the article are likely? What changes would you like to see in the future?

Units 9–10 Progress check

SELF-ASSESSMENT

How well can you do these things? Check (✓) the boxes.

I can . . .	Very well	OK	A little
Discuss professional services (Ex. 1)	☐	☐	☐
Give advice and make suggestions (Ex. 2)	☐	☐	☐
Understand and discuss historic events (Ex. 3)	☐	☐	☐
Make predictions about the future (Ex. 4)	☐	☐	☐

1 DISCUSSION Professional services

GROUP WORK Take turns asking questions about these services. When someone answers "yes," find out why and when the service was performed, and who performed it.

have a piece of clothing tailor-made for you
get your carpet cleaned
have your home redecorated or remodeled
get something translated
have your cell phone repaired

A: Have any of you ever had a piece of clothing tailor-made for you?
B: Yes, I have. I had a suit tailor-made when I got married.
C: Really? Why didn't you buy one in a store? . . .

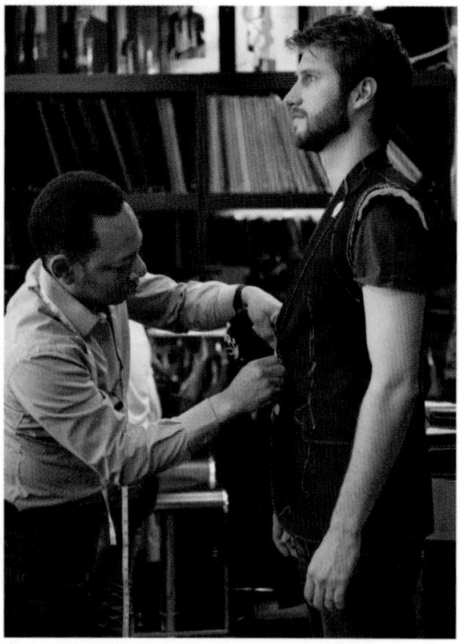

2 ROLE PLAY Advice needed

Student A: Choose one of these problems. Decide on the details of the problem. Then tell your partner about it and get some advice.

I want to move to my own place, but I don't make enough money.
I never have time to do any of the things I enjoy doing. I'm always busy with . . .
I have a job interview in English, and I'm feeling nervous about it.
My in-laws are coming to dinner, but I can't cook at all.

Student B: Your partner tells you about a problem. Ask questions about it. Then consider the situation and offer two pieces of advice.

Change roles and choose another situation.

useful expressions

Have you thought about . . . ?
It might be a good idea to . . .
Maybe you could . . .
Why don't you . . . ?

3 LISTENING Important world events

A Listen to people discuss the questions. Write the correct answers.

1. What date did people first land on the moon? ______________
2. When was the first World Cup? ______________
3. When was the Chernobyl disaster? ______________
4. How long did it take to build the *Titanic*? ______________
5. When did the Indian Ocean tsunami occur? ______________

B PAIR WORK Which of these events would you like to learn more about? Why?

C GROUP WORK Write three more questions about historic events. (Make sure you know the answers.) Then take turns asking your questions. Who has the most correct answers?

4 SURVEY What will happen?

A CLASS ACTIVITY How many of your classmates will have done these things in the next 5 years? Write down the number of "yes" and "no" answers. When someone answers "yes," ask follow-up questions.

	"Yes" answers	"No" answers
1. get a (new) job		
2. develop a new skill		
3. move to a new home		
4. learn another language		
5. travel abroad		
6. get a college or master's degree		

A: Five years from now, will you have moved to a new home?
B: Yes, I think I will be living in a new place.
A: Where do you think you'll be living?
B: I'd like to live in a bigger place. Our current apartment is too small.
A: Really? Would you rather live in a house or an apartment?

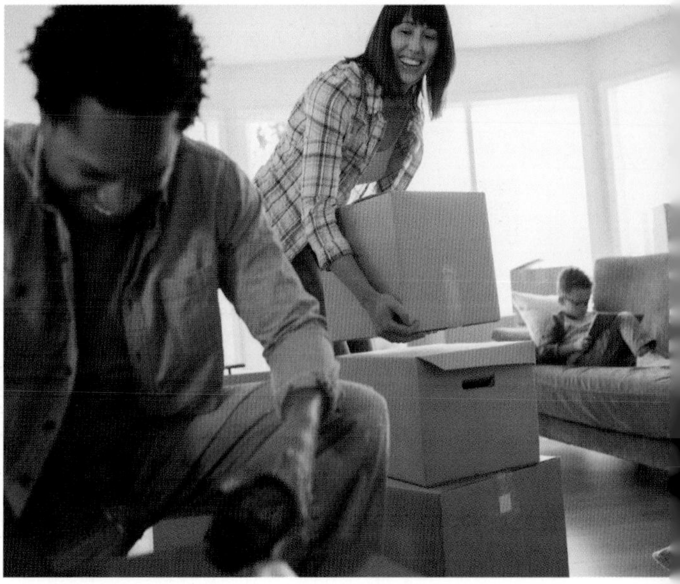

B GROUP WORK Tally the results of the survey as a group. Then take turns telling the class any additional information you found out.

"Most people think they will have moved to a new home. Only three people think they'll be living at their current address. One person thinks she'll be living in a big house in the suburbs, and . . . "

WHAT'S NEXT?

Look at your Self-assessment again. Do you need to review anything?

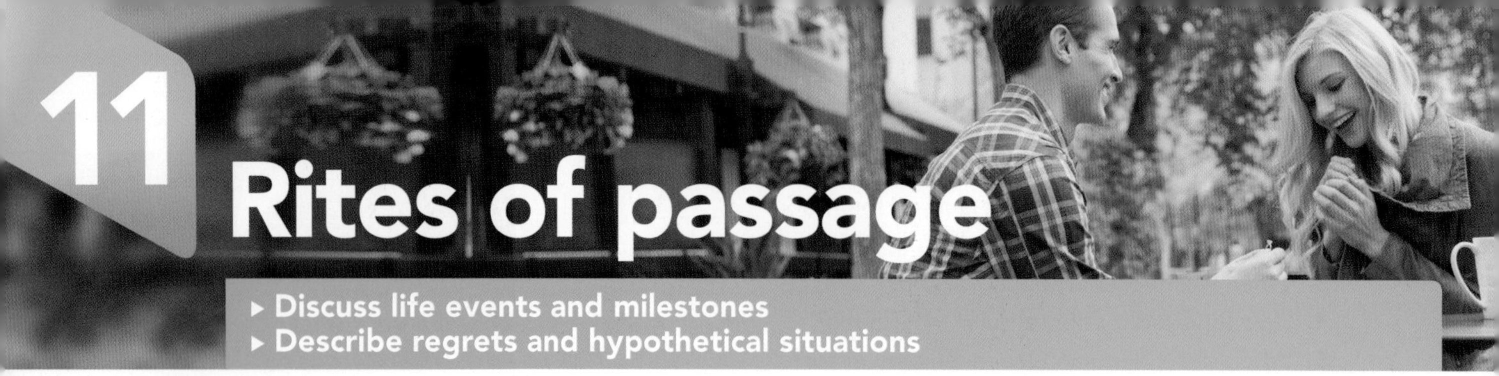

11 Rites of passage

- Discuss life events and milestones
- Describe regrets and hypothetical situations

1 SNAPSHOT

UNFORGETTABLE FIRSTS

Some moments that matter

- [ ] first sleepover
- [ ] losing your first tooth
- [ ] first day at school
- [ ] first pet
- [ ] first swim in the ocean
- [ ] first crush
- [ ] first trip with friends
- [ ] high school graduation
- [ ] first paycheck
- [ ] getting your driver's license
- [ ] entering college
- [ ] first heartbreak

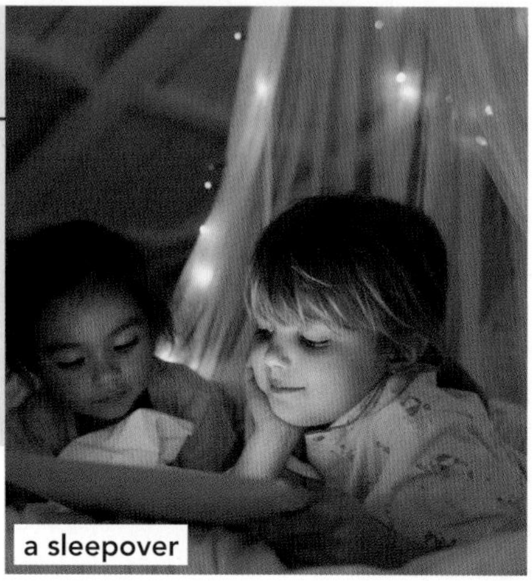
a sleepover

Which of these first experiences were important for you? Check (✓) them.
How did you feel when you had these experiences?
What other first experiences have you had that you will never forget?

2 CONVERSATION I was so immature.

A Listen and practice.

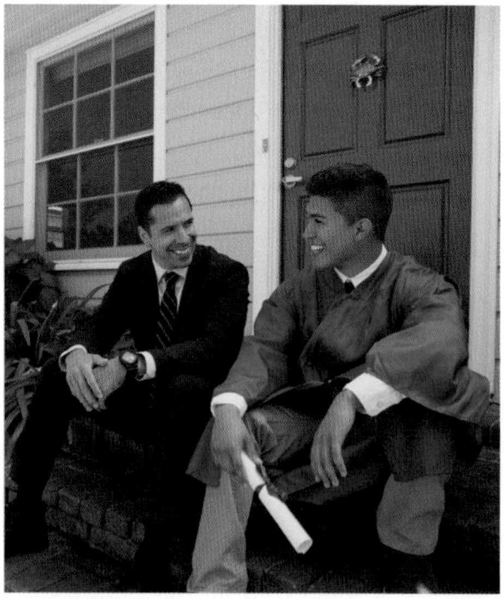

Jim: Congratulations, graduate! What's next for my favorite nephew?
Luke: I'm your *only* nephew, Uncle Jim!
Jim: But you're still my favorite! Anyway, what *are* your plans?
Luke: I'm looking for a job, so I can make some money before I go to college.
Jim: Ah! After *I* graduated, I went to Alaska to work as a fisherman. It was a tough job, but it helped me grow up.
Luke: How do you mean?
Jim: Until I started working, I'd never had any important responsibilities. I was so immature. But once I moved away from home, I learned to take care of myself.
Luke: So you became independent.
Jim: Yeah, but not for very long, actually. After two months, I moved back home . . . and got a job at your grandfather's store.
Luke: Hey, I think my search just ended. I'm going to talk to Grandpa about a job.

B Listen to the rest of the conversation. What was an important turning point for Jim? for Luke?

3 GRAMMAR FOCUS

Time clauses

Before I graduated from high school, I had never worked.
After I graduated, I went to Alaska to work as a fisherman.
Once I moved away from home, I learned to take care of myself.
The moment I moved away from home, I felt like a different person.
As soon as I got my own bank account, I started to be more responsible.
Until I moved to Alaska, I had never been away from home.
By the time I went to college, I had already lived away from home.

GRAMMAR PLUS *see page 142*

A Match the clauses in column A with appropriate information in column B. Then compare with a partner.

A	B
1. Until I went to college, ______	**a.** I learned the importance of teamwork.
2. Before I became a parent, ______	**b.** I understood why you shouldn't text and drive.
3. Once I joined a sports team, ______	**c.** I realized that I wasn't a child anymore.
4. The moment I had a car accident, ______	**d.** I learned that love can hurt!
5. As soon as I got my first paycheck, ______	**e.** I had never taken school very seriously.
6. By the time I was 15, ______	**f.** I began to understand the value of money.
7. After I began a relationship, ______	**g.** I had never cooked a real meal.
8. Until I left home, ______	**h.** I had never worried about the future.

B Which of the clauses in column A can you relate to your life? Add your own information to those clauses. Then compare with a partner.

"Until I left home, I had never bought my own clothes."

C **GROUP WORK** What do you think people learn from these events? Write sentences using time clauses in the present. Then take turns reading and talking about them.

1. moving in with roommates
2. buying your own home
3. having a pet
4. getting a credit card
5. getting your first paycheck
6. getting your driver's license
7. getting married
8. becoming a parent

1. *"Once you move in with roommates, you have to learn to work together."*

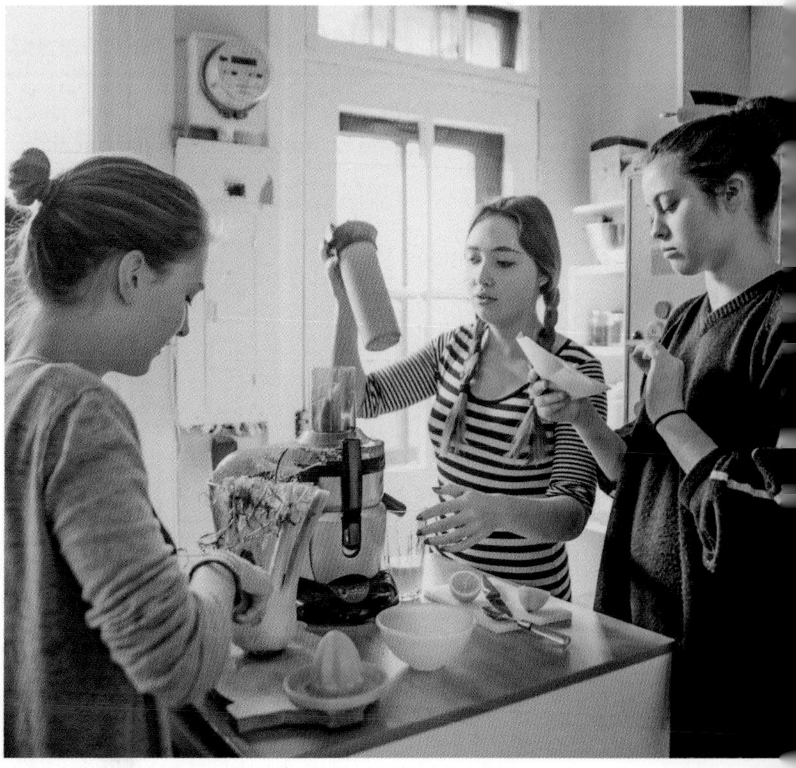

4 LISTENING Turning points

A Listen to three people describe important events in their lives. Complete the chart.

	Turning point	How it affected him or her
1. Nari		
2. Anthony		
3. Karina		

B Listen again. What do these three people have in common?

C PAIR WORK What has been a turning point in your life? Discuss with a partner.

5 SPEAKING Milestones

A PAIR WORK In your country, how old are people when these things typically happen?

get a first job
get a driver's license
move out of their parents' home
graduate from college
get married
retire

B GROUP WORK Choose three milestones. What do you think life is like before and after each one? Join another pair and discuss.

"Before you get a job, you depend on your family for everything. The moment you get your first paycheck, you . . ."

6 WORD POWER Personal characteristics

A PAIR WORK At what age do you think people possess these traits? Check (✓) one or more ages for each trait.

	In their teens	In their 20s	In their 30s	In their 40s	In their 60s
ambitious	☐	☐	☐	☐	☐
argumentative	☐	☐	☐	☐	☐
carefree	☐	☐	☐	☐	☐
dependable	☐	☐	☐	☐	☐
naive	☐	☐	☐	☐	☐
pragmatic	☐	☐	☐	☐	☐
rebellious	☐	☐	☐	☐	☐
sophisticated	☐	☐	☐	☐	☐
wise	☐	☐	☐	☐	☐

B GROUP WORK Use the words in part A to describe people you know.
"My mother is dependable. I can always count on her when I need help."

7 PERSPECTIVES That was a mistake.

A Listen to two recent college graduates talk about their regrets. Do you have any similar regrets?

1 I should have done an internship while I was in college.

3 If I hadn't been so irresponsible, I could have gotten better grades.

5 If I'd listened to my professors, I would have taken some additional courses.

2 If I'd been more ambitious in college, I could have learned to speak another language.

4 I shouldn't have taken out a student loan to pay for college.

6 If I hadn't wasted so much money last year, I would have saved enough to start graduate school.

B GROUP WORK What advice would you give to these recent grads?

8 GRAMMAR FOCUS

Expressing regret and describing hypothetical situations

Use *should have* + the past participle to express regret.
I should have done an internship while I was in college.
I shouldn't have taken out a student loan.

Use *would have* + the past participle to express probable outcomes in hypothetical situations.
Use *could have* + the past participle to express possible outcomes.
If I'd listened to my professors, I **would have taken** additional courses.
If I **hadn't been** so irresponsible, I **could have gotten** better grades.

GRAMMAR PLUS *see page 142*

A For each statement, write a sentence expressing regret. Then talk with a partner about which statements are true for you.

1. I didn't play any sports when I was younger.
2. I was carefree with money when I was a teenager.
3. I didn't stay in touch with my school friends after I graduated.
4. I was naive when I first started working.
5. I didn't study hard in school.

1. I should have played sports when I was a teenager.

B Match the clauses in column A with appropriate information in column B.

A	B
1. If I hadn't gone to so many parties, ______	**a.** I would have been nicer to my parents.
2. If I'd been more careful, ______	**b.** I wouldn't have borrowed money for a new car.
3. If I'd been wiser, ______	**c.** I would have done better in school.
4. If I'd listened to my financial advisor, ______	**d.** I wouldn't have lost all my documents.
5. If I hadn't been so rebellious, ______	**e.** I wouldn't have argued with my boss.

C Add your own information to the clauses in column A. Then compare in groups.

9 INTERCHANGE 11 Good choices, bad choices

Imagine if things were different. Go to Interchange 11 on page 125.

10 PRONUNCIATION Reduction of *have* and *been*

A Listen and practice. Notice how **have** and **been** are reduced in these sentences.

I should **have been** less selfish when I was younger.
If I'd **been** more ambitious, I could **have** gotten a promotion.

B PAIR WORK Complete these sentences and practice them. Pay attention to the reduced forms of **have** and **been**.

I should have been . . . when I was younger.
I should have been . . . in school.
If I'd been more . . ., I could have . . .
If I'd been less . . ., I would have . . .

11 LISTENING My biggest regret

A Listen to a conversation between three friends about regrets. Write two regrets that each person has.

	Regrets	
1. Ariana		
2. Ray		
3. Kira		

B Listen again. Which friend feels differently about regrets? How does he or she feel?

C PAIR WORK Do you agree with the attitude about regrets in part B? Why or why not?

12 WRITING An apology

A Think about something you regret doing that you want to apologize for. Consider the questions below. Then write a message of apology.

What did you do? What were the consequences?
Is there any way you can undo those consequences?

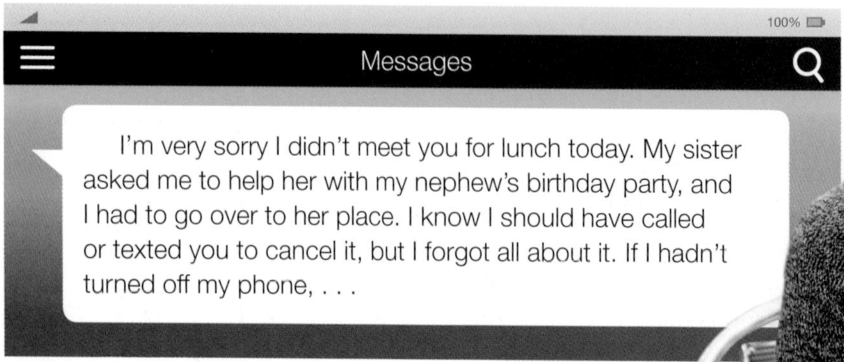

100%
Messages
I'm very sorry I didn't meet you for lunch today. My sister asked me to help her with my nephew's birthday party, and I had to go over to her place. I know I should have called or texted you to cancel it, but I forgot all about it. If I hadn't turned off my phone, . . .

B PAIR WORK Read your partner's message. Talk about what you would have done if you'd had a similar regret.

13 READING

A Skim the advice column. What is Paul's problem? What does he ask Stella?

STELLA'S ANSWERS

HOME | ABOUT | ADVICE | ASK STELLA | COMMUNITY | FOLLOW STELLA

Dear Stella,

I have a problem, and I'm not sure what to do about it. I was studying with my friend Karl, and he let me use his laptop for a minute to look something up. He had been busy typing an essay, so I opened the document again when I was done. But somehow I hit the wrong button, and I deleted the document. All of his work was gone. It was a total accident, and I did say, "Sorry," just so he wouldn't yell at me. But he got really angry and accused me of doing it on purpose. Now Karl is acting really cold towards me, and I can tell he's still angry. It really wasn't my fault, but I still feel bad. Should I apologize anyway just to make him feel better?

Paul in Philadelphia

Dear Paul,

When you've done something that hurt a friend, even by accident, it can be really uncomfortable. You obviously feel bad about deleting Karl's essay, and you didn't mean for it to happen. Unfortunately, it sounds like Karl has a pretty short fuse. Sure, if you'd apologized better at the time, and if you had offered to help him recover his work, it might have smoothed things over. After being accused of sabotage, however, I understand why you didn't apologize again.

What should you do now? First, ask yourself if an apology is necessary. If you don't feel you did anything wrong, it wouldn't mean very much. An apology has to be sincere and heartfelt to be effective. Second, if someone stops treating you like a friend because you made a mistake – which is a form of emotional blackmail – they probably won't believe your apology anyway. Third, a two-way discussion is often more effective than an apology. I think you need to sit down with Karl, tell him how badly you feel, avoid making excuses or trying to blame him, and get on with your friendship. If he still won't forgive you after that, maybe he's not such a great friend after all.

B Read the advice column. Find the words in *italics* in the text. Match the definitions to the words.

1. *short fuse* ______
2. *sabotage* ______
3. *heartfelt* ______
4. *blackmail* ______
5. *forgive* ______

a. act of demanding something from someone in exchange for a benefit
b. quick or violent temper
c. decide not to be angry at someone
d. act of destroying something to get an advantage
e. very sincere

C Check (✓) True, False, or Not given for each statement.

	True	False	Not given
1. The two boys are best friends from childhood.	☐	☐	☐
2. Paul mistakenly deleted some of Karl's work.	☐	☐	☐
3. Karl reacted very calmly at the time.	☐	☐	☐
4. Stella thinks Paul could have improved the situation at the time.	☐	☐	☐
5. Stella believes that both friends need to apologize.	☐	☐	☐
6. Stella thinks even an insincere apology is helpful.	☐	☐	☐
7. Karl's behavior shows that he is not very forgiving.	☐	☐	☐
8. Stella says that Paul and Karl's friendship is over.	☐	☐	☐

D **PAIR WORK** Do you agree with the advice Stella gave Paul? If not, what advice would you give him?

12 Keys to success

▸ Give personal views and describe qualities for success
▸ Give reasons

1 SNAPSHOT

HOW SOME MAJOR COMPANIES GOT THEIR NAMES

Nike The company got its name from the ancient Greek goddess of victory.

Google Google comes from *googol*, which is the math term for the number 1 followed by 100 zeros.

Facebook The name was taken from the term for a list with students' names and photos found at American universities.

Samsung In Korean, *sam* means "three" and *sung* means "star," so the name means "three stars." It represents the idea that the company should be everlasting, like stars in the sky.

Skype The original concept for the name was Sky-Peer-to-Peer, which became Skyper, and then Skype.

Häagen-Dazs The name of the American ice cream brand was invented to sound Danish and traditional, but it has no meaning in any language.

Pepsi The soft drink got its name from the word *dyspepsia*, which means indigestion, because its inventor believed it helped treat an upset stomach.

Which of these brands exist in your country? Are they successful?
Do you know the origin of the names of other companies or brands?

2 PERSPECTIVES Business strategies

A Listen to the survey. What makes a business successful? Number the choices from 1 (most important) to 3 (least important).

What makes a business successful?

1. **In order for an app to succeed, it has to be:**
   - ☐ easy to use ☐ inexpensive ☐ original
2. **To attract talented professionals, a company should offer:**
   - ☐ competitive salaries ☐ flexible working schedules ☐ a good career plan
3. **For a small company to be profitable, it should have:**
   - ☐ a good marketing plan ☐ a great product ☐ excellent professionals
4. **To build a successful start-up, it's important to:**
   - ☐ have a great product ☐ have a clear business plan ☐ control costs
5. **In order to finance a new business, it's a good idea to:**
   - ☐ try a crowd-funding platform ☐ get a bank loan ☐ borrow money from family
6. **For people to work from home, they need to have:**
   - ☐ self-discipline ☐ a separate working space ☐ a daily schedule

B GROUP WORK Compare your answers. Do you agree on the most important success factors?

3 PRONUNCIATION Reduced words

A Listen and practice. Notice how certain words are reduced in conversation.

In order **før a̸** hotel **tø** be successful, it needs **tø** have friendly service **a̸nd̸** reasonable prices.
Før a̸n entrepreneur **tø** be successful, they have **tø** invest in **a̸** good marketing campaign.

B PAIR WORK Take turns reading the sentences in Exercise 2 aloud. Use your first choice to complete each sentence. Pay attention to reduced words.

4 GRAMMAR FOCUS

Describing purpose

Infinitive clauses

To attract talented professionals,	a company should offer competitive salaries.
(**In order**) **to finance** a new business,	it's a good idea to get a bank loan.

Infinitive clauses with *for*

For a small company **to be** profitable,	it should have a good marketing plan.
(**In order**) **for** an app to succeed,	it has to be easy to use.

GRAMMAR PLUS *see page 143*

A Match each goal with a suggestion. Then practice the sentences with a partner. (More than one answer is possible.)

Goals

1. To run a popular convenience store, ______
2. In order to run a profitable clothing boutique, ______
3. To establish a successful language school, ______
4. In order for a health club to succeed, ______
5. For a restaurant to attract more customers, ______

Suggestions

a. it has to offer friendly service.
b. it's a good idea to know the competition.
c. you need to choose the right location.
d. you have to train your staff well.
e. it's important to understand your customers' needs.

B PAIR WORK Give another suggestion for each goal in part A.

C GROUP WORK What kind of business would you like to have? Talk to your classmates and get suggestions on how to make your business successful.

A: I think I'd like to set up a coffee shop.
B: For a coffee shop to succeed, it's important to choose a good location.
C: And in order to attract customers, you have to offer some tasty desserts, too.

5 WORD POWER Qualities for success

A PAIR WORK What qualities are important for success? Rank them from 1 to 5.

A personal trainer	A politician	A news website
☐ athletic	☐ clever	☐ affordable
☐ passionate	☐ charming	☐ attractive
☐ industrious	☐ knowledgeable	☐ entertaining
☐ muscular	☐ persuasive	☐ informative
☐ experienced	☐ tough	☐ well written

B GROUP WORK Add one more adjective to each list.

"For a personal trainer to be successful, he or she needs to be . . ."

6 ROLE PLAY The job is yours!

Student A:

Interview two people for one of these jobs. What qualities do they need for success? Decide who is more qualified for the job.

Students B and C:

You are applying for the same job. What are your best qualities? Convince the interviewer that you are more qualified for the job.

sales associate at a trendy boutique   public relations specialist   tour guide

A: To be a good sales associate, you need to be persuasive. Are you?
B: Oh, yes. I'm very good at convincing people. And I'm industrious.
C: I've worked at other stores before, so I'm experienced. And I'm fashionable, too.

7 CONVERSATION It's always packed.

A Listen and practice.

Kyle: What's your favorite club, Lori?
Lori: The Firefly. They have fabulous music, and it's never crowded, so it's easy to get in.
Kyle: That's funny. There's always a long wait outside my favorite club. I like it because it's always packed.
Lori: Why do you think it's so popular?
Kyle: Well, it just opened a few months ago, everything is brand-new and modern, and lots of trendy people go there. It's called the Dizzy Lizard.
Lori: Oh, right! I hear the reason people go there is just to be seen.
Kyle: Exactly! Do you want to go some night?
Lori: I thought you'd never ask!

B CLASS ACTIVITY What are some popular places in your city? Do you ever go to any of these places? Why or why not?

8 GRAMMAR FOCUS

Giving reasons

The Firefly is famous **for** its fantastic music.
I like the Dizzy Lizard **because** it's always packed.
Since it's always so packed, there's a long wait outside the club.
It's popular **because of** the trendy people.
Due to the crowds, the Dizzy Lizard is difficult to get into.
The reason (**that/why**) people go there **is** just to be seen.

GRAMMAR PLUS *see page 143*

A Complete the paragraphs with *because, since, because of, for, due to*, and *the reason*. Then compare with a partner. (More than one answer is possible.)

1. Apple is considered one of the most innovative companies in the world. The company is known ________ introducing original products, but it's also admired ________ its ability to predict what the market will need in the future. ________ Apple has been so successful is that it has become a symbol of status and high-end technology.
2. McDonald's is popular worldwide ________ customers know what to expect when they eat there. Whether you're in Florida or in France, your Big Mac is the same. The company is also known ________ its ability to adapt to different markets. ________ the company adjusts some items to local tastes, you can eat a pineapple pie in Thailand or a shrimp burger in Japan.

B PAIR WORK Match the situations with the reasons for success. Compare ideas with a partner. Then give two more reasons for each success.

Situation	Reason
1. FedEx is famous ______	**a.** because of its ability to attract new customers.
2. Samsung is a successful company ______	**b.** for its fast and reliable service.
3. Online stores are becoming very popular ______	**c.** for its innovative athletic wear.
4. Netflix has expanded quickly ______	**d.** for its wide selection of products.
5. People buy Levi's jeans ______	**e.** since prices are generally more affordable.
6. Many people like Amazon ______	**f.** due to its high investment in research.
7. Nike is known ______	**g.** since it's advertised worldwide.
8. People everywhere drink Coca-Cola ______	**h.** because they appeal to people of different ages and lifestyles.

A: FedEx is famous for its fast and reliable service.
B: I think another reason why FedEx is famous is . . .

C GROUP WORK What are some successful companies in your country? Why are they successful?

9 LISTENING What have you got to lose?

A Listen to radio commercials for three different businesses.
What are two special features of each place?

	Fitness For Life	Beauty To Go	Like-New Repair Services
1.			
2.			

B Listen again. Complete the slogan for each business.

1. "Fitness For Life, where ______________________."
2. "Beauty To Go. When and where you want, beauty ______________________."
3. "Like-New Repair Services. Don't let your phone ______________________."

C GROUP WORK Which business do you think would be the most successful in your city? Why?

10 INTERCHANGE 12 Advertising taglines

How well do you know the slogans companies use for their products?
Go to Interchange 12 on page 127.

11 DISCUSSION Ads and commercials

GROUP WORK Discuss these questions.

When you watch TV, do you pay attention to the commercials? Why or why not?
When you're online, do you click on any ads that you see?
What ads attract your attention?
What are some effective commercials or ads you remember?
What made them effective?
What is the funniest commercial you've ever seen? the worst? the most shocking?
Which celebrities have been in commercials or ads?
Has this affected your opinion of the product?
Has it affected your opinion of the celebrity?

12 WRITING A commercial

A Choose one of your favorite products. Read the questions and make notes about the best way to sell it. Then write a one-minute TV or online commercial.

What's good or unique about the product?
Why would someone want to buy or use it?
Can you think of a clever name or slogan?

Do you want a car that is dependable and economical? Do you need more space for your family? The new Genius SUV has it all. Genius offers the latest safety technologies and . . .

B GROUP WORK Take turns presenting your commercials. What is good about each one? Can you give any suggestions to improve them?

13 READING

A Scan the article. What does "sticky" mean in the advertising world?

BRAIN INVASION:
WHY WE CAN'T FORGET SOME ADS

Advertisements: They're all over our social media pages; they arrive as text messages; they interrupt our favorite shows; and they bombard us in the streets. In order to survive the constant barrage of advertising, we learn to ignore most of what we see. But what is it that makes certain ads "sticky"? In other words, why do we remember some ads while managing to completely forget others?

According to advertising experts, an ad needs three key elements to make it unforgettable. In the first place, it needs to be clear and simple. TV commercials usually last about 30 seconds, so a complicated or confusing presentation will not do the job. For an ad to be "sticky," it has to be obvious enough that we can pick up the message in a split second.

More importantly, ads should appeal to our senses and emotions. When we really feel something, it tends to stick in our brains much longer than if we simply understand it. This is the reason why so much advertising depends on emotional music and images of family, romance, or success that relate directly to our own hopes and dreams.

One more element necessary to make an ad successful is surprise. When we see something out of the ordinary, it makes us take notice whether we want to or not. A talking animal, a beautifully dressed model diving into a swimming pool, a car zooming through an ever-changing landscape – these are the types of things that grab our attention.

But do "sticky" ads actually make us buy the products? That's another story. Sometimes the most memorable ads make people laugh or mention them to their friends, but they don't actually convince people to buy anything. Still, after watching a "sticky" ad, we usually remember the name of the company it promotes. And in a world with so many brands and products, that is almost as important as sales.

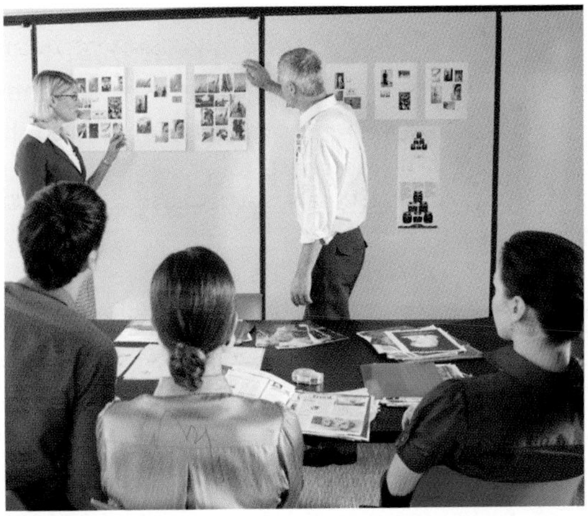

B Read the article. Check (✓) the three things that make an ad memorable.

- ☐ an uncomplicated concept
- ☐ a puzzle or mystery
- ☐ a short time span
- ☐ a sensual or emotional appeal
- ☐ a familiar scene or situation
- ☐ something unexpected or strange

C Read these descriptions of two ads. According to the article, are these "sticky" ads? Explain why.

A family of four is having breakfast together, and they're all looking tired. The father pours each of them a glass of "Super Juice," and as they all drink it, they are transformed into costumed superheroes. As they leave, the mother says, "Ready to save the world, team?"

A young couple are in a luxurious car; the woman is driving. They are driving quickly through lush countryside. They glance at other and smile. A voiceover says: "The Eternity: a car that feels like home."

D **PAIR WORK** Describe an advertisement that has stuck in your mind. Why do you think you remember it? Has it influenced what you buy in any way?

Units 11–12 Progress check

SELF-ASSESSMENT

How well can you do these things? Check (✓) the boxes.

I can . . .	Very well	OK	A little
Describe important life events and their consequences (Ex. 1)	☐	☐	☐
Describe and explain regrets about the past (Ex. 2)	☐	☐	☐
Describe hypothetical situations in the past (Ex. 2)	☐	☐	☐
Understand and give reasons for success (Ex. 3, 4)	☐	☐	☐
Give reasons (Ex. 4)	☐	☐	☐

1 SPEAKING Important events

A What are two important events for each of these age groups? Complete the chart.

Children	Teenagers	People in their 20s	People in their 40s

B GROUP WORK Talk about the events. Why is each event important? What do people learn from each event?

A: Learning to drive is an important event for teenagers.
B: Why is learning to drive an important milestone?
A: Once they learn to drive, . . .

useful expressions

after	once
as soon as	before
the moment	until
by the time	

2 GAME Regrets

A Write three regrets you have about the past.

1. *I wish I hadn't argued with my boss.*

B GROUP WORK What if the situations were different? Take turns. One student expresses a regret. The next student adds a hypothetical result, and so on, for as long as you can.

A: I shouldn't have argued with my boss.
B: If you hadn't argued with your boss, she wouldn't have fired you.
C: If she hadn't fired you, you could have . . .

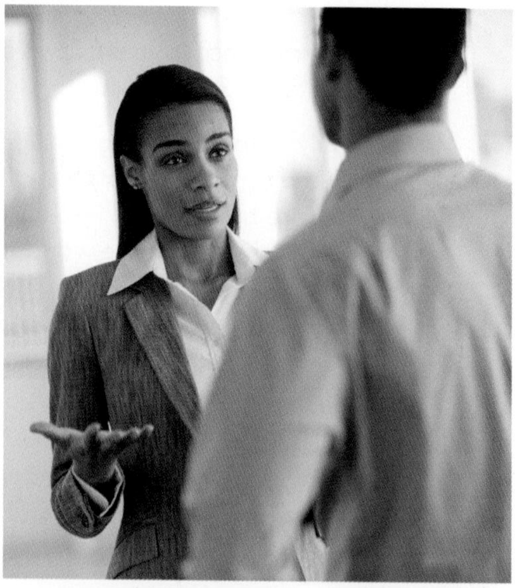

3 LISTENING The road to success

A Listen to a career coach discuss some factors necessary to work for yourself. Write down the three factors that you hear.

	Factor	Why is it important?
1.		
2.		
3.		

B Listen again. In your own words, write why each factor is important.

C PAIR WORK If you could work for yourself, what would you do? Why?

4 DISCUSSION Effective strategies

A PAIR WORK Choose two businesses and discuss what they need to be successful. Then write three sentences describing the most important factors.

- ☐ a convenience store
- ☐ a gourmet supermarket
- ☐ a dance club
- ☐ a beach hotel
- ☐ a juice bar
- ☐ a used clothing store

In order for a convenience store to be successful, it has to be open 24 hours.

B GROUP WORK Join another pair. Share your ideas. Do they agree?

A: We think in order for a convenience store to be successful, it has to be open 24 hours.

B: Really? But many convenience stores close at midnight.

C GROUP WORK Now choose a popular business that you know about. What are the reasons for its success?

"I think Mark's Comics is successful because their comic books are affordable and they don't mind if people hang out there and read."

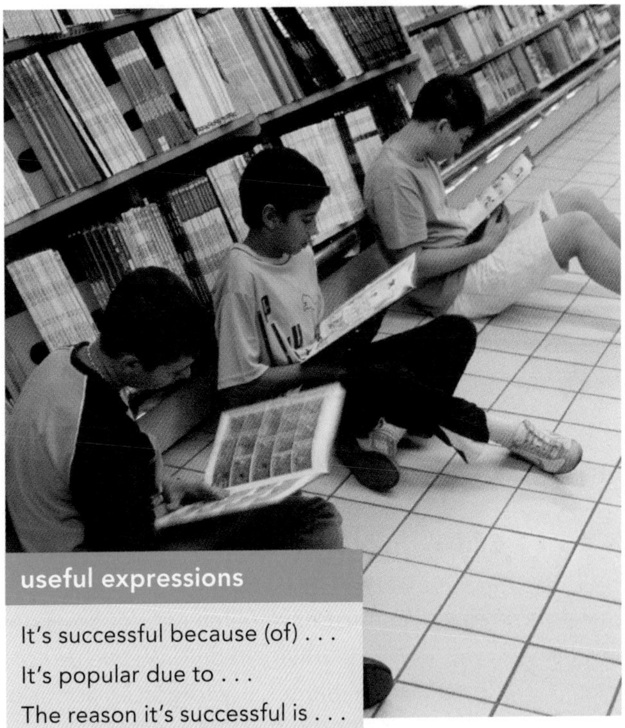

useful expressions

It's successful because (of) . . .
It's popular due to . . .
The reason it's successful is . . .
It's become popular since . . .
It's famous for . . .

WHAT'S NEXT?

Look at your Self-assessment again. Do you need to review anything?

13 What might have been

- Suggest explanations and reasons
- Give opinions and advice about past situations

1 SNAPSHOT

PET PEEVES

IT DRIVES ME CRAZY WHEN . . .

- people push too close to me on the subway.
- someone borrows my things without asking.
- people keep interrupting me.
- a couple starts arguing in public.
- people don't pay for their share at a restaurant.
- a friend criticizes another friend.
- someone is late for no reason.
- people chew with their mouths open.
- a friend constantly asks me for favors.
- someone cuts in line in front of me.

Which of the pet peeves do you have about people you know? Which one is the worst?
What other pet peeves do you have?
Do you do any of these things? When and why?

2 CONVERSATION He might have gone out.

A Listen and practice.

Chris: Didn't Tyler ask us to come at 7:30?
Ava: Yes, and it's almost 8:00 now. Why don't we ring the bell again? He must not have heard it.
Chris: That's impossible. We've been ringing the bell for more than 10 minutes.
Ava: He must have fallen asleep. You know Tyler has been working so hard on his new project.
Chris: Or he might have forgotten about our dinner and just gone out.
Ava: No, he couldn't have forgotten. I just talked to him about it this morning. Besides, the lights are on. He could have had an emergency. He might not have had time to call us.
Chris: Yeah, maybe. I'll call him and find out.
Ava: And?
Chris: He's not answering. . . . Now *I'm* getting worried.

B Listen to the rest of the conversation. What happened?

3 PRONUNCIATION Reduction in past modals

A Listen and practice. Notice how **have** is reduced in these sentences.

He may **have** fallen asleep. She might **have** gone out.

B Listen and practice. Notice that **not** is not contracted or reduced in these sentences.

He might **not** have had time to call us. She must **not** have heard the doorbell.

4 GRAMMAR FOCUS

Past modals for degrees of certainty

It's almost certain.

He **must have fallen** asleep.
He **must not have heard** the doorbell.

It's not possible.

He **couldn't have forgotten** about it.

It's possible.

He **may/might have gone out**.
He **may/might not have had** time to call us.
He **could have had** an emergency.

GRAMMAR PLUS *see page 144*

A Read each situation and choose the best explanation. Then practice with a partner. (Pay attention to the reduced forms in past modals.)

Situation	**Explanation**
1. Marcia seems very relaxed. ______	**a.** She must have gotten fired.
2. Claire is packing her things. ______	**b.** He might have worked late last night.
3. Jeff got a bad grade on his test. ______	**c.** She may have just come back from vacation.
4. Rodrigo looks very tired today. ______	**d.** He couldn't have heard good news.
5. Julia didn't talk to her friends in the cafeteria. ______	**e.** He might not have studied very hard.
6. Ahmed got a call and looked worried. ______	**f.** She must not have seen them.

B PAIR WORK Suggest different explanations for each situation in part A.

5 LISTENING What could have happened?

A GROUP WORK Look at the pictures. What do you think happened? Offer an explanation for each event.

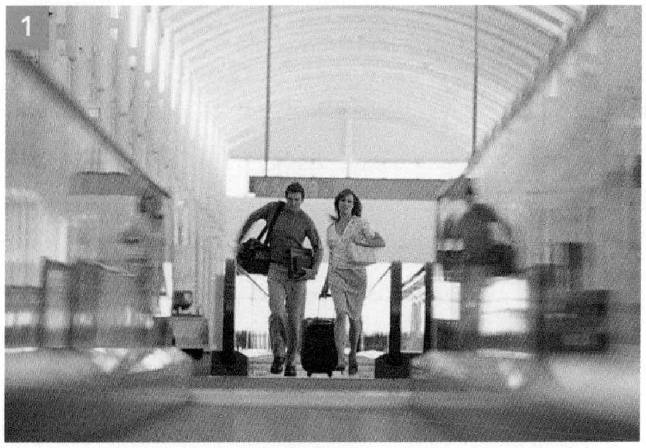

B Listen to the explanations for the two events in part A and take notes. What *did* happen? How similar were your explanations?

6 SPEAKING What's your guess?

A PAIR WORK What do you think were the reasons for these events? Suggest two different explanations for each.

1. The bride didn't show up for her wedding. She sent a bunch of flowers to the groom with a note: "Thank you."
2. A man arrived at the airport with a suitcase and saw his brother. He grabbed a cab and went back home.
3. It was a hot, sunny day. A man arrived home. He was soaking wet.

B GROUP WORK Each student thinks of two situations like the ones in part A. Others suggest explanations.

A: A man went around town and bought all the copies of the latest issue of a specific magazine.
B: Well, the magazine might have had an article about him.

7 INTERCHANGE 13 Think of the possibilities!

What's your best explanation for some unusual events? Go to Interchange 13 on page 128.

8 PERSPECTIVES I'm going nuts!

A Listen to a person complaining about her family members. Check (✓) the response you think is best for each problem.

Last night, my sister borrowed my car without asking. She did call me a couple of times, but I was in a meeting and couldn't answer the phone. We had a big fight, and now we're not speaking.

- ☐ She shouldn't have used your car without permission, no matter what.
- ☐ You could have been more understanding. After all, she tried to call you first.

My nephew is so inconsiderate. He called me at 3:00 in the morning to talk about his problems with his best friend, and I had to get up very early to work. I was really mad.

- ☐ You could have told him that you had to get up early the next day.
- ☐ Your nephew is always doing that. You shouldn't have answered his call.

My brother came over for the weekend with his wife and three kids. They made such a mess of the apartment! I'll never invite them over again.

- ☐ I would have asked them to help clean up the place.
- ☐ I wouldn't have invited them to spend the weekend. Having overnight guests can be really stressful.

B Do you talk about pet peeves with your friends? Do they give you advice?

9 GRAMMAR FOCUS

Past modals for judgments and suggestions

Judging past actions	Suggesting alternative past actions
You **should have asked** your sister to help.	You **could have told** her that you had to
He **shouldn't have used** your car.	I **would have asked** them to help clean
	I **wouldn't have invited** them to spend the weekend.

GRAMMAR PLUS *see page 144*

A Complete the conversations using past modals with the verbs given. Then practice with a partner.

1. **A:** My boss asked me to help her choose a gift for her husband, and I ended up spending all day at the mall.
   B: You ______________ (make up) an excuse not to help her. She ______________ (not ask) for such a personal favor in the first place.
2. **A:** I lent my sister-in-law some money a year ago, and she never paid it back.
   B: She ______________ (pay) it back already! Well, I ______________ (not lend) money to her anyway. I never lend money to relatives.
3. **A:** Austin invited me out to dinner, but when the check came, he said he was broke!
   B: I ______________ (not pay) for him. I ______________ (tell) him to wash the dishes. He ______________ (not invite) you if he didn't have enough money.
4. **A:** I can't believe my cousin came over and stayed until 1:00 in the morning!
   B: He ______________ (not stay) so late. You ______________ (start) yawning. Maybe he would have gotten the hint!

B PAIR WORK Think of another suggestion or comment for each situation above.

10 WORD POWER Reactions

A Helena's boyfriend forgot their anniversary. How does she react? Match each reaction with the best example.

Reaction	Example
1. an assumption ______	**a.** "Sometimes you're so selfish."
2. a criticism ______	**b.** "You could take me out to dinner."
3. a demand ______	**c.** "You must have wanted to break up with me."
4. an excuse ______	**d.** "I bet you went out with your friends."
5. a prediction ______	**e.** "Now you'll have to get me a really nice gift."
6. a suggestion ______	**f.** "I know you've been busy lately. It just slipped your mind."
7. a suspicion ______	**g.** "If you ever forget another important date, I'll never talk to you again."
8. a warning ______	**h.** "You'll probably forget my birthday, too!"

B GROUP WORK Imagine that someone was late for class, or choose another situation. Give an example of each reaction in the list above.

LISTENING What should they have done?

A Listen to descriptions of three situations. What would have been the best thing to do in each situation? Check (✓) the best suggestion.

1. ☐ Simon should have kept the ring for himself.
   ☐ He should have called the police.
   ☐ He did the right thing.
2. ☐ Jana shouldn't have mentioned her last job at all in her application.
   ☐ She should have been honest in her application and admitted she made a mistake.
   ☐ She did the right thing.
3. ☐ Martin should have reported what his boss did as soon as he found out.
   ☐ He should have withdrawn more money and blamed it on his boss.
   ☐ He did the right thing.

B PAIR WORK What would you have done in each situation in part A?

12 DISCUSSION How would you have reacted?

GROUP WORK Read each situation. Say what the person could have or should have done, and what you would have done.

"It was my friend's birthday, and he had invited a few close friends out to celebrate. I forgot all about it, so I called him the next day and pretended I'd had to take my mother to the hospital." –Warren

"My sister got a new haircut, and I thought it looked a little dated. I didn't want to hurt her feelings, so I told her I liked it." –Sonia

"I didn't have any money to buy my cousin a birthday present, so I gave her something I had received previously as a gift. My brother told my cousin about my regifting, and now she's mad at me." –Chase

"I went to my in-laws' house for dinner last night. My husband thinks his mother is a great cook, but the food was awful! I didn't know what else to do, so I ate it." –Fay

A: Warren should have told his friend the truth.
B: I agree. He could have taken his friend out to make up for it.
C: I think I would have . . .

13 WRITING A tricky problem

A Think of a complicated situation from your own experience. Write a paragraph describing the situation, but don't explain how you resolved it.

I have a close friend who doesn't get along with my other friends. He's a nice guy, friendly and funny, but every time we all go out, he makes a fuss over how much everyone should pay. Last week, my friends were going to dinner, and he wanted to come along. I didn't want to hurt his feelings . . .

B PAIR WORK Exchange papers. Write a short paragraph about how you would have resolved your partner's situation.

C PAIR WORK Read your partner's resolution to your situation. Tell your partner how you resolved it. Whose resolution was better?

14 READING

A Skim the article. What do the two unexplained events have in common?

Messages from **Outer Space**, or a Leaking Pipe?

Home | **Sciencenews** | **Technology** | **Articles** | **Blog** | **Community**

Even though we know so much about the world around us, unexplained events still take place. Read about these two events. What do you think may have happened?

Since 2008, people around the world have been reporting a mysterious sound that seems to come from the sky. Some people say it sounds like trumpets playing. Others say it is like sound effects from sci-fi movies. The phenomenon has caused both fear and fascination, and many people have been looking for explanations. One popular idea is that the sound is an announcement of the end of the world, and another

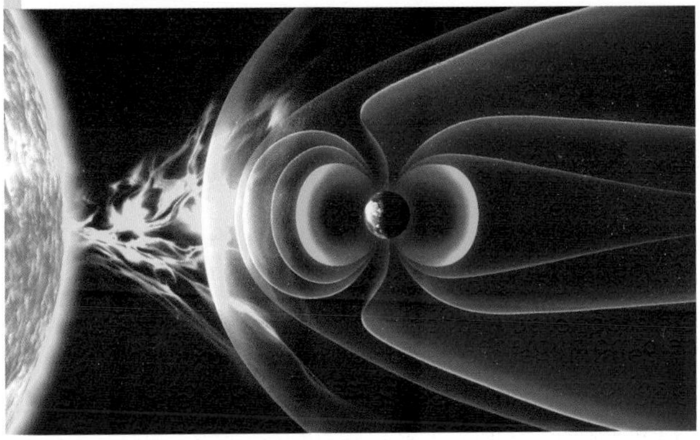

suggests that it's the sound of spaceships. But there may be a more scientific explanation. It involves flares from the sun and energy from the center of the earth. Which explanation do you think might be right?

Of course, there are some strange events that still baffle both the general public and experts. Take the high-pitched noise that has been driving people crazy in Forest Grove, Oregon. To some people, it sounds like a giant flute being played very badly, and to others, it sounds like a train slowing down or truck brakes squealing. The sound is coming from under the street, but gas, water, and sewer inspectors have said there is nothing wrong down there. One resident was so sure it was a serious gas leak that he was ready to flee. However, experts say that a leak would make a different sound, and people would definitely smell gas. How would you explain this mysterious and annoying event?

B Read the article. Then answer the questions.

1. To what two things have people compared the first sound?
2. What non-scientific explanations have been offered?
3. What sort of sound are people in Forest Grove hearing?
4. What explanation has been proven untrue?
5. If there had been a gas leak, what would be different?

C Which of these statements are facts? Which are opinions? Check (✓) Fact or Opinion.

	Fact	Opinion
1. Science has not explained everything that happens.	☐	☐
2. Some sounds mean the end of the world is coming.	☐	☐
3. The first sound is caused by energy from planets.	☐	☐
4. The sound in Forest Grove is very annoying.	☐	☐
5. The Forest Grove sound comes from under the street.	☐	☐
6. Gas lines and other systems in Forest Grove have no problems.	☐	☐
7. No local problems can explain the Forest Grove noise.	☐	☐

D **PAIR WORK** Which explanations of the events in the article do you think are the most likely? least likely? Can you think of any other possible explanations?

14 Creative careers

- Describe steps in a process
- Discuss jobs in entertainment and the media

1 SNAPSHOT

MILESTONES IN CONTEMPORARY CINEMATOGRAPHY

THE FIRST . . .

- movie with **Dolby Digital** sound. – *Batman Returns* (1992)
- **computer-animated** feature film. – *Toy Story* (1995)
- major movie **shot entirely in digital video.** – *Star Wars Episode II: Attack of the Clones* (2002)
- computer-animated **motion-captured** film. – *The Polar Express* (2004)
- movie to be **released simultaneously** in theaters, on DVD, and on the Internet. – *EMR* (2005)
- **film directed by a woman** to win the Oscar for Best Picture. – *The Hurt Locker* (2008)
- full-length feature film **shot on a phone.** – *Olive* (2011)
- major movie **filmed at 48 frames per second,** instead of the standard 24 fps. – *The Hobbit: An Unexpected Journey* (2012)

Have you seen any of these movies? Did you enjoy them?
What's the most popular movie playing right now? Have you seen it? Do you plan to?
Are there many movies made in your country? Name a few of your favorites.

2 CONVERSATION I have more control.

A Listen and practice.

Clara: Thanks for coming to the film festival! Directing this film was amazing, and I'm happy to answer your questions about it.
Diego: Yes, hi. What is it like to direct an animated movie? Is it different from live action?
Clara: Well, for one thing, I have a lot more control. There are no actors to argue with me!
Diego: I guess not! But how do you direct cartoon characters?
Clara: Well, after a screenplay is chosen, many drawings of the characters are presented to me . . .
Diego: And you get to choose which ones to use?
Clara: Even better: I can change them if I want. The characters have to be drawn just right – like I see them in my mind.
Diego: So you decide a lot about the characters early on.
Clara: Definitely. By the time the voice actors are picked, the characters feel like old friends!

B Listen to the rest of the conversation. Who helps Clara choose the voice actors?

3 GRAMMAR FOCUS

The passive to describe process

is/are + past participle	Modal + *be* + past participle
A screenplay **is chosen**.	The characters **have to be drawn** just right.
Many drawings **are presented**.	The drawings **might be changed** 10 times.

GRAMMAR PLUS *see page 145*

A The sentences below describe how an animated movie is made. First, complete the sentences using the passive. Then compare with a partner.

Storyboard and animation steps

1. First, storyboards ________________ (draw) by story artists. For some movies, over 200,000 storyboards might ________________ (draw).
2. Next, the storyboards need to ________________ (place) in order.
3. After the storyboarding process ________________ (complete), technical directors must ________________ (hire).
4. Then, the scenes and characters have to ________________ (create) on the computer by the technical directors.
5. Finally, movement ________________ (add) to the scenes by animators. In addition, the scenes ________________ (populate) with background characters.

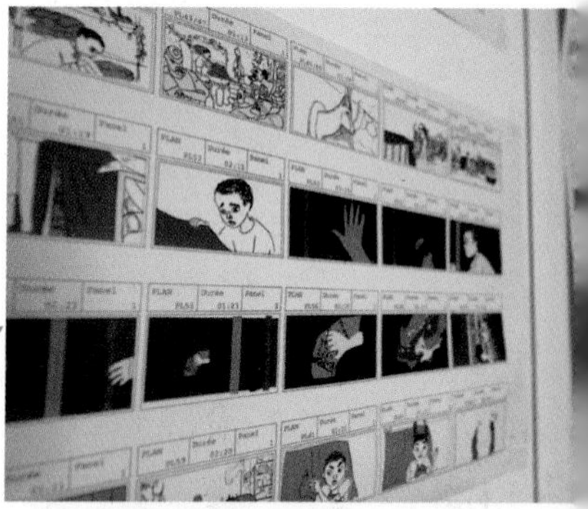

Voice-over steps

6. First, temporary "scratch" voices ________________ (record). Sometimes scratch voices are so good that they ________________ (not replace).
7. Later, professional actors ________________ (hire) to record the character voices. For some movies, studios hire famous actors so their names can ________________ (use) as a marketing tool.
8. The lines ________________ (rehearse) and the same line ________________ (record) in different ways.
9. Finally, the best recording ________________ (choose) for the final movie.

B PAIR WORK What are some steps that happen after the animated movie is complete? Discuss with a partner.

"After all that, the movie is sent to theaters."

4 LISTENING It was too predictable.

A Listen to Casey and Grant talk about things that often happen in movies. Number the parts of a movie in the order they are mentioned.

	Movie example
☐ A new plan is put into action.	*Luke planned to destroy the Death Star.*
☐ A problem is presented.	
☐ Something bad happens, and all hope is lost.	
☐ The main character is introduced.	
☐ The bad guy is defeated.	

B Listen again. For each movie part above, write an example from the movies the friends discuss.

5 SPEAKING Tutorials

A PAIR WORK What do you think is required to make a short movie? Put the pictures in order and describe the steps. More than one order may be possible. Use the vocabulary to help you.

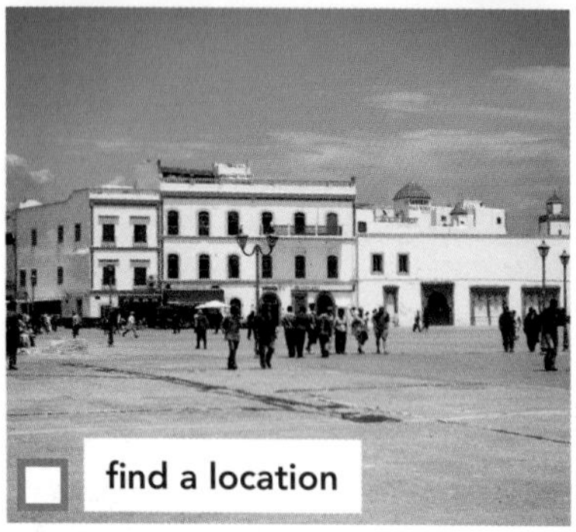

A: Making a short movie requires many steps. First, the script needs to be written.
B: Right! And after that, a location must be found.
A: I agree. Then . . .

B PAIR WORK Choose one of these topics. Come up with as many steps as you can.

preparing a school party	organizing a fundraising campaign	developing a mobile app
organizing a trip abroad	planning a wedding	putting on a school musical

C GROUP WORK Share your information from part B with another pair.

6 WRITING Describing a process

A Write about one of the topics from Exercise 5, part B or use your own idea. Describe the different steps in the process.

Developing a mobile app requires a lot of work. First, the objective of the app must be defined. Then, a prototype should be built. After that, the prototype can be tested by potential users or friends. Then a developer needs to be hired, and . . .

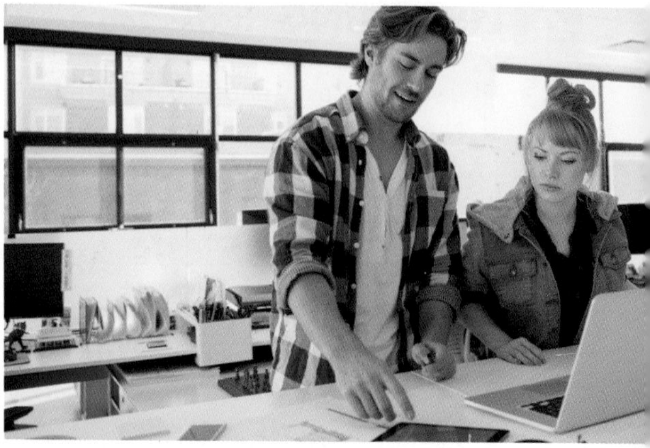

B PAIR WORK Read your partner's description. Can you think of any more steps?

7 WORD POWER Creative jobs

A What kind of jobs are these? Complete the chart with the compound nouns. (More than one answer is possible.)

band manager	game animator	songwriter	talk show host
club DJ	gameplay programmer	storyboard artist	quality assurance analyst
editorial director	news photographer	stunt person	web content manager

Film/TV jobs	Publishing jobs	Gaming jobs	Music jobs

B GROUP WORK Choose four jobs from part A. Describe each job.

"A band manager negotiates contracts for artists and helps promote their careers."

8 PERSPECTIVES Career questions

A Listen to the career questions that people have. How would you answer them?

I have a degree in journalism, and I'm an amateur photographer. I'm considering a career as a news photographer who covers conflicts around the world. Do you think that's too dangerous?

Videographers like me, who shoot weddings and other social events, often work evenings and weekends. I want to have a nine-to-five job, so I'm looking for a job with a major studio. Is that a good move?

I love movies and I love action, so I'm thinking of becoming a stunt person – you know, the person who takes the place of an actor in dangerous scenes. What do you think?

A talk show host, who interviews artists, politicians, and celebrities, gets to meet lots of people. I love to meet new people. Do you think that would be a good job for me?

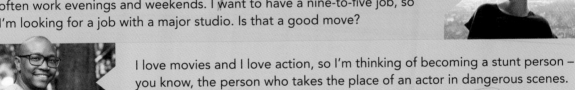

B PAIR WORK Which of these careers do you think would be the most interesting? Why?

9 PRONUNCIATION Review of stress in compound nouns

A Listen and practice. Notice how the first word in a compound noun usually receives greater stress.

band manager   talk show host   game animator   news photographer   stunt person

B Practice the sentences in Exercise 8. Pay attention to the word stress in the compound nouns.

10 GRAMMAR FOCUS

Defining and non-defining relative clauses

Defining relative clauses are used to identify people.

I want to become a photographer. I want to cover conflicts.	→	I want to become a photographer **who/that covers conflicts**.

Non-defining relative clauses give further information about people.

Videographers shoot weddings and social events. They work evenings and weekends.	→	Videographers, **who shoot weddings and social events**, work evenings and weekends.

GRAMMAR PLUS *see page 145*

A Do these sentences contain defining (**D**) or non-defining (**ND**) clauses? Write **D** or **ND**. Add commas to the non-defining clauses. Then compare with a partner.

1. The art editor who creates the look of a magazine should make it attractive. ______
2. A game programmer is the person who writes the computer code that runs and controls a game. ______
3. The extras are the people who appear in the background scenes. ______
4. The producer who is responsible for the budget is the big boss in an animation studio. ______

B Add the non-defining relative clauses in parentheses to the sentences.

1. A game designer works closely with the programmers. (who creates new games)
   ____
   ____
2. A lead vocalist is the main voice on stage. (who may also be a songwriter)
   ____
   ____
3. A news reporter collects information about news and events. (who should be impartial)
   ____
   ____
4. A photo editor selects the photos that go into magazines. (who is responsible for the quality and content of images)
   ____
   ____

C Write three sentences with relative clauses about jobs you know. Compare with a partner.

11 INTERCHANGE 14 Celebrities

Can you guess who the celebrities are? Go to Interchange 14 on page 129.

12 READING

A Scan the title and first paragraph of the article. Who do you think it was written for? Why?

Home | News | Entertainment | Articles | Blog | Community

THE TRUTH ABOUT BEING A FILM EXTRA

by Anna Murphy

When people discover that I work as a film and TV extra, they always ask me the same questions: *Is it easy to get work? Isn't it boring? Do you get to meet famous actors? Does it pay well?* My answers are pretty standard as well: yes, sometimes, once in a while, and . . . kind of. The life of an extra is both more interesting and more boring than you might imagine.

Extras, who play the people in crowds, on streets, or in the background of indoor scenes, can come from all walks of life. Unlike many extras, I'm a trained actor. I do get real speaking roles, but work can be hard to come by if you're not an in-demand star. I'm registered with an agency that deals exclusively with extras, so I get calls all the time. The agency explains who I'll be – someone in a crowd, a member of a jury, a clerk – and tells me where to go. Call time is usually bright and early, so I try to get to bed at a reasonable hour.

Sometimes being an extra is a "hurry up and wait" job. In my first extra role, I was one of a group of office workers who come out of a building just as a car explodes in the street. We waited for hours for the scene to be shot, and then went in and out of the building about fifty times, trying to act horrified by a nonexistent explosion. Then we had lunch, changed clothes, and spent the afternoon as customers in a department store.

It may sound like I don't enjoy the work, but I do. Being part of the background in a convincing way is challenging, and being on a film or TV set is always fascinating. A lot of famous actors don't even notice the extras, but the ones who do make the job a lot of fun for everyone. As for the money, it's nothing compared to what the big actors make, but it pretty much pays the bills. And, as a bonus, I've beaten my high scores on all my phone games, thanks to all the time I spend sitting around, waiting for something to happen.

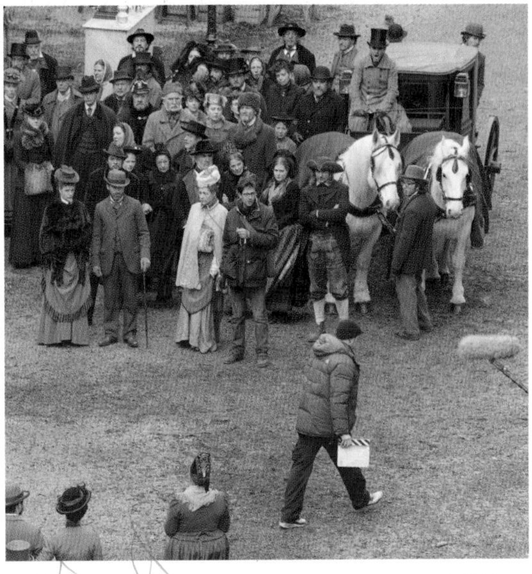

B Read the article. Underline a sentence in the article that answers each question below.

1. What training has the writer had?
2. How does she get work as an extra?
3. What was her first role as an extra?
4. What unexpected advantage of the work does she mention?

C Find words or phrases in the article that mean the same as the following.

1. have very different jobs and life experiences ______
2. wanted or needed by many people ______
3. first thing in the morning ______
4. imaginary ______
5. difficult ______

D **PAIR WORK** What job would you most like to have on a film or TV show? Why?

Units 13–14 Progress check

SELF-ASSESSMENT

How well can you do these things? Check (✓) the boxes.

I can . . .	Very well	OK	A little
Speculate about past events (Ex. 1)	☐	☐	☐
Give opinions and advice about past events (Ex. 2)	☐	☐	☐
Describe steps in processes (Ex. 3)	☐	☐	☐
Use relative clauses to give information about people (Ex. 4)	☐	☐	☐

1 LISTENING Something's not right.

A Listen to three conversations. Where do you think each conversation takes place? What do you think might have happened? Take notes.

	Location	What might've happened	What could've happened next
1.			
2.			
3.			

B PAIR WORK Decide what happened with your partner. Then decide what could have happened next in each situation. Complete the chart.

2 DISCUSSION Bad moves

A PAIR WORK React to these situations. First, make a judgment or suggestion using a past modal. Then add another statement using the reaction in parentheses.

1. Samantha didn't get to work on time today. (a suggestion)
2. Pat took a vacation, and now he doesn't have money for rent. (a warning)
3. Jim didn't study for the test, but he got all the answers correct. (a suspicion)
4. Nick was driving too fast, and the police stopped him. (an excuse)
5. Carl spent the night playing his favorite game online. (a prediction)

"Samantha should have left home earlier. She could have set an alarm."

B GROUP WORK Join another pair and compare your comments. Who has the most interesting reaction to each situation?

3 GAME Step by step

A GROUP WORK Look at these topics. Set a time limit. Talk with your group and write as many steps as you can between the first and last parts of each process.

making a grilled cheese sandwich

organizing a party

making a grilled cheese sandwich	organizing a party
First, the bread has to be sliced.	First, the guests have to be chosen.
______________________	______________________
______________________	______________________
______________________	______________________
______________________	______________________
______________________	______________________
Finally, the sandwich is served on a plate.	Finally, the guests are welcomed.

B CLASS ACTIVITY Compare your answers. Which group has the most steps?

4 SPEAKING Your social circle

A Complete these statements about people in your life.

My best friend is a person who ______________________.
My neighbor, who ______________________, always ______________________.
My mother is someone that ______________________.
My teacher, who ______________________, is ______________________.
______________________ is a ______________________ who ______________________.

B PAIR WORK Compare your answers. Ask two follow-up questions about each of your partner's statements.

A: My best friend is a person who always listens to me when I have a problem.
B: Does she give you good advice?

WHAT'S NEXT?

Look at your Self-assessment again. Do you need to review anything?

15 A law must be passed!

- ▸ Make recommendations about social issues
- ▸ Give opinions about laws and social issues

1 SNAPSHOT

8 UNUSUAL LAWS FROM AROUND THE WORLD

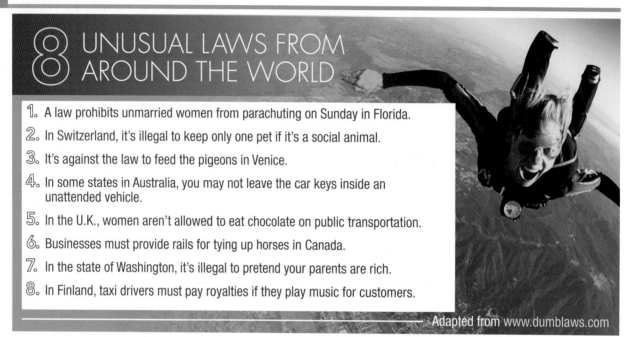

1. A law prohibits unmarried women from parachuting on Sunday in Florida.
2. In Switzerland, it's illegal to keep only one pet if it's a social animal.
3. It's against the law to feed the pigeons in Venice.
4. In some states in Australia, you may not leave the car keys inside an unattended vehicle.
5. In the U.K., women aren't allowed to eat chocolate on public transportation.
6. Businesses must provide rails for tying up horses in Canada.
7. In the state of Washington, it's illegal to pretend your parents are rich.
8. In Finland, taxi drivers must pay royalties if they play music for customers.

Adapted from www.dumblaws.com

Which of these laws would you like to have in your city or country? Why?
Can you think of reasons for these laws?
Do you know of any other unusual laws?

2 PERSPECTIVES Rules and regulations

A Listen to people make recommendations at a city council meeting. Would you agree with these proposals if they were made in your community? Check (✓) your opinion.

CITY OF BRISTOL

MEETING NOTES

	STRONGLY AGREE	SOMEWHAT AGREE	DISAGREE
1. Clubs should be required to install soundproof walls.	☐	☐	☐
2. Riding a bike on the sidewalk mustn't be permitted.	☐	☐	☐
3. Pet owners shouldn't be allowed to walk dogs without a leash.	☐	☐	☐
4. Something has got to be done about littering.	☐	☐	☐
5. A law must be passed to control the pollution from vehicles.	☐	☐	☐
6. Children ought to be required to wear a helmet when riding a bike.	☐	☐	☐
7. Schools should only be permitted to serve organic food.	☐	☐	☐

B **GROUP WORK** Compare your opinions. Try to get your classmates to agree with you.

3 GRAMMAR FOCUS

Giving recommendations and opinions

When you think something is a good idea

Clubs **should be required** to install soundproof walls.

Pet owners **shouldn't be allowed** to walk dogs without a leash.

People **ought (not) to be required** to wear a helmet when riding a bike.

When you think something is absolutely necessary

A law **must be passed** to control the pollution from vehicles.

Riding a bike on the sidewalk **mustn't be permitted**.

A rule **has to be made** to require bike lanes on city streets.

Something **has got to be done** to stop littering.

GRAMMAR PLUS *see page 146*

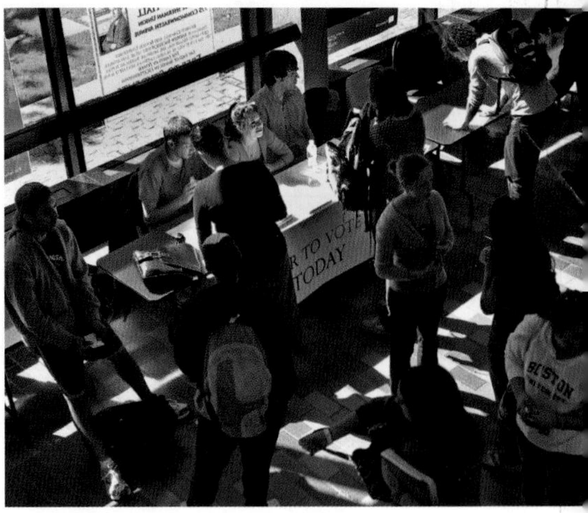

A Complete the sentences positively or negatively. Choose a modal that shows how strongly you feel about these issues.

1. Young people ______________ (permit) to vote before age 21.
2. Laws ______________ (pass) to protect people's online privacy.
3. People ______________ (allow) to use offensive language in social media.
4. Governments ______________ (require) to provide health care to all their citizens.
5. Children ______________ (allow) to play violent video games.
6. Scientists ______________ (permit) to use animals for research.
7. The sale of fur products ______________ (prohibit).
8. Something ______________ (do) to stop the pollution of rivers and oceans.

B GROUP WORK Compare your statements. Do you agree with one another? If not, why not?

A: Young people shouldn't be permitted to vote before age 21. They're not prepared.

B: You may have a point, but they could be better informed.

C: Maybe, but in my opinion, . . .

4 DISCUSSION Controversial topics

A GROUP WORK Think of three reasons for, and three reasons against, each idea below. Then discuss your views. As a group, form an opinion about each idea.

requiring employers to offer workers 12 weeks of parental leave

paying teachers less when their students fail

banning private cars from the downtown areas of big cities

A: What do you think about requiring employers to offer workers 12 weeks of parental leave?

B: I think it's a good idea. Parents should be allowed to stay with their babies . . .

offering a different opinion

That sounds interesting, but I think . . .

That's not a bad idea. On the other hand, I feel . . .

You may have a point. However, I think . . .

B CLASS ACTIVITY Share your group's opinions and reasons. Who has the most persuasive reasons for and against each position?

5 LISTENING Something has got to be done!

A Listen to people discuss annoying situations. Number the situations they describe in the correct order from 1 to 3. (There are three extra situations.)

- [ ] using the phone on speaker in public places
- [ ] using a cell phone on a plane
- [ ] posting selfies on social media
- [ ] taking selfies in crowded places
- [ ] not having signs about cell phones in public places
- [ ] texting in a movie theater

B Listen again. What solutions do they suggest for each situation?

1. ______________________________
2. ______________________________
3. ______________________________

C GROUP WORK Do you agree or disagree with the solutions? What do you think should be done about each problem?

6 INTERCHANGE 15 On the wrong side of the law

What if you could make the rules? Go to Interchange 15 on page 130.

7 WORD POWER Community issues

A PAIR WORK Which of these issues are problems in your community? Check (✓) the appropriate boxes.

- [ ] bullying
- [ ] homelessness
- [ ] inadequate health care
- [ ] irregular trash collection
- [ ] lack of affordable child care
- [ ] noise pollution
- [ ] overcrowded classrooms
- [ ] stray animals
- [ ] street crime
- [ ] vandalism

B GROUP WORK Join another pair of students. Which three problems concern your group the most? What should or can be done about them?

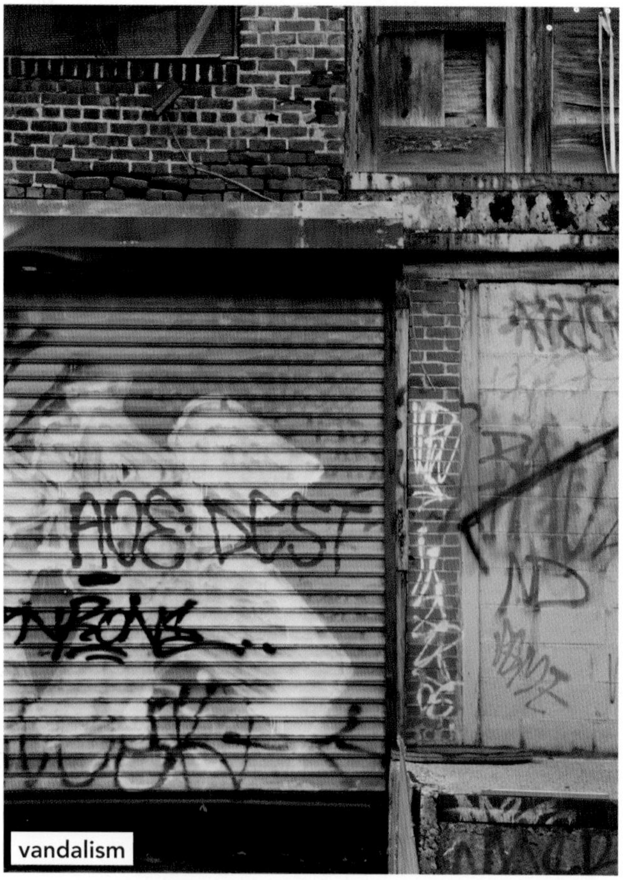

vandalism

8 CONVERSATION It's not easy, is it?

A Listen and practice.

Mara: I need to find a new apartment. I can't stand the noise from all those bars and clubs in my neighborhood anymore.

Ted: I can imagine. But it isn't easy to find a nice apartment in a quiet neighborhood, is it?

Mara: No, it's not! And my rent is already sky-high. I'm having a hard time making ends meet.

Ted: I know. Everything is really expensive nowadays, isn't it?

Mara: It sure is. You know, I'm looking for child care for my baby, but I just can't find anything affordable in the area.

Ted: The city should provide free child care to working families.

Mara: I think so, too. But unfortunately, the mayor doesn't.

B Listen to the rest of the conversation. What is Ted concerned about?

9 GRAMMAR FOCUS

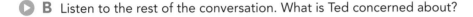

Tag questions for opinions

Affirmative statement + negative tag	Negative statement + affirmative tag
Everything is really expensive nowadays, **isn't it**?	It isn't easy to find a nice apartment, **is it**?
There are lots of clubs around, **aren't there**?	There aren't any noise pollution laws, **are there**?
Mara likes her apartment, **doesn't she**?	Her neighbors don't make much noise, **do they**?
The city should provide child care, **shouldn't it**?	You can't sleep because of the noise, **can you**?

GRAMMAR PLUS *see page 146*

A Add tag questions to these statements. Then compare with a partner.

1. There aren't enough shelters for the homeless, . . . ?
2. Vandalism makes a neighborhood very unpleasant, . . . ?
3. In overcrowded classrooms, teachers can't give enough attention to students, . . . ?
4. School bullying is a major problem in most schools, . . . ?
5. There are more street crimes in big cities than in small towns, . . . ?
6. The government should provide adequate health care to everyone, . . . ?
7. The city doesn't do enough for stray animals, . . . ?
8. It isn't easy to save money these days, . . . ?

B What are some things you feel strongly about in your school or city? Write six statements with tag questions.

C GROUP WORK Take turns reading your statements. Other students respond by giving their opinions.

A: Public transportation isn't adequate, is it?
B: No, it isn't. There should be more bus lines.
C: On the other hand, the subway system is very efficient . . .

10 PRONUNCIATION Intonation in tag questions

A Listen and practice. Use falling intonation in tag questions when you are giving an opinion and expect the other person to agree.

Noise pollution is a serious problem in our city, isn't it?

Governments should offer child care to all working families, shouldn't they?

B PAIR WORK Take turns reading the statements with tag questions from Exercise 9, part A. Give your own opinions when responding.

11 LISTENING Let's face it.

A Listen to people give their opinions about issues in the news. What issues are they talking about?

	Issue	Opinions for	Opinions against
1.			
2.			

B Listen again. Write the different opinions that you hear.

C GROUP WORK What do you think about the issues in part A? Give your own opinions.

12 WRITING There ought to be a law.

A Think about a local problem that needs to be solved, and write a persuasive essay suggesting a new law to help solve it. Be creative! Use these questions to help you.

What is the problem, and how does it affect your community?
What can be done to help solve it?
Who might disagree with you, and how will you convince him or her that your law is a good idea?

The water crisis affects people all over the world. I think cities should be required to recycle their water. Also, people shouldn't be permitted to use clean drinking water to wash their cars and water their gardens. If people used recycled water, . . .

B GROUP WORK Try to convince your classmates to pass your new law. Then vote on it.

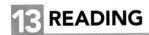

13 READING

A Look at the title and the picture. What do you think plagiarism is?

HOME NEWS ARTICLES COMMUNITY

THAT'S PLAGIARISM?

POSTED AUGUST 21

If a teacher or your boss called you aside and said that he or she suspected you of plagiarism, how would you react? You'd probably be honestly confused. Nowadays, there are so many sources of information available that you can copy from with a single click. Many people don't even realize that they're committing plagiarism. Whether it's intentional or not, using someone else's information is stealing, and stealing is definitely a big deal.

The confusion about ownership comes from the fact that articles, photos, blogs, and social media posts are so easy to access – and just as easy to copy. When you see the same article on various websites, it's fairly natural to assume that it's public property. If a resource like Wikipedia offers material that can be critiqued and changed by its readers, that must be free for the taking, right? But that simply is not the case. Everything that has been written, drawn, photographed,

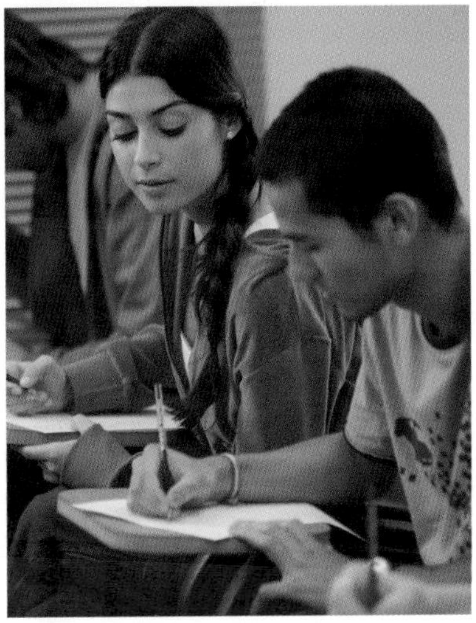

or recorded, and released to the public, belongs to someone. Even your friends' comments on your social media page belong to them, not to you.

To avoid plagiarism, here are a few basic points to keep in mind. When writing a paper, if you get ideas or wording from someone else's writing, you must include the name of the writer or the source. If you find a few articles that you want to use, and you think taking a few points from each article and combining them makes the content yours, it's just not the case. This kind of "masked" plagiarism is very easy to spot, and it will get you into trouble. But really, just asking yourself a simple question should be enough: "Are all of these words my own?" If the answer is yes, you're in the clear.

In the end, the best approach is to write down the source for any material you quote from directly, and to assume that if it's public, it isn't yours. Plagiarism is a serious problem and can have serious consequences – even if it's totally accidental. Besides, putting ideas into your own words can make you a better writer, and a better thinker as well.

B Read the article. Then answer the questions.

1. What is the author's main purpose in writing the piece?
2. Why might it be easy to commit plagiarism by accident?
3. What question should you ask yourself in order to avoid plagiarism?

C Look at the following situations. Do you think they are describing plagiarism or not? If they are, do you think it was accidental or intentional?

1. Stacy copied a paragraph from a travel website and pasted it into her essay about Aruba. She put it into quotation marks and included the name and link for the website.
2. John works for a bank. He copied a paragraph from a website. He changed some words and rearranged some of the sentences. He did not indicate where it came from. He used it in a brochure for the bank.
3. Julie read an article online and later wrote her own essay about the same subject. Some of her wording was exactly the same as the online article.
4. Mitch borrowed a friend's essay to get some ideas for his own. Their teacher said that their essays were almost identical.

D PAIR WORK Sometimes famous musicians get in trouble for putting out songs that sound like someone else's. Do you think this is plagiarism? What, if anything, should be done about it?

16 Reaching your goals

- ▸ Discuss personal accomplishments
- ▸ Discuss goals

1 SNAPSHOT

Some Common Goals and Dreams

- ☐ win a competition
- ☐ make a lot of money
- ☐ get a promotion
- ☐ become famous
- ☐ learn to travel light
- ☐ find true love
- ☐ run a marathon
- ☐ learn to live with less
- ☐ be able to help others
- ☐ be respected
- ☐ have a healthy lifestyle
- ☐ plant a tree

Which of these goals do you think are the most difficult to achieve? Which are the easiest? Why?
Do you have the same goals? Check (✓) them.
What other goals or wishes do you have?

2 PERSPECTIVES Personal accomplishments

A Listen to people talk about their accomplishments. Match the statements and the people.

1. For me, my greatest accomplishment is the feeling that I've been able to help kids develop their potential and achieve their goals. _____
2. I worked hard in school, but I never managed to get good grades. However, I've just published my first book – and it's a best seller! _____
3. Last year, I ran my first marathon. I didn't win, but I was able to finish it, and I was very proud of myself. _____
4. No one believed in me in the beginning, but I've managed to make a living from my music for the past 5 years. _____
5. I felt I had reached one of my lifetime goals when I managed to quit my nine-to-five job to make a living traveling and sharing my experiences. _____

a. an amateur athlete
b. a teacher
c. a writer
d. a travel blogger
e. a musician

B GROUP WORK Do you share any similar accomplishments? Which ones?

3 GRAMMAR FOCUS

Talking about past accomplishments

With the simple past	With the present perfect
I **managed** to quit my nine-to-five job two years ago.	**I've managed** to make a living with my music.
I **didn't manage** to get good grades in school.	I **haven't managed** to record an album yet.
I **was able** to finish the marathon last year.	**I've been able** to help kids achieve their goals.
I **wasn't able** to travel much on my last job.	I **haven't been able** to achieve many of my goals.

GRAMMAR PLUS *see page 147*

A What are some of your latest accomplishments? Complete the statements with *have*, *haven't*, *was*, or *wasn't* to make them true for you.

1. I __________ managed to eat a healthy diet.
2. I __________ been able to help others.
3. I __________ met the person who's right for me.
4. I __________ made an important career move.
5. I __________ able to get a degree.
6. I __________ learned important life skills.

B PAIR WORK Compare your sentences in part A. What accomplishments do you have in common?

C GROUP WORK Complete the statements with your own information. Then share them with your classmates.

I have been able to ____________________.
I have managed to ____________________.
I haven't been able to ____________________.
I haven't managed to ____________________.

A: I've managed to take a trip abroad.
B: What countries did you visit?
A: I went to New Zealand three years ago.
C: Really? I've always wanted to go to New Zealand. How did you like it?

4 PRONUNCIATION Stress and rhythm

A Listen and practice. Notice how stressed words and syllables occur with a regular rhythm.

I managed to accomplish a lot while I was in college.

I haven't managed to get a promotion yet.

I was able to share my experiences with the world.

B PAIR WORK Take turns reading the sentences in the grammar box in Exercise 3. Pay attention to stress and rhythm.

5 LISTENING A different perspective

A Listen to two people answer two interview questions. Write the obstacles they faced and what they did about them in the chart.

	Mr. Sandberg	**Ms. Rowe**
Obstacle		
What he or she did		
What he or she learned		

B Listen again. What did each person learn from his or her experience? Complete the chart.

C **PAIR WORK** Discuss an obstacle that you managed to overcome. What did you learn?

6 WORD POWER Antonyms

A Complete the pairs of opposites with the words in the box. Then compare with a partner.

compassionate cynical dependent rigid timid unimaginative

1. adaptable ≠ ______________
2. courageous ≠ ______________
3. insensitive ≠ ______________
4. resourceful ≠ ______________
5. self-sufficient ≠ ______________
6. upbeat ≠ ______________

B **GROUP WORK** How many words or things can you associate with each word in part A?

A: What words or things do you associate with *resourceful*?
B: Capable.
C: Good at solving problems.

7 DISCUSSION Inspirational sayings

A Read the quotes. Which one inspires you the most?

1. The greatest pleasure in life is doing what people say you can't do.
2. Discipline is the bridge between goals and achievements.
3. No matter what you have achieved, somebody helped you.
4. Fall down seven times, stand up eight.
5. Success isn't about how much money you make. It's about the difference you make in people's lives.

B **GROUP WORK** Discuss and justify your choices.

A: I like the first quote because, even though my friends weren't sure I could do it, I managed to graduate from high school early. That felt great!
B: You must have been resourceful! But someone helped you, too, didn't they?
C: That's why I like the third quote. No one achieves anything all on their own.

8 CONVERSATION Where do you see yourself?

A Listen and practice.

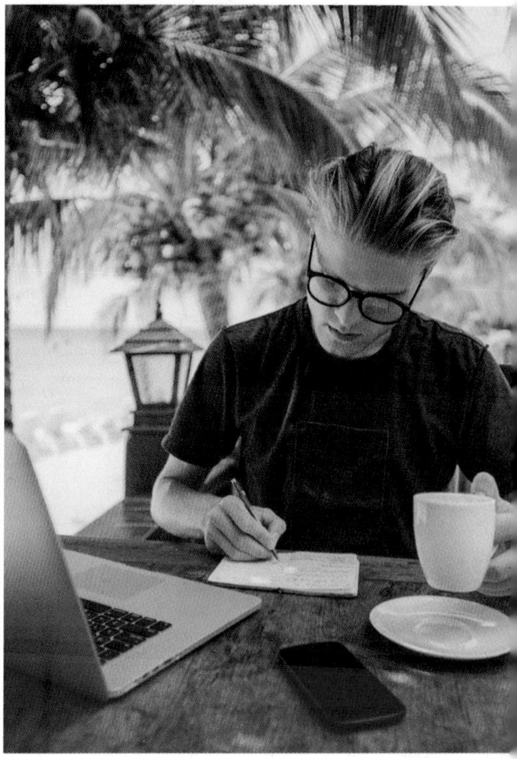

Interviewer: Tell me a bit more about yourself. What's your greatest accomplishment?

Mike: I think my most important accomplishment was the development of a mobile app during my internship last summer.

Interviewer: And did you manage to finish the project?

Mike: Yes, I was able to deliver the app before the end of my internship, and it has already received lots of positive reviews from customers.

Interviewer: That's interesting. And where do you see yourself in five years?

Mike: Well, I know your company already hires remote workers, and that's one of my goals for the future. So, five years from now, I hope I'll be working from my laptop in some tropical country . . . a true digital nomad.

Interviewer: I see. And what do you hope you'll have achieved by then?

Mike: I'd like to have developed many other successful apps. And I hope I'll have seen more of the world.

B CLASS ACTIVITY What do you think of Mike's answers? How would you have answered the interviewer's questions?

9 GRAMMAR FOCUS

Describing goals and possible future accomplishments

With the future perfect	With *would like to have* + past participle
What do you hope you**'ll have achieved**?	**What would you like to have** achieved?
I hope **I'll have seen** more of the world.	**I'd like to have developed** many successful apps.

GRAMMAR PLUS *see page 147*

A What are some goals you would like to have accomplished in the future? Complete the sentences.

1. By this time next year, I hope I'll have . . .
2. Three years from now, I'd like to have . . .
3. In 10 years, I'd like to have . . .
4. By the time I'm 60, I hope I'll have . . .

Montreal, Canada

B PAIR WORK Compare your sentences. What goals do you have in common?

A: By this time next year, I hope I'll have finished my English course.

B: Me, too. And I'd like to have spent some time in an English-speaking country, like . . .

10 LISTENING My dream career

A Listen to three young people describe their plans for the future. What do they hope they will have achieved by the time they're 30?

	 1. **Hugo**	 2. **Erin**	 3. **Danny**
What they hope they'll have achieved			
Their reasons			

B Listen again. Why does each person have his or her specific dream? List one reason for each person.

C **PAIR WORK** Who do you think has the most realistic expectations? the least realistic? Why?

11 INTERCHANGE 16 A digital nomad

Are you ready to work remotely? Take a quiz and find out.
Go to Interchange 16 on page 131.

12 WRITING A personal statement for an application

A Imagine you are applying to a school or for a job that requires a personal statement. Use these questions to organize your ideas. Make notes and then write a draft.

1. What has your greatest accomplishment been? Has it changed you in any way? How?
2. What are some interesting or unusual facts about yourself that make you a good choice for the job or school?
3. What is something you hope to have achieved 10 years from now? When, why, and how will you reach this goal? Will achieving it change you? Why or why not?

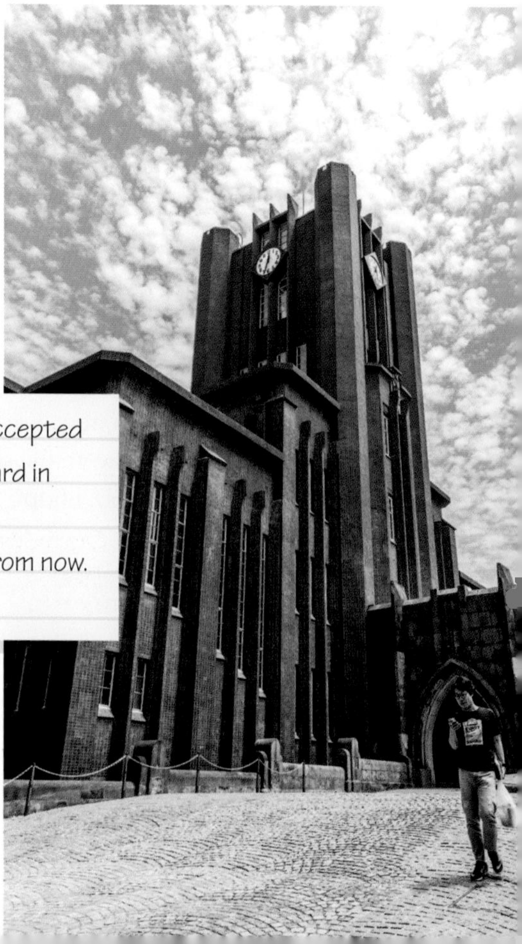

I think my greatest accomplishment has been getting accepted at a top university in my country. I've always worked very hard in school, and I've had some truly amazing teachers who . . .

There are two things I'd like to have achieved 10 years from now. First, I hope I'll have made a good start on my career . . .

B **GROUP WORK** Share your statements and discuss each person's accomplishments and goals. Who has the most unusual accomplishment or goal? the most realistic? the most ambitious?

13 READING

A Scan the article. Where is Michael Edwards from? What sport did he participate in?

Soaring Like an Eagle

Being highly successful in any field is pretty rare. It takes a combination of natural talent, luck, determination, and plenty of outside support for someone to make it big in sports, entertainment, or business. But what if competing is all that matters to you, whether you are likely to succeed or not? This was the goal of Michael "Eddie the Eagle" Edwards, and that he reached that goal was an amazing achievement.

Born in the U.K. in 1963, Michael was an enthusiastic downhill skier whose dream was to compete for Britain in world-class competitions. He would have liked to represent his country in the 1984 Winter Olympics, but there was a large number of downhill competitors, and Edwards didn't qualify. Seeing his chance elsewhere, he switched to ski jumping. Ski jumping training didn't cost nearly as much, and there was no competition for a place on the British team.

But a number of hurdles could have meant the end of Edwards's dream. He weighed more than most competitors, which put him at a disadvantage. He had no financial support for his training. Poor eyesight meant that he had to wear glasses under his goggles – not a good thing when they steamed up at high altitudes. But he didn't let any of this discourage him. He saw himself as a true lover of the sport who simply wanted the chance to compete. Winning wasn't the point. Having the opportunity to try was all he cared about. And nothing could stop him from trying.

In the end, Edwards took 55th place in the 1987 World Championships. He then went on to the Calgary Olympics in 1988, where he finished last in both of his events. Many athletes would have been embarrassed by this result, but he is proud of his achievement to this day. His determination to persevere against all the odds made him a global hero, and in 2016, the inspiring film *Eddie the Eagle* was made about his life.

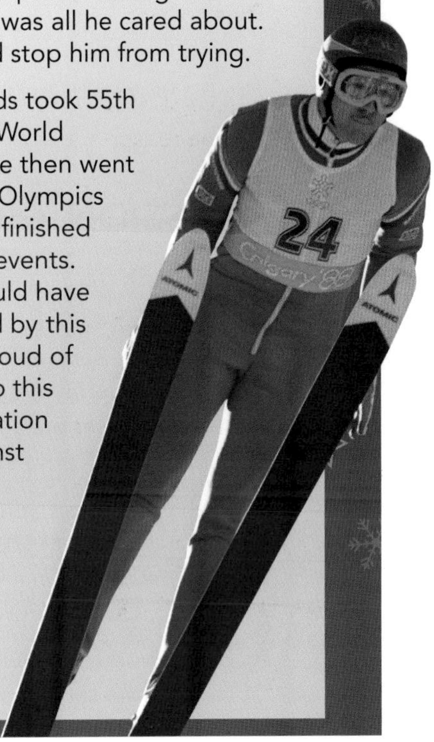

B Read the article. Answer the questions.

1. According to the writer, how often do people become highly successful?
2. What were two disadvantages that Michael Edwards overcame?
3. How did Edwards do at the Calgary Olympics in 1988?

C Choose the correct answers.

1. Michael Edwards chose ski jumping instead of downhill skiing because . . .
   a. it took less skill. **b.** the equipment was cheaper. **c.** there were few British ski jumpers.
2. After the Calgary Olympics, Edwards . . .
   a. felt he had reached his goal. **b.** was embarrassed by his results. **c.** was glad it was over.
3. Michael Edwards is outstanding because of . . .
   a. his determination to win. **b.** his ability to overcome physical disabilities. **c.** his enthusiasm for the sport.

D **PAIR WORK** Would you compete in something if you knew you were likely to lose? Why or why not?

Units 15–16 Progress check

SELF-ASSESSMENT

How well can you do these things? Check (✓) the boxes.

I can . . .	Very well	OK	A little
Give recommendations and opinions about rules (Ex. 1)	☐	☐	☐
Understand and express opinions, and seek agreement (Ex. 2)	☐	☐	☐
Describe qualities necessary to achieve particular goals (Ex. 3)	☐	☐	☐
Ask about and describe personal achievements and goals (Ex. 4)	☐	☐	☐

1 DISCUSSION It's the rule.

A PAIR WORK What kinds of rules do you think should be made for these places? Talk with your partner and make three rules for each. (Have fun! Don't make your rules too serious.)

office	public pool
a health club	an apartment building

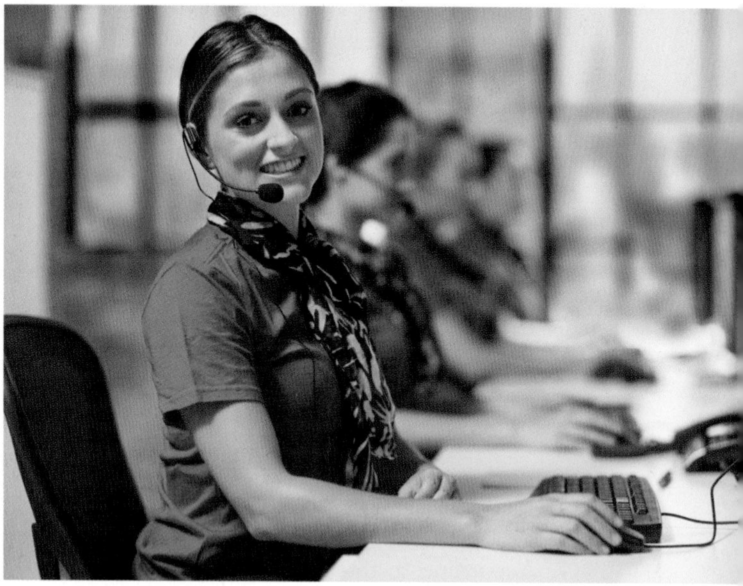

B GROUP WORK Join another pair. Share your ideas. Do they agree?

A: Office workers should all be required to wear the same outfit.
B: That sounds interesting. Why?
A: Well, for one thing, people wouldn't need to spend so much money on clothes.

2 LISTENING My city

A Listen to people give opinions about their city. Check (✓) the correct responses to agree with their statements.

1. ☐ Yes, it should.
   ☐ No, it shouldn't.
2. ☐ Yes, it is.
   ☐ No, it isn't.
3. ☐ Yes, they are.
   ☐ No, there aren't.
4. ☐ Yes, it does.
   ☐ Yes, they do.
5. ☐ Yes, we do.
   ☐ No, we don't.
6. ☐ No, there isn't.
   ☐ Yes, it is.

B PAIR WORK Come up with three more opinions about your city with a partner. Ask your classmates and see if they agree or disagree.

A: There aren't enough nightlife options for teenagers, are there?
B: No, there aren't!

3 DISCUSSION Do you have what it takes?

A GROUP WORK What qualities are needed if you want to accomplish these goals? Decide on two qualities for each goal.

Goals	Qualities		
start your own business	adaptable	dependent	self-sufficient
live abroad for a year	compassionate	insensitive	timid
make a low-budget movie	courageous	resourceful	unimaginative
hike across your country	cynical	rigid	upbeat

A: To start your own business, you need to be resourceful.
B: Yeah, and you should be courageous too.

B PAIR WORK Does your partner have what it takes to accomplish the goals in part A? Interview him or her and find out.

A: Do you think you're resourceful?
B: Yes, I think so. I'm usually good at solving problems.

4 ROLE PLAY Students' profiles

Student A: Student B is going to interview you for the school website. Think about your accomplishments and goals. Then answer the questions.

Student B: You are interviewing Student A for the school website. Add two questions to the notebook paper below. Then start the interview.

Change roles and try the role play again.

What have you managed to accomplish in school?
What would you like to have achieved by the time you graduate?

Are you happy with your home?
Do you hope you will move someday?
Where would you like to live?

Have you been able to accomplish a lot in your career?
Where do you hope you'll be in 5 years?

____

____

WHAT'S NEXT?

Look at your Self-assessment again. Do you need to review anything?

Interchange activities

INTERCHANGE 1 Personality quiz

A PAIR WORK What is your personality type? Take turns using the quiz to interview each other. Then tally your answers and find out which category best describes you.

What's your personality type?

1. When you fail a test, do you:
- **a.** get really upset and decide to try much harder next time?
- **b.** go over your answers and learn from your mistakes?
- **c.** not care much about it?

2. When you work on a big project, do you:
- **a.** try to finish it as quickly as possible?
- **b.** work at it over a long period of time?
- **c.** put it off as long as possible?

3. When you do an assignment, do you:
- **a.** try to do a first-class job so people will notice?
- **b.** do it as well as you can without worrying too much?
- **c.** do only what you must to get it done?

4. When faced with a difficult challenge, do you:
- **a.** look forward to facing it?
- **b.** worry about dealing with it?
- **c.** try to avoid it?

5. Do you think the best way to get the most out of a day is to:
- **a.** do as many things as possible?
- **b.** take your time to get things done?
- **c.** do only those things you really have to?

6. When something doesn't work out the way you want it to, do you:
- **a.** get angry with yourself and others?
- **b.** think calmly about what to do next?
- **c.** give up, because it wasn't important anyway?

7. When people take a long time to finish something, do you:
- **a.** get impatient and do it yourself?
- **b.** gently ask them to do it more quickly?
- **c.** let them take their time?

8. When you are learning a new skill, do you:
- **a.** work very hard to master it quickly?
- **b.** do your best and often ask for help?
- **c.** take your time and enjoy the learning experience?

9. If you compare your goals with your friends' goals, do you:
- **a.** want to accomplish greater things than they do?
- **b.** hope to achieve similar things in life?
- **c.** not care if they set higher goals for themselves than you do?

10. When people are late for appointments, do you:
- **a.** get angry and stressed out?
- **b.** remember that you are sometimes late, too?
- **c.** not worry, because you are usually late, too?

11. When people are talking to you, do you:
- **a.** not listen and think about other things?
- **b.** listen and participate in the conversation?
- **c.** let them talk and agree with everything they say?

Scoring

Count how many a, b, and c answers your partner has. If there are . . .

mostly a answers: This person is a high achiever but can get very stressed.

mostly b answers: This person is the cool and steady type.

mostly c answers: This person is the easygoing or carefree type.

B GROUP WORK Compare your scores. Then suggest four characteristics of each personality type.

"A high achiever is the kind of person who . . . . He or she can't stand it when . . ."

INTERCHANGE 2 Networking

A PAIR WORK Imagine you and your partner are organizing a dinner party for new entrepreneurs and potential investors.

Read about each person on the guest list.

Home | About | News | Business | Community | Sign in

ENTREPRENEURS

Gaston Lafont is 25, single, and a promising chef. He's friendly and ambitious, but he can be very moody. He's coming to the party to get celebrities and powerful business executives to invest in his restaurant.

Melissa Dominguez is 28, single, and a computer wizard. She puts her career ahead of her personal life and has few interests apart from her work. She needs funding for a new start-up company.

Don Hart is 32, married, and an environmentalist. He's egotistical, outspoken, and tends to start arguments. He wants to run for mayor and needs funding for his campaign.

Emma Stewart is 30, single, and a medical researcher. She's shy and introverted and has devoted her life to helping children around the world. She's currently developing a new vaccine for a widespread tropical disease.

INVESTORS

Mike Hunter is 54, a widower, and an oil tycoon. This millionaire is bossy and straightforward. His companies have been accused of destroying the environment in many countries.

Paola Di Matteo is 23, single, and a world-famous movie star. She's very private about her personal life, and she is interested in investing in young talent.

Joanne Parson is 42, single, and an art and nature lover. Wealthy and sociable, she takes part in several volunteer projects and gives substantial amounts of money to various causes around the world.

Ren Okawa is 38, married, and a stockbroker. He likes to invest in new companies and has helped many startups and young entrepreneurs succeed. He's smart, ambitious, and has sophisticated taste in art and food.

B PAIR WORK Discuss the possible seating arrangements for the party. Then complete this seating plan.

A: Let's seat Gaston next to Ren. Gaston is interested in finding investors for his new restaurant.

B: It might be better to put Ren next to Melissa. Ren likes to invest in start-ups, so . . .

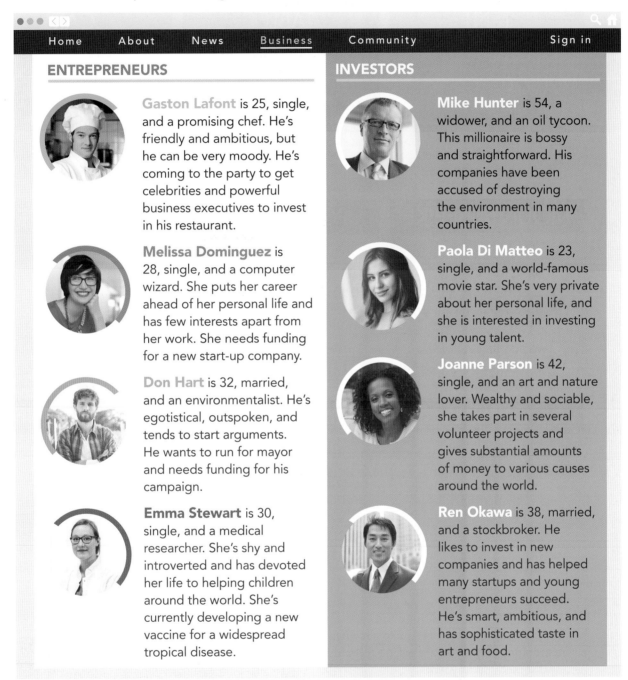

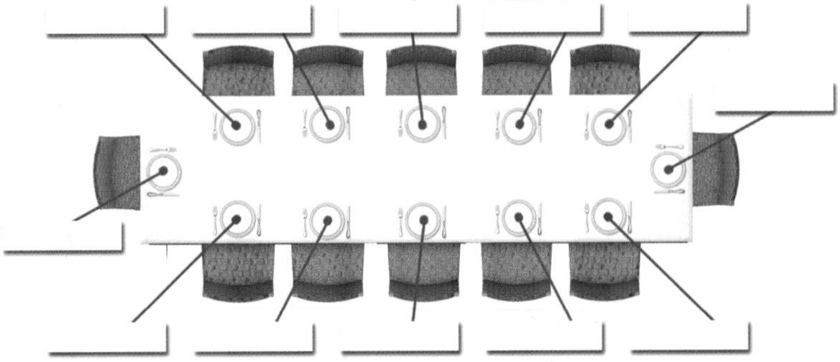

INTERCHANGE 3 Beg and borrow

A Imagine you own these items. Which ones would you be willing to lend to a friend? Which ones wouldn't you lend? Check (✓) a response for each item.

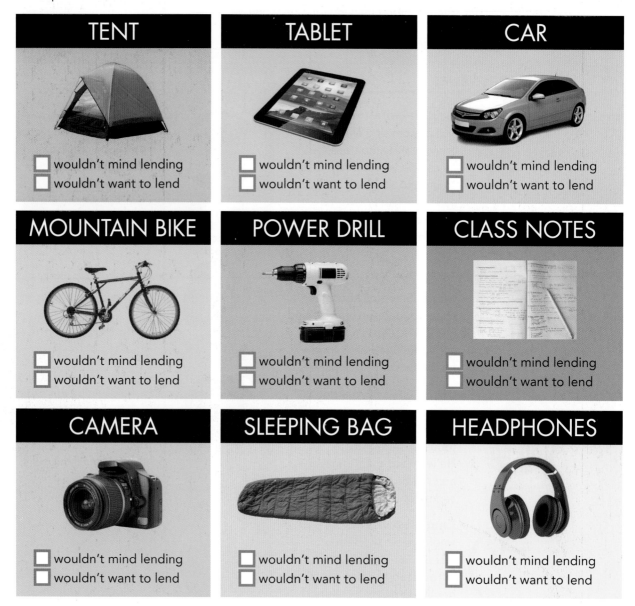

TENT

☐ wouldn't mind lending
☐ wouldn't want to lend

TABLET

☐ wouldn't mind lending
☐ wouldn't want to lend

CAR

☐ wouldn't mind lending
☐ wouldn't want to lend

MOUNTAIN BIKE

☐ wouldn't mind lending
☐ wouldn't want to lend

POWER DRILL

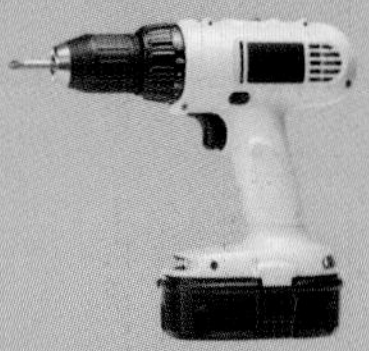

☐ wouldn't mind lending
☐ wouldn't want to lend

CLASS NOTES

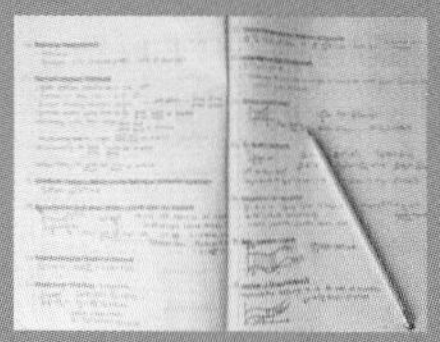

☐ wouldn't mind lending
☐ wouldn't want to lend

CAMERA

☐ wouldn't mind lending
☐ wouldn't want to lend

SLEEPING BAG

☐ wouldn't mind lending
☐ wouldn't want to lend

HEADPHONES

☐ wouldn't mind lending
☐ wouldn't want to lend

B CLASS ACTIVITY Go around the class and take turns asking to borrow each item in part A. Explain why you want to borrow it. When responding, say if you are willing to lend the item or not. If you won't lend something, say why.

A: Would you mind lending me your tent for the weekend? I want to go camping, but I got a hole in my tent.

B: I'm sorry, but I don't think I can. I might want to go camping this weekend, too!
OR

B: Sure. Just come over tonight and pick it up.

C CLASS ACTIVITY Who was able to borrow the most items?

INTERCHANGE 4 Spin a yarn

A GROUP WORK Place a pen on the CHARACTER spinner and spin it. Repeat for the other two spinners. Use the elements the pen points at to create a story. If the pen points at YOU DECIDE, you can use any element from that spinner, or you can invent a new one.

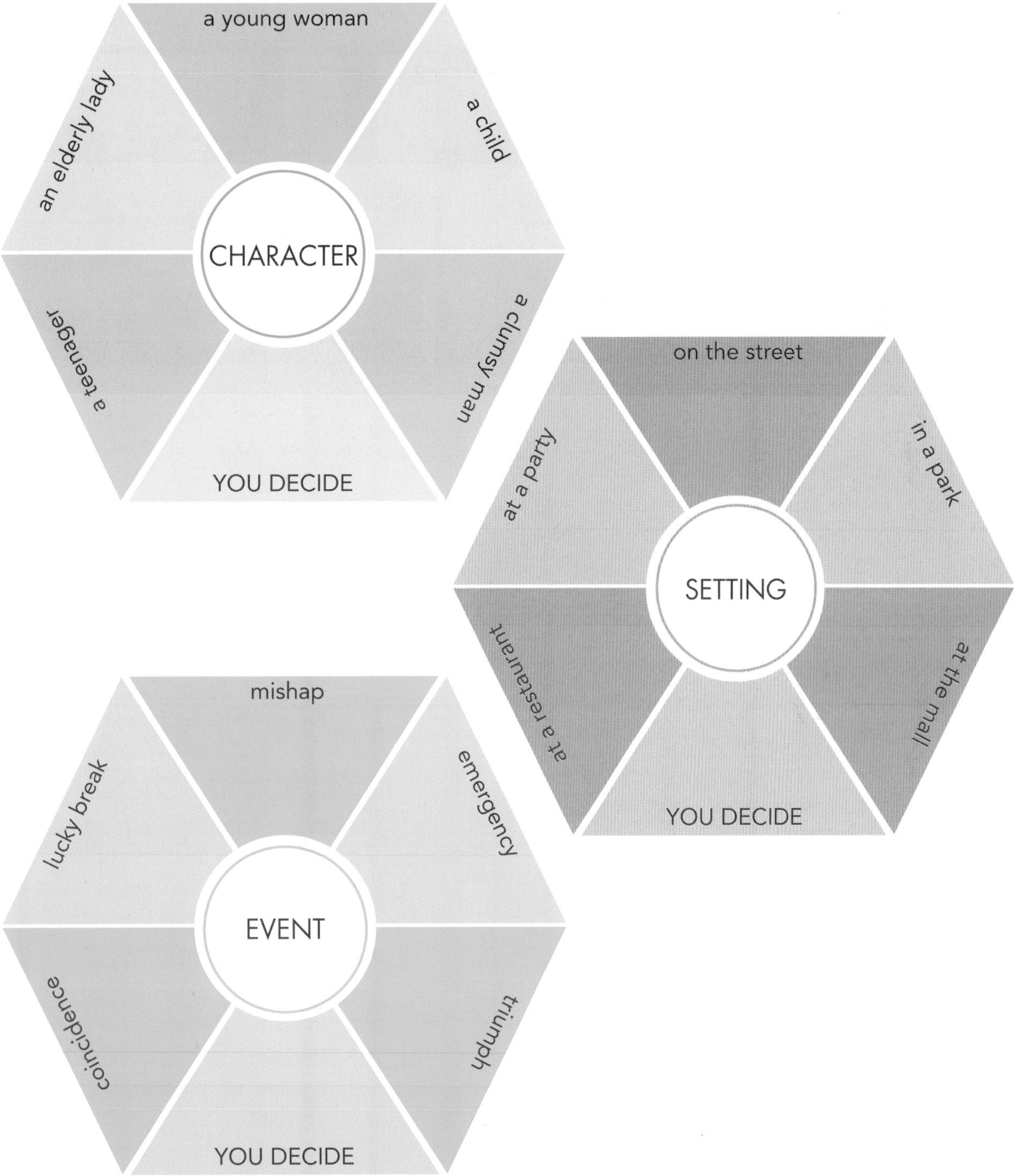

"One day a clumsy man was having dinner at a restaurant when . . ."

B CLASS ACTIVITY Share your group's stories with your classmates. Who created the most interesting story? the most unexpected? the most creative?

INTERCHANGE 5 Cultural dos and taboos

A These statements are generally true about cultural behavior in the United States. Check (✓) those that are true in your country.

COMPARING CULTURES

Find out how typical U.S. cultural behavior compares to yours!

SOCIALIZING AND ENTERTAINING

- ☐ **1.** It's OK to start a conversation with a stranger when waiting in line.
- ☐ **2.** People aren't supposed to stand too close to other people when talking.
- ☐ **3.** In general, people wear outdoor shoes inside their homes.
- ☐ **4.** Women often hug their female friends when they meet.
- ☐ **5.** It's not acceptable to ask people how much money they earn or how much they paid for things.
- ☐ **6.** People are expected to call or text before dropping by a friend's house.
- ☐ **7.** When invited to someone's home for dinner, people usually arrive on time.
- ☐ **8.** Gifts are normally opened when received.

DINING AND SHOPPING

- ☐ **9.** It's acceptable to eat while walking outside.
- ☐ **10.** Eating is not allowed while shopping in most stores.
- ☐ **11.** When eating in a restaurant, friends either split the cost of the meal or take turns paying.
- ☐ **12.** It's the custom to leave a 15–20% tip for the server at a restaurant.
- ☐ **13.** It's uncommon to bargain when you buy things in stores.

AT WORK AND SCHOOL

- ☐ **14.** In an office, people usually prefer to be called by their first names.
- ☐ **15.** Students remain seated when the teacher enters the classroom.

DATING AND MARRIAGE

- ☐ **16.** It's acceptable for most teenagers to go out on dates.
- ☐ **17.** People usually decide for themselves who they will marry.

B **PAIR WORK** Compare your answers with a partner. For the statements you didn't check, why do you think these behaviors are different in your country?

INTERCHANGE 6A Home makeover

Student A

A Look at this apartment. What's wrong with it? First, make a list of as many problems as you can find in each room.

B PAIR WORK Compare your lists. What are the similarities and differences in the problems between your picture and your partner's picture? Ask questions to find the differences.

A: What's wrong in the bedroom?

B: Well, in my picture, the walls need painting. And the curtains . . .

A: Oh, really? In my picture, the walls need to be painted, but the curtains . . . , and the window . . .

INTERCHANGE 6B Home makeover

Student B

A Look at this apartment. What's wrong with it? First, make a list of as many problems as you can find in each room.

B PAIR WORK Compare your lists. What are the similarities and differences in the problems between your picture and your partner's picture? Ask questions to find the differences.

A: What's wrong in the bedroom?

B: Well, in my picture, the walls need painting. And the curtains . . .

A: Oh, really? In my picture, the walls need to be painted, but the curtains . . . , and the window . . .

INTERCHANGE 7 Take action!

A Read about these issues. Which one would you most likely protest?

A baby food company has been using genetically modified fruit and vegetables in their recipes to lower costs.

Congress is discussing a law that allows the government to shut down any website it considers inappropriate.

The city is going to close a public park to build a new bus terminal.

B GROUP WORK Find other students who chose the same issue. Then look at methods of protest. Which are the most effective for the issue you chose? Complete the chart.

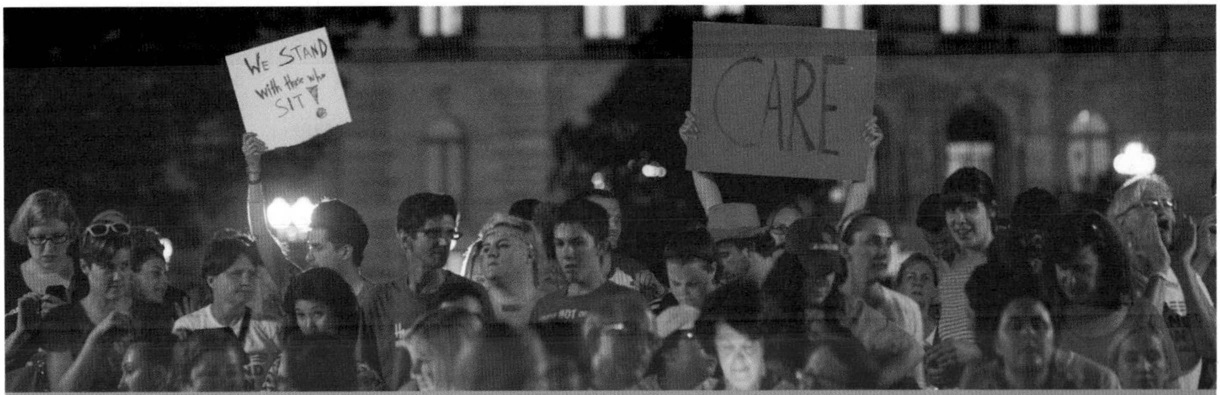

METHOD OF PROTEST	VERY EFFECTIVE	SOMEWHAT EFFECTIVE	NOT EFFECTIVE
start an online campaign	☐	☐	☐
stage a sit-in	☐	☐	☐
organize a demonstration	☐	☐	☐
boycott a product or service	☐	☐	☐
ask people to sign an online petition	☐	☐	☐
contact local news stations	☐	☐	☐
contact your local government representative	☐	☐	☐
distribute pamphlets about the issue	☐	☐	☐
hold an awareness campaign in the community	☐	☐	☐
create posters and signs to hang up around town	☐	☐	☐

Develop a strategy to make your voices heard using the above methods or your own ideas.

C CLASS ACTIVITY How did you decide to deal with the issue? Present your group's strategy to the class.

INTERCHANGE 8 Making choices

A Complete this chart with information about yourself. Add one idea of your own.

two artistic skills I'd like to develop		
two adventurous activities I'd like to try		
two dances I'd like to learn		
two topics I'd like to learn more about		
two foreign languages I'd like to speak		
two dishes I'd like to learn how to cook		
two volunteer activities I'd like to do		
two courses I'd like to take		
two sports I'd like to play		
two skills I'd like to improve		
two ________________		

B CLASS ACTIVITY Ask three classmates to help you choose between the things you wrote down in part A. Write their recommendations in the chart.

Names:			
artistic skill			
adventurous activity			
dance			
topic			
foreign language			
dish			
volunteer activity			
course			
sport			
skill			

A: I don't know if I'd rather be a graffiti artist or a painter. What do you think?
B: Hmm. If I were you, I'd choose graffiti.
A: Why graffiti and not painting?
B: Well, that kind of street art is very popular nowadays. You could become famous, and . . .

C GROUP WORK What are your final choices? Who gave the best advice? Why?

INTERCHANGE 9 Absolutely not!

A PAIR WORK Read these comments made by parents. Why do you think they feel this way? Think of two arguments to support each point of view.

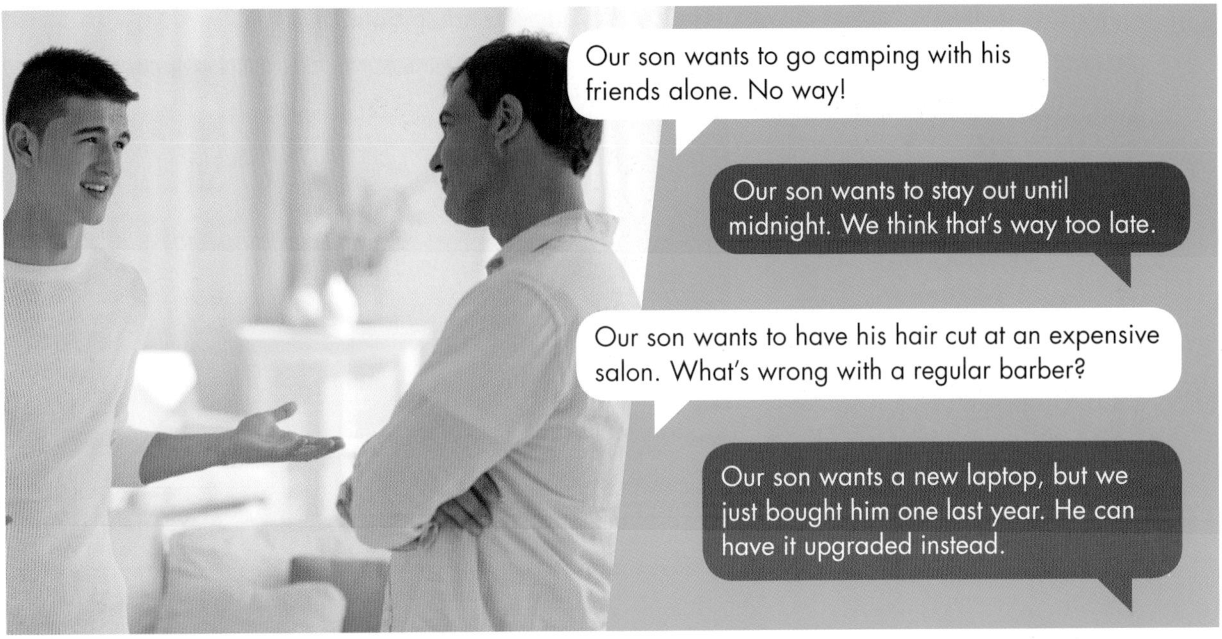

Our son wants to go camping with his friends alone. No way!
Our son wants to stay out until midnight. We think that's way too late.
Our son wants to have his hair cut at an expensive salon. What's wrong with a regular barber?
Our son wants a new laptop, but we just bought him one last year. He can have it upgraded instead.

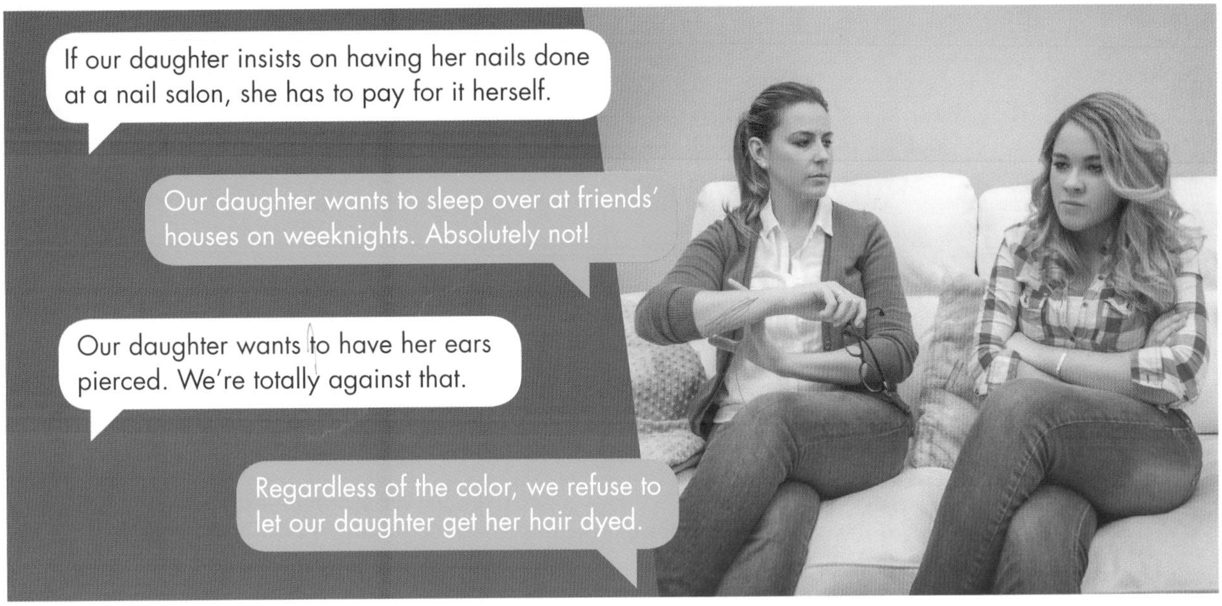

If our daughter insists on having her nails done at a nail salon, she has to pay for it herself.
Our daughter wants to sleep over at friends' houses on weeknights. Absolutely not!
Our daughter wants to have her ears pierced. We're totally against that.
Regardless of the color, we refuse to let our daughter get her hair dyed.

A: Why do you think they won't let their son go camping with his friends?
B: They probably think he's too young to take care of himself.
A: They may also feel that he . . .

B PAIR WORK Discuss the parents' decisions. Think of arguments for and against their points of view.

A: I think the parents should let their son go camping with his friends.
B: Why?
A: Because his friends are going, and he needs to learn to take care of himself.
B: I don't agree. I think he's too young. Teens shouldn't travel without an adult.

C CLASS ACTIVITY Take a vote. Do you agree with the parents? Why?

INTERCHANGE 10A History buff

Student A

A PAIR WORK Ask your partner these questions. Put a check (✓) if your partner gives the correct answer. (The correct answers are in **bold**.)

Frida Kahlo

Volkswagen Beetle

Alexander Fleming

TEST YOUR KNOWLEDGE

☐ 1. What nationality was the painter Frida Kahlo? Was she Spanish, **Mexican**, or Argentinian?

☐ 2. What was the first capital of the United States? Was it **Philadelphia**, New York, or Boston?

☐ 3. Who played 007 in the first James Bond movie? Was it Roger Moore, **Sean Connery**, or Pierce Brosnan?

☐ 4. When was the first Volkswagen Beetle car built? Was it during the 1920s, **1930s**, or 1940s?

☐ 5. Was Nelson Mandela a political activist from India, Angola, or **South Africa**?

☐ 6. When did the British return Hong Kong to China? Was it in 1987, **1997**, or 2007?

☐ 7. Who discovered penicillin? Was it **Alexander Fleming**, Charles Darwin, or Albert Einstein?

☐ 8. Which planet is closest to the sun? Is it Mars, **Mercury**, or Venus?

☐ 9. What Italian astronomer invented the thermometer in 1593? Was it Copernicus, Isaac Newton, or **Galileo**?

☐ 10. When did the first MP3 player hit the market in the US? Was it in 1978, 1988, or **1998**?

B PAIR WORK Answer the questions your partner asks you. Then compare quizzes. Who has the most correct answers?

C CLASS ACTIVITY Think of three more questions of your own. Can the rest of the class answer them?

INTERCHANGE 11 Good choices, bad choices

A PAIR WORK Play the board game. Follow these instructions.

1. Use small pieces of paper with your initials on them as markers.
2. Take turns tossing a coin:

Move one space.

Heads

Move two spaces.

Tails

3. When you land on a space, tell your partner what is true. Then say how things would have been different. For example:
   "When I was younger, I didn't pay attention in class. If I had paid attention in class, I would have gotten better grades."
   OR
   "When I was younger, I paid attention in class. If I hadn't paid attention in class, I wouldn't have won a scholarship."

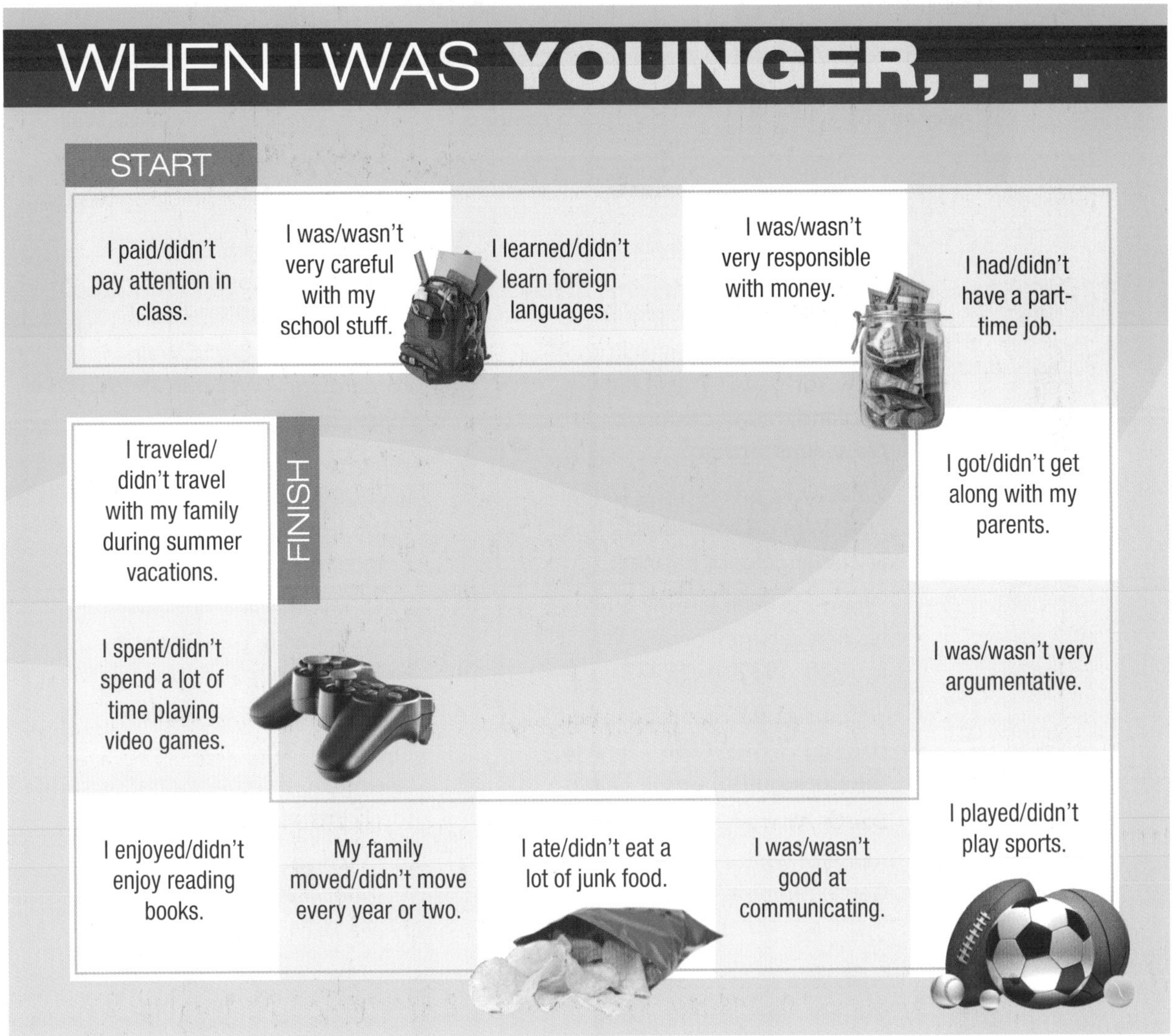

WHEN I WAS YOUNGER, . . .
START
I paid/didn't pay attention in class.
I was/wasn't very careful with my school stuff.
I learned/didn't learn foreign languages.
I was/wasn't very responsible with money.
I had/didn't have a part-time job.
I got/didn't get along with my parents.
I was/wasn't very argumentative.
I played/didn't play sports.
I was/wasn't good at communicating.
I ate/didn't eat a lot of junk food.
My family moved/didn't move every year or two.
I enjoyed/didn't enjoy reading books.
I spent/didn't spend a lot of time playing video games.
I traveled/didn't travel with my family during summer vacations.
FINISH

B CLASS ACTIVITY Who was responsible when they were younger? Who was rebellious? Tell the class.

INTERCHANGE 10B History buff

Student B

A PAIR WORK Answer the questions your partner asks you.

B PAIR WORK Ask your partner these questions. Put a check (✓) if your partner gives the correct answer. (The correct answers are in **bold**.) Then compare quizzes. Who has the most correct answers?

Mona Lisa

a compass

Berlin Wall

TEST YOUR KNOWLEDGE

- ☐ 1. What was the former name of New York City? Was it New England, New London, or **New Amsterdam**?
- ☐ 2. What artist painted the *Mona Lisa*? Was it **Leonardo da Vinci**, Michelangelo, or Raphael?
- ☐ 3. When did Walt Disney make his first cartoon movie? Was it in 1920, **1937**, or 1947?
- ☐ 4. Who used the first magnetic compass? Was it **the Chinese**, the Portuguese, or the Dutch?
- ☐ 5. Constantinople was an earlier name of what city? Was it Cairo, Mumbai, or **Istanbul**?
- ☐ 6. When did the Berlin Wall come down? Was it in 1979, **1989**, or 1999?
- ☐ 7. Where was Marie Curie, the first woman to receive a Nobel Prize, born? Was it in **Poland**, France, or England?
- ☐ 8. Who was the first human in space? Was it **Yuri Gagarin**, Neil Armstrong, or John Glenn?
- ☐ 9. What did Thomas Edison invent in 1879? Was it the television, the telephone, or the **lightbulb**?
- ☐ 10. In which year did Mexico gain its independence? Was it in 1721, **1821**, or 1921?

C CLASS ACTIVITY Think of three more questions of your own. Can the rest of the class answer them?

INTERCHANGE 12 Advertising taglines

A PAIR WORK Read these popular slogans for products. Match the slogans with the product types.

1. Think different. ______	**a.** a soft drink
2. Unforgettable happens here. ______	**b.** a technology company
3. Taste the feeling. ______	**c.** an amusement park
4. All the news that's fit to print. ______	**d.** sports clothing
5. Impossible is nothing. ______	**e.** potato chips
6. Bet you can't eat just one. ______	**f.** a daily newspaper
7. Stay with us, and feel like home. ______	**g.** fast food
8. Reach out and touch someone. ______	**h.** automobiles
9. I'm loving it. ______	**i.** a game console
10. Live in your world. Play in ours. ______	**j.** a hotel
11. Melts in your mouth, not in your hands. ______	**k.** a telephone service
12. Built for the road ahead. ______	**l.** chocolate candy

B PAIR WORK Join another pair and compare your answers. Then check your answers at the bottom of the page.

C GROUP WORK Think of a product. Then create your own slogan for it and add a logo. Consider a design and colors that are suitable for the product.

A: Any ideas for a product?
B: What about an online store for used toys?
C: Sounds interesting. Let's try to think of some catchy slogans.
D: How about, "Play again!"? Or maybe . . .

D CLASS ACTIVITY Present your slogans to the class. Who has the catchiest ones?

1. b; **2.** c; **3.** a; **4.** f; **5.** d; **6.** e; **7.** j; **8.** k; **9.** g; **10.** i; **11.** l; **12.** h

INTERCHANGE 13 Think of the possibilities!

A PAIR WORK What do you think might have happened in each situation? Talk about possibilities for each situation.

Pete made a fortune in the stock market. He's now working at a burger joint.

Lisa went grocery shopping yesterday afternoon. She hasn't come back home yet.

Jim was the best salesperson in the company for the past 10 years. He just got fired.

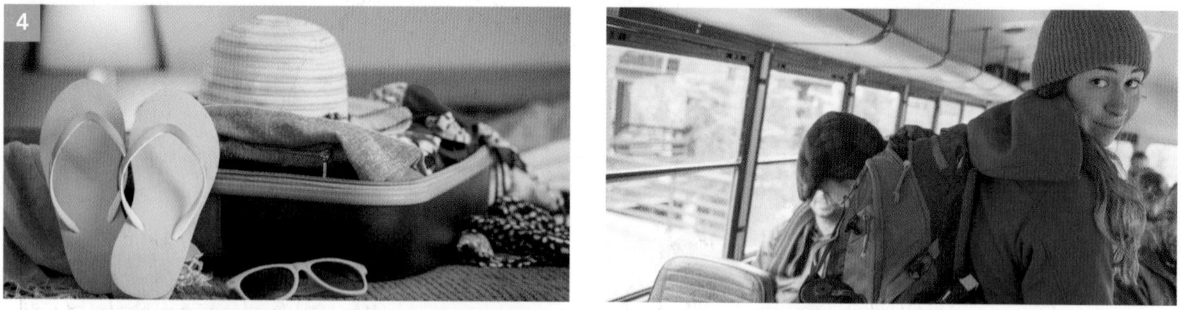

Clara had everything ready for her dream vacation in Tahiti. She's on the bus heading to her parents' home.

A: Maybe Pete made some bad investments.

B: Or he might have spent all his money on . . .

useful expressions	
Maybe he/she was . . . when . . .	He/She may have . . . when . . .
Or perhaps he/she was . . .	He/She might have . . .

B GROUP WORK Agree on one explanation for each situation and share it with the class. Be ready to answer any questions.

INTERCHANGE 14 Celebrities

A Prepare to play a guessing game.

- Write the names of five celebrities on slips of paper. Names can include people in history, movie stars, singers, politicians, writers, etc.
- Mix all the slips in a bag.

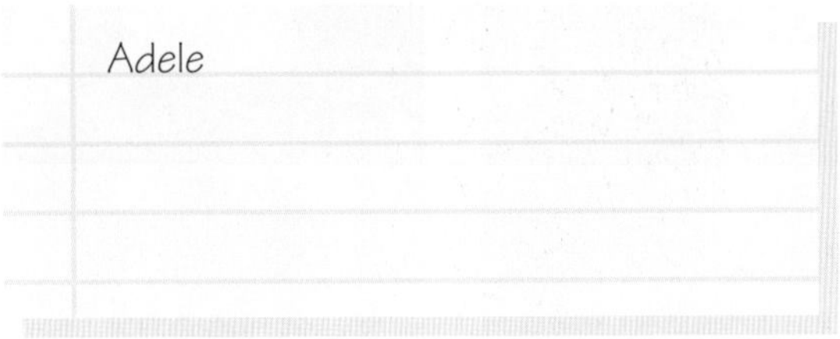

B GROUP WORK Each player takes turns picking a slip for his or her group to guess.

A: She's a celebrity who was born in London.
B: Is she a movie star?
A: No, she's a singer and songwriter who has a beautiful voice.
C: I think I know the answer. It's . . .

C CLASS ACTIVITY Which celebrities were easier to guess? Which were the most difficult? Who gave the best clues?

Nico Rosberg

Sofia Vergara

Albert Einstein

Sally Ride

INTERCHANGE 15 On the wrong side of the law

A PAIR WORK What punishment (if any) is appropriate for each possible offense? Why? Complete the chart.

OFFENSE	PUNISHMENT
1 parking in a disabled parking space without a permit	______________
2 posting offensive comments online	______________
3 leaving trash on public streets	______________
4 riding the subway without paying the fare	______________
5 failing to clean up after a dog	______________
6 pickpocketing	______________
7 scratching paint off another person's car	______________
8 crossing the street in dangerous places	______________
9 driving without a seat belt	______________
10 riding a motorcycle without a helmet	______________
11 hacking into a government computer	______________
12 ______________ (your own idea)	______________

A: What do you think should be done about people who park in a disabled parking space without a permit?

B: They should be required to pay a heavy fine because it may cause problems for people with disabilities.

A: I don't agree. I think . . .

possible punishments

- receive a warning
- spend some time in jail
- pay a fine
- lose a driver's license
- get suspended
- do community service
- be banned from using the Internet

B GROUP WORK Join another pair of students. Then compare and discuss your lists. Do you agree or disagree? Try to convince each other that you are right!

INTERCHANGE 16 A digital nomad

A PAIR WORK Interview your partner. Would he or she be a happy digital nomad?

Is the digital nomad lifestyle **right for you?**

Do you dream of working from a beach paradise? Are you ready to hit the road and make a living while traveling the world? Take our quiz and find out.

1. Have you traveled much before?
   - ☐ **a.** I've traveled with my family in our country.
   - ☐ **b.** Not yet, but I hope to have seen more of the world by the time I retire.
   - ☐ **c.** I've been to a couple of continents and seen some amazing things!
2. Are you resourceful?
   - ☐ **a.** Well, I can always count on my friends to help me when I need it.
   - ☐ **b.** Yes, and I can always find the answers I need on the Internet.
   - ☐ **c.** Yes, I'm good at finding opportunities everywhere.
3. When you pack for a long weekend, what do you take with you?
   - ☐ **a.** A big suitcase with everything I might need – you never know what might happen.
   - ☐ **b.** A small bag with the essentials.
   - ☐ **c.** A toothbrush and a change of clothes. I like to travel light.
4. Are you flexible and adaptable?
   - ☐ **a.** I try to be, but I don't always succeed.
   - ☐ **b.** Yes, if you give me some time to adjust.
   - ☐ **c.** Definitely. I've managed to survive under the most challenging circumstances.

5. Have you ever traveled all by yourself?
   - ☐ **a.** Of course not. I need family and friends around at all times.
   - ☐ **b.** No, but I think I'd enjoy it.
   - ☐ **c.** Sure. I often take vacations alone. It's a great opportunity to meet new people.
6. Are you ready to give up a fixed salary?
   - ☐ **a.** No. I need to have a steady income. It's important for me to know how much money I'll be making for the next 12 months.
   - ☐ **b.** Well, I can live on very little money – I've done it before.
   - ☐ **c.** I'm good at managing my money, and I always have some savings, so that wouldn't be a problem.
7. Are you self-motivated, or do you depend on others to get you going?
   - ☐ **a.** I need to know that my boss or my teachers are around and that I can count on them.
   - ☐ **b.** It depends. If I'm really involved with a project, I'm more independent; if not . . .
   - ☐ **c.** Definitely. I know what I have to do, and I always finish the work on time.
8. How do you feel about changes?
   - ☐ **a.** I like to have a set routine. Changes make me feel uncomfortable.
   - ☐ **b.** They can be a challenge, but they also help me grow.
   - ☐ **c.** Changes are always welcome. New things inspire and motivate me.

Score the quiz by counting the number of a's, b's, and c's.
Mostly a's: The digital nomad lifestyle is not for you.
Mostly b's: You'd probably be happy being a digital nomad, but you might miss your current life.
Mostly c's: What are you doing here? Go grab your things and hit the road!

B CLASS ACTIVITY Compare your findings. Who is ready to become a digital nomad?

Grammar plus

UNIT 1

1 Relative pronouns page 3

- A relative pronoun – *who* or *that* – is necessary when the pronoun is the subject of the clause: I'd love to meet someone **who/that** is considerate. (NOT: I'd love to meet ~~someone is considerate~~.)
- When the pronoun is the object of the clause, *who* and *that* can be left out: I'd like a roommate **who/that** I have a lot in common with. OR I'd like a roommate I have a lot in common with.

Complete the conversation with *who* or *that*. Put an ✗ when a relative pronoun isn't necessary.

A: Ana, have you met Clint – the guy __✗__ Laurie is going to marry?
B: Oh, Clint and I have been friends for years. In fact, I'm the one __who__ introduced Laurie and Clint.
A: Do you think they're right for each other?
B: Definitely. They're two people __that__ (who) have a lot in common – but not *too* much.
A: What does that mean?
B: Well, you don't want a partner __who__ (that) doesn't have his or her own interests. Couples __that__ (who) do everything together usually don't last very long.
A: I guess you're right, but the opposite isn't good, either. My last girlfriend was someone __X__ I had nothing in common with. She wasn't the kind of girl __X__ I could talk to easily.
B: Well, you can talk to *me* easily. . . .

2 *It* clauses + adverbial clauses with *when* page 6

- In sentences with an *it* clause + an adverbial clause with *when*, the word *it* refers to and means the same as the adverbial clause with *when*. The *it* in these sentences is necessary and cannot be left out: I hate **it when** people talk on a cell phone in an elevator. (NOT: ~~I hate when~~ people . . .) **It** bothers me **when** people talk on a cell phone in an elevator. (NOT: ~~Bothers~~ me when people . . .)

Rewrite the sentences using the words in parentheses.

1. I can't stand it when people call me before 8:00 A.M. (it really bothers me)
   It really bothers me when people call me before 8:00 a.m.
2. It upsets me when I don't have enough time to study for an exam. (I hate it)
   I hate it when I don't have enough time to study for an exam.
3. I don't mind it when friends talk to me about their problems. (it doesn't bother me)
   It doesn't bother me when friends talk to me about their problems.
4. I don't like it when I forget a co-worker's name. (it embarrasses me)
   It embarrasses me when I forget a co-worker's name
5. It makes me happy when my friends send me videos. (I love it)
   I love it when my friends send me videos
6. I hate it when I have to wait for someone. (it upsets me)
   It upsets me when I have to wait for someone

UNIT 2

1 Gerund phrases page 9

GERUND (ing)

- Preposition expressions (about, like)
- Preposition phrases (in, of, by, to, at)

- A gerund phrase as a subject takes a singular verb: Taking care of children **is** a rewarding job. (NOT: Taking care of children ~~are~~ a rewarding job.)
- There are some common verb + preposition expressions (for example, *dream about, feel like, talk about, think about*) and adjective + preposition phrases (for example, *good/bad at, excited by/about, interested in, tired of, used to*) that are followed by a gerund: I'm **thinking about looking for** a new job. I'm **tired of working** long hours.

Complete the sentences with the correct gerund forms of the verbs in the box.

✓ become	have	make	stand	travel
change	learn	solve	take	work

1. My brother's very interested in becoming a flight attendant. He dreams about traveling to new places.
2. I'm excited about taking a Japanese class next semester. I enjoy learning languages.
3. You wouldn't like working in a restaurant. You'd get tired of standing on your feet throughout the long shifts!
4. Our teacher is very good at solving problems. Maybe she should think about changing careers to become a guidance counselor.
5. making a living as a photographer could be challenging. having an impressive portfolio is really important to attract new clients and employers.

2 Comparisons page 11

- When making general comparisons with count nouns, use *a/an* + singular noun or no article + plural noun: **A pilot** earns (gana) more than **a flight attendant**. **Pilots** earn more than **flight attendants**. (NOT: ~~The~~ pilots earn more than ~~the~~ flight attendants.)

Make comparisons with the information below. Add articles and other words when necessary.

1. architect / more education / hairstylist
   An architect needs more education than a hairstylist.
2. college professor / earn more / elementary school teacher
   An college professor earns more than a elementary school teacher.
3. nurses / worse hours / psychiatrists
   Nurses have worse hours than psychiatrist
4. working as a police officer / as dangerous / being a firefighter
   working as a police officer is as dangerous as being a firefighter
5. taxi driver / not as well paid / electrician
   An Taxi driver is not as well paid as an electrician.
6. being a tour guide / less interesting / being an actor
   Being a tour guide sounds less interesting than being an actor.

1 Requests with modals, *if* clauses, and gerunds　page 17

■ Use the simple past form – not the gerund or simple present form – after *if* with *Would you mind* . . . ? and *Would it be all right* . . . ?: **Would you mind if I used** your car? **Would it be all right if I used** your car? (NOT: Would you mind if I using your car? OR Would it be all right if I use your car?)

Read the situations. Then complete the requests.

1. You want to borrow a friend's underwater camera for a diving trip.
 A: I was wondering if I could borrow your underwater camera.
 B: Sure. That's fine. Just please be careful with it.

2. You want to use your roommate's computer.
 A: Is it OK if I use your computer ? ✓
 B: You can use it, but please don't drink near it.

3. Your neighbor has a car. You need a ride to class.
 A: Would you mind if you giving me a ride to class ?
 B: I'd be glad to. What time should I pick you up?

4. You want your brother to help you move on Saturday.
 A: Can you help me to move on Saturday ? ✓
 B: I'm sorry. I'm busy all weekend.

5. You would like a second piece of your aunt's cherry pie.
 A: Would it be all right if I had a second piece of your cherry pie ?
 B: Yes, of course! Just pass me your plate.

6. You want to borrow your cousin's red sweater.
 A: Could you lend me your red sweater
 B: Sorry. I don't like it when other people wear my clothes.

2 Indirect requests　page 20

■ In indirect requests with negative infinitives, *not* comes before – not between – the infinitive: Could you tell Allie **not to be** late? (NOT: Could you tell Allie to not be late?)

Complete the indirect requests. Ask someone to deliver the messages to Susie.

1. Are you busy this weekend? → Could you ask Susie if she's busy this weekend?
2. Do you want to hang out with me? → Can you ask Susie if she wants hang out with me?
3. Text me. → Can you tell Susie no to forget text me
4. Do you know my address? → Can you'll ask Susie if she knows my adress
5. Don't forget to write. → Could you tell Susie not to forget to write
6. What are you doing Saturday? → Can you ask Susie what she's doing on satur
7. Do you have plans on Sunday? → Could you ask Susie if she has plans on sunday.

UNIT 4

1 Past continuous vs. simple past page 23

■ Verbs for non-actions or states are rarely used in the past continuous: I **wanted** to stop, but I couldn't. (NOT: I ~~was wanting~~ to stop . . .)

Circle the best forms to complete the conversations.

1. **A:** How **did you break** / **were you breaking** your arm?
   B: It's a crazy story! Ramon and I **rode** / **were riding** our bikes in the park when a cat **ran** / **was running** out in front of me. I **went** / **was going** pretty fast, so when I **tried** / **was trying** to stop, I **went** / **was going** off the road and **fell** / **was falling**.
   A: That's terrible! **Did you go** / **Were you going to** the hospital after it **happened** / **was happening**?
   B: Yes. Luckily, we **weren't** / **weren't being** too far from City Hospital, so we **went** / **were going** there.
2. **A:** You'll never guess what **happened** / **was happening** to me this morning!
   B: What?
   A: Well, I **brushed** / **was brushing** my teeth when suddenly the water **went** / **was going** off. I **had** / **was having** toothpaste all over my mouth, and I couldn't wash it off.
   B: So what **did you do** / **were you doing**?
   A: Fortunately, I **had** / **was having** a big bottle of water in the refrigerator, so I **used** / **was using** that water to rinse my mouth.

2 Past perfect page 25

■ Use the past perfect to show that one past action happened before another past action:
I **wasn't able to** pay for lunch because I **had left** my wallet at work.
PAST ———— X ———————— X ———— NOW
had left my wallet — wasn't able to pay

Combine the two ideas into one with a past event and a past perfect event. Use *when* or *because*.

1. The museum closed. A thief stole a famous painting earlier.
   The museum closed because a thief had stolen a famous painting earlier.
2. We finished cleaning the house. Then our guests arrived.
   we had finished cleaning the house when our guests arrived
3. Someone robbed my house yesterday. I left the window open.
   someone robbed my house yesterday because I had left the window open
4. There was no food in the house. We forgot to stop at the supermarket.
   There was no food in the house because we had forgot to stop at the supermarket
5. I called her three times. She finally answered.
   I had called her three times, when she finally answered
6. I knew about the problem. Your brother told me about it.
   I knew about the problem because your brother had told me about it

UNIT 5

1 Noun phrases containing relative clauses page 31

- The relative pronoun *who* or *that* can be left out in noun phrases as subjects and as objects. These four sentences have exactly the same meaning: One thing I'd be nervous about is getting lost. One thing that I'd be nervous about is getting lost. Getting lost is one thing I'd be nervous about. Getting lost is one thing that I'd be nervous about.

Answer the questions using the words in parentheses. Write each sentence two ways. Leave out the relative pronouns.

If you went to live in a foreign country, . . .

1. Who would you miss a lot? (person: my best friend)
   - **a.** One person I'd miss a lot is my best friend.
   - **b.** My best friend is one person I'd miss a lot.
2. What would you be very interested in? (things: the food and the music)
   - **a.** I'd be very interested in are the food an the music
   - **b.** In the food and the music are two things I'd be interested
3. What would you be worried about? (something: not understanding the customs)
   - **a.** Something I'd be worried about is not understanding the customs
   - **b.** Not understanding the customs is something I'd be worried about
4. Who would you stay in touch with? (people: my brother and sister)
   - **a.** I'd stay in touch with are my brother and sister
   - **b.** My brother and sister are two people I'd stay in touch with.
5. What would you feel insecure about? (thing: speaking a new language)
   - **a.** I'd be feel insecure about is speaking a new language
   - **b.** Speaking a new language is one thing I'd feel insecure.

2 Expectations page 33

- Use the base form of a verb – not the gerund – after these expressions for expectations: *be the custom to, be supposed to, be expected to, be acceptable to*: It's the custom to **arrive** a little late. (NOT: It's the custom to ~~arriving~~ a little late.)

Complete the sentences with the clauses in the box.

it's not acceptable to show up without calling first.
it's the custom for them to sit across from each other.
you're expected to reply within a few days.
you're supposed to bring a gift.
✓ you're supposed to shake his or her hand.

1. When you meet someone for the first time, you're supposed to shake his or her hand.
2. When a friend sends you an email, you're expected to reply within a few days
3. If you want to visit someone, it's not acceptable to show up without calling first
4. If you invite a married couple to dinner, It's the custom for them to sit across from
5. When you go to a birthday party, you're supposed to bring a gift

UNIT 6

1 Describing problems 1 page 37

■ The simple past and the past participle of regular verbs are the same: I **chipped** the vase. The vase is **chipped**. BUT Many irregular verbs have different simple past and past participle forms: I **tore** my jacket. My jacket is **torn**.

Complete the conversations with the correct words from the box.

are stained	**has a dent**	✓ **have a tear**	**is broken**	**is scratched**
has a chip	**has a stain**	**is a hole**	**is leaking**	**some damage**

1. **A:** Oh, no! These jeans *have a tear* in them.
   B: And they are stained, too.
2. **A:** This table has some damage on top.
   B: I know. The wood is scratched because my son drags his toy cars on it.
3. **A:** Why are you drinking out of that glass? It has a chip in it.
   B: Oh, I didn't see it. That's why it is leaking.
4. **A:** Someone hit my car today. Look! The door has a dent in it.
   B: I see that. Your back light is broken, too.
5. **A:** I bought this blouse yesterday, but I have to take it back. There is a hole in it.
   B: It's really cute, but that's not the only problem. It has a stain on it, too.

2 Describing problems 2 page 39

■ Use the past participle – not the present participle or gerund – with passive forms: The oven needs to be **fixed**. (NOT: The oven needs to be ~~fixing~~.)

A Complete the conversation with the verbs in parentheses. Use *need* + passive infinitive in A's lines and *need* + gerund in B's lines.

A: Look at this place! A lot of work *needs to be done* (do) before we move in.
B: You're not kidding. Let's make a list. First, the walls *need painting* (paint).
A: Right. And the windows need to be washed (wash). Add the rug to your list: It really needs to be cleaned (clean). Do you think it needs dry cleaned (dry-clean)?
B: No, I think we can do it ourselves. It needs shampooing (shampoo). We can rent a machine for that.
A: And what about the ceiling fan? I think it needs to be replaced (replace). Fans aren't too expensive.
B: OK. I've added it to the list. And what should we do with all this old furniture?
A: It needs to be throw out (throw out)! I think the landlord should take care of that, though.

B Complete the blog with the correct form of *keep* and the verb in parentheses.

I *keep having* (have) technical problems. My computer keeps crashing (crash), and my printer keeps jamming (jam). I have to keep putting (put) a new battery into my mouse because it keeps dying (die). The letters on my keyboard keep sticking (stick), too. I keep thinking (think) things will get better, but they just keep getting (get) worse. Time for some new electronics!

UNIT 7

1 Passive with prepositions page 45

- The prepositions *by, as a result of, because of, though,* and *due to* have similar meanings. They are used in sentences that describe cause and effect; they introduce the cause.

Match phrases from each column to make sentences. (More than one answer may be possible.)

Subject	Effect	Cause
1. The environment	is being contaminated due to	improper disposal of medical waste.
2. Our soil	is being harmed by	deforestation to make paper products.
3. Infectious diseases	are being endangered due to	hybrid cars.
4. Many different species	has been affected because of	the use of pesticides on fruits and vegetables.
5. Our air quality	has been reduced as a result of	the destruction of their habitats.
6. Smog pollution	have been spread through	climate changes like global warming.

2 Infinitive clauses and phrases page 47

- The form of *be* that follows the first infinitive must agree with the subject:
  The best way to reduce pollution **is** to improve public transportation.
  BUT The best ways to reduce homelessness **are** to build more public housing and provide free health care.

A Match the phrases.

1. What are the best ways to make ___
2. And the best way to do that is ___
3. The best ways to reduce ___
4. One way to improve ___
5. Another way to make ___

a. people safer is to make the air healthier.
b. to create a larger police force.
c. people's quality of life is to help them feel safe.
d. air pollution are to ban cars and control industry.
e. this city a better place to live?

B Complete the conversation with the sentences above.

A: *What are the best ways to make this city a better place to live?*
B: Well, ___
A: That's right. ___
B: I agree. ___
A: Yes. Good air quality is key. ___
B: Maybe it's time to share our ideas with the mayor. Get out your phone.

UNIT 8

1 *Would rather* and *would prefer* page 51

- In negative statements with *would rather* and *would prefer*, the word *not* comes after the verbs: I'**d rather not**/I'**d prefer not** to take any courses this semester. (NOT: I ~~wouldn't rather~~/I ~~wouldn't prefer~~ to . . .)

Write questions and responses using the words in parentheses.

1. **A:** *Would you prefer to take classes during the day or at night?*
   (prefer / take classes / during the day / at night)
   B: I'd rather take classes at night
   (rather / take classes / at night)
2. **A:** Would you rather study business or education?
   (rather / study / business / education)
   B: I'd prefer to become a teacher.
   (prefer / become / a teacher)
3. **A:** Would you prefer to sign up for an art course or a computer course?
   (prefer / sign up for / an art course / a computer course)
   B: I'd prefer not to take any classes this semester
   (prefer / not / take / any classes this semester)
4. **A:** Would you rather take up an individual sport or a team sport?
   (rather / take up / an individual sport / a team sport)
   B: I'd rather not take up either
   (rather / not / take up / either)

2 *By* + gerund to describe how to do things page 53

- In negative sentences that express comparison with *by* + gerund and *but*, *not* comes before *by*: A good way to improve your accent is **not by watching** TV **but by talking** to native speakers. In negative sentences with *by* that give advice without a comparison, *not* comes after *by*: A good way to improve your accent is **by not imitating** non-native speakers.

Combine the two ideas into one sentence using *by* + gerund.

1. You can build your vocabulary. Write down new words and expressions.
   One way to build your vocabulary is by writing down new words and expressions.
2. There is a good way to improve your accent. You can mimic native speakers.
   A good way to improve your accent is by mimicking native speakers
3. Students can improve their listening skills. They can listen to English-language podcasts.
   Students can improve their listening skills by listening to English-language podcasts
4. Hardworking students improve their grammar. They don't repeat common mistakes.
   Hardworking students improve their grammar by not reapeating common mistakes
5. You can become fluent. Don't translate everything. Try to think in English.
   You can become fluent not by translating everything but by trying to think in english
6. You can become a good conversationalist. Don't just talk with others. Talk to yourself when you're alone, too.
   You can become a good conversationalist not just by talking with others. but by talking to yourself when you're alone, too

UNIT 9

1 Get or have something done page 59

- Sentences with *get/have* + object + past participle are passive. BUT Don't use any form of *be* before the past participle: Where can I **have** my watch **fixed**? (NOT: Where can I have my watch ~~be~~ fixed?)

Rewrite the statements as questions with *Where can I get/have . . . ?* Then complete B's answers with the information in parentheses.

1. I want to have someone shorten these pants.
   A: Where can I have these pants shortened?
   B: You can have them shortened at Tim's Tailoring. (at Tim's Tailoring)
2. I need to get someone to repair my computer.
   A: Where can I get my computer repaired?
   B: You can get it repaired at Hackers Inc. (at Hackers Inc.)
3. I need to have someone prepare my taxes.
   A: Where can I have my taxes prepared?
   B: You can have them prepared by my accountant (by my accountant)
4. I'd like to get someone to cut my hair.
   A: Where can I get my hair cut?
   B: You can get it cut at Beauty Barn (at Beauty Barn)
5. I need to have someone paint my apartment.
   A: where can I have my apartament painted?
   B: You can have it painted by Peter the Painter (by Peter the Painter)

2 Making suggestions page 61

- Use the base form of a verb – without *to* – after *Maybe you could . . .* and *Why don't you . . . ?*: Maybe you could **join** a book club. (NOT: Maybe you could ~~to~~ join a book club.) Why don't you **join** a book club? (NOT: Why don't you ~~to~~ join a book club?)

Complete the conversations with the correct form of the verbs in parentheses.

A: I'm having trouble meeting people here in the city. Any ideas?

B: I know it's hard. Why don't you join (join) a gym? That's usually a good place to meet people. Or maybe you could take (take) a class at the community college.

A: What about checking out (check out) the personal ads? Do you think that's a good way to meet people?

B: I wouldn't recommend doing that. People never tell the truth in those ads. But it might be a good idea to find (find) a sports team. Have you thought about playing (play) a team sport – maybe baseball or volleyball?

A: I'm not very good at most sports, but I used to play tennis.

B: There you go! One option is to look up (look up) tennis clubs in the city and see which clubs have teams people can join.

A: Now, that's a great idea. And I could always use the exercise!

UNIT 10

1 Referring to time in the past page 65

- Use *since* with a particular time: The UN has been in existence **since** 1945. Use *for* with a duration of time: The UN has been in existence **for** about the last 70 years.
- Use *in* and *during* with a specific period of time: Rock 'n' roll became popular **in/during** the 1950s.
- Use *from* and *to* to describe when something began and ended: World War II lasted **from** 1939 **to** 1945.

Complete the conversation with the words in the box. (Use some of the words more than once.)

ago	during	for	from	in	since	to

A: Hey, Dad. Did you use to listen to the Beatles?

B: Of course. In fact, I just listened to one of their records a few days ___*ago*___. Do you realize that the Beatles's music has influenced other musicians ________ over 50 years? They were the greatest!

A: Well, I just found some interesting information about them. I'll read it to you: "The Beatles were a well-known British band ________ the 1960s. They performed together ________ 10 years – ________ 1960 ________ 1970. ________ 2003, the Beatles released *Let it Be*, even though one of the original members had been dead ________ 1980 and another had died ________ 2001. The original album had been recorded ________ 1969 and was in the studio safe ________ 34 years before the new, remixed album was released."

B: That *is* interesting. It's pretty amazing that people have listened to the Beatles ________ both the twentieth and the twenty-first centuries, isn't it?

2 Predicting the future with *will* page 67

- In sentences referring to time, the preposition *by* means "not later than." Don't confuse *by* with *within*, which means "some time during." Use *by* with points in time; use *within* with periods of time: **By** 2050, we will have eliminated starvation around the world. (NOT: ~~Within~~ 2050, . . .) **Within** the next five years, people will have invented mobile phone apps for nearly everything! (NOT: ~~By~~ the next five years, . . .)

Circle the correct verb forms to complete the conversation.

A: What do you think you **will do** / **will be doing** five years from now?

B: I'm not sure. Maybe I **will get** / **will have gotten** married by then. How about you?

A: I **will be finishing** / **will have finished** medical school, so I **will be doing** / **will have done** my internship five years from now.

B: So you **won't be living** / **won't have lived** around here in five years, I guess. Where do you think you **will live** / **will have lived**?

A: Wherever I get my internship.

UNIT 11

1 Time clauses page 73

- Use the past perfect in the main clause with *until* and *by the time*. This shows that one of the past events happened before the other: Until I got my driver's license, I **had** always **taken** public transportation. By the time I got my driver's license, all of my friends **had** already **gotten** theirs.

Circle the correct time expression to complete each sentence.

1. **After / Until** I traveled overseas, I hadn't known much about different cultures.
2. **After / Before** I got a full-time job, I had to live on a very limited budget.
3. **By the time / Once** I finished high school, I had already taken three college courses.
4. **As soon as / Before** I left for college, my mother turned my room into her office.
5. **Once / Until** I left home, I realized how much my family meant to me.
6. **By the time / The moment** you have a child, you feel totally responsible for him or her.

2 Expressing regret and describing hypothetical situations page 75

- Conditional sentences describing hypothetical situations often refer to both the present and the past:
  If I**'d finished** college, I**'d have** a better job now.
  past present
  (NOT: If I'd finished college, I'd ~~have had~~ a better job now.)

A Write sentences with *should (not) have* to express regret about each person's situation.

1. Sarah was very argumentative with her teacher, so she had to stay after school.
   Sarah shouldn't have been argumentative with her teacher.
2. Ivan didn't save up for a car, so he still has to take public transportation.
   ______
3. Jon was very inactive when he was in college, so he gained a lot of weight.
   ______
4. Lisa didn't stay in touch with her high school classmates, so now she has very few friends.
   ______
5. Tony didn't study Spanish in school, so he's not bilingual now.
   ______

B Rewrite your sentences in part A, changing them to hypothetical situations.

1. If Sarah hadn't been argumentative with her teacher, she wouldn't have had to stay after school.
2. ______
3. ______
4. ______
5. ______

UNIT 12

1 Describing purpose page 79

- Don't use *for* immediately before an infinitive: **To have** a successful business, you need a lot of luck. (NOT: ~~For~~ to have a successful business, you need a lot of luck.)

A Complete the sentences with *in order to* or *in order for*.

1. In order for a supermarket to succeed, it has to be clean and well organized.
2. ______________ stay popular, a website needs to be accurate and visually attractive.
3. ______________ run a profitable furniture store, it's important to advertise on TV.
4. ______________ a restaurant to stay in business, it needs to have "regulars" – customers that come often.
5. ______________ establish a successful nail salon, it has to have a convenient location.
6. ______________ an online business to survive, it needs to have excellent pictures of the merchandise it's selling.

B Rewrite the sentences in part A without *In order*.

1. For a supermarket to succeed, it has to be clean and well organized.
2. ______________________________
3. ______________________________
4. ______________________________
5. ______________________________
6. ______________________________

2 Giving reasons page 81

- *Because* and *since* have the same meaning, and they can begin or end a sentence: **Because/Since** the food is always fantastic, Giorgio's is my favorite restaurant. = Giorgio's is my favorite restaurant **because/since** the food is always fantastic.
- Don't confuse *because* and *because of*. *Because* introduces an adverb clause and is followed by a subject and verb, while *because of* is a preposition and is followed by a noun object: **Because** Giorgio's is so popular, we should get there early. Giorgio's is popular **because of** its food and service.

Circle the correct words to complete the conversation.

A: I had to go downtown today **because** / **because of** / **due to** I needed to mail a package at the post office. **Due to** / **For** / **Since** I was only a few blocks from Main Street, I went over to Martin's. Did you know that Martin's has gone out of business? I'm so upset!

B: That's too bad, but I'm not surprised. A lot of family-owned shops are closing **because** / **because of** / **since** the construction of shopping malls.

A: Yeah, and don't forget about all the megastores that are popping up everywhere. **Because** / **For** / **The reason why** people prefer to shop there is to save money. Everyone loves a megastore **because** / **due to** / **since** the low prices and the huge selection.

B: Not me! I loved Martin's **for** / **since** / **the reason that** their beautiful clothes and friendly salespeople. When you were there, you almost felt like family. You'll never get that at a megastore!

UNIT 13

1 Past modals for degrees of certainty page 87

- Use the past modal *could have* to express possibility. BUT Use *couldn't have* when you are almost 100% sure something is impossible: I suppose he **could have gotten** stuck in traffic, but he **couldn't have forgotten** his own birthday party.

Complete the conversations with past modals *must (not) have, could (not) have,* or *may/might (not) have.* Use the degrees of certainty and the verbs in parentheses. (More than one answer may be possible.)

1. **A:** Yoko still hasn't called me back.
   B: She _might not have gotten_ your message. (it's possible – not get)
2. **A:** What's wrong with Steven?
   B: Oh, you ____________ the news. His dog ran away. (it's almost certain – not hear)
3. **A:** I went to see the Larsens today, but they didn't answer the door.
   B: Was their car there? If so, they ____________ in the backyard. (it's possible – be)
4. **A:** Fabio said he was going to the party last night, but I didn't see him.
   B: Neither did I. He ____________ there then. (it's not possible – not be)
5. **A:** I can't find my glasses, but I know I had them at work today.
   B: You ____________ them at the office. (it's possible – leave)
6. **A:** Marc's new car looks really expensive.
   B: Yes, it does. It ____________ a fortune! (it's almost certain – cost)

2 Past modals for judgments and suggestions page 89

- In advice with *would have*, the speaker means, "If I were you, . . ."

Read each situation and choose the corresponding judgment or suggestion for an alternative past action.

Situation

1. Sue forgot her boyfriend's birthday. _b_
2. Tim got a speeding ticket. ______
3. Ruth still hasn't paid me back. ______
4. Bill lied to us. ______
5. I spent an hour making Joe dinner, and he didn't even thank me. ______
6. Carol came over for dinner empty-handed. ______

Judgment/Suggestion

a. I wouldn't have lent her money.
b. She should have put it on her calendar.
c. He should have told the truth.
d. He shouldn't have gone over the limit.
e. She should have brought something.
f. I wouldn't have cooked for him.

UNIT 14

1 The passive to describe process page 93

- The modals *have to* and *need to* must agree with the subject; other modals, like *may be*, have only one form: Each character **has to/needs to** be drawn by the animators.

Put the words in the correct order to make sentences.

1. overnight / business / A / started / small / isn't / .
   A small business isn't started overnight.
2. to / plan / business / a / written / First, / be / has / .
   ____
3. research / Next, / done / be / market / should / .
   ____
4. needs / competition / to / the / Then / identified / be / .
   ____
5. online / ads / posted / be / Classified / may / .
   ____
6. work / are / employees / hired / can / start / the / so / Finally, / .
   ____

2 Defining and non-defining relative clauses page 96

- Use either *who* or *that* in defining relative clauses about people: A set designer is an artist **who/that** makes important contributions to a theater production. BUT Use only *who* in non-defining relative clauses about people: A set designer, **who** makes important contributions to a theater production, has to be very creative. (NOT: A set designer, ~~that~~ makes . . .)
- Use commas before and after a non-defining clause: A gossip columnist**,** who writes about celebrities and scandals**,** often gets to go to fabulous parties.

Combine these sentences with *who* or *that*. Add a comma wherever one is necessary.

1. A cartoon animator creates animated scenes for movies and games. He or she needs to have a high level of technical know-how.
   A cartoon animator, who needs to have a high level of technical know-how, creates animated scenes for movies and games.
2. A screenwriter is a talented person. He or she develops a story idea into a movie script.
   A screenwriter is a talented person that develops a story idea into a movie script.
3. Voice-over actors are usually freelancers. They give voice to characters in animated movies and video games.
   ____
4. Casting directors choose an actor for each part in a movie. They have usually been in the movie business for a long time.
   ____
5. High-budget movies always use big stars. The stars are known around the world.
   ____
6. Movie directors are greatly respected. They "make or break" a film.
   ____

UNIT 15

1 Giving recommendations and opinions page 101

- *Ought to* has the same meaning as *should*, but it's more formal:
  Traffic signs **ought to** be obeyed. = Traffic signs **should** be obeyed.

A student committee is discussing rules for their school. Complete speaker B's sentences with appropriate passive modals. (More than one answer is possible.)

1. **A:** Students must be required to clean off the cafeteria tables after lunch.
   B: I disagree. Students shouldn't be required to do that. That's what the cafeteria workers are paid to do.
2. **A:** Teachers shouldn't be allowed to park in the student parking lot.
   B: Why not? Teachers ______________ to park wherever a space is available. After all, they're here for us.
3. **A:** A rule has to be made to ban the use of cell phones in school.
   B: I don't think a rule ______________. Students may need their phones for emergency purposes.
4. **A:** Students mustn't be permitted to use calculators during math exams.
   B: Sometimes we ______________ to use them, especially when we're being tested on more complicated concepts than simple arithmetic.
5. **A:** Something has got to be done to control the noise in the hallways.
   B: Students ______________ to talk to each other between classes, though. They aren't disturbing anyone when classes aren't in session.
6. **A:** Teachers must be required to remind students about important exams.
   B: That's unnecessary. On the contrary, students ______________ to follow the syllabus and check important dates on the course websites.

2 Tag questions for opinions page 103

- Tag questions added to statements in the simple present and simple past use the corresponding auxiliary verb in the tag: You **agree** with me, **don't** you? You **don't agree** with me, **do** you? You **paid** the rent, **didn't** you? You **didn't pay** the electric bill, **did** you?

Check (✓) the sentences if the tag questions are correct. If they're incorrect, write the correct tag questions.

1. Food is getting more and more expensive, ~~is it~~? isn't it
2. Supermarkets should try to keep their prices down, shouldn't they? ✓
3. People don't buy as many fresh fruits and vegetables as they used to, don't they? ______________
4. We have to buy healthy food for our children, don't we? ______________
5. Many children go to school hungry, won't they? ______________
6. Some people can't afford to eat meat every day, don't they? ______________
7. We can easily live without eating meat every day, can we? ______________
8. A lot of people are having a hard time making ends meet these days, haven't they? ______________

UNIT 16

1 Talking about past accomplishments page 107

■ When talking about past accomplishments and including a specific time, use the simple past – not the present perfect: I **was** able to complete my degree last year. (NOT: I~~'ve been~~ able to complete my degree last year.)

Complete the sentences about people's accomplishments. Use the verbs in parentheses. (More than one answer is possible.)

In the last 5 years, Ana . . .

1. managed to finish (finish) college.
2. ____________ (pay) all her college loans.
3. ____________ (start) her own company.
4. ____________ (move) to the city.
5. ____________ (make) some new friends.

In the past year, Bill . . .

6. ____________ (buy) a new car.
7. ____________ (take) a vacation.
8. ____________ (get) a promotion at work.
9. ____________ (learn) to cook.
10. ____________ (visit) his grandparents in the south.

2 Describing goals and possible future accomplishments page 109

■ When talking about future accomplishments and goals, use *in* to refer to a period of time: I hope I'll find a new job **in** the next two months. Use *by* to talk about a time limit in the future: I hope I'll find a new job **by** the end of September. = I hope I'll find a new job not later than the end of September.

Complete the conversation. Use the verbs in parentheses. (Sometimes more than one answer is possible.)

Louise: So, Mike, what do you hope you will have accomplished (accomplish) five years from now?
Mike: I hope I ____________ (complete) medical school, and I ____________ (start) my residence in a good hospital.
Louise: What about your personal goals? What ____________ (achieve) by then?
Mike: Well, I ____________ (meet) that special someone, and, maybe, I ____________ (get) married by then. What about you? What are your goals?
Louise: Well, I hope I ____________ (finish) culinary school in the next five years, and I ____________ (manage) to work with some famous chef.
Mike: Good plan! What about opening your own restaurant?
Louise: That will take some more time, but by the time I'm 35, I hope I ____________ (open) my own bistro – Chez Louise.
Mike: I can hardly wait. I just love your food.

Grammar plus answer key

Unit 1

1 Relative pronouns

A: Ana, have you met Clint – the guy **X** Laurie is going to marry?
B: Oh, Clint and I have been friends for years. In fact, I'm the one **who/that** introduced Laurie and Clint.
A: Do you think they're right for each other?
B: Definitely. They're two people **who/that** have a lot in common – but not *too* much.
A: What does that mean?
B: Well, you don't want a partner **who/that** doesn't have his or her own interests. Couples **who/that** do everything together usually don't last very long.
A: I guess you're right, but the opposite isn't good, either. My last girlfriend was someone **X** I had nothing in common with. She wasn't the kind of girl **X** I could talk to easily.
B: Well, you can talk to *me* easily. . . .

2 *It* clauses + adverbial clauses with *when*

2. I hate it when I don't have enough time to study for an exam.
3. It doesn't bother me when friends talk to me about their problems.
4. It embarrasses me when I forget a co-worker's name.
5. I love it when my friends send me videos.
6. It upsets me when I have to wait for someone.

Unit 2

1 Gerund phrases

1. My brother's very interested in **becoming** a flight attendant. He dreams about **traveling** to new places.
2. I'm excited about **taking** a Japanese class next semester. I enjoy **learning** languages.
3. You wouldn't like **working** in a restaurant. You'd get tired of **standing** on your feet throughout the long shifts!
4. Our teacher is very good at **solving** problems. Maybe she should think about **changing** careers to become a guidance counselor.
5. **Making** a living as a photographer could be challenging. **Having** an impressive portfolio is really important to attract new clients and employers.

2 Comparisons

Answers may vary. Some possible answers:

2. A college professor earns more than an elementary school teacher.
3. Nurses have worse hours than psychiatrists.
4. Working as a police officer is as dangerous as being a firefighter.
5. A taxi driver isn't as well paid as an electrician.
6. Being a tour guide is less interesting than being an actor.

Unit 3

1 Requests with modals, *if* clauses, and gerunds

Answers may vary. Some possible answers:

2. A: Is it OK **if I use your computer?**
   B: You can use it, but please don't drink near it.
3. A: Would you mind **giving me a ride to class?**
   B: I'd be glad to. What time should I pick you up?
4. A: Can you **help me move on Saturday?**
   B: I'm sorry. I'm busy all weekend.
5. A: Would it be all right **if I had another piece of pie?**
   B: Yes, of course! Just pass me your plate.
6. A: Could you **lend me your red sweater?**
   B: Sorry. I don't like it when other people wear my clothes.

2 Indirect requests

2. Can you ask Susie if she wants to hang out with me?
3. Can you ask/tell Susie to text me?
4. Can you ask Susie if she knows my address?
5. Could you tell Susie not to forget to write?
6. Can you ask Susie what she's doing on Saturday?
7. Could you ask Susie if she has plans on Sunday?

Unit 4

1 Past continuous vs. simple past

1. A: How **did you break** your arm?
   B: It's a crazy story! Ramon and I **were riding** our bikes in the park when a cat **ran** out in front of me. I **was going** pretty fast, so when I **tried** to stop, I **went** off the road and **fell**.
   A: That's terrible! **Did you go** to the hospital after it **happened**?
   B: Yes. Luckily, we **weren't** too far from City Hospital, so we **went** there.
2. A: You'll never guess what **happened** to me this morning!
   B: What?
   A: Well, I **was brushing** my teeth when suddenly the water **went** off. I **had** toothpaste all over my mouth, and I couldn't wash it off.
   B: So what **did you do**?
   A: Fortunately, I **had** a big bottle of water in the refrigerator, so I **used** that water to rinse my mouth.

2 Past perfect

2. We had finished cleaning the house when our guests arrived.
3. Someone robbed my house yesterday because I had left the window open.
4. There was no food in the house because we had forgotten to stop at the supermarket.
5. I had called her three times when she finally answered.
6. I knew about the problem because your brother had told me about it.

Unit 5

1 Noun phrases containing relative clauses

2. a. Two things (that) I'd be very interested in are the food and the music.
   b. The food and the music are two things (that) I'd be very interested in.
3. a Something (that) I'd be worried about is not understanding the customs.
   b. Not understanding the customs is something (that) I'd be worried about.
4. a. Two people (who/that) I'd stay in touch with are my brother and sister.
   b. My brother and sister are two people (who/that) I'd stay in touch with.
5. a. One thing (that) I'd feel insecure about is speaking a new language.
   b. Speaking a new language is one thing (that) I'd feel insecure about.

2 Expectations

2. When a friend sends you an email, **you're expected to reply within a few days.**
3. If you want to visit someone, **it's not acceptable to show up without calling first.**
4. If you invite a married couple to dinner, **it's the custom for them to sit across from each other.**
5. When you go to a birthday party, **you're supposed to bring a gift.**

Unit 6

1 Describing problems 1

1. A: Oh, no! These jeans **have a tear** in them.
   B: And they **are stained**, too.
2. A: This table has **some damage** on top.
   B: I know. The wood **is scratched** because my son drags his toy cars on it.
3. A: Why are you drinking out of that glass? It **has a chip** in it.
   B: Oh, I didn't see it. That's why it **is leaking**.
4. A: Someone hit my car today. Look! The door **has a dent** in it.
   B: I see that. Your back light **is broken**, too.

5. A: I bought this blouse yesterday, but I have to take it back. There **is a hole** in it.
   B: It's really cute, but that's not the only problem. It **has a stain** on it, too.

2 Describing problems 2

A

A: Look at this place! A lot of work **needs to be done** before we move in.
B: You're not kidding. Let's make a list. First, the walls **need painting**.
A: Right. And the windows **need to be washed**. Add the rug to your list: It really **needs to be cleaned**. Do you think it **needs to be dry-cleaned**?
B: No, I think we can do it ourselves. It **needs shampooing**. We can rent a machine for that.
A: And what about the ceiling fan? I think it **needs to be replaced**. Fans aren't too expensive.
B: OK. I've added it to the list. And what should we do with all this old furniture?
A: It **needs to be thrown out**! I think the landlord should take care of that, though.

B

I **keep having** technical problems. My computer **keeps crashing**, and my printer **keeps jamming**. I have to **keep putting** a new battery into my mouse because it **keeps dying**. The letters on my keyboard **keep sticking**, too. I **keep thinking** things will get better, but they just **keep getting** worse. Time for some new electronics!

Unit 7

1 Passive with prepositions

Answers may vary. Some possible answers:

2. Our soil is being contaminated due to the use of pesticides on fruits and vegetables.
3. Infectious diseases have been spread through improper disposal of medical waste.
4. Many different species are being endangered due to the destruction of their habitats.
5. Our air quality has been affected because of deforestation to make paper products.
6. Smog pollution has been reduced as a result of hybrid cars.

2 Infinitive clauses and phrases

A

2. b   3. d   4. c   5. a

B

B: Well, **one way to improve people's quality of life is to help them feel safe.**
A: That's right. **And the best way to do that is to create a larger police force.**
B: I agree. **Another way to make people safer is to make the air healthier.**
A: Yes. Good air quality is key. **The best ways to reduce air pollution are to ban cars and control industry.**
B: Maybe it's time to share our ideas with the mayor. Get out your phone.

Unit 8

1 *Would rather* and *would prefer*

1. A: Would you prefer to take classes during the day or at night?
   B: I'd rather take classes at night.
2. A: Would you rather study business or education?
   B: I'd prefer to become a teacher.
3. A: Would you prefer to sign up for an art course or a computer course?
   B: I'd prefer not take any classes this semester.
4. A: Would you rather take up an individual sport or a team sport?
   B: I'd rather not take up either.

2 *By* + gerund to describe how to do things

2. A good way to improve your accent is by mimicking native speakers.
3. Students can improve their listening skills by listening to English-language podcasts.
4. Hardworking students improve their grammar by not repeating common mistakes.
5. You can become fluent not by translating everything but by trying to think in English.
6. You can become a good conversationalist not just by talking with others but by talking to yourself when you're alone, too.

Unit 9

1 Get or have something done

2. A: Where can I get/have my computer repaired?
   B: You can get/have it repaired at Hackers Inc.
3. A: Where can I get/have my taxes prepared?
   B: You can get/have them prepared by my accountant.
4. A: Where can I get/have my hair cut?
   B: You can get/have it cut at Beauty Barn.
5. A: Where can I get/have my apartment painted?
   B: You can get/have it painted by Peter the Painter.

2 Making suggestions

A: I'm having trouble meeting people here in the city. Any ideas?
B: I know it's hard. Why don't you **join** a gym? That's usually a good place to meet people. Or maybe you could **take** a class at the community college.
A: What about **checking out** the personal ads? Do you think that's a good way to meet people?
B: I wouldn't recommend doing that. People never tell the truth in those ads. But it might be a good idea **to find** a sports team. Have you thought about **playing** a team sport – maybe baseball or volleyball?
A: I'm not very good at most sports, but I used to play tennis.
B: There you go! One option is **to look up** tennis clubs in the city and see which clubs have teams people can join.
A: Now, that's a great idea. And I could always use the exercise!

Unit 10

1 Referring to time in the past

A: Hey, Dad. Did you use to listen to the Beatles?
B: Of course. In fact, I just listened to one of their records a few days **ago**. Do you realize that the Beatles's music has influenced other musicians **for** over 50 years? They were the greatest!
A: Well, I just found some interesting information about them. I'll read it to you: "The Beatles were a well-known British band **during/in** the 1960s. They performed together **for** 10 years – **from** 1960 **to** 1970. **In** 2003, the Beatles released a new version of their classic album *Let it Be*, even though one of the original members had been dead **since** 1980 and another had died **in** 2001. The original album had been recorded **in** 1969 and was in the studio safe **for** 34 years before the new, remixed album was released."
B: That *is* interesting. It's pretty amazing that people have listened to the Beatles **in** both the twentieth and the twenty-first centuries, isn't it?

2 Predicting the future with *will*

A: What do you think you **will be doing** five years from now?
B: I'm not sure. Maybe I **will have gotten** married by then. How about you?
A: I **will have finished** medical school, so I **will be doing** my internship five years from now.
B: So you **won't be living** around here in five years, I guess. Where do you think you **will live**?
A: Wherever I get my internship.

Unit 11

1 Time clauses

2. **Before** I got a full-time job, I had to live on a very limited budget.
3. **By the time** I finished high school, I had already taken three college courses.
4. **As soon as** I left for college, my mother turned my room into her office.
5. **Once** I left home, I realized how much my family meant to me.
6. **The moment** you have a child, you feel totally responsible for him or her.

2 Expressing regret and describing hypothetical situations

A

2. Ivan should have saved up for a car.
3. Jon shouldn't have been inactive when he was in college.
4. Lisa should have stayed in touch with her high school classmates.
5. Tony should have studied Spanish in school.

B

Answers may vary. Some possible answers:

2. If Ivan had saved up for a car, he wouldn't have to take public transportation.
3. If Jon hadn't been inactive when he was in college, he wouldn't have gained a lot of weight.
4. If Lisa had stayed in touch with her high school classmates, she wouldn't have very few friends.
5. If Tony had studied Spanish in school, he would be bilingual now.

Unit 12

1 Describing purpose

A

2. **In order to** stay popular, a website needs to be accurate and visually attractive.
3. **In order to** run a profitable furniture store, it's important to advertise on TV.
4. **In order for** a restaurant to stay in business, it needs to have "regulars" – customers that come often.
5. **In order to** establish a successful nail salon, it has to have a convenient location.
6. **In order for** an online business to survive, it needs to have excellent pictures of the merchandise it's selling.

B

2. To stay popular, a website needs to be accurate and visually attractive.
3. To run a profitable furniture store, it's important to advertise on TV.
4. For a restaurant to stay in business, it needs to have "regulars" – customers that come often.
5. To establish a successful nail salon, it has to have a convenient location.
6. For an online business to survive, it needs to have excellent pictures of the merchandise it's selling.

2 Giving reasons

A: I had to go downtown today **because** I needed to mail a package at the post office. **Since** I was only a few blocks from Main Street, I went over to Martin's. Did you know that Martin's has gone out of business? I'm so upset!
B: That's too bad, but I'm not surprised. A lot of family-owned shops are closing **because of** the construction of shopping malls.
A: Yeah, and don't forget about all the megastores that are popping up everywhere. **The reason why** people prefer to shop there is to save money. Everyone loves a megastore **due to** the low prices and the huge selection.
B: Not me! I loved Martin's **for** their beautiful clothes and friendly salespeople. When you were there, you almost felt like family. You'll never get that at a megastore!

Unit 13

1 Past modals for degrees of certainty

Answers may vary. Some possible answers:

2. A: What's wrong with Steven?
   B: Oh, you **must not have heard** the news. His dog ran away.
3. A: I went to see the Larsens today, but they didn't answer the door.
   B: Was their car there? If so, they **could have been** in the backyard.
4. A: Fabio said he was going to the party last night, but I didn't see him.
   B: Neither did I. He **couldn't have been** there then.
5. A: I can't find my glasses, but I know I had them at work today.
   B: You **might have left** them at the office.
6. A: Marc's new car looks really expensive.
   B: Yes, it does. It **must have cost** a fortune!

2 Past modals for judgments and suggestions

2. d 3. a 4. c 5. f 6. e

Unit 14

1 The passive to describe process

2. First, a business plan has to be written.
3. Next, market research should be done.
4. Then the competition needs to be identified.
5. Classified ads may be posted online.
6. Finally, employees are hired so the work can start.

2 Defining and non-defining relative clauses

3. Voice-over actors, who give voice to characters in animated movies and video games, are usually freelancers.
4. Casting directors, who have usually been in the movie business for a long time, choose an actor for each part in a movie.
5. High-budget movies always use big stars that are known around the world.
6. Movie directors, who "make or break" a film, are greatly respected.

Unit 15

1 Giving recommendations and opinions

Answers may vary. Some possible answers:

2. A: Teachers shouldn't be allowed to park in the student parking lot.
   B: Why not? Teachers **should be allowed** to park wherever a space is available. After all, they're here for us.
3. A: A rule has to be made to ban the use of cell phones in school.
   B: I don't think a rule **has to be made**. Students may need their phones for emergency purposes.
4. A: Students mustn't be permitted to use calculators during math exams.
   B: Sometimes we **should be permitted** to use them, especially when we're being tested on more complicated concepts than simple arithmetic.
5. A: Something has got to be done to control the noise in the hallways.
   B: Students **should be allowed** to talk to each other between classes, though. They aren't disturbing anyone when classes aren't in session.
6. A: Teachers must be required to remind students about important exams.
   B: That's unnecessary. On the contrary, students **should be required** to follow the syllabus and check important dates on the course websites.

2 Tag questions for opinions

3. do they
4. ✓
5. don't they
6. can they
7. can't we
8. aren't they

Unit 16

1 Talking about past accomplishments

Answers may vary. Some possible answers:

2. has managed to pay
3. has been able to start
4. was able to move
5. managed to make
6. was able to buy
7. has managed to take
8. has managed to get
9. has been able to learn
10. has managed to visit

2 Describing goals and possible future accomplishments

Louise: So, Mike, what do you hope you will have accomplished five years from now?
Mike: I hope I**'ll have completed** medical school and I**'ll have started / 'd like to have started** my residence in a good hospital.
Louise: What about your personal goals? What **would you like to have achieved** by then?
Mike: Well, I**'d like to have met** that special someone, and, maybe I**'ll have gotten** married by then. What about you? What are your goals?
Louise: Well, I hope I**'ll have finished** culinary school in five years, and I**'ll have managed / 'd like to have managed** to work with some famous chef.
Mike: Good plan! What about opening your own restaurant?
Louise: That will take some more time, but by the time I'm 35, I hope I**'ll have opened** my own bistro – Chez Louise.
Mike: I can hardly wait. I just love your food.

Credits

The authors and publishers acknowledge the following sources of copyright material and are grateful for the permissions granted. While every effort has been made, it has not always been possible to identify the sources of all the material used, or to trace all copyright holders. If any omissions are brought to our notice, we will be happy to include the appropriate acknowledgements on reprinting and in the next update to the digital edition, as applicable.

Key: Ex = Exercise, T = Top, B = Below, C = Centre, CR = Centre Right, TR = Top Right, BR = Below Right, TL = Top Left, TC = Top Centre, BL = Below Left, BC = Below Centre, L = Left, R = Right, CL = Centre Left, B/G = Background.

Illustrations

Mark Duffin: 39, 115, 119, 120; **Thomas Girard** (Good Illustration): 86; **Dusan Lakicevic** (Beehive Illustration): 18, 24; **Gavin Reece** (New Division): 43.

Photos

Back cover (woman with whiteboard): Jenny Acheson/Stockbyte/GettyImages; Back cover (whiteboard): Nemida/GettyImages; Back cover (man using phone): Betsie Van Der Meer/Taxi/GettyImages; Back cover (woman smiling): PeopleImages.com/DigitalVision/GettyImages; Back cover (name tag): Tetra Images/GettyImages; Back cover (handshake): David Lees/Taxi/GettyImages; p. v (TL): Hill Street Studios/Blend Images/GettyImages; p. v (BR): Hill Street Studios/Blend Images/GettyImages; p. v (BL): track5/E+/GettyImages; p. v (TR): fstop123/E+/GettyImages; p. 2 (header), p. vi (Unit 1): Tony Anderson/Taxi/GettyImages; p. 2 (T): Steve West/Taxi Japan/GettyImages; p. 2 (B): PhotoInc/E+/GettyImages; p. 4 (CR): Thomas Barwick/Iconica/GettyImages; p. 4 (BR): monkeybusinessimages/GettyImages; p. 5 (T): Shawna Hansen/Moment Open/GettyImages; p. 5 (B): Andersen Ross/Stockbyte/GettyImages; p. 6: Caiaimage/Tom Merton/OJO+/Cultura/GettyImages; p. 7: Heath Korvola/Stone/GettyImages; p. 8 (header), p. vi (Unit 2): Kelvin Murray/Taxi/GettyImages; p. 8 (TR): Paul Bradbury/Caiaimage/GettyImages; p. 8 (Lia): Tetra Images/Brand X Pictures/GettyImages; p. 8 (Josh): NicolasMcComber/E+/GettyImages; p. 8 (Ed): XiXinXing/GettyImages; p. 8 (Rose): Tim Robberts/The Image Bank/GettyImages; p. 8 (Jeff): T2 Images/Cultura/GettyImages; p. 8 (Mei): Yagi Studio/DigitalVision/GettyImages; p. 8 (Anna): Ron Levine/DigitalVision/GettyImages; p. 8 (Mike): Jon Feingersh/Blend Images/GettyImages; p. 9 (student): Nycretoucher/Stone/GettyImages; p. 9 (volunteer): asiseeit/E+/GettyImages; p. 9 (business): Thomas Barwick/Stone/GettyImages; p. 9 (movie set): bjones27/E+/GettyImages; p. 10: Sue Barr/Image Source/GettyImages; p. 11: JP Greenwood/The Image Bank/GettyImages; p. 12: Edge Magazine/Future/Future Publishing/GettyImages; p. 13 (T): Gary Burchell/Taxi/GettyImages; p. 13 (C): Hero Images/GettyImages; p. 13 (B): asiseeit/E+/GettyImages; p. 14: Juanmonino/E+/GettyImages; p. 15 (CR): Hero Images/GettyImages; p. 15 (BR): kali9/E+/GettyImages; p. 16 (header), p. iv (Unit 3): Ascent Xmedia/Stone/GettyImages; p. 16 (T): PeopleImages/DigitalVision/Getty Images Plus/GettyImages; p. 16 (B): Tetra Images/GettyImages; p. 17: Maskot/GettyImages; p. 18 (Sara): Tim Robberts/Taxi/GettyImages; p. 18 (Kim): monkeybusinessimages/iStock/Getty Images Plus/GettyImages; p. 19 (T): Maskot/Maskot/GettyImages; p. 19 (Ex 9): Tetra Images-Rob Lewine/Brand X Pictures/Getty Images; p. 20: Roy Mehta/Iconica/GettyImages; p. 21: Tetra Images/GettyImages; p. 22 (header), p. iv (Unit 4): Tom Merton/Caiaimage/GettyImages; p. 22 (news): Rune Johansen/Photolibrary/GettyImages; p. 22 (health): Peter Dazeley/Photographer's Choice/GettyImages; p. 22 (trending topics): Jess Nichols/EyeEm/GettyImages; p. 22 (arts): Daniel Allan/Cultura/GettyImages; p. 22 (science): Don Klumpp/The Image Bank/GettyImages; p. 22 (tech): Georgijevic/E+/GettyImages; p. 23: Tetra Images/Brand X Pictures/GettyImages; p. 25: Rachel Lewis/Lonely Planet Images/GettyImages; p. 25 (Carol): Jetta Productions/Blend Images/GettyImages; p. 25 (Milo): JohnnyGreig/E+/GettyImages; p. 26: elvira_gumirova/GettyImages; p. 26 (B/G): Anna Bryukhanova/GettyImages; p. 27: artpipi/E+/GettyImages; p. 28: JGI/Jamie Grill/Blend Images/GettyImages; p. 29: Matt Dutile/Image Source/GettyImages; p. 30 (header), p. iv (Unit 5): Image Source/DigitalVision/GettyImages; p. 30 (T): William King/Taxi/GettyImages; p. 30 (B): PBNJ Productions/Blend Images/GettyImages; p. 31: Buena Vista Images/DigitalVision/GettyImages; p. 32: Nachosuch/iStock/Getty Images Plus/GettyImages; p. 33: John Fedele/Blend Images/GettyImages; p. 34 (T): Dave & Les Jacobs/Blend Images/GettyImages; p. 34 (B): Kay Chernush/Stockbyte/GettyImages; p. 35 (B): Westend61/GettyImages; p. 35 (TR): Rafael Elias/Moment/GettyImages; p. 36 (header), p. vi (Unit 6): Caiaimage/Trevor Adeline/Caiaimage/GettyImages; p. 36 (CR): Peter Cade/The Image Bank/GettyImages; p. 37 (photo 1): p6opov/iStock/Getty Images Plus/GettyImages; p. 37 (photo 2): Michael Blann/DigitalVision/GettyImages; p. 37 (photo 3): Shannon Miller/Moment/GettyImages; p. 37 (photo 4): xril/iStock/Getty Images Plus/GettyImages; p. 38 (TR): Creatas/Creatas/Getty Images Plus/GettyImages; p. 38 (BR): Mel Yates/Photodisc/Getty Images Plus/GettyImages; p. 38 (Leory): Monty Rakusen/Cultura/GettyImages; p. 38 (Heather): Sam Edwards/Caiaimage/GettyImages; p. 40: Jupiterimages/PHOTOS.com/Getty Images Plus/GettyImages; p. 41: Image Source/GettyImages; p. 42: Jamie Grill/GettyImages; p. 43: Klaus Vedfelt/DigitalVision/GettyImages; p. 44 (header), p. vi (Unit 7): Hero Images/GettyImages; p. 44 (B): Todd Wright/Blend Images/GettyImages; p. 45 (TL): narvikk/E+/GettyImages; p. 45 (TC): TongRo Images Inc/TongRo Images/GettyImages; p. 45 (TR): Visuals Unlimited, Inc./Thomas Marent/Visuals Unlimited/GettyImages; p. 45 (BL): mshch/iStock/Getty Images Plus/GettyImages; p. 45 (BC): Marcos Alves/Moment/GettyImages; p. 45 (BR): Helmut Meyer zur Capellen/imageBROKER/Getty Images Plus/GettyImages; p. 46: Michael Krasowitz/Photographer's Choice/GettyImages; p. 47: Photofusion/Universal Images Group/GettyImages; p. 48 (TL): jinga80/iStock/Getty Images Plus/GettyImages; p. 48 (TR): sestovic/E+/GettyImages; p. 48 (BL): 101cats/iStock/Getty Images Plus/GettyImages; p. 48 (BR): inFocusDC/iStock/Getty Images Plus/GettyImages; p. 49 (TR): Cigdem Sean Cooper/Moment Open/GettyImages; p. 49 (BL): Antonio Busiello/robertharding/GettyImages; p. 50 (header), p. vi (Unit 8): akindo/DigitalVision Vectors/GettyImages; p. 51: Hill Street Studios/Blend Images/GettyImages; p. 52: Wavebreakmedia Ltd/Wavebreak Media/Getty Images Plus/GettyImages; p. 53: MarioGuti/iStock/Getty Images Plus/GettyImages; p. 54 (T): Dave & Les Jacobs/Blend Images/Getty Images Plus/GettyImages; p. 54 (B): JGI/Jamie Grill/Blend Images/GettyImages; p. 55: Apeloga AB/Cultura/GettyImages; p. 56: John Lund/DigitalVision/GettyImages; p. 57: mediaphotos/iStock/Getty Images Plus/GettyImages; p. 58 (header), p. viii (Unit 9): Dusty Pixel photography/Moment/GettyImages; p. 58 (automotive): Reza Estakhrian/Iconica/GettyImages; p. 58 (car wash): gilaxia/E+/iStock/Getty Images Plus/GettyImages; p. 58 (computer repair): Tetra Images/GettyImages; p. 58 (security repair): fatihhoca/iStock/Getty Images Plus/GettyImages; p. 58 (carpet cleaning): leezsnow/E+/GettyImages; p. 58 (home repair): sturti/E+/GettyImages; p. 58 (laundry cleaning): kali9/E+/GettyImages; p. 58 (tutoring): Hill Street Studios/Blend Images/GettyImages; p. 59 (Jessica): imagenavi/GettyImages; p. 59 (Peter): g-stockstudio/iStock/Getty Images Plus/GettyImages; p. 59 (Barry): Maskot/GettyImages; p. 59 (Tricia): Andersen Ross/GettyImages; p. 60: MachineHeadz/iStock/Getty Images Plus/GettyImages; p. 61: Morsa Images/DigitalVision/GettyImages; p. 62 (L): James And James/Photolibrary/GettyImages; p. 62 (C): Jose Luis Pelaez Inc/Blend Images/GettyImages; p. 62 (R): Dan Dalton/Caiaimage/GettyImages; p. 63: Paul Morigi/Getty Images Entertainment/Getty Images North America/GettyImages; p. 64 (header), p. viii (Unit 10): Kimberley Coole/Lonely Planet Images/GettyImages; p. 64 (1975): Jason Todd/DigitalVision/GettyImages; p. 64 (1982): Photofusion/Universal Images Group Editorial/GettyImages; p. 64 (1986): Kimberly Butler/The LIFE Images Collection/GettyImages; p. 64 (2004): Graffizone/E+/GettyImages; p. 64 (2006): Future Publishing/Future/GettyImages; p. 64 (2013): Jacob Ammentorp Lund/iStock/Getty Images Plus/GettyImages; p. 65 (T): Mark Dadswell/Getty Images Sport/Getty Images AsiaPac/GettyImages; p. 65 (B): andresr/E+/GettyImages; p. 66: Steve Sands/FilmMagic/GettyImages; p. 67 (T): Walter Bibikow/AWL Images/GettyImages; p. 67 (B): ferrantraite/Vetta/GettyImages; p. 68 (BR): JGI/Jamie Grill/Blend Images/GettyImages; p. 68 (crossing slackline): Ascent Xmedia/The Image Bank/GettyImages; p. 69 (B/G): vladimir zakharov/Moment/GettyImages; p. 69: PASIEKA/Science Photo Library/GettyImages; p. 70: Jonas Gratzer/LightRocket/GettyImages; p. 71 (T): NASA/The LIFE Picture Collection/GettyImages; p. 71 (B): Hero Images/GettyImages; p. 72 (header), p. viii (Unit 11): Hero Images/GettyImages; p. 72 (T): PeopleImages/DigitalVision/GettyImages; p. 72 (B): Hero Images/GettyImages; p. 73: martinedoucet/E+/GettyImages; p. 74: Jamie Kingham/Image Source/GettyImages; p. 75 (L): Rick Gomez/Blend Images/GettyImages; p. 75 (R): Simon Winnall/Taxi/GettyImages; p. 76: Elenathewise/iStock/Getty Images Plus/GettyImages; p. 77 (R): FilippoBacci/E+/GettyImages; p. 77 (L): Comstock Images/Stockbyte/GettyImages; p. 78 (header), p. viii (Unit 12): Jose Luis Pelaez Inc/Blend Images/GettyImages; p. 78: Martin Barraud/Caiaimage/GettyImages; p. 79: Martin Poole/The Image Bank/GettyImages; p. 80 (T): Tim Robberts/GettyImages; p. 80 (B): Chris Ryan/Caiaimage/GettyImages;

p. 81: Anadolu Agency/Anadolu/GettyImages; p. 82: Car Culture/Car Culture®Collection/GettyImages; p. 83 (T): UpperCut Images/GettyImages; p. 84: Tetra Images/GettyImages; p. 85: ullstein bild/GettyImages; p. 86 (header), p. viii (Unit 13): Manfred Gottschalk/Lonely Planet Images/GettyImages; p. 86: Image Source/GettyImages; p. 87 (L): James Lauritz/Photodisc/GettyImages; p. 87 (R): RichLegg/E+/GettyImages; p. 88 (T): Sweet Wedding/GettyImages; p. 88 (B): Gogosvm/iStock/Getty Images Plus/GettyImages; p. 89: LisaValder/E+/GettyImages; p. 91 (T): serdjophoto/iStock/Getty Images Plus/GettyImages; p. 91 (B): Ian Cuming/Ikon Images/GettyImages; p. 92 (header), p. viii (Unit 14): bjones27/E+/GettyImages; p. 92 (BR): GUILLAUME SOUVANT/AFP/GettyImages; p. 93 (T): GUILLAUME SOUVANT/AFP/GettyImages; p. 93 (B): Highwaystarz-Photography/iStock/Getty Images Plus/GettyImages; p. 94 (TL): B. O'Kane/Alamy; p. 94 (TC): Hill Street Studios/Blend Images/GettyImages; p. 94 (TR): Tom and Steve/Moment/GettyImages; p. 94 (CL): Daniela White Images/Moment/GettyImages; p. 94 (C): Lucia Lambriex/Taxi/GettyImages; p. 94 (CR): Caiaimage/Sam Edwards/OJO+/GettyImages; p. 94 (B): Hero Images/GettyImages; p. 95 (TL): Mads Perch/Iconica/GettyImages; p. 95 (TR): Plume Creative/DigitalVision/GettyImages; p. 95 (BL): Sam Edwards/Caiaimage/GettyImages; p. 95 (BR): asiseeit/E+/GettyImages; p. 96: Gary Houlder/Taxi/GettyImages; p. 97 (R): FREDERICK FLORIN/AFP/GettyImages; p. 97 (L): Tim Robberts/The Image Bank/GettyImages; p. 98: Image Source/GettyImages; p. 99 (TL): Vico Collective/Michael Shay/Blend Images/GettyImages; p. 99 (TR): Eric Audras/ONOKY/GettyImages; p. 99 (BR): Morsa Images/DigitalVision/GettyImages; p. 100 (header), p. viii (Unit 15): 04linz/iStock/GettyImages; p. 100: Joe McBride/Stone/GettyImages; p. 101: Boston Globe/GettyImages; p. 102 (T): Toby Burrows/DigitalVision/GettyImages; p. 102 (B): andipantz/iStock/GettyImages; p. 103: Maskot/GettyImages; p. 104: John Lund/Marc Romanelli/Blend Images/GettyImages; p. 105: Commercial Eye/The Image Bank/GettyImages; p. 106 (header), p. viii (Unit 16): David Trood/Stone/GettyImages; p. 106 (T): Hero Images/GettyImages; p. 106 (B/G): Klaus Vedfelt/DigitalVision/GettyImages; p. 106 (B): Tetra Images - Daniel Grill/Brand X Pictures/GettyImages; p. 107: Tara Moore/Taxi/GettyImages; p. 108: Ariel Skelley/Blend Images/GettyImages; p. 109 (T): Lumina Images/Blend Images/GettyImages; p. 109 (B): Nino H. Photography/Moment Open/GettyImages; p. 110 (TL): David Malan/Photographer's Choice/GettyImages; p. 110 (TC): Sam Edwards/OJO Images/GettyImages; p. 110 (TR): m-imagephotography/iStock/Getty Images Plus/GettyImages; p. 110 (BR): John S Lander/LightRocket/GettyImages; p. 111 (T): Samir Hussein/WireImage/GettyImages; p. 111 (B): AFP/GettyImages; p. 112: Zero Creatives/Image Source/GettyImages; p. 113: andresrimaging/iStock/Getty Images Plus/GettyImages; p. 115 (Gaston): Serge Krouglikoff/The Image Bank/GettyImages; p. 115 (Melissa): Sam Edwards/OJO Images/GettyImages; p. 115 (Don): Neustockimages/E+/GettyImages; p. 115 (Emma): Tom Werner/Taxi/GettyImages; p. 115 (Mike): Hero Images/GettyImages; p. 115 (Paola): filadendron/E+/GettyImages; p. 115 (Joanne): digitalskillet/iStock/Getty Images Plus/GettyImages; p. 115 (Ren): Stewart Cohen/Taxi/GettyImages; p. 116 (TL): Bluemoon Stock/Stockbyte/GettyImages; p. 116 (TC): scanrail/iStock/Getty Images Plus/GettyImages; p. 116 (TR): sihuo0860371/iStock/Getty Images Plus/GettyImages; p. 116 (CL): Comstock/Stockbyte/GettyImages; p. 116 (C): EasyBuy4u/E+/GettyImages; p. 116 (CR): Rebekah Logan/Moment Mobile/GettyImages; p. 116 (BL): JosT Elias/Hemera/Getty Images Plus/GettyImages; p. 116 (BC): Zoonar RF/Zoonar/Getty Images Plus/GettyImages; p. 116 (BR): tiler84/iStock/Getty Images Plus/GettyImages; p. 118 (TL): Yellow Dog Productions/The Image Bank/GettyImages; p. 118 (TR): Cultura Exclusive/MoofCultura Exclusive/GettyImages; p. 118 (BL): Alix Minde/PhotoAlto Agency RF Collections/GettyImages; p. 121: Pete Marovich/Getty Images News/Getty Images North America/GettyImages; p. 122: Michael Marquand/Lonely Planet Images/GettyImages; p. 123 (TL): Tetra Images/GettyImages; p. 123 (BR): doble-d/iStock/Getty Images Plus/GettyImages; p. 124 (Frida Kahlo): Michael Ochs Archives/GettyImages; p. 124 (Volkswagen): 8c061bbf_466/iStock Editorial/Getty Images Plus/GettyImages; p. 124 (Alexander): Bettmann/GettyImages; p. 125 (R): jmb_studio/iStock/Getty Images Plus/GettyImages; p. 125 (L): jmb_studio/iStock/Getty Images Plus/GettyImages; p. 125 (backpack): Songbird839/iStock/Getty Images Plus/GettyImages; p. 125 (dollar jar): IcemanJ/iStock/Getty Images Plus/GettyImages; p. 125 (balls): Ian McKinnell/Photographer's Choice/GettyImages; p. 125 (chips): MarkGillow/E+/GettyImages; p. 125 (video game): Angelo Angeles/Hemera/Getty Images Plus/GettyImages; p. 126 (L): Stuart Dee/Photographer's Choice/GettyImages; p. 126 (C): Riccardo Livorni/EyeEm/GettyImages; p. 126 (R): 3D_generator/iStock/Getty Images Plus/GettyImages; p. 127: Daviles/iStock/Getty Images Plus/GettyImages; p. 128 (photo 1a): Carl Court/Getty Images News/Getty Images Europe/GettyImages; p. 128 (photo 1b): Helen H. Richardson/Denver Post/GettyImages; p. 128 (photo 2a): GabryC/iStock/Getty Images Plus/GettyImages; p. 128 (photo 2b): Tom Merton/Hoxton/GettyImages; p. 128 (photo 3a): Multi-bits/The Image Bank/GettyImages; p. 128 (photo 3b): Stuart O'Sullivan/The Image Bank/GettyImages; p. 128 (photo 4a): scyther5/iStock/Getty Images Plus/GettyImages; p. 128 (photo 4b): Bread and Butter Productions/The Image Bank/GettyImages; p. 129 (TR): Dave J Hogan/Getty Images Entertainment/Getty Images Europe/GettyImages; p. 129 (CL): Dan Istitene/Getty Images Sport/Getty Images Europe/GettyImages; p. 129 (CR): Allen Berezovsky/WireImage/GettyImages; p. 129 (BL): Fred Stein Archive/Archive Photos/GettyImages; p. 129 (BR): Bettmann/GettyImages; p. 130 (L): Image Source/GettyImages; p. 130 (C): Jen Grantham/iStock Editorial/Getty Images Plus/GettyImages; p. 130 (R): Mauro Speziale/The Image Bank/GettyImages; p. 131: Jay Reilly/UpperCut Images/GettyImages.

interchange

FIFTH EDITION

Video Activity Worksheets

3

Jack C. Richards

Revised by Lynne Robertson

CAMBRIDGE
UNIVERSITY PRESS

Credits

Illustration credits

Andrezzinho: 7, 22; Ralph Butler: 17, 40; Paul Daviz: 6, 18 (*top*), 42; Carlos Diaz: 12, 36; Chuck Gonzales: 5, 14 (*top*), 35, 45; Jim Haynes: 2, 34; Trevor Keen: 14 (*bottom*), 44; KJA-artists.com: 4, 54; Robert Schuster: 18 (*bottom*), 56; James Yamasaki: 8, 16, 24

Photo Acknowledgements

The authors and publishers acknowledge the following sources of copyright material and are grateful for the permissions granted. While every effort has been made, it has not always been possible to identify the sources of all the material used, or to trace all copyright holders. If any omissions are brought to our notice, we will be happy to include the appropriate acknowledgements on reprinting and in the next update to the digital edition, as applicable.

Key: T = Top, L = Left, B = Below, TC = Top Centre, TR = Top Right, CL = Centre Left, C = Centre, CR = Centre Right, BC = Below Centre, BR = Below Right.

p. 2 (T): Fuse/Getty Images; p. 10 (T): damircudic/E+/Getty Images; p. 21 (B): Monkey Business Images/Shutterstock; p. 22 (T): Steve Dunwell/Photolibrary/Getty Images; p. 25 (B): kak2s/Shutterstock; p. 26 (T): Peter Harrison/Photolibrary/Getty Images; p. 26 (B): U.S. Coast Guard/Science Faction/SuperStock; p. 30 (T): Adalberto R_os Szalay/age fotostock; p. 30 (B): Comstock Images/Getty Images; p. 32 (BR): Tim Robberts/Riser/Getty Images; p. 32 (notebook): Igor Bondarenko/Hemera/Getty Images; p. 32 (TC): © GoGo Images Corporation/Alamy; p. 32 (TR): Nick White/Digital Vision/Getty Images; p. 32 (BL): Masterfile; p. 33 (B): © Erik Isakson/Tetra Images/Corbis; p. 34: forestpath/Shutterstock; p. 38 (CL): 06photo/iStock/Getty Images; p. 38 (T): © Norbert Michalke/imagebroker/Alamy; p. 38 (BL): David M. Grossman/The Image Works; p. 38 (BR): Yuri Arcurs/Shutterstock; p. 38 (C): Mixa/age fotostock; p. 38 (BC): Masterfile; p. 46: Lonely Planet/Getty Images; p. 50: © Marcia Chambers/db Images/Alamy; p. 51 (L), p. 51 (CL): Adam Stanford/Aerial-Cam Photography; p. 52 (CL): Scherl/SZ Photo/The Image Works; p. 52 (CR): Nataiki/Shutterstock; p. 54: © GoGo Images Corporation/Alamy; p. 58 (T): Spencer Platt/Getty Images; p. 60: Brigette Sullivan/PhotoEdit; p. 62: © David Grossman/Alamy.

Video credits

Unit 7 ©BBC Worldwide Americas Inc. Used with permission. Unit 10 ©ABC News. Used with permission. Footage from The Crayon Marketing Firm used with permission. Unit 13 ©A&E Television Networks. All rights reserved. Used with permission. Unit 16 courtesy of *60 Minutes*. ©Copyright CBS News. Used with permission.

Plan of Video 3

1 Dream Date A young woman chooses one of three men for her date on a dating game show.

Functional Focus Expressing feelings; describing personalities
Grammar Clauses containing *it* with adverbial clauses
Vocabulary Adjectives to describe personalities

2 Career moves A career advisor talks about the importance of someone's personality type in choosing a major and profession.

Functional Focus Describing personality types
Grammar Gerunds as subjects and objects
Vocabulary Words related to jobs and personality types

3 Common ground A woman asks her friend to look after her younger sister overnight.

Functional Focus Asking favors
Grammar Indirect requests
Vocabulary Requests and responses

4 Around the campfire Three friends on a camping trip share a spooky story and meet a mysterious stranger.

Functional Focus Telling a story in the past
Grammar Past tense verbs: past continuous, simple past, past perfect
Vocabulary Unusual events

5 Travel World Reporters around the world ask people about cross-cultural experiences.

Functional Focus Describing customs
Grammar Expectations: (*not*) *expected to*, (*not*) *supposed to*, (*not*) *customary to*, (*not*) *acceptable to*
Vocabulary Words related to traveling abroad

6 What's the problem? A couple's hope for a relaxing weekend at a quaint hotel is dashed.

Functional Focus Describing problems; making complaints
Grammar *Need* with passive infinitives and gerunds
Vocabulary Words to describe problems

7 Endangered islands A BBC reporter explains how climate change threatens the island nation of Tuvalu.

Functional Focus Describing environmental problems
Grammar The passive and prepositions of cause
Vocabulary Words related to the environment and climate change

8 Tango! A reporter talks to several people about learning to dance the tango.

Functional Focus Talking about learning methods
Grammar Gerunds and infinitives; *would rather* and *would prefer*
Vocabulary Words related to learning

9 Stressed out A woman seeks advice from a co-worker on how to relieve stress.

Functional Focus Making suggestions
Grammar Making suggestions with gerunds, infinitives, base-form verbs, and negative questions
Vocabulary Idioms related to stress

10 The Virtual Office ABC News presents a report on the changing face of the workplace.

Functional Focus Comparing old and new ways of doing things
Grammar Predicting the future with *will*
Vocabulary Terms to describe the modern office

11 Live and learn A host asks people to share embarrassing stories.

Functional Focus Talking about past mistakes
Grammar *Should have/shouldn't have* + past participle; *if* clauses + past perfect
Vocabulary Words to describe embarrassment

12 Good business A student interviews a local business owner about her secrets of success.

Functional Focus Discussing what makes a business successful
Grammar Infinitive clauses and phrases of purpose
Vocabulary Words to describe a café

13 Stonehenge The History Channel presents current scientific theories on the mysterious origin and purpose of Stonehenge.

Functional Focus Explaining past events
Grammar Past modals for degrees of certainty
Vocabulary Words to describe an ancient civilization

14 Making music A look at how a song is written, is produced, and gets played on the air.

Functional Focus Describing the steps in a process
Grammar The passive to describe process
Vocabulary Words related to music production

15 The streets of Montreal A reporter in Montreal, Quebec, Canada, interviews people about bicycling in the city.

Functional Focus Expressing opinions about city rules
Grammar Passive modals
Vocabulary Words related to traffic and safety

16 The Harlem Children's Zone An interview with Geoffrey Canada, an education reformer in the U.S., excerpted from the CBS News program *60 Minutes*.

Functional Focus Talking about challenges
Grammar Complex noun phrases with gerunds
Vocabulary Words related to education

1 Dream Date

Preview

1 CULTURE

In North America, many people start dating in their teens and early twenties. They meet at school or work, or they're introduced by friends. On dates, they go out in couples or in groups to movies, sporting events, and meals. Traditionally, the man paid for the date, but modern couples may decide to split the bill or let the person who made the invitation pay for both people.

How do people in your country meet each other? What do friends or dating couples like to do together? Where are some popular places to go? When a man and a woman (or a group of friends) go out together, who pays?

2 VOCABULARY Personality types

PAIR WORK How would you describe the people below? Choose a description from the box.

a good conversationalist	easygoing	generous
ambitious	✓ egotistical	straightforward

1. Jill is always talking about herself. She thinks she's better than other people.
   A: I think she's *egotistical*.
   B: Yes, I agree.
2. Mike is very relaxed. Nothing seems to upset him.
3. Paul always tells people exactly what he thinks. He doesn't hide his feelings.
4. Erika has big plans and works hard to achieve them.
5. John asks a lot of questions, and he's interested in what I have to say.
6. Leah is a great friend. She gives others a lot of her time and energy, and she also forgives others easily.

3 GUESS THE STORY

Elizabeth is going to choose one of these men to be her date. How do you think she will decide? Who will she choose?

Bachelor 1 **Bachelor 2** **Bachelor 3**

Watch the video

4 GET THE PICTURE

A Look at your answers to Exercise 3. Did you guess correctly?

B Check (✓) the things Elizabeth said to the bachelors. Then compare with a partner.

- [ ] Describe to me your ideal date.
- [ ] How old are you?
- [ ] What's your favorite sport?
- [ ] Tell me two things about yourself: one positive and one negative.
- [ ] Finish this sentence: "I think it's disgusting when . . . "
- [ ] Finish this sentence: "My ideal date has . . . "

C What words describe Elizabeth and the bachelors? Write the correct word under each picture. Then compare with a partner.

easygoing **egotistical** **excited** **straightforward**

1. ....
2. ....
3. ....
4. ....

5 WATCH FOR DETAILS

Correct the mistakes below. Then compare with a partner.

Bachelor 1 is a ~~reporter~~ writer and a former college soccer coach who loves playing or watching almost every kind of game. Bachelor 2 is a model, who also studies languages. Everyone should recognize him from his latest jeans ad on buses and in magazines. Bachelor 3 is the Director of Educational Programs at a high school. In his free time, he enjoys swimming, running, and dancing. He and Elizabeth went to college together.

6 WHO SAID WHAT?

Who said the sentences below? Check (✓) the correct answers. Then compare with a partner.

	Bachelor 1	Bachelor 2	Bachelor 3
1. I'd be too embarrassed to tell you the truth.	☐	☐	☐
2. It bothers me when people lie.	☐	☐	☐
3. It's hard to split my time among so many people!	☐	☐	☐
4. I'd take you out for a nice dinner.	☐	☐	☐
5. I think I'm a pretty good friend, very reliable.	☐	☐	☐
6. Well, I'm actually a pretty good guy.	☐	☐	☐
7. I'd probably say I had car trouble.	☐	☐	☐

Follow-up

7 ROLE PLAY *Let's play Dream Date!*

A PAIR WORK Imagine you are Elizabeth. Add two more questions to ask the bachelors.

1. Describe to me your ideal date.
2. Tell me two things about yourself: one positive and one negative.
3. Finish this sentence: "I can't stand it when . . ."
4. ....
5. ....

B GROUP WORK Now join another pair. Three of you are bachelors. The fourth person is Elizabeth.

Elizabeth: Take turns asking the three bachelors your questions. Then choose your dream date.

Bachelors: Answer Elizabeth's questions. Try to get Elizabeth to choose you as her dream date.

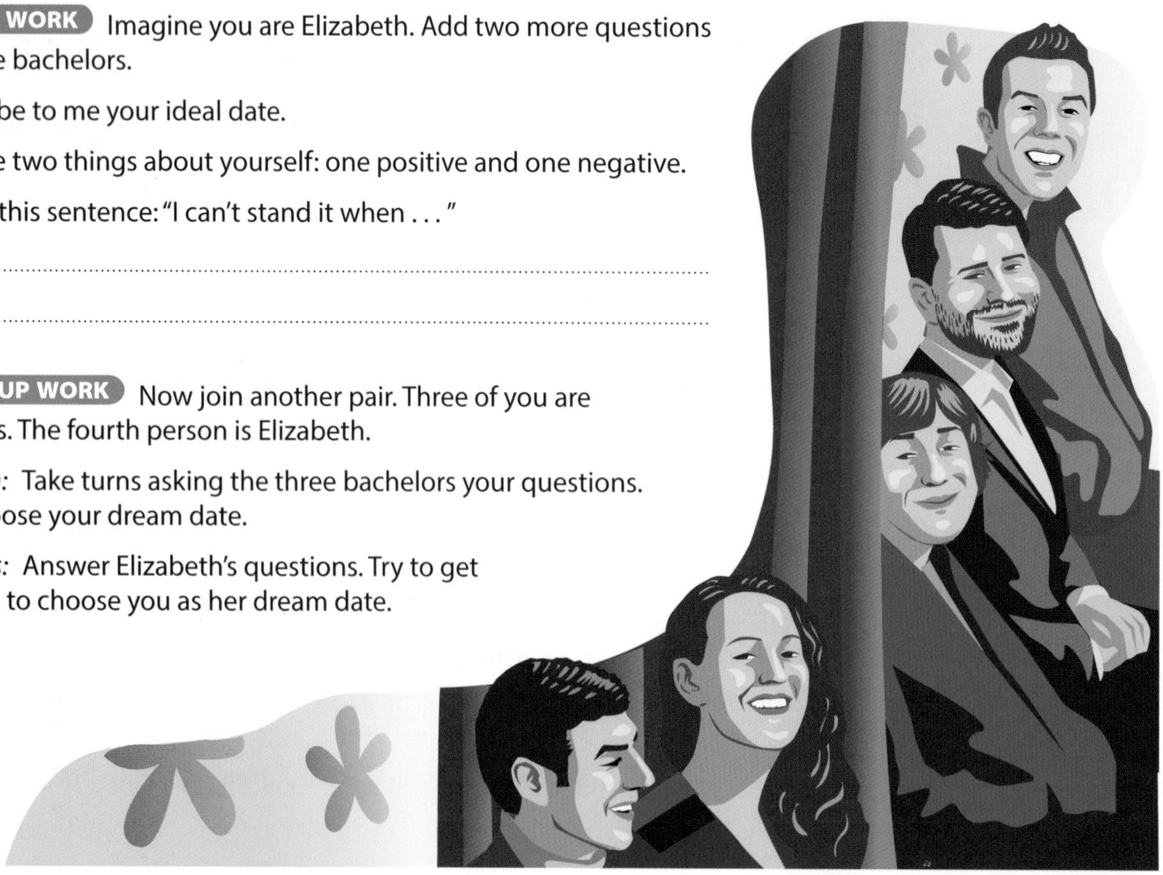

Language close-up

8 WHAT DID THEY SAY?

Watch the video and complete the conversation. Then practice it.

Elizabeth is asking the bachelors to complete a few sentences.

Elizabeth: Bachelor Number 1, finish this sentence:
"I .... it when . . ."

Bachelor 1: I .... it when . . . people
.... when I'm ....
.... the soccer match on TV.

Elizabeth: Bachelor Number 3, finish this sentence:
"I .... it's .... when . . ."

Bachelor 3: I .... it's .... when . . .
when I go to a fancy .... and I don't get
the .... I deserve.

Elizabeth: Bachelor Number 2, finish this sentence: "It .... me when . . ."

Bachelor 2: It .... me when . . . people .... over unimportant
things. I just think people should be less .... and more ....

9 CLAUSES CONTAINING IT WITH ADVERBIAL CLAUSES

A Complete the sentences about dates or friendships with phrases from the box. Then add two more statements of your own.

✓ arrive late
forget to call me
lie to me
make me feel special
send me flowers
talk during a movie

1. I can't stand it *when my date arrives late* .
2. It makes me happy ....
3. I like it ....
4. It bothers me ....
5. It really upsets me ....
6. It embarrasses me ....
7. ....
8. ....

B PAIR WORK Compare your statements with a partner. Which of your partner's statements are true for you?

2 Career moves

Preview

1 CULTURE

Choosing a career can be difficult if you're not sure what job is best for you. Experts suggest the following to help you make a decision:

- Take a career assessment test to find out what professions are a good match for you.
- Look at your educational and work achievements to determine your strengths and weaknesses.
- Think about your hobbies and free-time activities, and what they say about your interests, abilities, and values.
- Talk with a friend or family member who is a good listener, or consult with a career counselor.

Talk about your career plans. Which skills and abilities would you use in this future career? How is this type of work related to what you want to accomplish in life? How sure are you of your current career choice?

2 VOCABULARY Attributes at work

A Complete each sentence with a word from the box.

creative	collaborative	✓ independent	physical	practical	precise

1. My brother is very independent, so he prefers to work by himself.
2. My friend Elena is a graphic designer, which lets her use her imagination and be ....
3. My boss comes up with the big ideas, but I enjoy planning out the .... details.
4. Building a house requires .... strength and stamina.
5. The best part of working in a team is the .... process of making decisions together.
6. In finance, it's important to be .... and not make mistakes!

B PAIR WORK Describe yourself or someone you know well. Your partner describes the person's personality using one of the words from the box.

A: My friend makes a list of all the things he has to do each day.
B: He sounds like a practical person.

3 GUESS THE STORY

Watch the first minute of the video with the sound off.
Answer these questions.

1. Where is the conversation taking place?
2. Who do you think the man and woman are?
3. What do you think they are discussing?

Watch the video

4 GET THE PICTURE

A Look at your answers to Exercise 3. Did you guess correctly?

B What personality type did Ms. Auden think would be best suited to the jobs below? Write the correct word under each picture. Then compare with a partner.

librarian

....

repair person

....

teacher

....

lawyer

....

5 MAKING INFERENCES

Which statements are probably true? Which are probably false?
Check (✓) your answers. Then compare with a partner.

	True	False
1. A conventional type would make a good actor.	☐	☐
2. Good waiters are often social types.	☐	☐
3. An enterprising type would not work for other people.	☐	☐
4. Most accountants are artistic types.	☐	☐
5. Someone who runs his or her own business is an investigative type.	☐	☐
6. Mechanics are often realistic types.	☐	☐
7. Studying animals in the wild would appeal to some investigative types.	☐	☐

6 WHAT'S YOUR OPINION?

A Read the description of each person's personality type below. Then write notes in the chart about which job at an advertising agency you think the person would enjoy, if any. Be sure to give reasons.

	Manager	Ad designer	Accountant
1. Bernie is a conventional type.	No; prefers to follow rules and procedures	No; doesn't enjoy creative things as much	Yes; likes details
2. Fatima is an enterprising type.			
3. Yoko is an investigative type.			
4. Carlos is an artistic type.			

B GROUP WORK Compare your answers with your group. Come up with one other job at the agency that would suit each person.

Follow-up

7 ARE THEY DOING THE RIGHT JOBS?

A Write the names of three people you know well. Tell what job each one does. Then describe each worker's personality type and explain why his or her job is right for them.

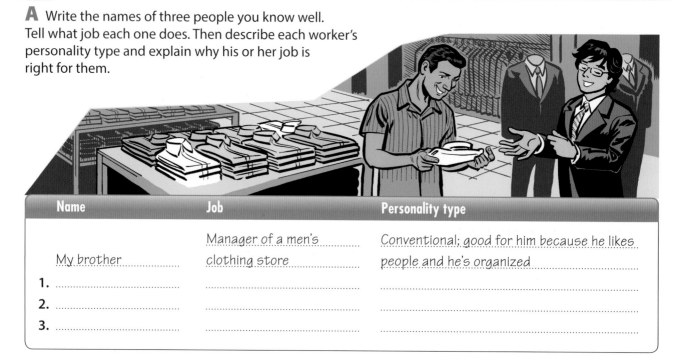

Name	Job	Personality type
My brother	Manager of a men's clothing store	Conventional; good for him because he likes people and he's organized
1.		
2.		
3.		

B PAIR WORK Take turns describing each person you wrote about to your partner. Answer any questions your partner may have.

Language close-up

8 WHAT DID THEY SAY?

Watch the video and complete the conversation. Then practice it.

Jacquelyn Auden talks with Jamie about personality types.

Ms. Auden: There are six .... personality types: .... , conventional, enterprising, investigative, realistic, and .... The .... type is artistic. These .... are .... and imaginative, and they .... to work on one .... at a time, rather than multi-tasking.

Jamie: What .... should artistic .... pursue?

Ms. Auden: The most .... thing for .... type of people is being in .... of a .... project. So, ... to consider are landscaping, graphic .... , web design.

Jamie: I .... The .... personality type is conventional. Tell us .... that one.

Ms. Auden: Yes. Conventional types are .... and orderly. They .... well to rules, ... , schedules, ... like that.

9 GERUNDS AS SUBJECTS AND OBJECTS *Describing a job*

A Complete the sentences about a job using the gerund forms of the words and phrases in the box. Then guess the job described.

encourage	organize the game schedule	work on weekends
improve their skills	stay in shape	✓work with children

1. I enjoy working with children ; it helps me feel young.
2. .... is easy with all the running around I have to do.
3. I don't always enjoy .... , but that's when our games are held.
4. At the end of the season, we have a big tournament, so I spend a lot of time .... for that event.
5. I help players concentrate on ....
6. .... weaker players helps the whole team improve.

Job described: ....

B PAIR WORK Choose a job and describe your duties. Can your partner guess your job?

3 Common ground

Preview

1 CULTURE

Read this advice to babysitters in North America.

- Ask parents to show you the location of emergency exits, smoke detectors, and fire extinguishers.
- Make sure you have the telephone number of where the parents are going.
- If the children are up, know their location at all times and never leave them alone for too long. If the children are asleep, check on them about every fifteen minutes.
- Always get approval if you would like to have a visitor.
- In an emergency, call 911. Identify yourself by name, say you are babysitting, and state the problem. Say where you are and give the phone number you are calling from.

Is babysitting popular in your country? What would you enjoy about babysitting? What would be challenging? Write some suggestions or rules for babysitters to add to the list above.

2 VOCABULARY Requests and responses

PAIR WORK Match each request with a response. Then practice the requests and responses.

...d... 1. Is it all right if I use your phone?
.... 2. Would you mind my using your car?
.... 3. Is it OK if I drop her off?
.... 4. Could you ask her to bring something?
.... 5. I was wondering if you could help me out.
.... 6. Would you mind if she stayed with you?

a. No, go ahead. The keys are on the table.
b. OK. I'll tell her.
c. Sure. What can I do?
d. No, sorry. I'm expecting a call.
e. Not at all. I'd be happy to have her.
f. Sure. Or I can pick her up.

3 GUESS THE STORY

Watch the first minute of the video with the sound off.
What do you think the women are talking about?

Watch the video

4 GET THE PICTURE

First put the pictures in order (1 to 6). Then write the correct request under each picture. Compare with a partner.

Could you please turn down the volume?
Is it OK if I watch the movie now?
Could I have something to eat?
Can we watch them?
Would you mind if she stayed with you tonight?
Could we watch the second movie after this one is over?

....
....

....
....

....
....

....
....

....
....

....
....

5 MAKING INFERENCES

Which statements are probably true? Which are probably false? Check (✓) your answers. Then compare with a partner.

	True	False
1. Anne is in a hurry.	☐	☐
2. Anne and Megan live together.	☐	☐
3. Rachel thinks it will be easy to get along with Megan.	☐	☐
4. Rachel is worried that Megan might interfere with her work.	☐	☐
5. Megan doesn't want to do her homework.	☐	☐
6. Megan doesn't care what food she eats.	☐	☐
7. Anne is surprised that Megan and Rachel became friends.	☐	☐

6 WHO SAID WHAT?

Who said the sentences below? Check (✓) the correct answers. Then compare with a partner.

	Anne	Rachel	Megan
1. I need a big favor.	☐	☐	☐
2. Hey, you've got the *Twilight* movies!	☐	☐	☐
3. How's the homework coming?	☐	☐	☐
4. I'm starving.	☐	☐	☐
5. You've never read any of the books or seen the movies?	☐	☐	☐
6. You two really seemed to hit it off.	☐	☐	☐

Follow-up

7 ROLE PLAY

A PAIR WORK

Student A: You're planning a big party for this weekend. You want your friend (Student B) to help you. Write your requests in the box below. Then ask your friend for help.

Student B: Accept or decline your friend's (Student A's) requests.

1. I was wondering if I could borrow your vacuum cleaner.
2. ....
3. ....

A: I was wondering if I could borrow your vacuum cleaner.
B: Of course. Go right ahead!

B PAIR WORK

Student B: You're moving to a new apartment. You want your friend (Student A) to help you. Write your requests in the box below. Then ask your friend for help.

Student A: Accept or decline your friend's (Student B's) requests.

1. Is it OK if I borrow these boxes?
2. ....
3. ....

Language close-up

8 WHAT DID THEY SAY?

Watch the video and complete the conversation. Then practice it.

Anne asks her friend Rachel for a favor.

Anne: Rachel! I am so .... you're home. I was .... if you could help me out.

Rachel: Yeah. .... , Anne?

Anne: I .... a big .... My .... just called, and he wants me to go out of town .... to meet with a client.

Rachel: ....

Anne: Yeah. But my .... are out of town, too, and my little sister, Megan, is .... with me. .... if she stayed with you .... ? I .... pick her up .... by ten.

Rachel: No, I .... at all. What .... did you want to .... her over?

Anne: How about .... ?

9 INDIRECT REQUESTS *Asking favors*

A Anne has asked Rachel to look after her apartment while she is away. Anne has several requests for Rachel. Complete their phone conversation with the correct form of the expressions in the box.

feed the fish
spend the weekend
✓take in the mail every day
water the plants
walk the dog

Anne: Would you mind taking in the mail every day .... ?

Rachel: Sure, no problem. I'll leave it on the table.

Anne: Great. And could you .... ?

Rachel: I'd love to. I've got some fish at home.

Anne: And let's see. I was wondering if you could .... ?

Rachel: Sure. I'll water them once a day.

Anne: Great. Oh, and I was wondering if you'd mind .... ?

Rachel: Yeah, I guess. How often does he need a walk?

Anne: Only three times a day. Anyway, one more thing. Is it OK if Megan .... ?

Rachel: Are you kidding? Of course it's OK. Megan and I get along just fine.

B PAIR WORK Imagine you are going away for a weekend, and your partner is going to look after your apartment or house. Write several requests. Then take turns asking each other the favors.

4 Around the campfire

Preview

1 CULTURE

North Americans enjoy telling stories, especially spooky stories about scary and mysterious things. Spooky stories are popular around the campfire, at sleepovers, and during the fall and winter months, especially near Halloween. People tell and listen to these stories as a way of dealing with their fear of the unknown. It's also fun to experience the thrill of fear while knowing that you're really safe.

Do you enjoy telling and listening to stories? Do you enjoy spooky or scary stories? Why or why not? Are stories about mysterious people and events popular in your culture? If you can, share a well-known story from your culture with some classmates.

2 VOCABULARY *Descriptions*

For each pair of pictures write the correct description.

1.

surprised .... freaked out ....

freaked out
surprised

2.

....

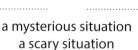

a mysterious situation
a scary situation

3.

....

a scream
a hoot

4.

....

a farm
a campground

3 GUESS THE STORY

Check (✓) what you think is happening in each of the following situations.

- ☐ She has just taken a shower.
- ☐ She has just gone on a hike.

- ☐ She is going to make dinner.
- ☐ She is going to tell a story.

- ☐ He is greeting the girls.
- ☐ He is telling a spooky story.

Watch the video

4 GET THE PICTURE

A Check your answers to Exercise 3. Did you guess correctly?

B Check (✓) **True** or **False**. Correct the false statements. Then compare with a partner.

	True	False	
1. Ellen heard a story at the restaurant.	☐	☐	....
2. Molly doesn't like scary stories.	☐	☐	....
3. The campground used to be a farm.	☐	☐	....
4. Ted McShane died in a fire.	☐	☐	....

5 WATCH FOR DETAILS

Complete the sentences. Then compare your answers with a partner.

1. Ellen overheard a woman telling this story to her ....*daughter*.... .
2. Vanessa tells Molly not to be a ....
3. The McShanes inherited the farm from a ....
4. When the McShanes walked down the street, they always ....
5. Every evening, Mr. McShane brought his wife ....
6. Mr. McShane's wife was named ....
7. The girls get frightened when .... arrives.

6 MAKING INFERENCES

Which statements are probably true? Which are probably false? Check (✓) your answers. Then compare with a partner.

	True	False
1. Vanessa likes scary stories.	☐	☐
2. The man in the story was a farmer.	☐	☐
3. The fire started because of a hot and dry summer.	☐	☐
4. The park ranger wanted to scare the girls.	☐	☐
5. Vanessa is embarrassed that they were so easily frightened.	☐	☐
6. The ranger is the same person from the story.	☐	☐

Follow-up

7 DO YOU BELIEVE THESE STORIES?

GROUP WORK Read the descriptions of the creatures below. Do you believe they ever existed? Do you think they exist now? Have conversations like this:

A: Do you think the Loch Ness Monster exists?
B: I think it's just a story. There are no such things as monsters!
C: I hate to disagree, but many people say that they have seen strange creatures.

The Loch Ness Monster, Scotland

This creature was first seen in 565 BCE, and sightings are still reported every year. Some people believe that it is a dinosaur, an eel, or a type of whale. Many photos of "Nessie" have been taken, but some have turned out to be fakes and others are too dark or blurry to really show the creature.

Alien Big Cats, England

Some people believe that large, wild cats, such as panthers and leopards, exist in some areas of the English countryside. Called "alien" because they are foreign (not extraterrestrial!), none has ever been captured. Photos and videos have never been clear enough to prove their existence, yet there have been as many as 2,000 sightings in a single year.

Language close-up

8 WHAT DID THEY SAY?

Watch the video and complete the conversation. Then practice it.

The ranger surprises the girls while Ellen is telling the story.

Ranger: Oh, I'm .... I didn't mean to .... you ladies. I was making my .... and .... to see if .... is all right.

Molly: Yes. A park ranger, of .... Yes, everything's .... Ellen was .... us a .... story when you came by.

Ranger: Campfire .... , huh? That's .... fun. Well, OK, then. I'll let you .... back to it.

Vanessa: Thanks for .... on us. And sorry .... the ....

Ranger: That's OK. I'm .... to it. Hey, in the .... you .... should take a look .... that path. There's a .... full of wildflowers, and .... in bloom right now – very ....

Vanessa: Oh! That's good to .... We'll .... that. Thanks.

9 PAST TENSE VERBS *Telling a story*

A Write the correct form of the verbs in parentheses (past perfect, past continuous, or simple past) to complete this story.

Last Saturday, I .... (walk) down Elm Street when I .... (notice) something strange. A very fancy sports car .... (sit) in front of the entrance to the First Bank building. No one .... (be) in the car, but the engine .... (run). I .... (stop) next to the car to take a look. It was the first time I .... (see) a car like that. Suddenly, a man with a large bag .... (run) out of the bank and .... (jump) into the car. He .... (drive) away so fast, he almost .... (hit) me. Then I realized: I .... (witness) a bank robbery!

B PAIR WORK

A: Think of something unusual that has happened to you. Tell a story about what happened.
B: Listen and ask questions. Then change roles.

5 Travel World

Preview

1 CULTURE

Culture shock, the emotional and physical distress you may feel when you visit a foreign country or culture, has three stages. The first stage, sometimes called the "honeymoon" stage, is characterized by exaggerated happiness and excitement. In the second stage, you might feel angry or sad at not being able to communicate or understand the other culture. You might even get physically ill. Finally, in the third stage, you realize that the new culture offers rewards as well as challenges, and you feel ready and able to adapt to a new lifestyle.

Have you ever seen a visitor to your country experiencing culture shock? What kind of person do you think experiences culture shock the most severely? the least severely? Have you ever experienced culture shock? Describe your experiences.

2 VOCABULARY *Travel abroad*

Put the words below in the word map. Add at least one more word to each list. Then compare answers with a partner.

afraid to make a mistake	**eating a huge meal at lunch**	**shaking hands**
beautiful	**kissing in public**	**spectacular**
confused	**picturesque**	**surprised**

Feelings
afraid to make a mistake
....
....
....

Customs
....
....
....
....

Scenery
....
....
....
....

3 GUESS THE FACTS

What things do you think cause people to experience culture shock?

- ☐ climate
- ☐ clothing
- ☐ families
- ☐ food
- ☐ greetings
- ☐ hotels
- ☐ language
- ☐ transportation

Watch the video

4 GET THE PICTURE

A Check your answers from Exercise 3. Then compare with a partner.

B Complete the information for each person.

Camilla

Lives in: ....
Visited: ....

Andrew

Is from: ....
Lives in: ....

Delfino

Is from: ....
Lives in: ....

5 GUESSING MEANING FROM CONTEXT

Read these sentences from the video. Guess the meanings of the underlined words. Check (✓) your answers. Then compare with a partner.

1. When you get home, you often have some interesting and perhaps humorous stories to tell about your cross-cultural experiences.
   - ☐ experiences that made you angry
   - ☑ experiences in different cultures
   - ☐ experiences in similar cultures
2. Rio de Janeiro – that picturesque city of beautiful beaches, Carnaval, and the samba.
   - ☐ old-fashioned
   - ☐ expensive
   - ☐ pretty
3. You're invading my space.
   - ☐ making me uncomfortable
   - ☐ taking too much of my time
   - ☐ causing me pain
4. It is customary in my culture to have a huge meal in the middle of the day.
   - ☐ rare
   - ☐ polite
   - ☐ usual

6 WATCH FOR DETAILS

According to the video, to which country do the following customs refer? Write the name of a country next to each custom.

Brazil
Mexico
Peru
Sweden
the United States

1. People shake hands when they meet. ....
2. It's customary to eat a huge meal around noon. ....
3. People kiss on the cheek when they meet. ....
4. People often eat just a soup and sandwich for lunch. ....
5. Bus drivers call out to people on the street. ....

7 WHAT'S YOUR OPINION?

A Which customs and situations discussed in the video would make you feel uncomfortable when visiting a foreign country? Rank them from 1 (most uncomfortable) to 6 (least uncomfortable).

.... using public transportation
.... greeting someone by kissing on the cheeks
.... eating a huge meal in the middle of the day
.... having only soup and a sandwich for lunch
.... using a private bus system
.... greeting someone by shaking hands

B PAIR WORK Take turns talking about the customs. Use sentences like these:

One thing I'd be most uncomfortable about . . .
Something I wouldn't be uncomfortable about . . .
The thing that I'd be most uncomfortable about . . .
The thing that I'd be least uncomfortable about . . .

Follow-up

8 CROSSING CULTURES

A Choose a country you know well. Make a list of customs that visitors to that country might find different or unusual. Complete the chart.

Country	Customs	
....	....	....
	....	....

B PAIR WORK Take turns asking about the customs in the countries you and your partner chose in part A.

9 WHAT DID HE SAY?

Watch the video to complete the commentary. Then compare with a partner.

Chris Brooks talks about culture shock.

Hi. I'm Chris Brooks. .... to *Travel World*. Have you ever .... to a .... with a .... different .... ? If you have, you .... know what ".................... ...." is. It's a feeling of .... you get from .... being in a new .... The .... and .... may seem .... are different. You don't know exactly what you're .... do. You may .... be a little .... of making a .... In .... , you get .... everything. But .... you get .... , you often have some .... and perhaps .... stories to .... about your .... experiences.

10 EXPECTATIONS *Noun, adjective, and verb forms*

A Complete the sentences about expectations with the correct word in parentheses.

1. It is .... (tradition / traditional) to have a large meal at noon in Mexico.
2. You are .... (expected / expectation) to kiss people on both cheeks in Brazil.
3. It is .... (custom / customary) for people to take public transportation in Peru.
4. Are you .... (suppose / supposed) to kiss people on both cheeks in Mexico?
5. My family has a .... (tradition / traditional) of eating dessert at every meal.
6. What is the .... (custom / customary) of greeting people in your country?
7. I didn't have any .... (expect / expectations) about what life was like in Peru.
8. What do you .... (suppose / supposed) I should do when I want more food?

B PAIR WORK Compare your statements with a partner.

6 What's the problem?

Preview

1 CULTURE

Travelers in North America looking for quaint, old-fashioned charm or personalized service sometimes choose to stay in a bed and breakfast, or "B & B." Herb and Ruth Boven opened Castle in the Country in Allegan, Michigan. "Our guests come here to relax, enjoy the countryside, or shop at antique markets and specialty shops," says Ruth. Castle in the Country offers special mystery or romance weekends and services such as horse-drawn wagon rides and holiday dinners. "We enjoy meeting guests from different states and countries and showing them what's special about our area."

Have you ever stayed in a B & B? Would you like to stay in one? Talk about different types of hotels in your country with your classmates.

2 VOCABULARY *Problems*

Complete the sentences with words from the box. Then match each sentence with a picture. Compare with a partner.

cracked	scratched
✓dirty	stained
broken	stuck
peeling	fixed

1. The room needs cleaning. It's very ...dirty... .
2. The paint is coming off the walls. It's ....
3. Oh, no. I spilled jam on my shirt. Now it's ....
4. My cat sharpened her claws on the table. Now it's ....
5. I dropped the glass on the floor and now it's ....
6. I can't open the window. It's ....
7. The remote control works now. It's ....
8. The cup isn't completely broken, but it is ....

☐ 

☐ 

☐ 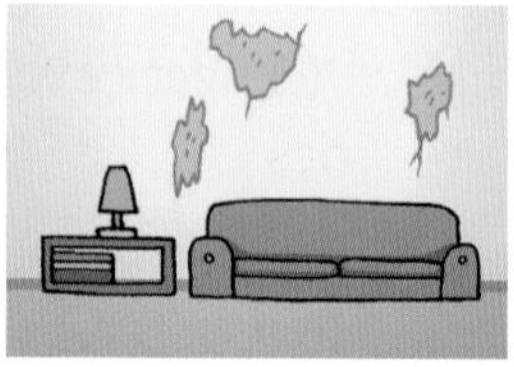

1 

☐ 

☐ 

☐ 

☐ 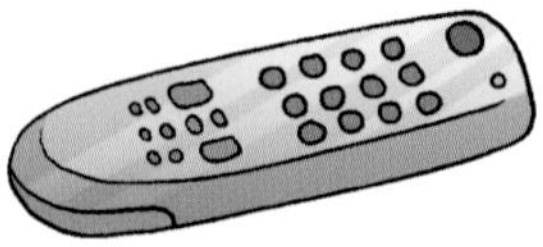

3 GUESS THE STORY

Check (✓) what you think is happening in each of the following situations.

- ☐ The older man is checking in.
- ☐ The older man is giving instructions.

- ☐ The couple is here to relax.
- ☐ The couple is here on business.

- ☐ The man is calling home.
- ☐ The man is calling the front desk.

Watch the video

4 GET THE PICTURE

Complete the chart. Check (✓) the word that describes each problem.
More than one answer may be possible.

	broken	dirty	peeling	scratched	stuck
1. temperature control	☐	☐	☐	☐	☐
2. paint	☐	☐	☐	☐	☐
3. furniture	☐	☐	☐	☐	☐
4. window	☐	☐	☐	☐	☐
5. rug	☐	☐	☐	☐	☐

5 WATCH FOR DETAILS

Complete the sentences with **George**, **Norman**, **Ed**, or **Michelle**.

1. .... needs to go to the hardware store.
2. .... says they don't have much luggage.
3. .... thinks the front desk clerk is strange.
4. .... checks the couple into the hotel.
5. .... calls the front desk to report a problem.
6. .... tries to repair the window.
7. .... says it feels cold in the room.
8. .... returns after the guests leave.

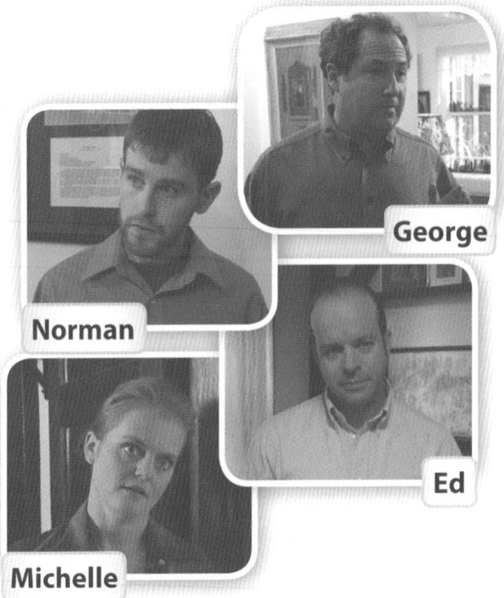

6 WHAT'S YOUR OPINION?

PAIR WORK Answer these questions.

1. Do you agree with Michelle and Ed's decision to check out of the hotel? What would you have done?
2. Think of an experience you've had where there were problems. What were the problems? What did you do to solve them?

Follow-up

7 ROLE PLAY

A **PAIR WORK** How many problems can you find in the picture below? Take turns describing the problems to each other.

B **GROUP WORK** Now join another pair. Three of you are customers. The fourth person is the waiter.

Customers: Complain to the waiter about the problems in the restaurant.

Waiter: Offer solutions to the customers' complaints.

Start like this:

Customer 1: Excuse me, but our dinners are cold.

Waiter: Oh, I'm sorry. I'll take them back and heat them up.

Customer 2: OK. That would be fine.

Customer 3: Actually, could I order something else instead?

8 WHAT DID THEY SAY?

Watch the video and complete the conversation. Then practice it.

Ed and Michelle complain to Norman about their room.

Norman: Hi. What's the .... ?

Michelle: Oh, it's ....

Norman: .... the heat.

Ed: The heat ....

Norman: Well, what's .... with it?

Michelle: The dial's .... It came off in my ....

Norman: That should .... it.

Ed: .... That window needs .... , too.

It's .... and it's letting the .... air in.

Norman: That should .... it.

Michelle: .... ?

Norman: You're ....

9 NEED *WITH PASSIVE INFINITIVES AND GERUNDS*

A Read the list of additional problems at the hotel that Norman needs to fix. Then write two sentences with *need* for each problem. Use the verbs in the box.

Norman's List

- ☐ the heat is stuck on high
- ☐ the wastebasket is full
- ☐ the chair is damaged
- ☐ the hair dryer is broken
- ☐ the rooms are dirty
- ☐ the floors are dirty

✓adjust	fix
clean	repair
empty	wash

1. The heat needs adjusting. / The heat needs to be adjusted.
2. ....
3. ....
4. ....
5. ....
6. ....

B Now think of two things that need to be done at your school or at your home. Then write two sentences to describe what needs to be done.

1. ....
2. ....

7 Endangered islands

Preview

1 CULTURE

Scientists estimate that the average temperature on Earth has increased by about 0.6 degrees Celsius (one degree Fahrenheit) in the last century. They call this phenomenon global warming, or climate change. Sea levels have risen dramatically because of global warming, increasing as much as eight inches in some places. Low-lying areas and islands are in danger of being covered by the rising water. Some experts predict that if the rising tides continue, many islands and coastal areas around the world will become uninhabitable.

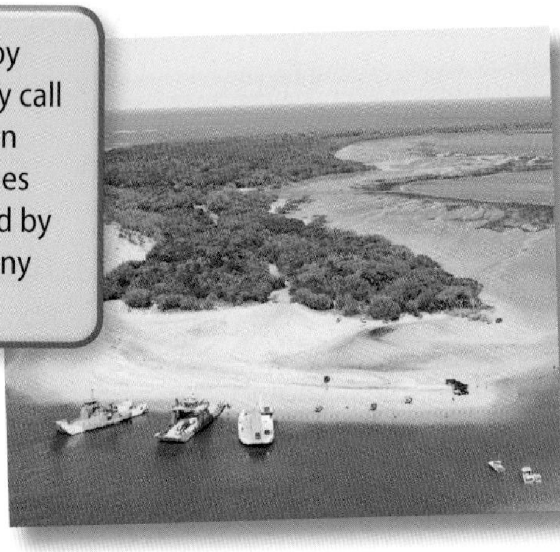

What do you know about the causes of global warming? What effect do you think rising sea levels might have on your country? What other effects do you think global warming might have?

2 VOCABULARY Environmental change

Complete the sentences with phrases from the box. Compare with a partner.

catastrophic event	**coastal areas**	**global warming**
climate panel	**high tide**	**technological fix**

1. Less than two days after the levees broke in New Orleans during Hurricane Katrina, 80 percent of the city was under water. It was a catastrophic event .
2. Engineers are likely to search for a .... to a problem, rather than a natural solution or a change in how people behave.
3. Tsunamis are usually more damaging to the .... of a country than the inland areas.
4. The government appointed a .... made up of scientific experts to find out how changing weather patterns might affect the country in the future.
5. Many scientists believe that .... is causing the glaciers to melt.
6. During a .... , many areas by the ocean that are usually above ground may be under water.

3 GUESS THE FACTS

Watch the first two minutes of the video with the sound off. Which of the following do you think are concerns of people living on the island of Tuvalu?

- ☐ cold water
- ☐ flooding
- ☐ high tides
- ☐ hot weather
- ☐ unsafe drinking water
- ☐ strong winds

Watch the video

4 GET THE PICTURE

A Look at your answers to Exercise 3. Did you guess correctly? Correct your answers. Then compare with a partner.

B What are some threats faced by the people living on Tuvalu? Match each threat with the correct picture.

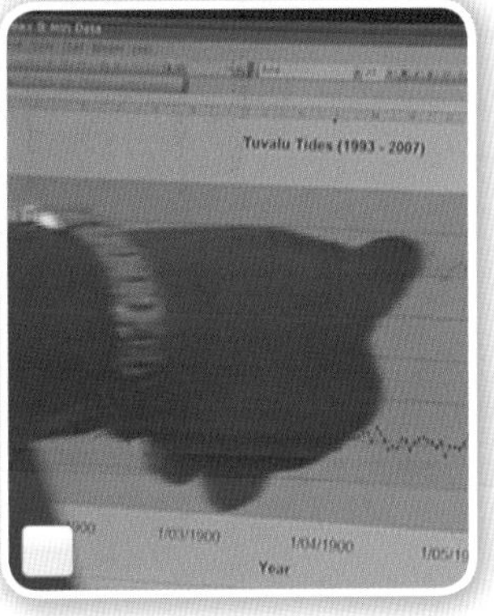

1. Forecasts show that the tides will continue to get higher.
2. The main roads on the island are sometimes flooded.
3. The airport runway may disappear.
4. Plants won't grow in the salty water.

5 WATCH FOR DETAILS

Fill in the blanks. Then compare with a partner.

1. It's difficult to grow anything on Tuvalu because the soil is too ....
2. An Australian system has been monitoring the tides in Tuvalu for .... years.
3. Scientists predict that most coastal areas of Tuvalu will be washed out in .... years.
4. A typical high tide reaches about .... meters.
5. The highest point on Tuvalu is only about .... meters.
6. Without help, Tuvalu can survive for only about .... more years.
7. The island nation of Tuvalu has .... inhabitants.

6 GUESSING MEANING FROM CONTEXT

Read these sentences from the video. Choose the best meaning of each underlined word. Check (✓) your answers. Then compare with a partner.

1. Incredibly beautiful, but incredibly vulnerable.
   - ☐ expensive ☐ easily damaged ☐ ancient
2. The water also surges up from underground, through the coral the islands are built on.
   - ☐ floats ☐ moves sideways ☐ rises suddenly
3. This isn't like other floods that I've covered, with a single catastrophic event.
   - ☐ fortunate ☐ terrible ☐ interesting
4. At the harbor, the rising swell is monitored by an Australian system.
   - ☐ controlled ☐ ignored ☐ measured
5. These [islands] are so narrow, you can cross from one side to the other in a few short paces.
   - ☐ steps ☐ miles ☐ minutes

Follow-up

7 FOR OR AGAINST

A PAIR WORK Imagine you are in charge of an organization that is considering helping the island nation of Tuvalu. List three reasons for and against trying to save these islands.

For	Against
....	....
....	....
....	....

B GROUP WORK Now join another pair. Discuss the reasons you listed. Use language like this:

In my opinion . . .	On the other hand . . .
That's an interesting idea. However, . . .	That's a good point. Nevertheless, . . .
I feel that . . .	I don't think that . . .

Language close-up

8 WHAT DID HE SAY?

Watch the video and complete the commentary. Then compare with a partner.

A reporter is talking about what Tuvalu needs to survive.

For the children of Tuvalu, the .... are fun. But for them to .... their .... on these islands will require .... international .... And with .... 11,000 people here, will the .... world think it's .... it? Now, of course, Tuvalu does get some .... , but not .... enough to keep the .... sea at bay. So the .... community .... very soon a difficult .... of .... to draw a line between .... who get .... and those who don't. And in the .... , people here are getting ready for .... king tide. Right now it's .... ; it's due to get very .... in about eight hours' time.

9 THE PASSIVE

Rewrite these sentences from the active to the passive. Use the prepositions in parentheses to indicate the cause. Then compare with a partner.

1. King tides are washing out some of Tuvalu's coastal areas. (because of)
   Some of Tuvalu's coastal areas are being washed out because of king tides.
2. Salty seawater is killing off most of the plant life. (due to)
   ....
   ....
3. An Australian system monitors the changes in sea level on Tuvalu. (by)
   ....
   ....
4. In five to ten years, rising sea levels will cover many coastal areas. (as a result of)
   ....
   ....
5. The international community must set up a global fund to save Tuvalu. (by)
   ....
   ....

8 Tango!

Preview

1 CULTURE

Tango dancing began in Argentina and Uruguay in the mid-1800s. The music of tango blended African, Cuban, and European elements. Over time, tango music and tango dancing united people from many different cultures and social classes in South America. As sailors from Argentina traveled to Europe and North America, they taught the dance to local residents, and its popularity spread. Today there are tango schools all over the world, and new styles of the dance are constantly evolving. One of the latest styles, *nuevo tango*, brings in electronic and alternative music and adds new life to this ever-popular dance form.

Why do you think people like to dance? Give as many reasons as you can.
What kinds of dances are popular in your country? What kinds have you tried?
What kinds of music are popular in your country now? Are there dances that go with each type of music?

2 VOCABULARY Learning

A PAIR WORK What are some phrases used to talk about learning? Match each verb on the left to a word or phrase on the right.

1. decide to	to ski
2. earn	take lessons
3. brush up on	hitting the ball
4. learn how	a diploma
5. practice	classes
6. take	my skills

B Complete the sentence below with phrases from part A. Change the verb form if necessary.

1. I heard you're interested in playing the violin. Did you decide to take lessons ?
2. If you want to get better at tennis, you'll have to .... !
3. I already know how to do karate, but I'm taking lessons just to ....
4. It's hard to learn to dance by myself. I'm going to .... with a friend.
5. Kim graduated from college last May. She .... in engineering.
6. This winter, James wants to ....

3 GUESS THE FACTS

Why do you think tango dancing is so popular? What are some ways people can learn or improve tango dancing?

Watch the video

4 GET THE PICTURE

What reasons do people give for wanting to learn the tango? Check (✓) your answers. Then compare with a partner.

- ☐ They're just interested in dancing.
- ☐ Their friends told them to learn the tango.
- ☐ They want to keep fit and have fun.
- ☐ The tango is exotic and challenging.
- ☐ They didn't like any other dances.
- ☐ The tango has a great rhythm.

5 WATCH FOR DETAILS

How do these people recommend learning or improving tango dancing? Match each person with a recommendation.

.... By starting with group classes or private classes.
.... By practicing with a guy.
.... By going to a tango club.
.... By practicing hard.
.... By taking the initiative and taking a class.

6 WHAT'S YOUR OPINION?

A How important do you think these qualities are for learning to dance? Rank them from 1 (most important) to 9 (least important).

.... athletic ability	.... curiosity	.... patience
.... competitiveness	.... intelligence	.... self-confidence
.... creativity	.... motivation	.... willpower

B PAIR WORK Compare your answers with a partner. Explain how you made your choices. Then talk about these activities. Would your rankings change? Why or why not?

learning a foreign language   learning to play tennis   learning to cook

Follow-up

7 ADVICE TO LEARNERS

A Think of a sport, game, or activity that you have learned. Make a list of different ways to learn it.

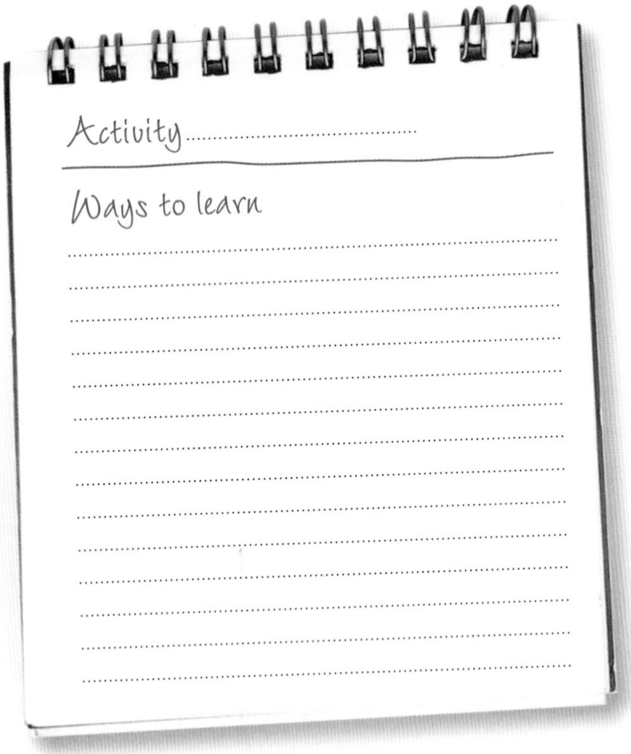

B GROUP WORK Take turns asking and answering questions about the activities the group members have chosen. Use language like this:

How did you learn to . . . ?	I learned . . . by . . .
Why do you enjoy . . . ?	I enjoy . . . because . . .
What's the best way to learn . . . ?	The best way to learn . . . is by . . .
What's a good way to improve . . . ?	A good way to improve . . . is to . . .

Language close-up

8 WHAT DID THEY SAY?

Watch the video and complete the conversation. Then practice with a partner.

A dance teacher talks about learning the tango.

Kevin: Why do you think tango is so .... ?
Uche: I think tango is .... because it's very .... and it's also very .... for people, and once people .... something that they find .... and it's very .... , I think they .... very rewarded.
Kevin: What do you .... for people who .... to learn tango?
Uche: I would recommend starting with .... classes or .... classes.
Kevin: And .... you've learned the .... of tango, what's a good way to .... your moves?
Uche: By going out .... with the people that you've .... the .... with, ... at home, listening to the .... , just feeling very .... with the music, and then .... dancing again.

9 GERUNDS AND INFINITIVES *Talking about preferences*

A For each pair of expressions, complete the questions.

1. earn a degree / learn for fun
   Would you prefer *to earn a degree or learn for fun* .... ?
2. learn English in Australia / in Canada
   Would you rather .... ?
3. learn how to cook / how to dance the tango
   Would you prefer .... ?
4. brush up on skills you already have / learn something new
   Would you rather .... ?
5. read English magazines / English novels
   Would you rather .... ?
6. study in the morning / at night
   Would you prefer .... ?

B GROUP WORK Ask several classmates the questions in part A. Then share their answers with the class.

"Mari would prefer to start a business. Juan would rather learn to dance at home."

9 Stressed out

Preview

1 CULTURE

What is stress? There are three main types:
- Mechanical stress, caused by carrying heavy objects, not getting enough exercise, or sleep disorders.
- Mental stress, caused by things such as relationship problems, financial worries, or career concerns.
- Chemical stress, caused by air and water pollution, detergents and cleaning products, and chemicals used in manufacturing.

Our bodies react to stress with the "fight or flight" response; you may want to challenge what stresses you, or you may want to run away!

What other kinds of mechanical, mental, and chemical stresses can you think of? Make a list with a partner or group. How many of these do you think affect you? What are some solutions to stress? What is your favorite way to relax?

2 VOCABULARY *Stress*

Choose from the expressions in the box to complete the paragraph below. Each expression is used only once.

blow off steam	**in knots**	**take some time off**	**very relaxing**
get some exercise	**stressed out**	**under pressure**	**what I needed**

Last year, I felt completely ......stressed out...... by my job. Every day it seemed like I was .... from my boss. My stomach was .... all the time. I used to .... by complaining to my co-workers, but that only made them feel stressed, too! Someone in my office said I should .... , but I felt too tired to go. Finally, my boss suggested, "Why don't you .... and go to a health spa for a few days? It'll be ...." It turned out to be just ....! When I got back, I felt calm and ready to handle anything.

3 GUESS THE STORY

Watch the first minute of the video with the sound off.
Answer these questions.

1. What is the woman's problem?
2. What do you think the man is telling her?

Watch the video

4 GET THE PICTURE

A Check (✓) the suggestions for stress relief that Carmen and Hugo talk about.

aromatherapy

dance lessons

hypnotherapy

ice-skating

sleeping

swimming

taking a vacation

talking to friends

yoga

B PAIR WORK Which of the activities above have you tried? Which would you like to try?

5 WATCH FOR DETAILS

Why doesn't Carmen like these suggestions for stress relief? Check (✓) the reason Carmen rejects each suggestion.

1. skating	☐ Her skate broke.	☐ The lessons were expensive.
2. dance lessons	☐ She couldn't find a partner.	☐ She got hurt.
3. yoga	☐ It was too slow.	☐ It twisted her in knots.
4. hypnotherapy	☐ It didn't work.	☐ It worked too well.
5. aromatherapy	☐ She's allergic to perfumes.	☐ She already tried it.

6 WHAT'S YOUR OPINION?

A PAIR WORK Imagine that Hugo suggests these activities for reducing stress to Carmen. Write the reasons Carmen might give for rejecting them.

playing tennis

get hit by a ball

running

....

listening to music

....

doing aerobics

....

B PAIR WORK Now act out Hugo and Carmen's conversation. Start like this:

Hugo: Have you thought about playing tennis?
Carmen: I've already tried that, but I got hit by the ball!

Follow-up

7 HOW STRESSED ARE YOU?

A PAIR WORK How much stress do you feel in the situations below? Add one more idea and check (✓) your answers. Then compare with a partner. Have conversations like this:

A: How much stress do you feel at school?
B: A lot. I have too much homework every night. How about you?

	none at all	a little	some	a lot
1. at school	☐	☐	☐	☐
2. with friends	☐	☐	☐	☐
3. on weekends	☐	☐	☐	☐
4. when visiting relatives	☐	☐	☐	☐
5. when traveling	☐	☐	☐	☐
6. .... *(your idea)*	☐	☐	☐	☐

B CLASS ACTIVITY Ask your classmates about how much stress they feel in the situations. Check (✓) their answers in the chart. Which things are the most stressful? the least stressful?

Language close-up

8 WHAT DID THEY SAY?

Watch the video and complete the conversation. Then practice it.

Carmen and Hugo talk about some possible solutions to her problem.

Hugo: There's always ....

Carmen: I've tried that, too. Now, ... time I .... the word "ocean," it's supposed to .... me. Oh, and it .... ! The other day, I was in a .... Someone .... talking about the .... problems in the world's .... People said the .... "ocean" so many times, I ....

Hugo: Oh, yeah. I .... about that. That must've been ....

Carmen: Now half the .... knows. See what I mean? I .... to get the hypnotherapy ....

Hugo: I have an idea. You could .... aromatherapy.

Carmen: .... ?

Hugo: It's .... a massage, but they .... your skin .... scented oils.

9 SUGGESTIONS

A Hugo would like some advice for his problems. Write a suggestion for each of his problems. Use the expressions in the box.

Have you thought about . . . ?	**Maybe you could . . .**	**Why don't you . . . ?**
It might be a good idea to . . .	**One thing you could do is . . .**	**What about . . . ?**

1. I'd really like to learn Spanish, but I never seem to have enough time.
   ....
2. Sometimes I can't finish my work because I get too many phone calls.
   ....
3. I want to go on vacation next month, but the boss wants me to be in the office.
   ....
4. I'd like to do something interesting on my lunch hour.
   ....
5. I love to read at night, but I usually fall asleep as soon as I begin to read.
   ....

B PAIR WORK Write two problems you have for which you would like advice. Then take turns reading your problems and offering suggestions.

1. ....
2. ....

10 The Virtual Office

Preview

1 CULTURE

In today's world, people have more choices than ever about where they do their jobs. Many companies are still located in office buildings, but the convenience of the Internet gives businesses new and exciting options. Many jobs, like website development and public relations, can be done from home, a café, or anywhere there's an Internet connection. Some companies also encourage employees to use instant messaging, online discussions, and video conferencing to communicate effectively with co-workers and clients.

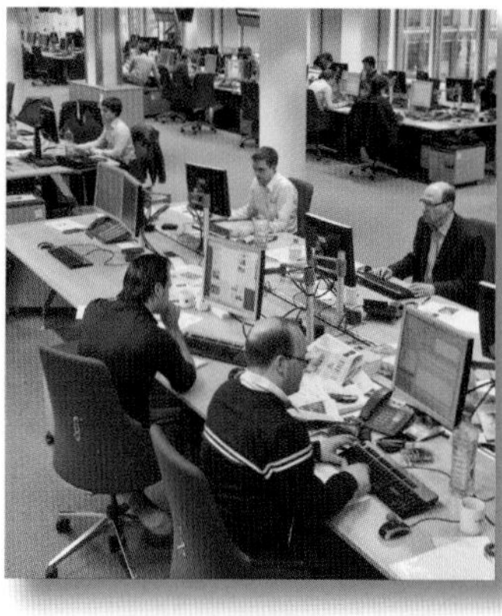

What are some virtual jobs you know about? Do you think all jobs will become virtual someday? Why do you think people might not want to work in an office building?

2 VOCABULARY *Today's office*

Match the word in the box to the correct picture below.

commute	kiosk
corporate headquarters	meeting
cyberspace	✓ workspace

1 workspace

2 ....

3 ....

4 ....

5 ....

6 ....

3 GUESS THE FACTS

What percentage of employees at IBM do you think work somewhere outside the office?

Watch the video

4 GET THE PICTURE

A Check your answer to Exercise 3. How close was your guess?

B Check (✓) **True** or **False**. Correct the false statements. Then compare with a partner.

	True	False	
1. IBM has 250,000 employees.	☐	☐	....
2. Bob Flavin works as a volunteer at an ambulance corps.	☐	☐	....
3. The CEO of Accenture has an office with his name on the door.	☐	☐	....
4. Accenture employees can reserve a workspace if they need it.	☐	☐	....
5. Crayon's workers often meet in the physical world.	☐	☐	....
6. The reporter met Crayon's CEO in person.	☐	☐	....

5 MAKING INFERENCES

Which statements are probably true? Which are probably false? Check (✓) your answers and compare with a partner.

	True	False
1. Bob Flavin works in the same office every day.	☐	☐
2. Bob Flavin likes working outside the regular office.	☐	☐
3. Janet Hoffman would like to have a big comfortable office.	☐	☐
4. Crayon Marketing has an office building with a rooftop space for parties.	☐	☐
5. Crayon workers communicate with each other regularly.	☐	☐
6. Joseph Jaffe believes that regular offices are necessary.	☐	☐

6 WATCH FOR DETAILS

Which new ideas about working were mentioned in the video? Check (✓) all the correct answers. Then write one more idea of your own.

1. Meetings in cyberspace ☐
2. Playing video games in the workplace ☐
3. Reserving a workspace only when you need it ☐
4. Bringing people together, no matter where they are in the world ☐
5. Cloud computing ☐
6. Having a virtual office party ☐
7. ....

Follow-up

7 CREATE YOUR OWN VIRTUAL OFFICE

A Imagine you have a new job where you work outside the traditional office building. Complete the chart with the location of the job, when it would begin and end, how you would stay in touch with colleagues, and how you would hold meetings.

Your job: ....

Location	Hours	Colleagues	Meetings
....	....	....	....
....	....	....	....
....	....	....	....

B PAIR WORK Compare your answers in part A with your partner.

A: What is your new job?
B: I am a web developer. I work from home. . . .

Language close-up

8 WHAT DID THEY SAY?

Watch the video and complete the commentary. Then compare with a partner.

A TV anchor introduces reporter Betsey Stark and her story on the virtual office.

Anchor: Finally from us, the virtual office. For better or .... , technology and .... are creating startling .... in what it .... to be " ...." Betsey Stark is tracking the .... order of .... and .... begins our series, "The .... of Work."

Reporter: Imagine a work .... with no commute, no corporate .... , maybe no .... in the .... world at all. For Bob Flavin, Janet Hoffman, and Joseph Jaffe, the .... is .... here.

Bob Flavin: These days we .... so .... stuff by .... and things, um, that it .... where you ....

9 PAST, PRESENT, AND FUTURE

A Complete the sentences below. Use the correct preposition or the correct form of the verb in parentheses.

1. ....In.... the 1960s, people listened to music on record players. Nowadays, people mostly ....use.... (use) MP3 players. Some experts believe that people in the future .... (listen) to music through chips in their brains.
2. .... the Middle Ages, most people have lived in rural areas and towns. However, this trend .... (change). In fact, most people now .... (live) in cities.
3. .... many years, people didn't spend time on computers and mobile devices. Now, of course, they .... (be) common. Some experts think that in the next few years, most people .... (spend) almost 60 hours a week on electronic devices!

B PAIR WORK Write two sentences based on the information in the table. Then compare your answers with a partner.

Average human lifespan		
1900	**Now**	**2050**
50 years	78 years	84 years

1. In 2050, people will live longer than they do now.
2. ....
3. ....

11 Live and learn

Preview

1 CULTURE

Most people remember at least one time when they made an embarrassing mistake – oversleeping and missing an exam, spilling food at a dinner party, calling someone by the wrong name. These mistakes can feel awful at the time. However, experts say that worrying too much about mistakes can keep people from trying new things. Some science suggests that the brain needs to do things incorrectly in order to build new knowledge. In the words of John Enoch Powell,, "The only real mistake is the one from which we learn nothing."

How do you feel when you make a mistake? Do you forget about it quickly, or think about it a lot afterward? What advice would you give a friend who made a mistake?

2 VOCABULARY *Mistakes at work*

A Put the words in the chart. Then add one more word to each list.

advertising agency	meeting	technology company
✓conference	performance	theater
embarrassed	spellbound	unprofessional

Events	Types of businesses	Feelings
conference		

B PAIR WORK Think about a mistake you made in the past in school or at work. Then take turns asking and answering the questions below.

1. What was the mistake you made?
2. How did the mistake make you feel?
3. What did you learn from the mistake?

3 GUESS THE STORY

Watch the first minute of the video with the sound off. What question do you think the interviewer is asking?

Watch the video

4 GET THE PICTURE

Where did these people's stories take place? Write it under the picture.
Add two more pieces of information about each person's story.

Where: ....
Other: ....
....

Where: ....
Other: ....
....

Where: ....
Other: ....
....

5 WATCH FOR DETAILS

Check (✓) **True** or **False**. Then correct the false statements. Compare with a partner.

	True	False	
1. Amber was still in college.	☐	☐	....
2. Amber was embarrassed at lunch.	☐	☐	....
3. Amber was wearing sandals.	☐	☐	....
4. Evan was on vacation.	☐	☐	....
5. Evan was staying with an old friend.	☐	☐	....
6. Evan broke a lamp.	☐	☐	....
7. Alexis took tickets at the theater.	☐	☐	....
8. Alexis's phone rang very quietly.	☐	☐	....

6 MAKING INFERENCES

Which statements are probably true? Which are probably false? Check (✓) your answers. Then compare with a partner. Give reasons for your answers.

	True	False
1. Amber knew what the office dress codes were.	☐	☐
2. Amber worries a lot about her past mistakes.	☐	☐
3. Evan didn't mean to break the vase.	☐	☐
4. Evan bought a new vase to replace the one he broke.	☐	☐
5. Alexis likes hip-hop music.	☐	☐
6. Alexis usually turns off her cell phone during a performance.	☐	☐

Follow-up

7 I SHOULD HAVE . . .

A Make notes about two situations in which you or someone you know made a mistake or did something embarrassing. Then suggest one or two things the person could or should have done differently.

Situation	I should have . . .
I was late to my sister's wedding.	I should have set my alarm clock. I should have asked my brother to wake me up.
....	....
....	....

B PAIR WORK Take turns sharing your situations and solutions. Talk about what happened and what the person should have done.

Language close-up

8 WHAT DID HE SAY?

Watch the video and complete the story. Then compare with a partner.

Evan talks about an embarrassing moment in his life.

I was attending a .... out of town and .... with an old friend, Ed, and his .... The first morning, I .... I was rushing to leave the .... when I knocked over a .... and .... it. No one was awake yet, and I was .... , so I just threw away the .... By the time I .... it up, I was really .... , so I left. I .... Ed and told him about it, but, honestly, I .... That night, when I got back to the .... , Ed and his wife, Michelle, were having an .... with their son, Ben. They thought Ben .... the vase and then tried to .... it.

9 PAST CONDITIONALS

A Rewrite the sentences using **if** clauses + past perfect.

1. I didn't go to bed early, so I fell asleep during the test.
   If I had gone to bed early, I wouldn't have fallen asleep during the test.
2. She took summer classes, so she graduated early.
   ....
3. He didn't know the answer, so he was embarrassed.
   ....
4. They brought a map, so they didn't get lost.
   ....
5. You didn't hear the announcement, so you missed your train.
   ....
6. We bought a new car, so we didn't have money for a vacation.
   ....

B GROUP WORK Talk about how your life would have been different if . . .

your parents had been millionaires.
you had been born a member of the opposite sex.
you had lived 200 years ago.
you had never gone to school.

12 Good business

Preview

1 CULTURE

Cafés are very popular in North America. In a café or coffeehouse, customers can sit for hours in a comfortable chair, talk with friends, and drink coffee. Many cafés are small, family-run businesses, but others are part of a chain run by a larger company. Some studies show that when a coffeehouse chain opens a store, the smaller coffee shops in the neighborhood attract more business as well. It may be that seeing a new coffeehouse just reminds people how much they like visiting their favorite café.

What do you like about your favorite coffee shop or café? Is it close to your home, work, or school? Do they play nice music? What's your favorite thing to eat or drink there?

2 VOCABULARY A café

A PAIR WORK Complete the conversation with words from the box.

comfortable
convenient
cozy
fresh
✓great
loud
popular
successful

A: I'm looking for a place to get a ......great...... cup of coffee.
B: How about Gino's Grind? It's nearby, so it's very ....
A: Do they have .... chairs?
B: Yes, they do. Gino's is small and .... It's .... with all the students.
A: I want to be able to have a conversation without shouting. Is the music very .... ?
B: No, it's not. And they have nice things to eat there, too. The owner makes .... pastries every morning.
A: That's good, but you know the real secret to a .... coffee shop is delicious coffee.
B: You said it! And Gino's coffee is fantastic. Let's go!

B PAIR WORK Take turns guessing the words in part A.

A: This word describes a place that is easy to get to.
B: Convenient.

3 GUESS THE FACTS

Who are these people?

- ☐ café owner
- ☐ reporter

- ☐ café owner
- ☐ reporter

Watch the video

4 GET THE PICTURE

A Check the reasons the café owner gives for the success of her business.

- ☐ Students like to do their homework at the café.
- ☐ The café stays open late.
- ☐ The music is always good.
- ☐ There are comfortable chairs.
- ☐ They serve unusual foods.
- ☐ The café is close to campus.

B Match each picture to the correct description.

1. People can sit outside.
2. People come here to study or read.
3. The food is made fresh every morning.
4. The chairs are comfortable.

5 WATCH FOR DETAILS

Complete the sentences. Then compare your answers with a partner.

1. Lili is the .... of Choice Café.
2. Choice Cafe's .... makes it easy for students to find.
3. Central Café closed because ....
4. People come to drink a few cups of coffee and have ....
5. While some customers eat their food inside the café, others eat ....
6. Lili encourages people who come to the café to ....
7. The .... isn't too loud, so people can chat together or read.
8. Lili lets the .... who work at the café choose the music.

6 WHAT'S YOUR OPINION?

A GROUP WORK Ask three of your classmates what they think about cafés and coffee shops. Be sure to ask for reasons. Take notes in the chart.

	.... (name)	.... (name)	.... (name)
1 Do you think a café is a good place to study?			
2 Do you think most cafés are affordable?			
3 Do you enjoy meeting your friends at a café?			
4 Do you want to work at a café?			
5 (your own question)			

B Share your information with the class. Did any comments surprise you?

Follow-up

7 OPEN YOUR OWN CAFÉ

A PAIR WORK Make plans for opening your own café. Answer the questions.

What is the name of your business?
Where will it be located in your community?
How large will it be?
What hours will it be open?
What will the furniture be like?
What kind of music will be played?
What kind of foods will you serve?

B GROUP WORK Join another pair and take turns describing your cafés.

Language close-up

8 WHAT DID THEY SAY?

Watch the video and complete the conversation. Then compare with a partner.

Jacob and Lili talk about the food and atmosphere at Choice Café.

Jacob: What .... the food?

Lili: Our food is made here .... every morning. We have a .... take-out business. People order food to take home or to eat ....

Jacob: .... ? You mean, on the .... , on campus?

Lili: .... We do have tables outside, too. But .... do eat on campus. It's really .... there.

Jacob: But it's nice to sit ...., too. The atmosphere is great .... Talk about that for a minute: the ...., the ....

Lili: Music is key to a café's .... You need to .... you have good music. I'm not an .... I mean, I don't know .... about music. But people who work here are .... They're .... They know what's .... So I let them .... the music.

9 INFINITIVE CLAUSES AND PHRASES OF PURPOSE

A Complete these sentences about starting a café. Use **in order for** or **in order to**.

1. ....In order to.... open a café, you will probably need to borrow money.
2. .... the café to be legal, you need to get a license.
3. .... people to learn about the place, you will need to advertise.
4. .... make money, you have to charge enough money to cover your costs.

B Complete these sentences with **because, because of, for,** and **the reason**.

1. We decided to open a café ....because.... we love coffee so much.
2. .... it took us so long to open our café was that we had to raise the money.
3. We had to open a week late .... a big storm in the area.
4. Now our café is known .... its fresh coffee and comfortable atmosphere.

13 Stonehenge

Preview

1 CULTURE

For reasons scientists do not completely understand, ancient cultures all around the world made monuments by arranging stones in a particular pattern. Archaeologists have discovered stone structures in Great Britain, Europe, South America, and Africa. Some, like the stone circles at Gobekli Tepe in Turkey, are also carved with designs and figures of animals and humans. Others, like Stonehenge in the United Kingdom, are exceptional because of their size and sophisticated engineering. Most of these monuments were created before written language. Archaeologists must use a wide variety of clues to uncover the true purpose for these amazing structures. In some cases, we may never know.

Have you ever visited an ancient historical site? What did it look like? Who built it? Why was it built? What did you find particularly interesting or meaningful about your visit?

2 VOCABULARY *Ancient history*

Check (✓) the best meaning for the underlined word in each sentence. Compare with a partner.

1. Anthropologists don't know how people could have built such colossal structures without the help of modern construction equipment.
   - [ ] expensive
   - [ ] beautiful
   - [x] huge
2. Experts found religious items at the ruins, which made them suspect it was a shrine.
   - [ ] market
   - [ ] holy place
   - [ ] school
3. The creators of Stonehenge only had primitive tools, but their knowledge of engineering was sophisticated.
   - [ ] useful
   - [ ] basic
   - [ ] metal
4. The Aztecs wore ceremonial masks with faces of their deities on them.
   - [ ] used for business
   - [ ] used for special rituals
   - [ ] used in everyday life
5. After death, the cremated remains of important people were buried in a special graveyard.
   - [ ] family members
   - [ ] burned bodies
   - [ ] clothes or possessions
6. The first scientists to excavate the ancient burial mound discovered very old pottery, tools, and weapons.
   - [ ] cut down with a saw
   - [ ] examine with binoculars
   - [ ] uncover by digging out earth

3 GUESS THE FACTS

Watch the first minute of the video with the sound off. What kinds of experts do you think will give opinions about Stonehenge?

- ☐ archaeologists
- ☐ astronomers
- ☐ construction experts
- ☐ geologists
- ☐ historians
- ☐ reporters

Watch the video

4 GET THE PICTURE

A Match each fact to the correct picture.

a. Stonehenge is made up of colossal standing stones.
b. Archaeologists have uncovered hundreds of human bones.
c. A second circle called Blue Stonehenge was discovered.
d. Stonehenge may have been a temple of the dead.

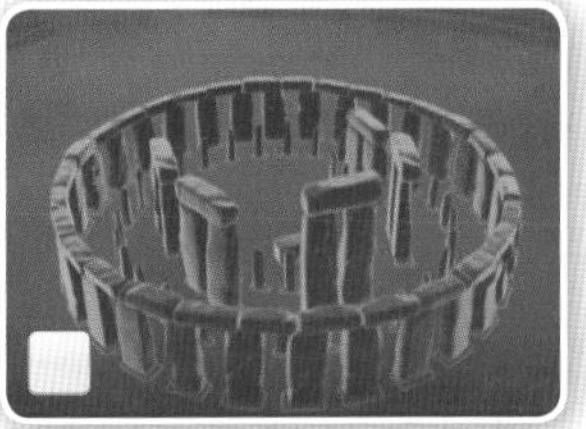
....

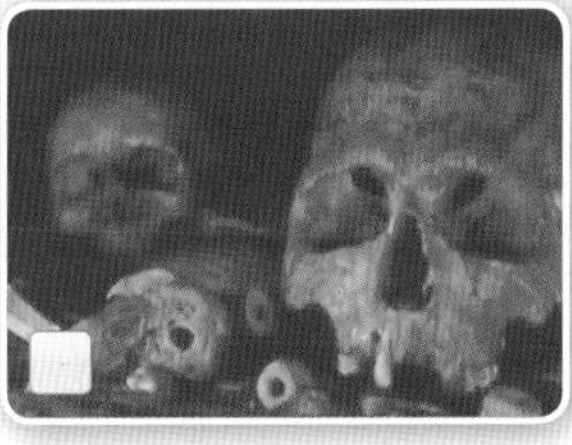
....

....

....

B Write each phrase under the correct picture.

an excavation
a monumental undertaking
a place to commune with the spirits
a part of the ceremonial complex

5 WATCH FOR DETAILS

Check (✓) **True** or **False**. Then correct the false statements. Compare with a partner.

	True	False	
1. Stonehenge is located in Wales.	☐	☐	....
2. Stonehenge contains about 53 standing stones.	☐	☐	....
3. Some of the stones weigh 40 tons.	☐	☐	....
4. Experts know who built Stonehenge.	☐	☐	....
5. Some people think Stonehenge was an alien landing site.	☐	☐	....
6. Most of the people buried at Stonehenge were men.	☐	☐	....
7. Blue Stonehenge was discovered in 2008.	☐	☐	....
8. Blue Stonehenge is shaped like a circle.	☐	☐	....

6 WHAT'S YOUR OPINION?

A Which of the sentences below do you think is the most likely explanation for the origin of Stonehenge? Rank them from 1 (most likely) to 5 (least likely).

.... It was built by aliens from another part of the universe.

.... It was a temple built to worship the sun.

.... It was a kind of hospital where sick people came to be healed.

.... It was a shrine, a holy place for the ancient Druid people who lived in the area.

.... It was a burial place where people came to commune with the dead.

B PAIR WORK Tell your partner which explanation you thought was the most likely, and why. Then talk about any other possible explanations for the building of Stonehenge.

Follow-up

7 WHAT DO YOU THINK HAPPENED?

A Read the descriptions of the mysterious events below.

What was the Tunguska event?

On June 30, 1908, a massive explosion took place in Siberia, Russia. Eighty million trees over an area of more than 2,000 square kilometers were destroyed by the blast. Some people believe that the destruction was caused by the crash of an alien spaceship. Scientists agree that it was caused by something from outer space, but they think it was a meteorite or a small comet.

What happened to the Maya?

Between the 8th and 9th centuries CE, the Mayan people in the lowlands of Central America suddenly abandoned many of their cities. Their disappearance is still a mystery. Some people believe that the Mayans fled after predicting the end of their own civilization. Archaeologists think that drought, foreign invasion, or disease might have caused the Mayan civilization in this area to collapse.

B GROUP WORK What do you think might have caused these mysterious events? Share your opinions with the group. Have conversations like this:

A: What do you think caused the Tunguska event?
B: I think it must have been a small comet.
C: I'm not sure. I think it could have been aliens.

Language close-up

8 WHAT DID THEY SAY?

Watch the video to complete the commentary. Then compare with a partner.

Scientist Julian Richards talks about Stonehenge.

Julian Richards: The .... we're .... with here is our .... , and what .... prehistory is that we've got no .... about .... So .... that we understand about it comes from archaeology, from .... we can excavate and what we can ....

Narrator: In 2008, ... of .... bones were .... at the .... , primitively burned and .... The bones were dated across a .... years of prehistory.

Julian Richards: The first .... of all the cremated .... that were .... at Stonehenge .... that it's .... adult .... , adult men that were .... there. So it's quite a .... group of people, and only probably very .... people came .... to be buried.

9 PASSIVE AND PAST MODALS

Rewrite the sentences using the passive voice.

1. Ancient peoples must have used stone circles for rituals.
   Stone circles must have been used by ancient peoples for rituals.
2. Better farming practices might have saved the Mayan people.
   ....
3. An infectious disease could have killed the Mayans.
   ....
4. A small comet may have destroyed eighty million trees in Tunguska.
   ....
5. The builders of Stonehenge couldn't have used vehicles with wheels.
   ....
6. The discovery of a second circle at Stonehenge must have surprised archaeologists.
   ....

14 Making music

Preview

1 CULTURE

Musicians are always looking for new ways to share their music with the world. These days, they may not need a record contract to attract an audience. Many small bands and solo artists use the Internet as their musical outlet. They can upload their songs to a music-sharing website, so anyone with access to the Internet can hear their music. These innovations are allowing independent artists to get noticed online, and to connect with other musicians and new fans.

Where do you get the music you listen to – radio, the Internet, CDs, or other places? Do you ever go to concerts? Where do you hear about new music?

2 VOCABULARY *Writing and recording songs*

A Choose words from the box to complete the sentences.

accompany	mix	set up
✓ compose	record	tune

1. The first thing a songwriter must do is ......compose...... a song.
2. Before playing an electric piano, a musician must .... the keyboard.
3. Before playing a guitar, a musician must .... the instrument.
4. A piano player may .... a singer.
5. When musicians .... their songs, they can hear what they sound like.
6. At a recording studio, an engineer will .... the voices and instruments together.

B PAIR WORK Compare your answers. Take turns using the words from the box in original sentences.

3 GUESS THE FACTS

What do you think these people who work in the music industry do?

recording engineer   DJ   program director   accompanist

Watch the video

4 GET THE PICTURE

What is each person's job? Write it under the picture. Use the words in the box.

Josh McBride

....

Richard Marr

....

- accompanist
- DJ
- program director
- recording engineer
- songwriter

Aldous Collins

....

Melanie Oliver

....

Matthew Hawkes

....

5 WATCH FOR DETAILS

A Complete the sentences with a job from Exercise 4.

1. The .... uses a multitrack recorder.
2. The .... speaks with listeners on the radio.
3. The .... plays along with the singer in the recording studio.
4. The .... writes music as a way to make sense of the world.
5. The .... decides what music is played on the air.

B PAIR WORK Tell your partner another detail about each of these jobs.

"The songwriter uses a thesaurus to write his songs."

6 WRITING A SONG

A Imagine that you are a songwriter, and you have just written a great new song. Write your answers to the questions below.

1. What is the song about?
2. What instrument(s) do you use on your song?
3. Where do you want to record the song?
4. How will people hear your song (on the radio, in clubs, on the Internet, other)?
5. Who do you want to listen to your song?

B PAIR WORK Compare your song ideas with a partner. Explain the reasons for your decisions.

7 WHICH JOB WOULD YOU LIKE?

A PAIR WORK Which music industry job appeals to you most – a singer, a songwriter, a DJ, or something else? Tell your partner why you would be good at the job you chose.

B GROUP WORK Join another pair. Compare your choices. Give reasons for your decisions.

8 WHAT DID THEY SAY?

Watch the video and complete the commentaries. Then compare with a partner.

Two people in the music industry talk about their jobs.

Matthew: Making music is my .... outlet: the way I make .... of the world .... me. .... I sit down to .... , the first thing I do is .... my guitar. Once the .... is tuned up and .... , I set up the keyboard. The .... has multiple .... and multiple .... What comes .... of .... is a .... of .... I'm .... that .... Sometimes I can .... hours writing .... piece. I'm .... this song. I .... it "Revelations."

* * *

Melanie: Hi, my name's Melanie Oliver. I'm the .... here at the .... The program director's job is to .... what music is .... on air. So I .... the songs and tell the DJs .... songs to play.

9 PASSIVE *How a song becomes a hit*

A Complete the sentences below about how a song becomes a hit by using the passive form of the verbs in parentheses.

.... The song .... (record) on a multitrack recorder.

.... The song .... (play) on the radio by the DJ.

.... The recording .... (take) to program directors at radio stations and .... (add) to their playlists.

....1.... The song .... (compose) by the songwriter.

.... The song .... (choose) for airplay by the program director.

.... The vocals and instruments .... (mix) together.

B PAIR WORK Put the sentences above in order. Then take turns describing how a song becomes a hit. Use **first**, **next**, **then**, **after that**, and **finally**.

15 The streets of Montreal

Preview

1 CULTURE

Most North Americans rely on their cars for transportation, but recently more people are choosing to ride their bicycles to work instead. Some cities are investing in bicycle paths and other changes to the roads, so it's easy and safe for cyclists to get around. Why are more people cycling to work? Cyclists say it improves physical fitness, protects the environment, and cuts down on traffic noise and crowding. Plus, there's an added benefit: It's fun!

How do you feel about cycling? Do you ever cycle to work or to school? How would you like drivers of cars to change their behavior? What would you like to see cyclists do differently?

2 VOCABULARY *City traffic*

Complete these sentences with the words in the box. Use the plural form when necessary.

bike helmet	**bus**	**cycle path**	**cyclist**	**commuter**
driver	**traffic**	**parking**	**pedestrian**	**✓sidewalk**

1. People walking on the ......sidewalk...... avoid traffic from bicycles and cars.
2. Some .... take the train to work every day.
3. .... should always keep their bicycles in good repair.
4. .... generally stay on the sidewalk.
5. Cyclists should not ride into oncoming ....
6. As more bicycles crowd the roads, ... have to share the road with cyclists.
7. .... reduce traffic and encourage public transportation.
8. Every cyclist should wear a ....
9. A .... is the safest place for cyclists to ride.
10. Drivers who commute to work may have trouble finding a .... spot.

3 GUESS THE FACTS

Watch the first minute of the video with the sound off.
Answer these questions.

1. Who is this man?
2. Where is he?
3. What do you think he's talking to people about?

Watch the video

4 GET THE PICTURE

Which issue does each person discuss? Check (✓) your answers.

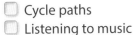

- ☐ Cycle paths
- ☐ Listening to music

- ☐ Bicycles and buses
- ☐ Driving toward traffic

- ☐ Cycling with children
- ☐ Restricting driving downtown

- ☐ Checking mirrors
- ☐ Cycling with children

- ☐ Bicycles and buses
- ☐ Driving toward traffic

- ☐ Wearing bike helmets
- ☐ Riding with headphones

- ☐ Cycle paths
- ☐ Cycling with children

5 WHO SAID WHAT?

Who said the sentences below? Match each person from Exercise 4 with a sentence. Then compare with a partner.

.... "I think it would be best if bicycles and buses were not on the same street."
.... "Cyclists should have their own bike lane and drive towards the oncoming traffic."
.... "I think cycling on the sidewalk is fine, with kids."
.... "There should be a law that says all children starting from age six should be educated on the rules of bicycling."
....1.... "I think the city should try to expand the system of cycle paths."
.... "Maybe some restrictions to driving downtown . . . "
.... "I'd like to bike and listen to music too, but . . . I think you should do that in a park."

6 GUESSING MEANING FROM CONTEXT

Read these sentences from the video. Guess the meanings of the underlined words. Check (✓) your answers. Then compare with a partner.

1. More bicycles means more bicycle traffic, and that means sharing the road.
   - ☐ allowing others space on the road ☐ expanding the road ☐ decreasing the space on the road
2. Wherever bikes and cars share the road, people are going to have opinions about how they ought to interact.
   - ☐ think about each other ☐ avoid each other ☐ relate to each other
3. I think most pedestrians are at ease with cycling on the sidewalk.
   - ☐ comfortable ☐ angry ☐ excited
4. Cyclists should be more aware of cars, automobiles, and pedestrians.
   - ☐ be afraid of ☐ pay attention to ☐ try to avoid
5. Sometimes we cut corners in terms of moving through traffic.
   - ☐ don't stop at street corners ☐ turn corners too quickly ☐ try to save time
6. Montreal is no exception.
   - ☐ is a special situation ☐ makes exceptions ☐ is the same as other places

Follow-up

7 FOR OR AGAINST

A You are a resident of Pleasantville, a small town about fifty kilometers from a large city. City officials have proposed replacing many of the parking places on the roads with bike lanes. Make a list of reasons for and against the bike lanes.

For	Against
would encourage cycling	would make it harder to park

B GROUP WORK Work in groups of four. Discuss the reasons **for** and **against** building the bike lanes. Then decide whether or not to build them. Use language like this:

In my opinion . . .	That's a good point. Nevertheless, . . .	On the other hand . . .
I feel that . . .	That's an interesting idea. However, . . .	I don't think that . . .

Language close-up

8 WHAT DID THEY SAY?

Watch the video and complete the commentaries. Then compare with a partner.

Montreal residents talk about their opinions on cycling in the city.

Sebastian: I think the city should try to .... the system of .... paths. One thing I .... this morning is that one .... drive .... traffic because that's a .... Sometimes there are corners where .... just cannot see you coming, and so you should really try to .... driving against the .... , if possible.

* * *

Nitai: Cyclists should have their own bike .... and drive towards the .... traffic .... they will be able to better see .... the other .... cars are doing, ... they're driving or .... , the cyclist will have more ....

9 PASSIVE MODALS *Giving opinions on cyclists and drivers*

Read these complaints from cyclists and drivers.

Common Complaints on the Road

Cyclists say:

"Many drivers go much faster than the speed limit."

"Sometimes drivers park in our bike lanes."

"Drivers don't check their rearview mirrors before opening their doors."

Drivers say:

"Cyclists don't put lights on their bikes when riding at night."

"Some cyclists don't wear bike helmets."

"Some cyclists ignore traffic signals."

What do you think about these complaints? Choose a modal from the box that shows how strongly you feel and rewrite each complaint. You can add words such as **allowed**, **required**, and **permitted.**

ought to be	**should be**	**must be**
shouldn't be	**have to be**	**mustn't be**

1. Drivers shouldn't be permitted to go faster than the speed limit.
2. ....
3. ....
4. ....
5. ....
6. ....

16 The Harlem Children's Zone

Preview

1 CULTURE

In some low-income neighborhoods in cities in the United States, public school students are struggling. They lag far behind those attending schools in higher-income neighborhoods in terms of academic success and college admission. Some experts say the following factors contribute to the difference in educational outcomes:

- the number of days students are absent from school
- the number of hours they spend watching television
- the number of pages they read for homework
- the quantity and quality of reading material in the students' homes

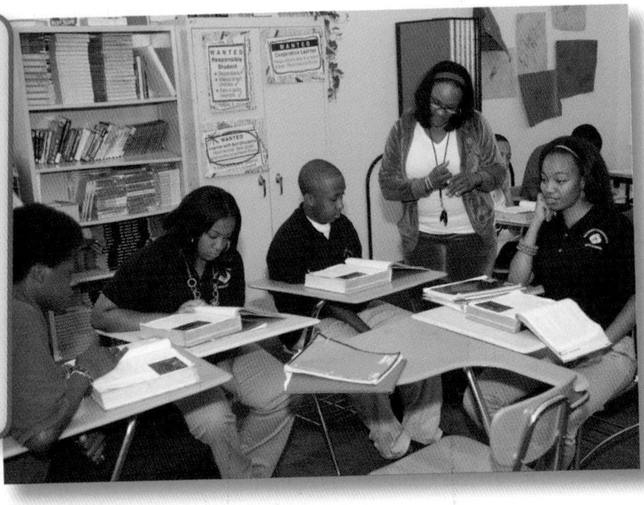

What kinds of educational challenges are you facing right now? Talk about some challenges you have faced in the past. Are you interested in going to college? If so, what are you thinking about studying? What is your ultimate career goal?

2 VOCABULARY *Education*

A Choose phrases from the box to complete the sentences.

achievement gap	**✓ break the cycle**	**inner city**	**scientific data**
affluent suburbs	**grade level**	**remarkable job**	**statistical study**

1. In order to ....break the cycle.... of poverty, it is necessary to improve schools.
2. Students in the .... often attend overcrowded and poorly-run schools.
3. Students who go to school in .... usually have more educational opportunities than urban students.
4. An .... occurs when one group of students performs better in school than another group.
5. In some schools, students are performing below .... , which means they're not learning as much as they should.
6. Researchers presented .... to show how well students are performing.
7. Many teachers do a .... of teaching students in difficult situations.
8. In a .... , researchers collect information to understand more about a subject.

B PAIR WORK Compare your answers. Take turns using the phrases in original sentences.

3 GUESS THE FACTS

Watch the first minute and a half of the video with the sound off.
Answer these questions.

1. Who are the two men?
2. What are they talking about?
3. Where do the scenes with children take place?

Watch the video

4 GET THE PICTURE

Check (✓) the items that describe the school in the video.

- ☐ It is a school for kids from the suburbs.
- ☐ It is a school for kids from the inner city.
- ☐ It is a charter school run by Geoffrey Canada.
- ☐ It is part of the public school system.
- ☐ Students are in class more often than in other schools.
- ☐ Summer vacation is longer than at most schools.
- ☐ It improves learning skills and test scores for its students.

5 WATCH FOR DETAILS

A Check (✓) **True** or **False**. Then compare with a partner.

	True	False
1. The Children's Zone covers 97 blocks in Harlem.	☐	☐
2. Geoffrey Canada doesn't want his students to go to college.	☐	☐
3. Canada grew up in Harlem.	☐	☐
4. There is one adult for every 20 children in the school.	☐	☐
5. There are 1200 children enrolled in Canada's school.	☐	☐
6. Children at Canada's school attend classes on Saturday.	☐	☐
7. One hundred percent of Canada's third graders scored at or above grade level.	☐	☐
8. Canada will know the Children's Zone has worked when they get more students.	☐	☐

B PAIR WORK Tell a partner how you would correct the false statements in part A. Then share some more details that you remember with your partner.

6 GUESSING MEANING FROM CONTEXT

Read these sentences from the video and guess the meanings of the underlined words. Check (✓) your answers. Then compare with a partner.

1. Geoffrey Canada may have figured out a way to close the racial achievement <u>gap</u>.
   - ☐ difference
   - ☐ cause
   - ☐ problem
2. <u>Abandoned</u> by his father, he and three brothers were raised by their mother.
   - ☐ loved
   - ☐ left forever
   - ☐ confused
3. His laboratory is a 97-block neighborhood in Harlem, which he's flooded with a wide <u>array</u> of social, medical, and educational services.
   - ☐ building
   - ☐ list
   - ☐ variety
4. Today, however, results are in and they are nothing short of <u>stunning</u>, so much so that the White House is now taking notice.
   - ☐ disappointing
   - ☐ amazing
   - ☐ normal
5. Right now, there are some twelve hundred kids enrolled from kindergarten to the tenth grade. It'll <u>eventually</u> expand all the way through the twelfth grade.
   - ☐ carefully
   - ☐ immediately
   - ☐ in the future

Follow-up

7 WHAT'S YOUR OPINION?

A Which features discussed in the video do you think are the most important in improving education for all students? Rank them from 1 (most important) to 6 (least important). Then add your own ideas.

.... smaller class size
.... weekend classes
.... a longer school day
.... free social and medical services
.... shorter summer vacation
.... more teachers

....

....

....

B PAIR WORK Take turns describing the features that are most important to you. Use sentences like these:

A: I think small classes are the best way to improve education.
B: I'm not sure. As far as I'm concerned, weekend classes are more important, because . . .

Language close-up

8 WHAT DID THEY SAY?

Watch the video and complete the commentaries. Then compare with a partner.

A reporter talks with Dr. Roland Fryer about the Harlem Children's Zone.

Reporter: What is the .... achievement gap?

Dr. Fryer: Black .... in our schools are not .... at even .... the rate as white children in our schools. The .... black seventeen-year-old .... at the proficiency .... of the .... white thirteen-year-old. A four-year .... in effective .... : that's . . . that's ....

Reporter: But when Dr. Fryer .... four years' worth of Promise Academy .... scores, he .... something ....

Dr. Fryer: At the .... school level, he .... the achievement .... in .... subjects: .... and reading.

Reporter: .... eliminating the .... in elementary .... ?

Dr. Fryer: Absolutely. We've .... seen . . . we've .... seen anything .... that.

9 COMPLEX NOUN PHRASES WITH GERUNDS

A PAIR WORK Interview a partner about a challenge that he or she has faced in life, such as taking a trip, learning a new skill, or accomplishing a goal. Use five of the questions below in your interview. Write your partner's responses below.

What was the most challenging part of . . . ?
What was one of the rewards of . . . ?
What was the most dangerous part of . . . ?
What was the easiest part of . . . ?
What was the most surprising thing about . . . ?
What was the most exciting thing about . . . ?
What was the scariest thing about . . . ?
What was the funniest thing about . . . ?

1. *The most challenging part of Anita's marathon was going up the hills.*
2. ....
3. ....
4. ....
5. ....

B GROUP WORK Join another pair. Explain your partner's challenge to them.

This page is intentionally left blank

interchange

FIFTH EDITION

3

Workbook

Jack C. Richards

with Jonathan Hull and Susan Proctor

CAMBRIDGE
UNIVERSITY PRESS

This page is intentionally left blank

Contents

Credits

The authors and publishers acknowledge the following sources of copyright material and are grateful for the permissions granted. While every effort has been made, it has not always been possible to identify the sources of all the material used, or to trace all copyright holders. If any omissions are brought to our notice, we will be happy to include the appropriate acknowledgements on reprinting and in the next update to the digital edition, as applicable.

Key: BL = Below Left, BR = Below Right, C = Centre, CL = Centre Left, CR = Centre Right, TC = Top Centre, TL = Top Left, TR = Top Right.

Illustrations

337 Jon (KJA Artists): 51; **Mark Duffin**: 31, 80; **Pablo Gallego** (Beehive Illustration): 10, 20; **Thomas Girard** (Good Illustration): 4, 28, 53; **Dusan Lakicevic** (Beehive Illustration): 1, 14, 22, 33, 96; **Yishan Li** (Advocate Art): 6, 13, 65; **Quino Marin** (The Organisation): 29; **Gavin Reece** (New Division): 3, 64; **Paul Williams** (Sylvie Poggio Artists): 15, 66.

Photos

Back cover (woman with whiteboard): Jenny Acheson/Stockbyte/GettyImages; Back cover (whiteboard): Nemida/GettyImages; Back cover (man using phone): Betsie Van Der Meer/Taxi/GettyImages; Back cover (woman smiling): PeopleImages.com/DigitalVision/GettyImages; Back cover (name tag): Tetra Images/GettyImages; Back cover (handshake): David Lees/Taxi/GettyImages; p. 2 : Michael H/DigitalVision/GettyImages; p. 5 (TL): Jade/Blend Images/Getty Images Plus/GettyImages; p. 5 (TR): Jamie Grill/GettyImages; p. 5 (BL): Blend Images - Jose Luis Pelaez Inc/Brand X Pictures/GettyImages; p. 5 (BR): Tomasz Trojanowski/Hemera/Getty Images Plus/GettyImages; p. 7: John Rowley/Photodisc/GettyImages; p. 8: KidStock/Blend Images/GettyImages; p. 9: monkeybusinessimages/iStock/Getty Images Plus/GettyImages; p. 12 (TL): ColorBlind/The Image Bank/GettyImages; p. 12 (TR): Sigrid Gombert/MITO images/GettyImages; p. 12 (CL): 4x6/E+/GettyImages; p. 12 (CR): Roy Hsu/Photographer's Choice RF/GettyImages; p. 13 (TR): mediaphotos/iStock/Getty Images Plus/GettyImages; p. 16: Purestock/GettyImages; p. 17 : PeopleImages/DigitalVision/GettyImages; p. 18: Phil Boorman/Cultura/GettyImages; p. 19 (TL): Robert George Young/Photographer's Choice/GettyImages; p. 19 (BR): dangdumrong/iStock/Getty Images Plus/GettyImages; p. 21 (TR): Chris Dyball/Innerlight/The Image Bank/GettyImages; p. 21 (CL): MattStansfield/iStock/Getty Images Plus/GettyImages; p. 23: EXTREME-PHOTOGRAPHER/E+/GettyImages; p. 24 (Johnson): George Doyle/Stockbyte/GettyImages; p. 24 (Marshall): Digital Vision./Photodisc/GettyImages; p. 24 (James): Yellow Dog Productions/The Image Bank/GettyImages; p. 24 (Grant): wdstock/iStock/Getty Images Plus/GettyImages; p. 24 (Simpson): Dave and Les Jacobs/Blend Images/GettyImages; p. 25 (TR): asiseeit/iStock/Getty Images Plus/GettyImages; p. 25 (BR): hadynyah/E+/GettyImages; p. 26: Thomas_EyeDesign/Vetta/GettyImages; p. 30: Education Images/Universal Images Group/GettyImages; p. 32 (George): snapphoto/E+/GettyImages; p. 32 (airport): Philippe TURPIN/Photononstop/Photolibrary/GettyImages; p. 32 (Diane): Vesnaandjic/E+/GettyImages; p. 32 (car): lisegagne/E+/GettyImages; p. 34: Whiteway/E+/GettyImages; p. 35 (wrench): TokenPhoto/E+/GettyImages; p. 35 (TR): John E. Kelly/Photodisc/GettyImages; p. 36: pixelfusion3d/iStock/Getty Images Plus/GettyImages; p. 37 (drain): belovodchenko/iStock/Getty Images Plus/GettyImages; p. 37 (plane): incposterco/E+/GettyImages; p. 37 (smoke): Harrison Shull/Aurora/GettyImages; p. 37 (land): Sierralara/RooM/GettyImages; p. 38 (forest): Ro-Ma Stock Photography/Photolibrary/GettyImages; p. 39: Howard Shooter/Dorling Kindersley/GettyImages; p. 40: VCG/Contributor/Visual China Group/GettyImages; p. 41: Travel Ink/Gallo Images/The Image Bank/GettyImages; p. 42: SolStock/iStock/Getty Images Plus/GettyImages; p. 43: Doug Armand/Oxford Scientific/GettyImages; p. 44: Wilfried Krecichwost/DigitalVision/GettyImages; p. 45: cglade/E+/GettyImages; p. 46 (TL): Lew Robertson/StockFood Creative/GettyImages; p. 46 (TC): Alina555/iStock/Getty Images Plus/GettyImages; p. 46 (TR): Jose Luis Pelaez Inc/Blend Images/GettyImages; p. 47 (photo 1): Hemera Technologies/PhotoObjects.net/Getty Images Plus/GettyImages; p. 47 (photo 2): Picturenet/Blend Images/GettyImages; p. 47 (photo 3): Zoran Milich/Photodisc/GettyImages; p.47 (photo 4): DragonImages/iStock/Getty Images Plus/GettyImages; p. 48 (TR): BrianAJackson/iStock/Getty Images Plus/GettyImages; p. 48 (CR): reka prod./Westend61/GettyImages; p. 49 (TR): simazoran/iStock/Getty Images Plus/Getty Image; p. 49 (CR): ONOKY - Eric Audras/Brand X Pictures/GettyImages; p. 49 (BR): michaeljung/iStock/Getty Images Plus/GettyImages; p. 50: leaf/iStock/Getty Images Plus/GettyImages; p. 52 (TL): IP Galanternik D.U./E+/GettyImages; p. 52 (TR): Lady-Photo/iStock/Getty Images Plus/GettyImages; p. 54: Westend61/GettyImages; p. 55 (CR): Andy Sheppard/Redferns/GettyImages; p. 55 (BR): by Roberto Peradotto/Moment/GettyImages; p. 56 (L): Mint/Hindustan Times/GettyImages; p. 56 (R): Michael Runkel/imageBROKER/GettyImages; p. 57: Bettmann/GettyImages; p. 58 (TL): Bettmann/GettyImages; p. 58 (BR): Ron Levine/Photographer's Choice/GettyImages; p. 59: Windsor & Wiehahn/Stone/GettyImages; p. 60: Javier Pierini/Stone/GettyImages; p. 61: blackred/iStock/Getty Images Plus/GettyImages; p. 62: izusek/iStock/Getty Images Plus/GettyImages; p. 63: ADRIAN DENNIS/AFP/GettyImages; p. 67: Greg Vaughn/Perspectives/GettyImages; p. 68: Caiaimage/Robert Daly/GettyImages; p. 69 (TL): marco wong/Moment/GettyImages; p. 69 (TR): Oscar Wong/Moment Open/GettyImages; p. 69 (CL): Otto Stadler/Photographer's Choice/GettyImages; p. 69 (CR): David Hannah/Lonely Planet Images/GettyImages; p. 69 (BL): LOOK Photography/UpperCut Images/GettyImages; p. 69 (BR): lightkey/E+/GettyImages; p. 70: Thomas Kokta/Photographer's Choice RF/GettyImages; p. 71 (Calgary Farmers' Market): Ken Woo/Calgary Farmers' Market; p. 71 (WWF): © naturepl.com/Andy Rouse/WWF; p. 72: Christian Hoehn/Taxi/GettyImages; p. 73 (TL): Rosanna U/Image Source/GettyImages; p. 73 (TC): Mark Weiss/Photodisc/GettyImages; p. 73 (TR): i love images/Cultura/GettyImages; p. 73 (BL): monkeybusinessimages/iStock/Getty Images Plus/GettyImages; p. 73 (BC): Photo and Co/The Image Bank/GettyImages; p. 73 (BR): Alija/E+/GettyImages; p. 74 (stonehenge): Maxine Bolton/EyeEm/GettyImages; p. 74 (people): Peter Dennis/GettyImages; p. 74 (boats): De Agostini/M. Seemuller/De Agostini Picture Library/GettyImages; p. 75 (bigfoot): Big_Ryan/DigitalVision Vectors/GettyImages; p. 75 (footprints): Danita Delimont/Gallo Images/GettyImages; p. 76: Steve Bronstein/Stone/GettyImages; p. 77: kbeis/DigitalVision Vectors/GettyImages; p. 78: mediaphotos/Vetta/GettyImages; p. 79 (T): Oscar Garces/CON/LatinContent Editorial/GettyImages; p. 81: Theo Wargo/Getty Images North America/GettyImages; p. 82 (TL): ColorBlind Images/Blend Images/GettyImages; p. 82 (TR): track5/E+/GettyImages; p. 83: imagenavi/GettyImages; p. 84 (TL): John Wildgoose/Caiaimage/GettyImages; p. 84 (TR): Bloomberg/GettyImages; p. 84 (CL): Chris Ryan/Caiaimage/GettyImages; p. 84 (CR): numbeos/E+/GettyImages; p. 84 (BL): Tom Merton/OJO Images/GettyImages; p. 84 (BR): Ariel Skelley/Blend Images/GettyImages; p. 85 (TL): marcoventuriniautieri/E+/GettyImages; p. 85 (TR): Anadolu Agency/GettyImages; p. 85 (CL): Caspar Benson/GettyImages; p. 85 (CR): Jake Olson Studios Blair Nebraska/Moment/GettyImages; p. 86 (house): Peter Baker/GettyImages; p. 86 (traffic): Levi Bianco/Moment/GettyImages; p. 86 (bike): Billy Hustace/The Image Bank/GettyImages; p. 86 (using mobile): SolStock/E+/GettyImages; p. 87: Image Source/DigitalVision/GettyImages; p. 89: Caiaimage/Paul Bradbury/Riser/GettyImages; p. 90: Dawid Garwol/EyeEm/GettyImages; p. 92: FatCamera/E+/GettyImages; p. 93: c.Zeitgeist/Everett/REX/Shutterstock; p. 94 (TR): shapecharge/E+/GettyImages; p. 94 (BR): borgogniels/iStock/Getty Images Plus/GettyImages; p. 95: Lucidio Studio, Inc./Moment/GettyImages.

1 That's my kind of friend!

1 Complete these descriptions with the words from the list.

✓ modest
✓ outgoing
✓ supportive
✓ temperamental
✓ unreliable

1. Eric is so ___modest___! He always has such great ideas and never takes any credit for them.
2. The Wongs like meeting new people and having friends over for dinner. They're one of the most ___outgoing___ couples I know.
3. You can't trust Alice. She always promises to do something, but then she never does it. She's pretty ___unreliable___.
4. James wants to be an actor. It's hard to break into the business, but his family is very ___supportive___ of his dream.
5. I never know how to act around Lisa! One minute she's in a good mood, and the next minute she's in a bad mood. She's so ___temperamental___

2 Opposites

A Complete the chart by forming the opposites of the adjectives in the list. Use *in-* and *un-*. Then check your answers in a dictionary.

✓ attractive	✓ dependent	✓ formal
✓ reasonable	✓ competent	✓ experienced
✓ helpful	✓ reliable	✓ cooperative
✓ flexible	✓ popular	✓ sensitive

• dis
disproportionate
dishonest

Opposites with *in-*		Opposites with *un-*	
incompetent	inexperienced	unattractive	unhelpful
inflexible	informal	unreliable	unpopular
independent	insesitive	unreasonable	uncooperative

B Write four more sentences using any of the words in part A.

1. Alan is very incompetent at work. He makes a lot of mistakes.
2. Minds don't have information. She is unhelpful for this work.
3. The appointment's with that Doctor is very inflexible
4. Roby has an insensitive sense of humor.
5. The Vegan Restaurants are very unpopular in this city.

3 Add *who* or *that* to the conversation where necessary. Put an ✗ where *who* or *that* is not necessary.

A: I'm looking for someone ___✗___ I can go on vacation with.

B: Hmm. So what kind of person are you looking for?

A: I want to travel with someone ___who___ is easygoing and independent.

B: Right. And you'd probably also like a person ___that/who___ is reliable.

A: Yeah, and I want someone ___X___ I know well.

B: So why don't you ask me?

A: You? I know you too well!

B: Ha! Does that mean you think I'm someone ___that/who___ is high-strung, dependent, and unreliable?

A: No! I'm just kidding. You're definitely someone ___X___ I could go on vacation with. So, . . . what are you doing in June?

4 Complete the sentences with *who* or *that* and your own information or ideas.

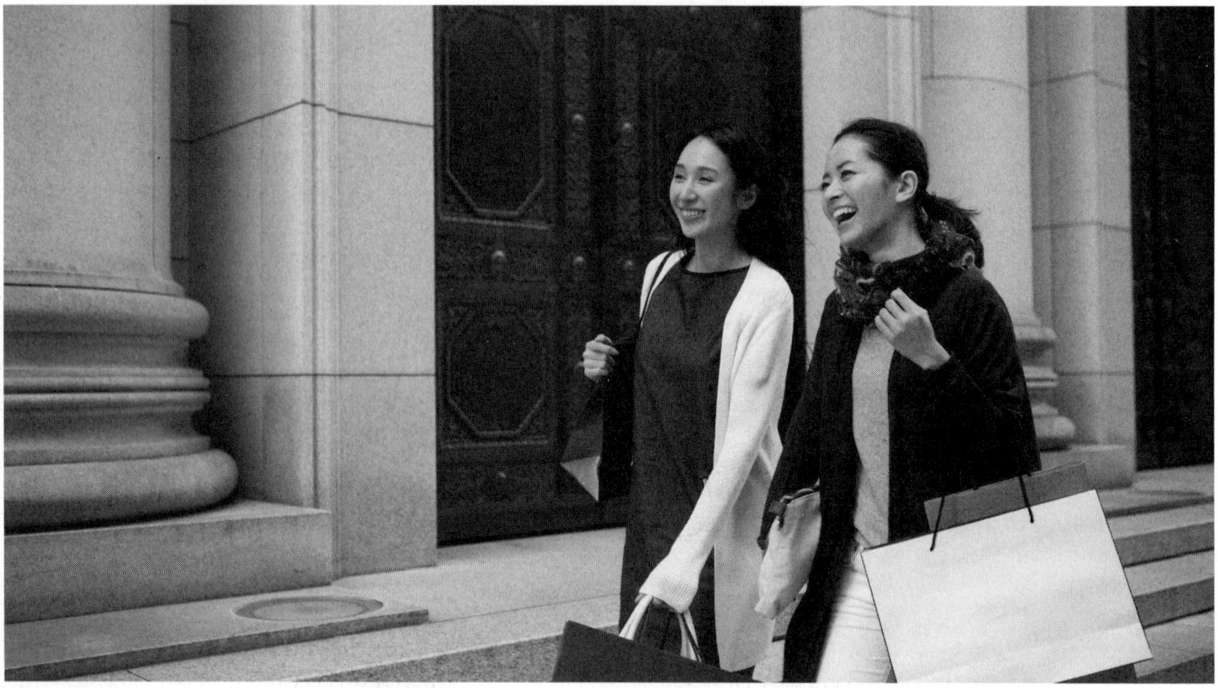

1. I generally like to go out with people *who are easygoing and have a sense of humor*.
2. I'd rather travel with someone ___who was very outgoing. I'll like have fun times___
3. I don't really want a roommate ___that his don't like clean your clothes constan___
4. My classmates and I like teachers ___who are supportive and friendly in the classro___.
5. My best friend and I want to meet people ___who like them travel frequently___.
6. Most workers would prefer a boss ___who leader them of one way more compassionate___
7. Some people don't like stingy types ___that complaining all the time. They are very negative person___
8. I don't want to have inflexible friends ___who never have any time for nothing___.
9. I feel comfortable discussing my problems with friends ___who listen to me with attention___
10. My favorite friends are people ___who like to say the things as they think___.

5 Two of a kind?

A Read the article. What six personality types are discussed?

DO OPPOSITES ATTRACT EACH OTHER?

Some psychologists believe that we are attracted to people who seem to have the characteristics that we wish we had. For example, if you love music but don't play an instrument, you might be attracted to someone who is a musician. Being with that person allows you to be close to something that is important to you and that you want more of in your life.

Because people are very complex, we can be attracted to several different kinds of people who are our opposites in one way or another. So let's take a look at six principal kinds of characteristics in people, and you can decide which type you are most like and which type is your opposite.

Let's begin with introverted and extroverted people. Introverted people often spend a lot of time inside their minds and can be quiet and reserved. Extroverted people enjoy getting out and spending time with other people. If opposites attract, then there will always be an interest between introverted and extroverted people. Introverted people will get out of their minds and into the world with their extroverted friends or partners, while extroverted people will appreciate the quiet space of the inner world of their introverted friends or partners.

Then there are people who relate to the world from a thinking perspective and others who relate to it from a feeling perspective. Thinkers can be cool and objective in their judgments, while feelers may be warm and passionate about theirs. Because people who spend a lot of time thinking want to feel deeply too, they may be attracted to a feeling kind of person. And someone who is very aware of their own powerful feelings may enjoy the company of a relaxed and logical thinker.

Two other characteristics are those of people who use their five senses to understand the world we live in as opposed to those who use their intuition. Sensing people are very aware of the present moment; they are realistic and practical people. Intuitive people, on the other hand, often spend their time in a future of infinite possibilities where their imagination is as free as a bird. The attraction here could be that intuitive people realize they need the practical know-how of sensing people in order to make their dreams come true. Likewise, the sensors are attracted to the imaginative possibilities they see in intuitive people.

These three different pairs of personality characteristics – the introvert and the extrovert, the thinker and the feeler, and the sensor and the intuitive – are of course found in each individual person. Yet many psychologists believe that a person will more often use one characteristic of each pair, in the same way that people use either their left hand or their right. And, according to the idea that opposites attract, the left hand needs the right hand in the same way that the right hand needs the left!

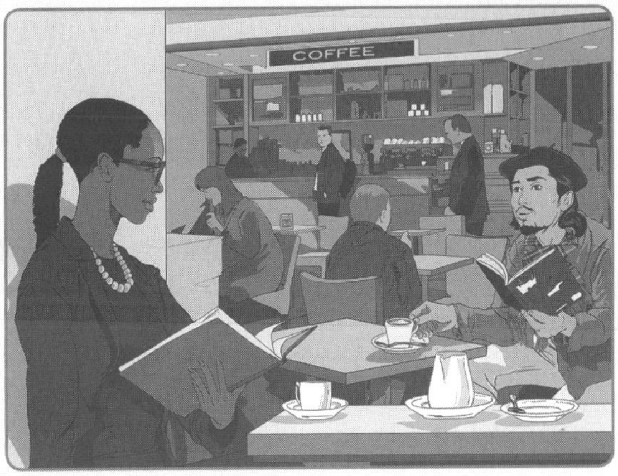

B Based on the information in the article, what kind of people are you attracted to? Circle the words. Then, using the idea that opposites attract, complete the next sentence with the type of person *you* must be.

1. I am more attracted to a person who is (introverted / extroverted). Therefore, I am introverted.
2. I am more attracted to a person who is a (thinker / feeler). Therefore, I am a thinker.
3. I am more attracted to a person who is the (sensing type / intuitive type). Therefore, I am a Sensing type

C Do you agree with the kind of person you seem to be according to part B? Why or why not?

Yes. Because the explanation define me very well

6 Match the clauses in column A with the most suitable clauses in column B.

A	B
1. I like it b	**a.** when someone criticizes me in front of other people.
2. I don't mind it d	**b.** when people are easygoing and friendly.
3. It upsets me c	**c.** when rich people are stingy.
4. It embarrasses me a	**d.** when people are a few minutes late for an appointment.

7 Write sentences about these situations. Use the expressions in the box.

I love it . . .	I can't stand it . . .	I don't like it . . .
It upsets me . . .	It bothers me . . .	I don't mind it . . .
I really like it . . .	It makes me happy . . .	It makes me angry . . .

1. I don't like it when people cut in line.

2. It makes me happy when I receive one surprise gift

3. It bothers me when the people sing with strong voice besde m

4. I Really like it when the workers arrive your work on time.

5. It upsets me when the traffic in the city is very slowly

6. I can't stand it when the person near me at the theather talk with his phone.

8 What are some things you like and don't like about people? Write two sentences about each of the following. Use the ideas in the pictures and your own ideas.

1. What I really like:

- I love it when someone is generous and gives me flowers.
- It makes me happy when the people say to me kind words for describe me

2. What I don't like:

- It's make me angry when the people are not respectful
- It bothers me when the couples are discussing about your personal problems loudly in the public space

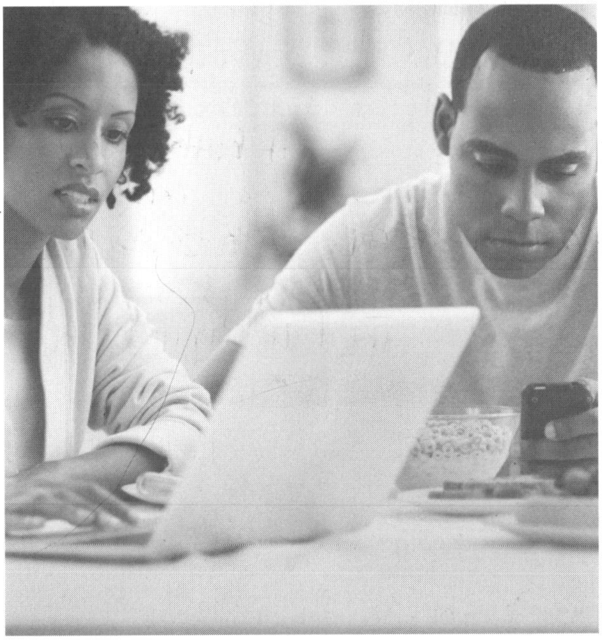

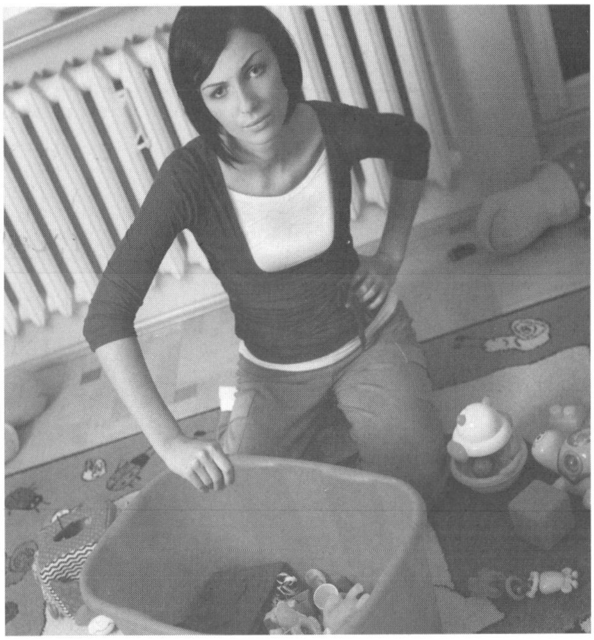

3. What doesn't bother me:

- I don't mind it when my friend use his phone while we are working
- I don't mind when during the work we can eat some snacks

4. What upsets me:

- It upsets me when the kids don't pick up your toys after play with them
- I don't like to put my feet on his toys. It's hurt me

9 It really bugs (upset) me!

Choose one thing from Exercise 8 that really embarrasses, bothers, or upsets you. Write two paragraphs about it. In the first paragraph, describe the situation. In the second paragraph, say why this situation is difficult for you and describe a situation you would prefer.

It really embarrasses me when someone is too generous to me. Recently, I dated a guy who was always giving me things. For my birthday, he bought me an expensive necklace, and he treated me to dinner and a movie.

The problem is, I don't have enough money to treat him in the same way. I'd prefer to date someone I have more in common with. In fact, my ideal boyfriend is someone who is sensible and saves his money!

• It really embarrasses me when I have to see my phone for any reason when I am with people who I know they wait for my attention, but there are time when really I need it. The places more incomfortable for me is in the restaurants, this situation makes me feel unrespectful and shy

• But I don't mind when the people near me make it. I understand and I know that there are situation's that is not controllable, the problem is when the ninety porcent of the time they see your screen. That if that bother me.

10 Choose the correct word to complete each sentence.

1. I can tell Simon anything (cualquier cosa), and I know he won't tell anyone else. I can really trust him. (believe / treat / trust)
2. Kay has a very high opinion of herself. I don't like people who are so egotistical. (egotistical / temperamental / supportive)
3. It bothers me when people are too serious. I prefer people who are easygoing and have a good sense of humor. (easygoing / inflexible / reliable (confianza))
4. I like it when someone expresses strong opinions. Hearing other people's views can really make you think. (accomplishments / compliments / opinions)
5. Lisa is very rich, but she only spends her money on herself. She's very stingy. (generous / modest / stingy)

2 Working 9 to 5

1 What's your job?

A Match the jobs with their definitions.

A/An . . .	is a person who . . . .
1. comedian f	**a.** researches environmentally friendly technologies
2. green researcher a	**b.** helps students with their problems
3. guidance counselor b	**c.** controls a company's brand online
4. organic food farmer e	**d.** creates computer applications
5. social media manager c	**e.** grows food without chemicals
6. software developer d	**f.** makes people laugh for a living

B Write a definition for each of these jobs: accountant, fashion designer, and flight attendant.

1. An accountant is someone who manage the financial situation of one company
2. A fashion Designer is someone who creates clothes
3. An flight Attendant is someone who attend people on a plane

2 Challenging or frightening?

A Which words have a positive meaning, and which ones have a negative meaning? Write *P* or *N*.

awful N
boring N
challenging P
dangerous N
difficult N
fantastic P
fascinating P
(aterrador) frightening N
interesting P
(gratificante) rewarding P

B Write about four more jobs you know. Use the words in part A and gerund phrases.

1. I think being a comedian would be fascinating.
2. I believe working as a doctor would be stessing (stressful)
3. I think being a veterinarian is very rewarding
4. I don't know if being a chef would be my job in the future
5. Designing stuff seems like a challenging career

3 Career choices

A Match each career and the most appropriate job responsibility.

Careers		Job responsibilities
work	for an airline	do research
	with computers	teach discipline and fitness
	as a high school coach	learn new software programs
be	a university professor	work independently
	a writer	travel to different countries

B Use the information from part A and gerund phrases to complete this conversation.

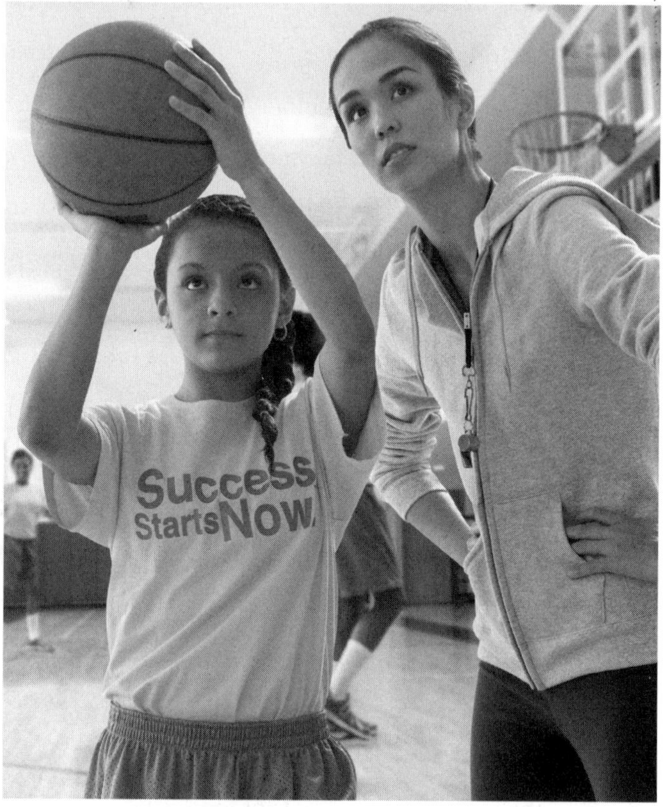

Teri: So, what kind of career would you like, Jack?

Jack: Well, I'm not exactly sure. Being a writer could be interesting. Maybe blogging about something I'm interested in.

Teri: Hmm. I don't know if I'd like that because I'd have to write every day.

Jack: What do you want to do, then?

Teri: Well, I'm not sure either! I'd love working as a high school coach. I'd really enjoy being with teenagers all day and teaching disciplice and fitness. On the other hand, I'd be interested in working for an airline.

Jack: Really? What would you like about that?

Teri: Well, I'd love traveling to different coutnes all over the world.

Jack: Oh, I could never do that! I think it would be very tiring work.

C Write a short conversation like the one in part B. Use the remaining information in part A or your own ideas.

A: So, what kind of career would you like?

B: Well, I'm not exactly sure. But I think would be an good architect

A: That sounds interesting. But I wouldn't like it because I think is dangerous

B: What do you want to do then?

A: Well, I'd love being a pediatrician

B: Is interesting career. I think I couldn't, I don't like kids.

A: I like the kids, for that I think this career is good for me.

4 What a job!

A Read the magazine interviews. Write the correct job title above each interview. There are two extra jobs.

☑ architect	☑ freelance artist	☐ preschool teacher	☐ university professor
☑ bus driver	☑ house painter	☐ train conductor	☑ website designer

TELL US ABOUT YOUR JOB

1 ARCHITECT

I have always enjoyed making things, and what's more interesting than building something that people will use for years? The challenge of discovering exactly how a space needs to be constructed for maximum usefulness and beauty is what makes me wake up with a smile. I often work late at the office, but that's part of the job.

2 FREELANCE ARTIST

Working for yourself is hard because you're responsible for everything. If no one calls you and asks you to work for them, you have to go out and look for work. Luckily, I now have some regular clients. I paint pictures for some expensive hotels. Right now, I'm doing some paintings for the rooms of a new hotel in Hawaii.

3 HOUSE PAINTER

My friends say my work is less demanding than theirs, but I work just as hard as they do. I spend a lot of time alone because my job can't begin until all the construction work is completed. Usually, the rooms look great when I've finished my work. Sometimes I don't like the colors that customers choose, but I have to do what they want.

4 WEBSITE DESIGNER

These days a lot of people are doing what I've been doing for fifteen years. I work closely with my clients to find out exactly what they want to show on the Internet and how to make it look as attractive as possible. My work requires a good eye for art, a command of clear and precise language, and of course, knowledge of the latest technology.

5 BUS DRIVER

I meet all kinds of people: some are the best and others aren't so good. Sometimes I have a great conversation with someone I've never met before. And of course, I have my regulars, people I see every day, and we talk about life. But I always keep my attention on the road.

6 PRESCHOOL TEACHER

Being with kids all day isn't for everyone, but I love it. I take care of children when their parents are away. I do all kinds of things – I teach, I play games, and I read books. I make sure the children are safe and happy. I have a lot of responsibility, but I love my job. It's very rewarding work even though the pay isn't great.

B Underline the words and phrases that helped you find the answers in part A.

5 First, use words from the list to complete each job title. Then choose the best expressions to compare the jobs in each sentence.

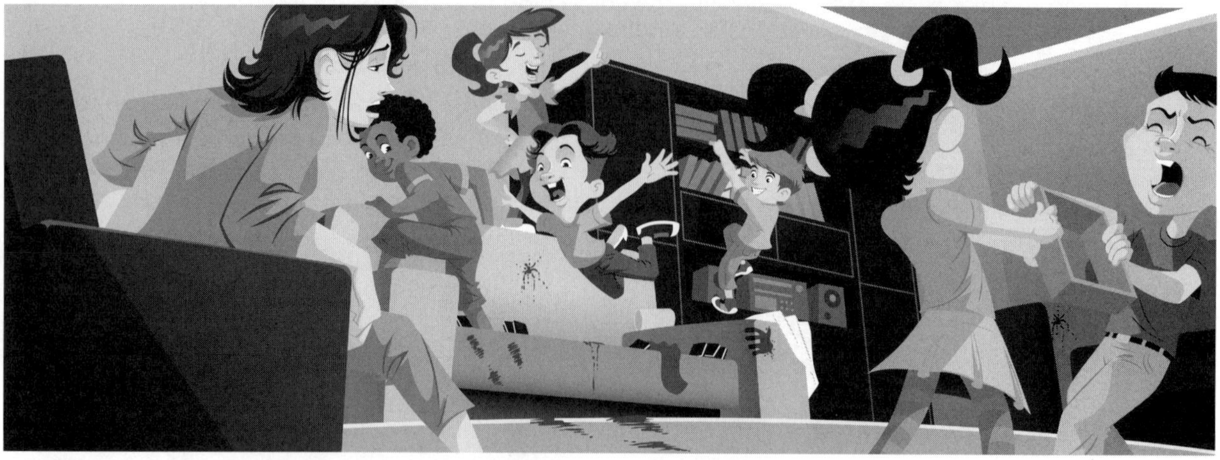

☑ assistant	☑ decorator	☑ painter	☑ walker
☑ counselor	☑ instructor	☑ ranger *guardabosque*	☑ worker

1. A child-care *worker* doesn't earn *(ganar)* *as much as* an accountant.
   - ☑ as much as ☐ greater than ☐ worse than
2. A chef's *assistant* has *worse hours than* a waiter.
   - ☑ worse hours than ☐ not as good hours ☐ as worse hours as
3. A dog *Walker* is *better paid than* a student intern.
   - ☐ more interesting than ☐ not as boring as ☑ better paid than
4. A house *painter* earns *more than* a camp counselor.
   - ☐ as bad as ☑ more than ☐ not more than
5. A park *ranger* is *not as well paid as* a landscaper.
   - ☐ as bad as ☑ not as well paid as ☐ worse than
6. Being a yoga *Instructor* is *not as difficult as* being a professor.
   - ☐ more than ☐ as much as ☑ not as difficult as
7. Being an interior *decorator* is *more interesting than* being a sales assistant.
   - ☐ greater than ☐ earns more than ☑ more interesting than
8. A guidance *counselor* has *more responsability than* a gardener.
   - ☑ more responsibility than ☐ not more than ☐ not as long as

6 Complete these sentences with the correct prepositions. Some of the prepositions may be used more than once. More than one answer may be possible.

☑ as
☑ at
☑ in
☑ on
☑ with

1. Chonglin works *at/in* the best Chinese restaurant in Los Angeles.
2. I think working *with* other people is more fun than working alone.
3. I would hate working *in/with* the media. It would be nerve-racking!
4. Working *as/with* a dance instructor sounds great.
5. Working *in/at* an office is less interesting than working *on* a cruise ship.

7 Use the words in parentheses to compare the jobs.

Assistant needed at an outdoor swimming pool. Must be able to swim. Responsible for keeping pool and changing rooms clean. $12/hour. Tues.–Fri. 12–7.

Learn web design!
In search of a bright young person to work as an intern for an advertising agency. Some clerical work. $15/hour. Mon.–Fri. 9–5.

1. A: An assistant at a swimming pool has shorter hours than an intern.
(shorter hours)
B: Yes, but working as an intern is more interesting than being a swimming pool assistant.
(interesting)

Travel agency needs energetic people. Knowledge of a second language is a plus. Mostly answering the phone. $18/hour. Flexible hours. Five vacation days a year.

Tutors in math, science, English, and music wanted at private summer school. Challenging work with gifted teenagers. Salary negotiable. Mon.–Sat. 3–7.

2. A: Working in a travel agency has better benefits. than working as a tutor
(better benefits)
B: Yes, but working as a tutor is more challenging than being a travel agency
(challenging)

Tennis instructor needed at summer camp for 12- and 13-year-olds. Must be excellent tennis player and good with kids. $18/hour. Mon.–Fri. 1–7.

Tour company seeks **guide** to lead bus tours. Great attitude and good speaking voice a must! Fun work, but must be willing to work long hours. $15/hour.

3. A: A tour guide doesn't make as much money as a tennis instructor
(make as much money)
B: that's true. And a tour guide has to work longer hours than a tennis instructor
(work longer hours)

City seeks **taxi drivers** for morning shift. No experience necessary; driver's license required. $15/hour plus tips. Mon.–Thu. 7 A.M.–2 P.M.

Office assistant required in small, friendly office. Computer skills an advantage. Interesting work. Some management skills necessary. $20/hour. 6-day week.

4. A: Working as taxi driver has a shorter work week than office assistants
(a shorter work week)
B: Yes, but being an office assistant is less boring than being a taxi driver
(less boring)

8 Choose four pairs of jobs from the box below to compare. Say which job you would prefer and give two reasons.

- a graphic designer/a TV news director
- an architect/a teacher
- a guidance counselor/a coach
- a doctor/a musician
- a police officer/a politician
- a secret agent/a psychiatrist
- working on a construction site/working in an office
- being self-employed/working for a company

Example: Working as a TV news director sounds more interesting than being a graphic designer. A TV news director has more responsibility than a graphic designer. Also, directing the news is better paid.

1. Working as an architect is more challenging than working as a teacher. The architect need more creativity than a teacher. Also I think being an architect is better paid
2. Being an musician sounds more interesting than working as a doctor. The musician has more fun and less stress Than a doctor. But the Doctor has a better paid
3. Working as a police officer is more dangerous than being a politician. The Police officer working all the time in the streets. But Being a Politician is safe all the time.
4. Being self-emplayed is more stressfull than working for a company. Being self-employed working more than working for a company. Also many times has better paid.

3 Lend a hand.

1 Would you mind . . . ?

A Complete the request for each situation.

1. You want to borrow a classmate's pen.

   Can I borrow your pen?

2. You want a classmate to give you a ride home after class.

   Would you mind giving me a ride home after class

3. You want to turn down your roommate's TV.

   Is it OK if I turn down your TV?

4. You want to use a friend's cell phone.

   Do you mind if I use your cell phone?

5. You want to borrow a friend's car for the weekend.

   I was wondering if I could borrow your car for the weekend?

6. You want someone to tell you how to get to the subway.

   Could you tell me how to get to the subway?

B Think of four more things you would need to have done if you were going on a long vacation. Write requests asking a friend to do the things.

1. Could you water the plants?
2. Could you put food for the fishes?
3. Do you mind feed the cat? • would you mind feeding my cat?
4. Is it OK if you care my fish?
5. Can you open the windows?

• I was wondering if you could collect my mail?
• Do you mind checking on my house a few times?

2 Accept or decline these requests. For requests you decline, give excuses. Use the expressions in the chart or expressions of your own.

Accepting	Declining
That's OK, I guess.	Sorry, but . . .
I'd be glad to.	I'd like to, but . . .
Fine. No problem.	Unfortunately, . . .

1. **A:** Can I use your computer? My computer crashed.
   B: Sorry, but I'm going to use it myself in a few minutes.
2. **A:** I've just finished this ten-page paper. Could you check it for me, please?
   B: fine, No Problem
3. **A:** I was wondering if I could stay at your place for a week while my landlord fixes the roof.
   B: That's ok, I guess
4. **A:** Would you mind if I used your cell phone to make a long-distance call to Nigeria?
   B: I'd like to, but my cell phon don't have batterie.

3 Look at the pictures and write the conversations. Speaker A makes a request. Speaker B declines it. Each speaker should give a reason.

1. **A:** Could you carry these boxes for me? I have a bad back.
   B: Sorry, but I have a bad back, too.

2. **A:** Do you mine washing the dishes?
   B: Sorry, but is not my turn.

3. **A:** Would you mind helped with this list?
   B: That's ok, I guess

• can you do this chores for me?

4 Getting what you want

A Scan the magazine article about making requests. What strategies can you use for less formal requests? What strategies can you use for more formal requests?

The Art of Making Requests

When you make a request, it helps to be clear about two things: Firstly, how well do you know the other person? Secondly, how important is it for you to get what you want? Are you willing to take "no" for an answer?

Let's say that you would like to borrow someone's car to go out on Friday night. Because borrowing a car is a big favor, we can assume that you'd probably only ask someone you know well for this favor. In general, when making requests of friends or close acquaintances, you can use a less formal approach.

Now let's imagine that it's very important for you to have that car on Friday night; you have to have it. In that case, you can let the other person know in a less formal, direct way. Here are two possible strategies:

1. Make a statement with *need*: "I need to borrow your car."
2. Use an imperative: "Please lend me your car."

By avoiding questions, this approach makes it more difficult for the other person to say no. If you are willing to put the other person in a possibly awkward situation, then this is definitely the clearest, and perhaps most effective, way of getting what you want.

But maybe you expect the other person to say no, and you can live with that. This attitude allows you to have a cooler, more objective perspective, so you can make your request in a more formal, indirect way.

Here are some examples:

3. Ask about ability: "Could/Can you lend me your car?"
4. Be polite – use *may*: "May I borrow your car?"
5. Ask for permission: "Would it be OK if I borrowed your car?"
6. Express curiosity: "I wonder if I could borrow your car."
7. State the request negatively: "I don't suppose you could lend me your car."
8. Apologize: "I hope you don't mind my asking, but could I borrow your car?"
9. Give a hint: "I have plans for Friday night, but I don't have a car."

This approach gives the other person a polite way to refuse if, for any reason, they don't want to or cannot lend you their car. And even though you know the person well, taking a more formal approach proves to the listener that you realize what a big favor you're asking. It shows them respect and appreciation – which makes it more likely that you'll get the result you want!

B Read the article. Check (✓) if each request is less formal or more formal. Then write the correct number from the article (1–9) for each type of request. Only eight of the numbers will be used.

	Less formal	More formal	Type
1. Close the door.	☑	☐	2 ✓
2. It's really cold in here.	☐	☑	9 ✓
3. Could you possibly move your car?	☐	☑	3 ✓
4. May I borrow your dictionary?	☐	☑	4 ✓
5. I was wondering if you could help me with this assignment.	☐	☑	6 ✓
6. I need some help moving to my new apartment.	☑	☐	1 ✓
7. I'm sorry, but I can't stand loud music.	☐	☑	8 ✓
8. I don't suppose I could borrow your camera.	☐	☑	7 ✓

5 Nouns and verbs

A Complete this chart. Then check your answers in a dictionary.

Noun	Verb	Noun	Verb
apology	apologize	invitation	invite ✓
compliment	compliment ✓	permission	permit ✓
explanation	explain ✓	request	request ✓

B Check (✓) the phrase that describes what each person is doing.

1. Don't worry. I know you didn't mean to break it.
 - ☐ returning a favor
 - ☑ accepting an apology

2. I really like your new haircut.
 - ☐ giving a reason
 - ☑ giving a compliment

3. Can I borrow your laptop?
 - ☑ asking for a favor
 - ☐ giving a gift

4. I can't lend you my bike because I need it myself. *Prester*
 - ☑ declining a request
 - ☐ accepting an invitation

5. Could you help me cook dinner?
 - ☑ making a request
 - ☐ returning a compliment

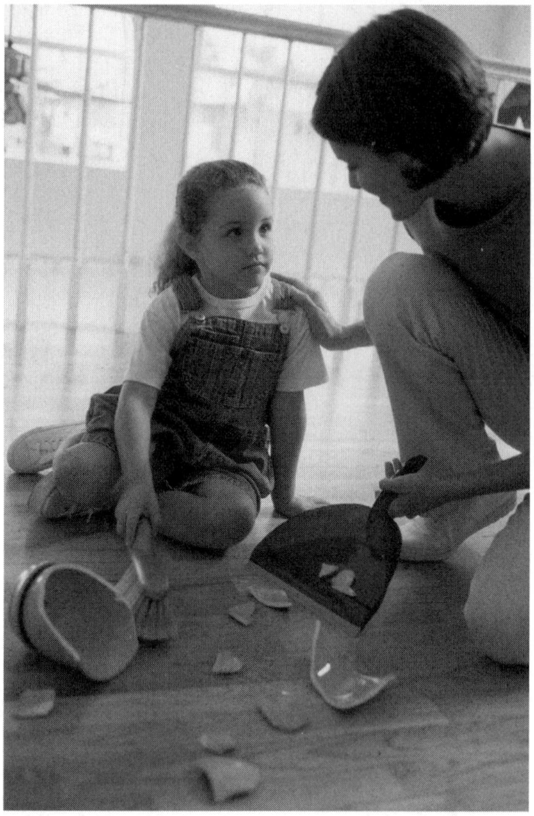

6 Choose the correct words.

1. My phone didn't work for a week. The phone company _offered_ ✓
 an apology and took $20 off my bill. (accepted / denied / offered)

2. A friend of mine really loves to _receive_ compliments, but he
 never gives anyone else one. I don't understand why he's like that. ✓
 (do / owe *deber* / receive)

3. Diane is always talking on the phone. She makes a lot of calls, but she
 rarely _returns_ mine. Maybe she never listens to her voice mail! ✓
 (makes / offers / returns)

4. I need to _ask for_ a favor. Could you please give me a ride to
 school tomorrow? My bike has a flat tire! (ask for / give / turn down) ✓

7 Use these messages to complete the phone conversations. Use indirect requests.

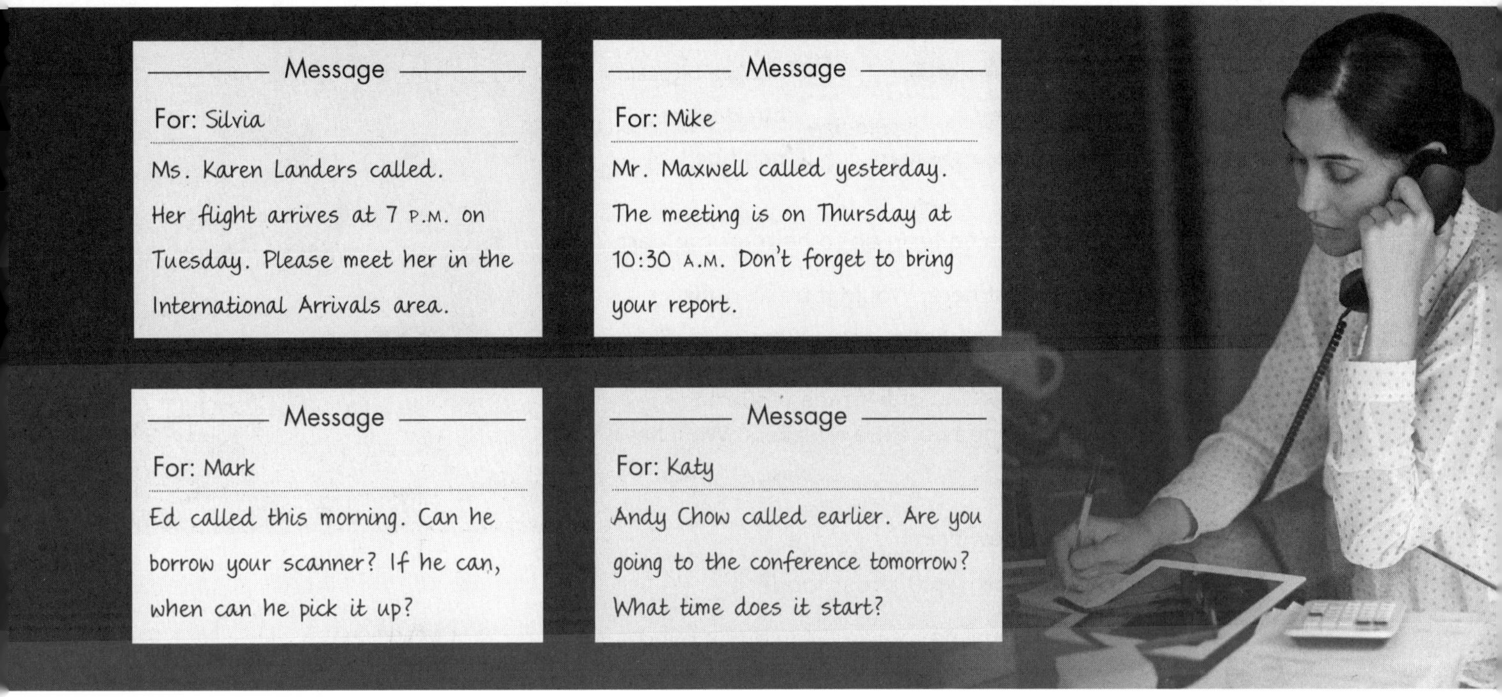
Message
For: Silvia
Ms. Karen Landers called.
Her flight arrives at 7 P.M. on Tuesday. Please meet her in the International Arrivals area.
Message
For: Mike
Mr. Maxwell called yesterday.
The meeting is on Thursday at 10:30 A.M. Don't forget to bring your report.
Message
For: Mark
Ed called this morning. Can he borrow your scanner? If he can, when can he pick it up?
Message
For: Katy
Andy Chow called earlier. Are you going to the conference tomorrow? What time does it start?

1. **A:** Is Silvia Vega there, please?
   B: No, she isn't. Would you like to leave a message?
   A: Yes, please. This is Karen Landers calling from Toronto.
   Could you tell her that my flight arrives at 7 P.M. on Tuesday?
   Would you ask Silvia if she meet me in the international Arrivals area? ✗
   • she mind meeting me in the international arrival area
   B: OK, I'll give her the message.
2. **A:** Can I speak to Mark, please?
   B: I'm afraid he's not here. Do you want to leave a message?
   • ask him if I can borrow his scanner?
   A: Yes, please. This is Ed. Please can you ask his if he's borrowed your scanner? ✗
   And if it's OK, could you tell me when I can pick it up? ✗ ?
   • ask him when I can pick it up?
   B: Sure, I'll leave him the message.
3. **A:** Could I speak to Mike, please?
   B: I'm sorry, but he's not here right now.
   A: Oh, OK. This is Mr. Maxwell. I'd like to leave a message.
   Could you tell him that the meeting is on Thursday at 10:30 am?
   Could you also tell him no to forget to bring his reports ✓ ?
4. **A:** I'd like to speak to Katy, please.
   B: She's not here right now. Can I take a message?
   A: Yeah. This is Andy Chow.
   Can you ask Katy if she's going to the conference tomorrow ✓ ?
   And would you ask her what time it starts ✓ ?
   B: OK, I'll give Katy your message.

8 Complete the conversation with the information in the box. Add any words necessary and use the correct form of the verbs given.

☑ ask Kelly to get some soda	☑ bring a big salad
☑ borrow some money	☑ buy dessert
☑ borrow your wireless speaker	☑ don't be late

Dan: So, is there anything I can do to help for the party?

Mark: Yeah. I have a list here. Would it be all right _if I borrowed your wireless speaker_? Mine isn't working very well.

Dan: Sure. And I'll bring two extra speakers. We'll have amazing sound.

Mark: Thanks.

Dan: No problem. Now, what about food?

Mark: Well, I thought maybe a salad. Would you mind _bringing a big salad_, too?

Dan: Well, OK. And how about drinks?

Mark: Well, could you _ask Kelly to get some soda_? And please tell her _not to be late_. Last time we had a party, she didn't arrive till eleven o'clock, and everyone got really thirsty!

Dan: I remember.

Mark: One more thing – I was wondering if you could _buy dessert_.

Dan: Um, sure. All right. But, uh, would you mind if I _borrowed some money_ to pay for it?

9 Rewrite these sentences. Find another way to say each sentence using the words given.

1. Can I use your cell phone?
   Would it be OK if I used your cell phone? (OK)
2. Please ask Annie to stop by and talk to me.
   Would you ask Annie to stop by on talk to me (would)
3. Could I borrow your guitar?
   I was wondering if I could borrow your guitar (wonder)
4. Would you ask Mitch what time he's coming over?
   could you ask Mitch when he's coming over? (could / when)
5. Lend me your hairbrush.
   Would you mind lending me your hairbrush. (mind)

What happened?

1 Complete these news stories using the verbs from the box.

1.

☑ broke	☑ found	☑ locking	☑ stayed	☑ went
☑ drank	☑ heard	☑ shouted	☑ waiting	☐ wondered

grito *Preguntarsal*

WOMAN TRAPPED IN BATHROOM FOR 20 DAYS

A 69-year-old grandmother in Paris _____went_____ to the bathroom – and __stayed__ ✓ there for twenty days. What happened? As she was __locking__ ✓ the door, the lock __broke__ ✓. She could not open the door. She __shouted__ ✓ for help, but no one __heard__ ✓ her because her bathroom had no windows. After nearly three weeks, the woman's neighbors __wondered__ where she was. Firefighters broke into her apartment and __found__ her *debilitado* in a "very weakened" state. While she was __waiting__ ✓ to be rescued, she __drank__ ✓ warm water.

2.

☐ became	☑ checking in	☑ entered	☐ opened	☑ sleeping
☑ behaving	☐ decided	☐ had	☑ showed	

TIGER CUB FOUND IN LUGGAGE

A woman was __behaving__ */extrañamente* strangely when she __entered__ the Bangkok airport. While she was __checking in__ for an overseas flight, she __had__ ✓ difficulty with a very large bag. The check-in clerk __became__ suspicious and __decided__ to X-ray the bag. The X-ray __showed__ ✓ an image that looked like an animal. When airport staff __opened__ the bag, they saw that a baby tiger was __sleeping__ ✓ under lots of toy tigers. The tiger was taken to a rescue center for wildlife, and the woman was arrested.

2 Join each sentence in column A with an appropriate sentence in column B. Use *as*, *when*, or *while* to join the sentences.

A	B
I was crossing the road.	My racket broke.
I was using my computer.	A car nearly hit me.
We were playing tennis.	The water got cold.
I was taking a shower.	I burned my finger.
I was cooking dinner.	It suddenly stopped working.

1. As I was crossing the road, a car nearly hit me.
2. When I was using my computer, it suddendly stopped workin
3. While we were playing tenny, my racket broke
4. When I was taking a shower, the water got cold
5. As I was cooking dinner, I burned my finger

3 Complete these conversations. Use the simple past or the past continuous of the verbs given.

1. **A:** Guess what happened to me last night! As I was getting (get) into bed, I heard (hear) a loud noise like a gunshot in the street. Then the phone rang (ring).

   B: Who was it?

   A: It was Luisa. She always calls me late at night, but this time she had a reason. She was driving (drive) right past my apartment when she got (get) a flat tire. It was very late, so while we were changing (change) the tire, I invited (invite) her to spend the night.

2. **A:** I'm sorry I'm so late, Erin. I was at the dentist.

   B: Don't tell me! While you were sitting (sit) in the waiting room, you met (meet) someone interesting. I know how you are, Matt!

   A: Well, you're wrong this time. The dentist was cleaning (clean) my teeth when she suddenly got (get) called away for an emergency. So I just sat there waiting for two hours with my mouth hanging open!

4 Lost and found

A Read this news story. Who is it about? Where did it take place?

Thank you, Andre Botha!

Surfing at the Pipeline

On December 6, 2015, Andre Botha was in the water, watching the big waves at the Pipeline off the island of Oahu, Hawaii, when he noticed something strange. The two-time world bodyboarding champion realized that professional champion surfer Evan Geiselman was in big trouble. Since the Pipeline has some of the biggest waves in the world and is considered to be the most dangerous place on the planet for surfing, situations like this are, unfortunately, not uncommon.

Botha realized that the surfer, who had entered the inside of a huge wave and was riding it, was knocked off his surfboard when the wave crashed on him. Normally a surfer will come up to the surface of the water a few moments after falling off the board. But there was no sign of Geiselman. Botha began to swim on his bodyboard as fast as he could to where the surfboard was being thrown around by the huge waves. When he reached the surfboard, he saw Geiselman, who looked like he might be dead. The surfer was unconscious and his face was turning blue as Botha tried to bring him back to life in the water. Botha breathed into Geiselman's mouth and hit him on the chest to get him breathing again. Then he began to swim to shore with the surfer's unconscious body. Two lifeguards swam out to meet him, and they brought Geiselman to a hospital.

Surfers and bodyboarders agree that Evan Geiselman would probably not be alive today if Andre Botha had not rescued him. They don't always agree about which sport is best, but surfers and bodyboarders do agree that taking care of each other in the big waves is important. This respect and care for people is a wonderful part of these exciting sports.

Bodyboarding

B Use the article to answer these questions.

1. In what sport is Andre Botha a two-time champion?
   Bodyboarding
2. What sport does Evan Geiselman excel at as a champion?
   Professional champion surfer - Surfing
3. Where is the Pipeline located?
   Island of Oahu - Hawaii
4. What is one way you can help an unconscious person start breathing?
   breathe into their mouth and hit their chest (CPR)
5. Who brought Geiselman to the hospital?
   Two lifeguards.
6. What helps make bodyboarding and surfing such wonderful sports?
   The respect and care of each other

5 Think of a real or imaginary problem like the one in Exercise 4. Write two paragraphs. In the first paragraph, describe your problem. In the second, say how you solved it.

A couple weeks ago, I was shopping in the supermarket because I needed many stuff for the bath time, things for my child and something for cooking. I spent around three hour searching everthin, at the moment for pay I noted my wallet not were in my purse, I felt frustrated, tired and a litterbit angry, So I decided call my mother in law and she went and she paid for everything.

A couple of years ago, I got lost in the mountains. I was hiking when it suddenly got foggy (nublado). I was really frightened (asustado) because I couldn't see anything, and it was getting cold (enfriandose). I decided to put up my tent and stay there for the night.

While I was putting up my tent, though, the fog began to clear. . . .

6 Choose the correct verbs to complete the story.

Grammar note: *After*

In sentences using *after* that show one past event occurring before another, the clause with *after* usually uses the past perfect.
After she **had called** her friend, her cell phone battery died.

Andy and I ___had just gotten___ (acababamos) engaged, so we (just got / had just gotten) went to a jewelry store to buy a wedding ring. We ___had just chosen___ a ring when a (just chose / had just chosen) masked man ___came in___. After the robber ___took___ Andy's (came in / had come in) (took / had taken) wallet, he ___had demanded___ the ring. I ___had just handed___ it to him when the (demanded / had demanded) (just handed / had just handed) alarm ___started___ to go off, and the robber ___ran off___. We were (started / had started) (ran off / had run off) so relieved! But then the sales assistant ___told___ us we had to pay for the ring (told / had told) because I ___gave___ it to the robber. We ___just told___ her (gave / had given) (just told / had just told) that we wouldn't pay for it when the police ___arrived___ and (arrived / had arrived) ___arrested___ us! What a terrible experience! (arrested / had arrested)

7 What a story!

A Choose the best headline for each of these news stories.

What a disaster! **What a triumph!**

What an emergency! **What a lucky break!** **What a dilemma!**

1. WHAT AN EMERGENCY

Karen Lane was seven months pregnant when she and her husband, Scott, went on vacation to a small **remote** island off the coast of South America. On the first night, Karen was in a lot of pain. There were no doctors on the island, so Scott called a hospital on the **mainland**. They told him they could not send a helicopter because a typhoon was coming. During the night, Karen thought she was going to die. Luckily, the typhoon had passed over the island by the following morning. A helicopter picked Karen up and took her to the hospital – just in time for her to have a beautiful baby girl.

2. WHAT A TRIUMPH

Serena Mills was very sick for several months before her final exams this summer. She couldn't study at all. Her parents suggested she should **skip** a year and take the exams the next summer. **Remarkably** (notablemente), Serena suddenly (repentinamente salió bien) got well just before the exams, spent two weeks studying, and got the highest grade in her class!

3. WHAT A DILEMMA

Mark Blaine had waited years for a **promotion**. Finally, a week ago, he was offered the position he had always wanted – Regional Manager. On the same day, however, he won $6 million in the lottery. Mark's wife wants him to **resign** from his job and take her on a trip around the world. Mark says he cannot decide what to do.

B Look at the words in bold in the articles. What do you think they mean?

remote far away skip miss promotion higher position

mainland larger land / continent remarkably amazingly resign quit

8 Complete the sentences. Use the simple past, the past continuous, or the past perfect of the verbs given.

1. In 2011, two divers discovered (discover) the remains (permanece) of a 200-year-old shipwreck (naufragio) while they were diving (dive) off the coast of Rhode Island, in the eastern United States.
2. After an art show opened (open) in New York, it was discovered that someone had hung (hang) a famous painting by Henri Matisse upside down.
3. In 2015, workers found (find) a chemistry lab from the 1840s while they work repairing (repair) a building at the University of Virginia in the United States. The lab was behind a wall of the current building.
4. Chile's Calbuco volcano surprised (surprise) residents of Santiago when it erupted in 2015. Before that, an eruption of Calbuco had not happened (not happen) for over 40 years.

MPLE PAST: I went to the movies last night
ST CONTINOUS I was taking a shower when the phone rang
ST PERFECT when Obama came to power I had already bought my house

9 Read this situation. Then use the information and clues to complete the chart. Write the name of each reporter and each country. (You will leave one square in the chart blank.)

Five news reporters – two women and three men – arrived for an international conference on Sunday, Monday, and Tuesday.

No more than two people came on the same day. The reporters came from five different countries.

Clues

The women: Ms. Johnson and Ms. Marshall

The men: Mr. James, Mr. Grant, and Mr. Simpson

The countries: Australia, Mexico, Brazil, Singapore, and the United States

The arrivals:

- Mr. Simpson arrived late at night. No one else had arrived that day.
- Ms. Johnson and Mr. Grant arrived on the same day.
- The man who came from Singapore had arrived the day before.
- The reporters who came from Brazil and Australia arrived on the same day.
- Mr. James and the woman who came from Brazil arrived on Tuesday, after Mr. Grant.
- The reporter from Australia arrived the day after the person who came from the United States.
- Mr. Grant came from North America but not the United States.

Reporters' countries and arrival days				
Sunday	Name:	Mr Simpson	Name:	
	Country:	Singapore	Country:	
Monday	Name:	Mr Grant	Name:	Ms Johnson
	Country:	Mexico	Country:	United States
Tuesday	Name:	Mr James	Name:	Ms Marshal
	Country:	Australia	Country:	Brazil

5 Expanding your horizons

1 **Complete these sentences. Use words from the box.**

☑ confident	☑ depressed	☑ fascinated	☐ uncomfortable
☑ curious	☑ embarrassed	☑ uncertain	☑ worried

1. In my country, people never leave tips. So when I first went abroad, I kept forgetting to tip servers. I felt really ___embarrassed___.

2. The first time I traveled abroad, I felt really ___depressed___. I was alone, I didn't speak the language, and I didn't make any friends.

3. I just spent a year in France learning to speak French. It was a satisfying experience, and I was ___fascinated___ by the culture.

4. At first I really didn't like shopping in the open-air markets. I felt ___uncomfortable___ because so many people were trying to sell me something at the same time.

5. When I arrived in Lisbon, I was nervous because I couldn't speak any Portuguese. As I began to learn the language, though, I became more ___confident___ about living there.

6. Before I went to Alaska last winter, I was very ___worried___ about the cold. But it wasn't a problem because most buildings there are well heated.

7. When I was traveling in Southeast Asia, I couldn't believe how many different kinds of fruit there were. I was ___curious___ to try all of them, so I ate a lot of fruit!

8. It was our first trip to Latin America, so we were ___uncertain___ about what to expect. We loved it and hope to return again soon.

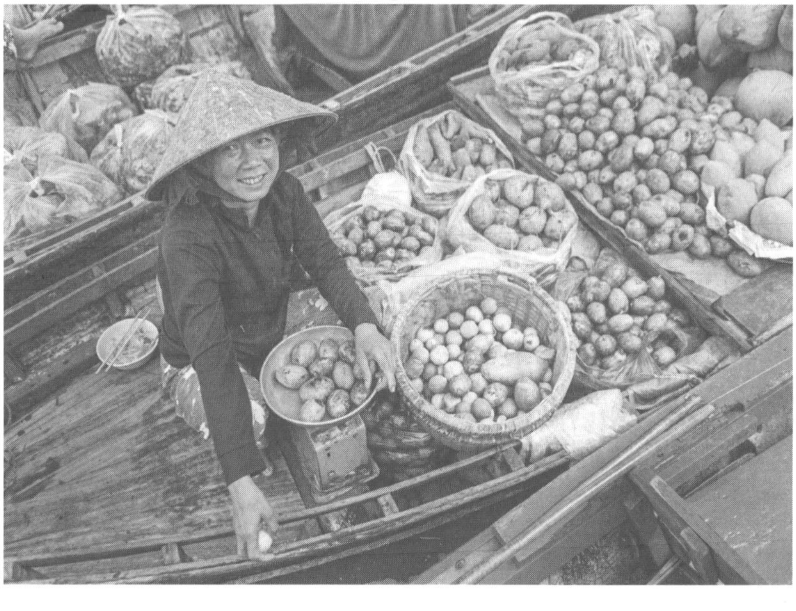

2 Imagine you are going to travel to a country you have never visited before. Write sentences using the factors and feelings given. Then add another sentence explaining your feelings.

Factors	Feelings
✓public transportation	✓anxious (about)
✓shopping	comfortable (with)
✓the climate	curious (about)
the food	enthusiastic (about)
the language	fascinated (by)
the money	nervous (about)
the music	uncertain (about)
the people my age	uncomfortable (with)

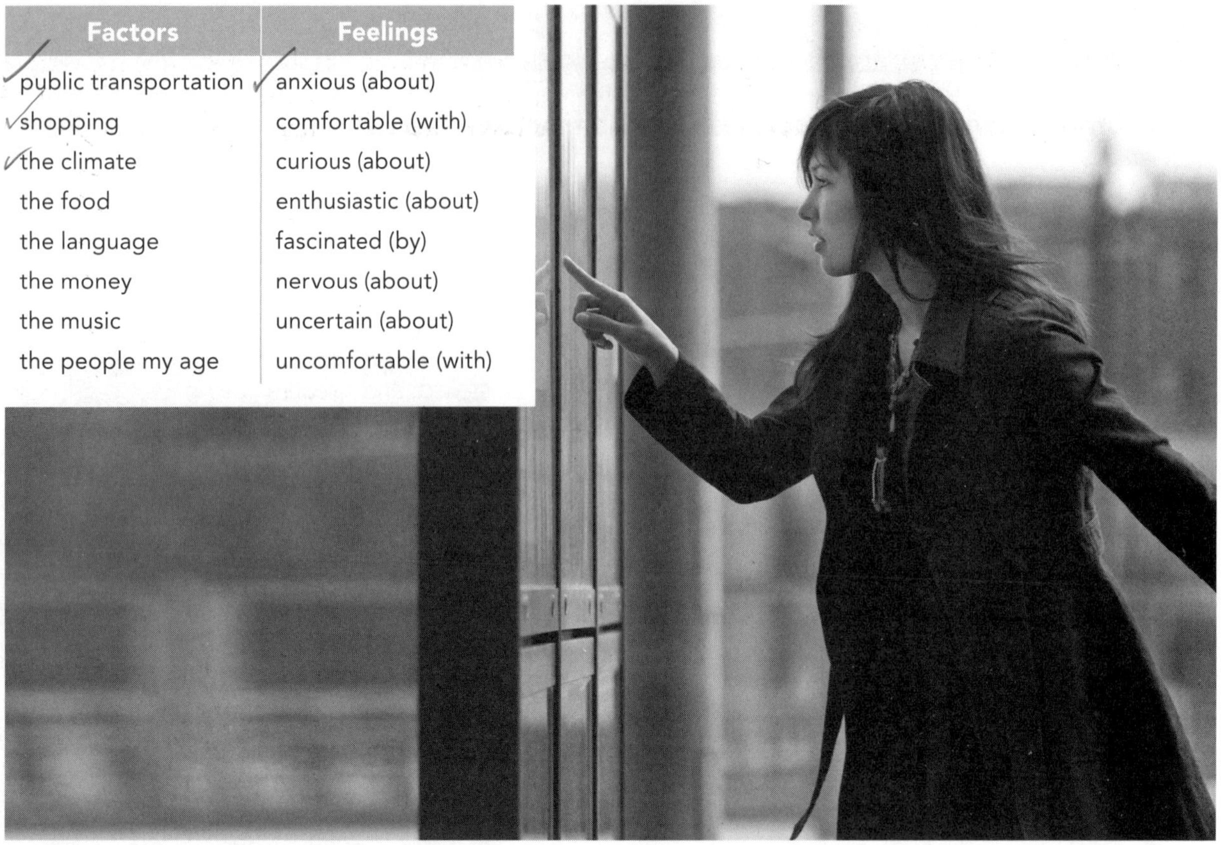

1. Public transportation is something I'd be anxious about. I'd be afraid of getting lost.

2. Shopping is something I'd be comfortable with. I'd be entertened

3. The climate

4. The food is something I'd be curious about.

5. The language is

6. The money

7. The music is something I'd be uncertain

8. The people my age is with I'd feel uncomfortable.

9. _____

3 Culture shock!

A Make a list of four pieces of advice to help people feel comfortable about traveling abroad.

B Scan the article about cultural differences. Where can you find articles like this? Who was it written for?

Culture Shock

Each society has its own beliefs, attitudes, customs, behaviors, and social habits. These things give people a sense of who they are and how they are supposed to behave.

People become conscious of such rules when they meet people from different cultures. For example, the rules about when to eat vary from culture to culture. Many North Americans and Europeans organize their timetables around three mealtimes a day. In other countries, however, it's not the custom to have strict rules like this – people eat when they want to, and every family has its own timetable.

When people visit or live in a country for the first time, they are often surprised at the differences between this culture and the culture in their own country. For some people, traveling abroad is the thing they enjoy most in life; for others, cultural differences make them feel uncomfortable, frightened, and insecure. This is known as "culture shock."

When you're visiting a foreign country, it is important to understand and appreciate cultural differences. This can help you avoid misunderstandings, develop friendships more easily, and feel more comfortable when traveling or living abroad.

Here are several things to do in order to avoid culture shock.

1 Instead of criticizing, enjoy the new customs you discover each day on your trip as much as possible.

2 If you read or understand the language, read a local newspaper or listen to the radio to find out what news they're likely to be talking about.

3 Talk to people in order to understand their ideas about their own country as well as their thoughts about yours.

4 Remember the proverb, "When in Rome, do as the Romans do." It's a great way to start learning new things!

5 For instance, try one new thing every day, like a food you've never had before, instead of choosing something on the menu that you can have in your own country.

6 Read a book about the history of the place you are in so you will understand it better while you are there.

7 Go to concerts, museums, theatrical performances, and sporting events to appreciate the culture of this country.

8 Remember that traveling is an educational experience, so be ready to question the stereotypes you may have of another country, and learn about the stereotypes people in that country may have about the place you come from.

C Read the article. Use your own words to write definitions for these words.

1. culture ______
2. culture shock ______
3. appreciate ______
4. stereotypes ______

D After reading the article, would you make any changes to the pieces of advice you listed in part A?

4 Complete these sentences by giving information about customs in a country you know.

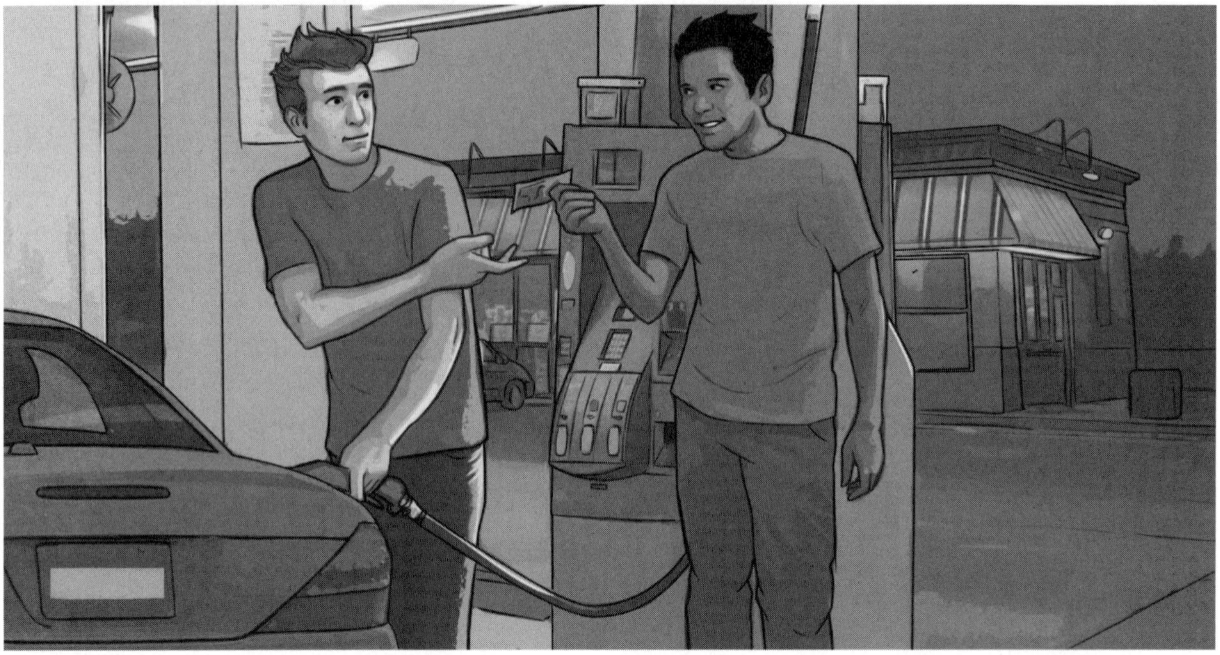

1. If you go for a long ride in a friend's car, it's the custom to offer to pay for some of the expenses.
2. When a friend graduates from school or college, It's the custom to send them a congratulation card
3. If you borrow something from a friend, give it back.
4. When a friend invites you to dinner, to bring a small gift

5 Contrasting customs

A Read the information about the different customs and find four pairs of countries with contrasting customs. Write the countries on the lines below.

Country	Custom
Brazil	Friends kiss each other three or four times on the cheeks as a greeting.
Denmark	People generally arrive on time for most occasions.
Egypt	People allow their hosts to treat them to meals in restaurants.
France	Service is usually included in the price of a meal in restaurants.
Japan	People bow when they see or meet someone they know.
New Zealand	People usually pay for their own meals in restaurants.
Spain	People usually arrive late for most appointments.
United States	People leave a tip of 15–20 percent in restaurants.

1. Brazil and Japan
2. United states, France
3. Denmart, Spain
4. New Zealand, Egypt

B Read these five cross-cultural situations. Write sentences describing what the visitors did wrong. Use the expressions in the box.

you're (not) supposed to
you're (not) expected to
it's (not) the custom to
it's (not) acceptable to

1. Enni is from Denmark. When she was on vacation in Spain, some Spanish friends invited her to dinner at 9:00. She arrived at exactly 9:00, but her friends had not even arrived home yet.

   In Spain, you're expected to arrive to dinner a few Minutes late

2. Kayla is from the United States. During her first week in Paris, she went to a restaurant with some new friends. She was so happy with the service that she left a tip of 20 percent. Her friends were a little embarrassed.

   In France, It's not the custom to tip restaurants.

3. James is from New Zealand. When he went to Egypt, he was invited to dinner at a restaurant. When the bill came, he offered to pay for his dinner. His Egyptian friend was kind of upset.

   In Egypt, when you are invited to dinner it's not acceptable to offer to pay for your dinner

4. Clara is from Brazil. She was working for a year in Osaka, Japan. One day, when she saw a Japanese co-worker in a bookstore, she went to say hello and kissed him on the cheeks. Her friend was very surprised.

   Because in Japan your not supposed to kiss your friends.

5. Brian is from Canada. He was on vacation in Bali, Indonesia, and some new friends invited him to a temple to watch a special dance performance. He arrived on time wearing a clean T-shirt and shorts, but they said he couldn't go inside the temple because he wasn't dressed properly.

   In Bali Indonesia it's not acceptable to wear short's an a T-shirt an a temple

6 Complete these sentences with information about yourself (1–4) and about a country you know well (5–8).

1. One reason I'd feel homesick abroad is ______
2. Something that would fascinate me would be ______
3. Traveling alone is something ______
4. Getting used to hot weather is one thing ______
5. In ______, it's the custom to ______
6. If you have good service in a restaurant, ______
7. You're expected to ______ when ______
8. It's just not acceptable to ______ if ______

7 Write about living in a foreign country. In the first paragraph, write about two things you would enjoy. In the second paragraph, write about two things you might worry about.

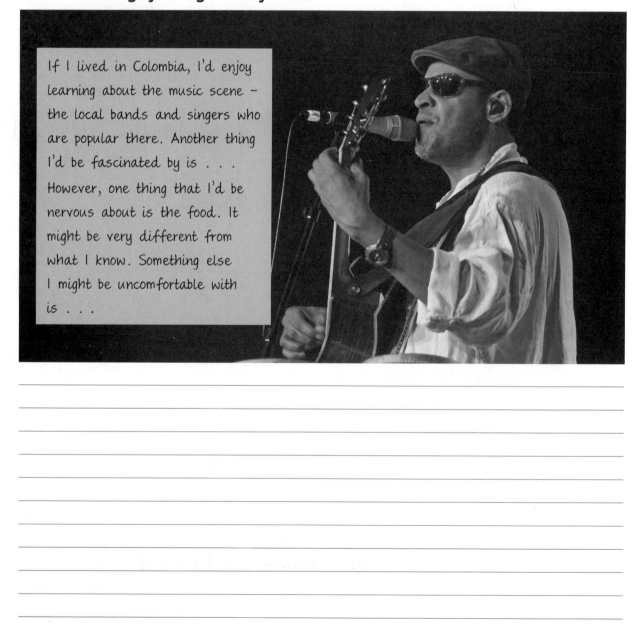

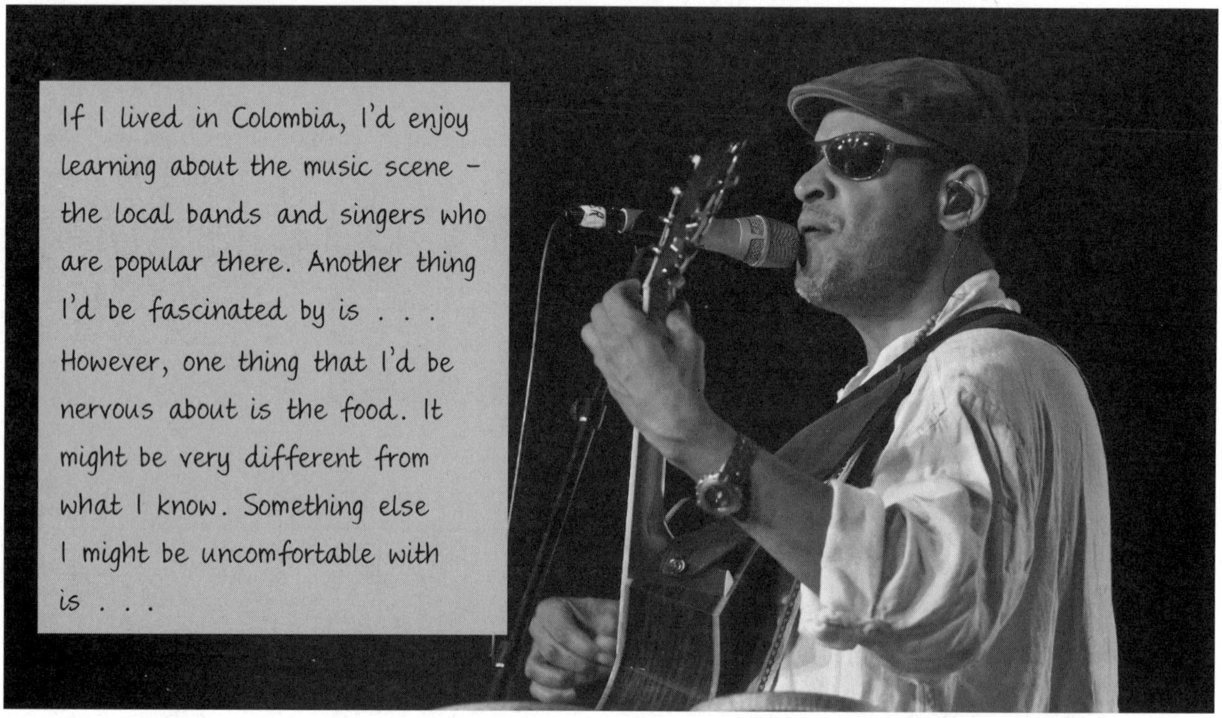
If I lived in Colombia, I'd enjoy learning about the music scene – the local bands and singers who are popular there. Another thing I'd be fascinated by is . . .
However, one thing that I'd be nervous about is the food. It might be very different from what I know. Something else I might be uncomfortable with is . . .

6 That needs fixing.

1 What's wrong with it?

A What can be wrong with these things? Put these words in the correct categories. (Most words go in more than one category.)

~~bike~~ ~~blouse~~ ~~car~~ ~~carpet~~ ~~chair~~ ~~glasses~~ ~~plate~~ ~~sink~~ ~~tablecloth~~

astillado chipped	grieta cracked	abollado dented	leaking	scratched	stained	rasgado torn
glasses	plate	bike car	sink	chair	blouse carpet	tablecloth

B What is wrong with these things? Use the words in part A to write a sentence about each one.

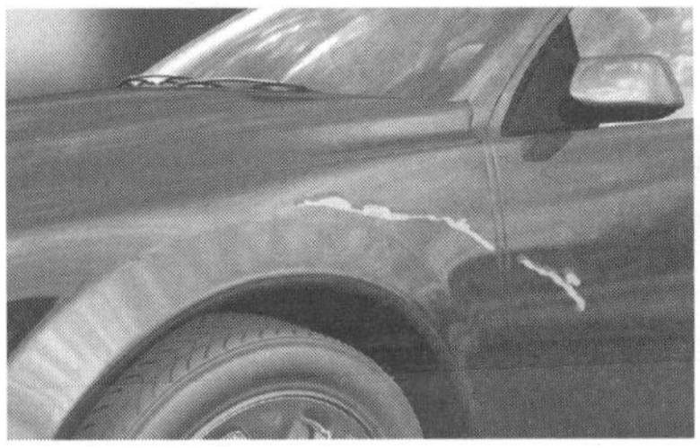

1. The car is scratched. OR There's a scratch on the car.

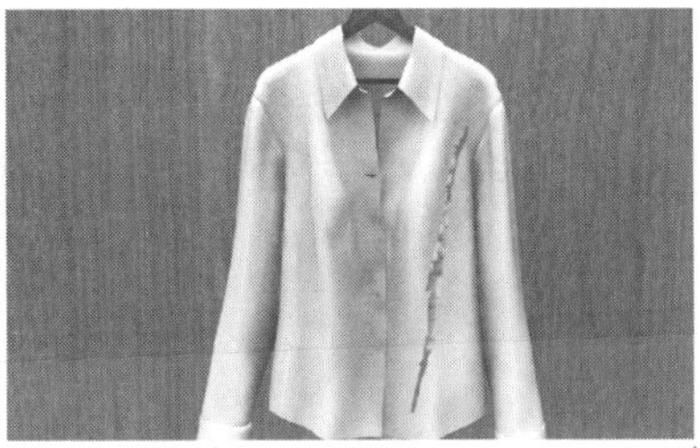

2. The blouse is stained. There's a stain on the blouse.

3. The carpet has a stain. The carpet is staned.

4. The bike is dented. There's a dent on the bike.

5. The sink is leaking. there's a leak on the sink.

6. The chair is scratched. There's a scratch on the chair.

7. The plate is chipped. There's a chip on the plate.

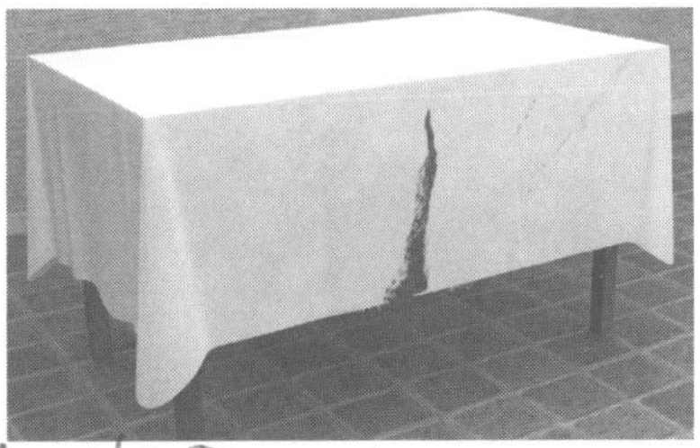

8. the Tablecloth is torn. there's a tear on the tablecloth.

9. The glasses is cracked. there're a crack on the glasses.

2 Problems, problems, problems!

A Scan the articles in *Consumer* magazine. Who would read articles like these? Why?

George's Class Trip

George Humphrey is a Spanish teacher at Crockett College in Duluth, Minnesota. Last year, George took his summer class from Duluth to Madrid, Spain. At the end of the six-week trip, George and the twenty students had a delayed flight at the airport in Madrid when they were coming home. Because of the six-hour delay in Madrid, they missed their plane from New York to Minnesota. Everyone had to stay at a hotel in New York City, and they all spent a lot more money than they had expected. They were also more than 24 hours late when they finally got back to Duluth. When George asked the airline office in New York to pay for their hotel and restaurant bills, the airline refused.

George contacted *Consumer* magazine. We talked to a representative of the airline office in Madrid and discovered that, in Europe, airlines must pay for delays – but that does not apply to airlines in the U.S. However, because the delay first occurred in Madrid, George and each student received 400 euros. George was very pleased, especially for his students. In his email to us, George wrote that he believes the law regarding airline delays needs changing in the U.S.

Diane's Vacation

Diane Gleason is a clothing designer in Cincinnati, Ohio. For her vacation last year, she decided to go somewhere she had never been – the southwestern part of the U.S. When she arrived at the airport in Phoenix, Arizona, she rented a beautiful red convertible for her trip. She planned to drive from Phoenix to the Grand Canyon to go hiking with friends for a few days. After she left the airport, Diane spent the night in Phoenix. The next morning, Diane discovered that someone had stolen the car from the parking lot. She called the car-rental agency, and they told her she was responsible for the cost of the car because she had left the keys in it. They would not let her rent another car until she paid for the stolen one. Diane didn't know what to do. She went back to the motel and contacted *Consumer* magazine.

We called the rental agency, and they told us that Diane had not bought special insurance for a stolen car. We told the agency that Diane needed help: she was all alone and feeling worried and depressed about what happened. The agency suggested that we contact Diane's credit card company. We did, and they told us that Diane was protected because of her credit card. They would pay for the stolen car! By evening, Diane had rented another car from the same agency and, that night, she had dinner at the Grand Canyon with her friends.

B Read the articles and complete the chart. Did George and Diane receive money?

	Problems	What *Consumer* magazine did	Received money? Yes	No
1. George's trip	delay in Madrid		☐	☐
2. Diane's vacation			☐	☐

3 Choose appropriate verbs to complete the sentences. Use passive infinitives (*to be* + past participle) or gerunds.

Language note: Verbs ending in *-en* or *-n*

Some verbs are formed by adding *-en* or *-n* to a noun or adjective.

These verbs mean "to make more of something."

Noun		**Verb**	**Adjective**		**Verb**
length	→	length**en**	loose	→	loose**n**
(make something longer)			(make something looser)		

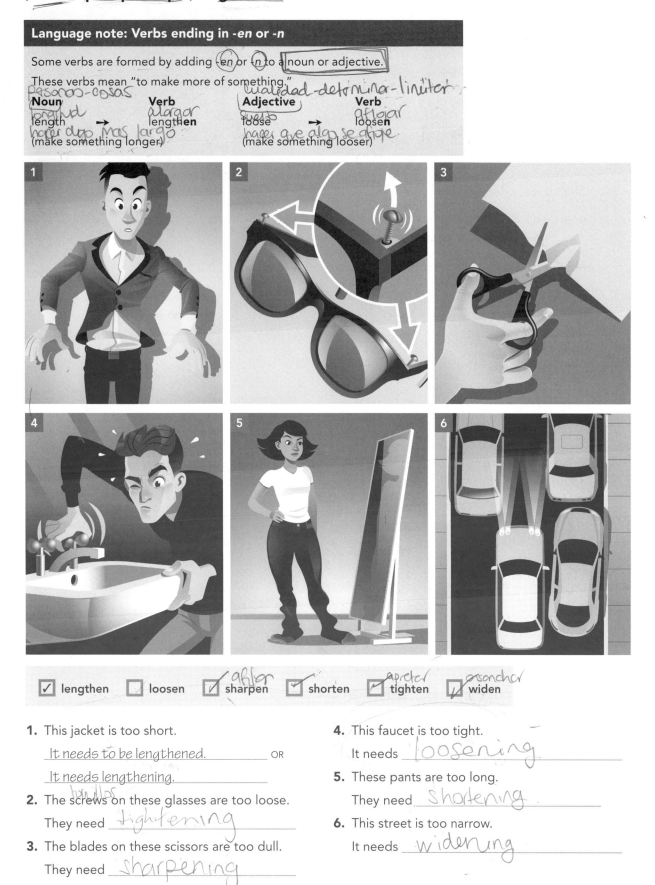

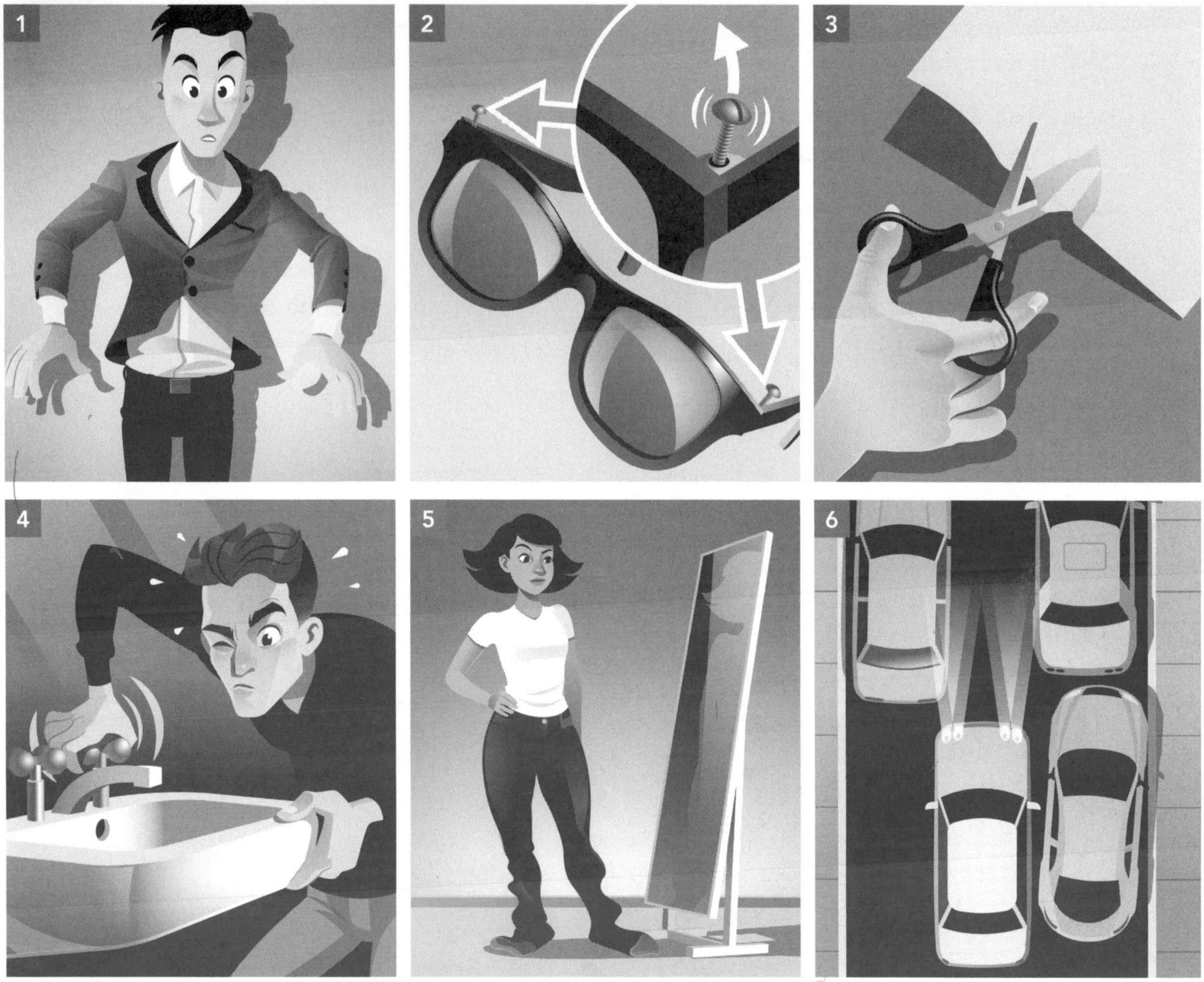

☑ lengthen ☐ loosen ☐ sharpen ☐ shorten ☐ tighten ☐ widen

1. This jacket is too short.
   It needs to be lengthened. OR
   It needs lengthening.
2. The screws on these glasses are too loose.
   They need tightening
3. The blades on these scissors are too dull.
   They need sharpening
4. This faucet is too tight.
   It needs loosening
5. These pants are too long.
   They need shortening
6. This street is too narrow.
   It needs widening

4 Complete the conversation. Use *keep, keeps, need,* or *needs* with passive infinitives or gerunds of the verbs given.

Jack: Guess what? Someone broke into my car last night!

Mia: Oh, no. What did they take?

Jack: Nothing! But they did a lot of damage. The lock needs to be repaired (repair). And the window to be replaced (replace).

Mia: It was probably some young kids having "fun."

Jack: Yeah, some fun. I think they had a party in my car! The seats needs cleaning (clean).

Mia: How annoying. Does the car drive OK?

Jack: No, it feels strange. The gears to be sticking (stick), so they needs fixed (fix). And the brakes keeps checking (check) right away.

Mia: Well, I guess you're lucky they didn't steal it!

Jack: Yeah, lucky me.

5 Write about something you bought that had something wrong with it. In the first paragraph, describe the problem. In the second paragraph, explain what you did about it.

Recently, I bought an espresso machine. While I was unpacking it, I could see it was already damaged. The glass carafe was chipped and needed to be replaced. And to make matters worse, the machine leaked!

I took it back to the store. I was worried because the machine had been on sale, and I had lost my receipt. Luckily, the clerk didn't ask me for it. She said a lot of customers had recently had the same problem, and she gave me a better machine at the same price.

6 Paul will fix it!

A Match each problem with the repair needed.

PAUL'S REPAIR SHOP

ITEM	PROBLEM	REPAIR NEEDED
1. ~~dishwasher~~	~~doesn't work~~ f	a. tighten and glue the legs
2. DVD player	DVD is stuck c	~~b.~~ repair the wire
3. speakers	(cable) wire is damaged b	~~c.~~ remove the DVD
4. dresser	mirror is cracked e	~~d.~~ repaint the door
5. stove	metal door is scratched d	~~e.~~ replace the mirror
6. table	legs are loose a	~~f.~~ check the motor

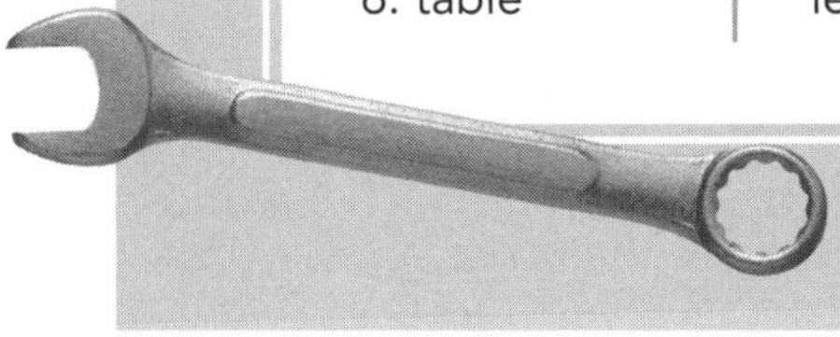

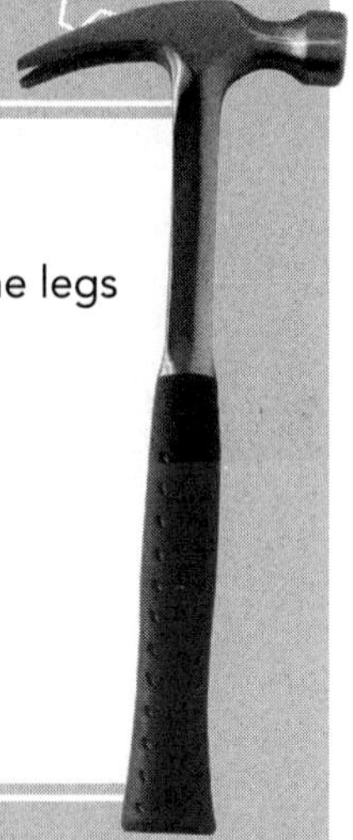

B Write a sentence describing each problem. Then add a sentence describing the action needed to fix it. Use passive infinitives or gerunds.

1. The dishwasher doesn't work. The motor needs to be checked. OR The motor needs checking.
2. The DVD is stuck. The DVD needs to be remoned. The DVD needs remoing
3. The wire Speakers is damage. The wire needs to be repaired. The wire needs repairing
4. The mirror of the dresser is cracked. The mirror needs to be replaced. The mirror needs replacing
5. The metal door of the stove has a scratch. The metal door needs to be repainted. The metal door needs repainting
6. the legs of the table are loose. The legs need to be tightened and glue. The legs needs tightening and glue.

C Think of three items you own that are damaged (or were damaged) in some way. Write a sentence describing each problem. Then write another sentence describing the action needed to fix it.

1. ______

2. ______

3. ______

7 Complete the sentences with the correct forms of the words in the box.

☑ chip	☑ drop	☑ freeze	☑ scratch
☑ clean	☑ fix	☐ jam	☑ stick
☑ die	☑ flicker	☑ leak	☑ torn

1. This cell phone is driving me crazy! My calls keep dropping.
2. Your computer screen is so dirty. It needs to be cleaned.
3. Something is wrong with your TV screen. It keeps flickring. It's time to get a new one.
4. I hate this printer. It keeps dying. The copies won't come out.
5. Be careful – your cup is chiped. I don't want you to cut yourself.
6. The buttons on this remote control keep stacking. Do you have something to clean it with?
7. Do you realize your jeans are torn in the back?
8. Your bathroom faucet keeps leaking. Do you want me to try to fix it?
9. My new glasses already have a scratched on one of the lenses. How did that happen?
10. Did your laptop freezing again? I find that so annoying.
11. This old scanner doesn't work at all anymore. It needs to be fixed.
12. The battery in my cell phone keeps jamming. I should buy a new one.

7 What can we do?

1 **Use the information in the pamphlet and the verbs and prepositions given below to change the sentences from the active to the passive.**

HERE ARE JUST SOME OF THE DANGERS FACING YOU AND YOUR CHILDREN.

The water we drink

1. Agricultural runoff is contaminating the water supply.
2. Chlorine and other additives have ruined the taste of our drinking water.

The food we eat

3. Certain agricultural pesticides have caused new illnesses.
4. Pollution from cars and trucks is destroying our crops.

The air we breathe

5. Factories are releasing dangerous chemicals.
6. Breathing smog every day has damaged many people's health.

The world we live in

7. The lack of rainfall has created more severe droughts.
8. Global warming is threatening our forests and wildlife.

Join **Save Our Planet** today!

1. The water supply is being contaminated due to agricultural runoff. (due to)
2. The taste of our drinking water has been ruined by the chlorine and other additives (by)
3. New illnesses are being caused by agricultural pesticides. (by)
4. Our crops are being destroyed because of pollution from cars and trucks (because of)
5. Dangerous chemicals are being released by factories (by)
6. Peoples health has been damaged as result of breathed smog every day (as a result of)
7. Severe droughts has been created through the lack of rainfall (through)
8. Our forests and wildlife is being threated by Global warming (by)

2 Verbs and nouns

A Complete the chart.

Verb	Noun	Verb	Noun
contaminate	contamination	educate	education
contribute	Contribution	pollute	pollution
Create	creation	populate	population
deplete	duplection	protect	protection
destruct	destruction	reduct	reduction

B Write four sentences like the ones in Exercise 1 using words from the chart.

Example: Many rivers and streams have been badly contaminated by industrial waste.

1. ______________________________
2. ______________________________
3. ______________________________
4. ______________________________

3 Choose the correct words or phrases.

1. Green organizations are trying to save rain forests that have been threatened by developers and farmers. (created / ruined / threatened)
2. One way to inform the public about factories that pollute the environment (medio ambiente) is through educational programs on TV. (agricultural / educational / industrial)
3. In many countries around the world, threatened (amenaza) animal and plant species are being protected by strict laws. (created / polluted / protected)
4. Agricultural pesticides are damaging the soil in many countries. (damaging / eating up / lowering)
5. poverty is an enormous problem in many large cities where whole families can only afford (permitirse) to live in one room. (pollution / poverty / waste)

El Yunque rain forest

4 How safe is the fleece you are wearing?

A Scan the title and first two paragraphs of this article. What is fleece? Do you own clothing made of fleece? What clothing?

The Fleece that Came to Dinner

Today, half of the clothing bought by people is made of a synthetic fiber. And that figure is almost 70% in the developing world. Synthetics – or fibers that are created by science, not by nature – are very attractive to customers because, for example, some of them are water-resistant, which is particularly desirable for rain gear and hiking shoes. Moreover, synthetics don't require the amount of water, labor, and land that is needed to cultivate cotton and other natural fibers.

One of the most popular synthetic fabrics is called fleece, a name that originally referred to the wool from a sheep, which is still used to make fall and winter clothes. But in the twenty-first century, the word "fleece" refers to the inexpensive, lightweight, and often water-resistant synthetic material that more and more people are wearing today.

One of the most interesting things about fleece is the fact that it can be made from recycled plastic bottles. This means that fleece can be far less expensive than wool or other natural fibers. For many people, recycling plastic bottles is thought of as friendly to the natural environment since we are reusing the plastic, not burying it in the ground or dumping it in the oceans. However, in the last few years, scientists have discovered that fleece may not be as environmentally friendly as we once supposed.

Scientists are now finding very small particles of plastic at the bottom of the ocean that they believe are the remains of fleece that is washed in washing machines every day all over the world. When it is washed, more than 1,500 particles may separate from a fleece product into the water. When that water is drained, some of it will make its way back into the lakes, rivers, and oceans of our world. That is what seems to be happening now. When the synthetic particles reach natural bodies of water, the plastic is going to be eaten by fish because it looks like food to them. And sooner or later, those fish are going to be caught, delivered to the food market, and end up on your plate at dinner.

What can be done? Shall we return to more costly, heavier, and traditional natural fibers such as cotton and wool? Are people willing to spend more money to possibly save the environment? Or is economics so important to people who have very little money that they believe they cannot afford to give up their synthetic fibers?

B Read the article. Check (✓) the true statements. For statements that are false, write the true information.

1. ☐ In the developing world, 50% of people buy clothing made of synthetic fiber.

   ____

2. ☐ The word "fleece" originally meant sheep's wool.

   ____

3. ☐ Fleece is made from recycled plastic bottles.

   ____

4. ☐ More than 2,000 particles of fleece may separate during washing.

   ____

5. ☐ Fortunately, fish will not consume particles of fleece.

   ____

6. ☐ We now know that people are going to stop using fleece because of its dangers.

   ____

5 World issues

A Match the nouns and definitions.

Nouns		Definitions
1. infectious diseases	d	a. physical actions that are meant to cause destruction or injury
2. global warming	i	b. a period of time when businesses are not doing well and a large number of people cannot find jobs
3. government corruption	g	c. an extreme lack of money
4. famine hambruna		d. illnesses that can be passed on to other people
5. political unrest distrubios	f	e. a situation in which people do not have enough food
6. poverty	c	f. a situation in which citizens become angry or violent due to their dissatisfaction with their government
7. recession	b	g. illegal or dishonest activity by people with political power
8. violence	a	h. a situation in which a number of people are not working because they cannot find jobs
9. unemployment	h	i. an increase in the world's average temperatures

B Choose the correct noun from part A to complete each sentence. You will not use all of the words.

1. It seems like there are more dangerous infectuos diseases these days, like swine flu and the Zika virus.
2. During the recent unemployment, 30 percent of the businesses in my town closed, and a large part of the population didn't have jobs.
3. There's so much poverty in this city. I'm afraid to walk on the streets alone at night because I don't feel safe.
4. Before you travel to a foreign country, make sure there are no dangerous political situations going on there. It can be unsafe to visit countries that are experiencing political unrest.
5. In the 1800s, a large portion of Irish potato crops were destroyed by disease. Because potatoes were a major part of the Irish diet, there was a major famine and over 1.5 million people died.
6. People in this country don't trust the police or city officials because there is a lot of goverment corruption

6 Complete the conversations. Use the expressions in the box and the information in the list.

One thing to do . . .	The best way to fight . . .
Another thing to do . . .	One way to help . . .

- [✓] complain to the Parks Department about it
- [✓] create more government-funded jobs
- [✓] create more public housing projects
- [✓] organize a public meeting to protest the threat of public property
- [ ] educate young people about its dangers
- [✓] report it to the local newspaper
- [✓] donate money to charities that provide shelters and food

A new housing development?

1. **A:** A big housing developer wants to build an apartment complex in Forest Hill Park. I think that's terrible, but what can we do?
   B: *One thing to do is to complain to the Parks Department about it.*
   A: That's a good idea.
   B: Another thing to do is report it to the local newspaper
2. **A:** Personally, I'm worried about violence in the city. The streets are not safe at night.
   B: The best way to fight is educate young people about its dangers
3. **A:** You know, there's a lot of corruption in our city government.
   B: One way to help is organize a public meeting to protest
   A: Yeah, the bad publicity might help to clean things up a bit.
4. **A:** There are so many unemployed people in this city, I just don't know what can be done about it.
   B: One way to help is create more government funded jobs
5. **A:** What worries me most is the number of homeless people on the streets.
   B: One thing to do is create more public housing projects
   A: I agree.
   B: Another thing to do is donate money to charities that provide shelters and food

7 Complete the sentences using the present continuous passive or the present perfect passive. Then suggest a solution to each problem.

1. A lot of jobs ___have been lost___ (lose) in recent years.
   One way to deal with unemployment ___is to bring more businesses___ into the area.
2. These days, a lot of endangered animals ___are being___ (kill) by hunters and poachers.
   The best way to stop this practice ______________________________
   ______________________________.
3. During the past few years, lots of trees ___have been___ (destroy) by acid rain.
   One thing to do about it ______________________________
   ______________________________.
4. Underground water ___is being___ (contaminate) by agricultural pesticides.
   The best way to deal with the problem ______________________________
   ______________________________.
5. Too many people ___have been___ (affect) by infectious diseases in the past few years.
   The best way to stop this ______________________________
   ______________________________.

8 Write two paragraphs about a charity, an organization that helps people. In the first paragraph, describe what the charity does. In the second paragraph, explain why you think the charity is useful.

A good charity in my city is Shelter. This organization works to reduce the number of homeless people on our streets. Shelter believes the best way to do this is to . . .

Shelter is my favorite charity because homelessness is, in my opinion, the greatest problem facing my city. Many people cannot find jobs, and . . .

____
____
____
____
____
____
____
____

8 Never stop learning.

1 Choose the correct words or phrases.

1. I'm interested in human behavior, so I'm planning to take a class in ____________________. (geography / psychology / math)
2. I want to take a course in ____________________, such as commerce or accounting. (education / business / social science)
3. I'd prefer not to study ____________________ because I'm not very comfortable in hospitals. (engineering / new media / nursing)
4. I'd really like to work in Information Technology, so I'm thinking of taking courses in ____________________. (computer science / finance / English)

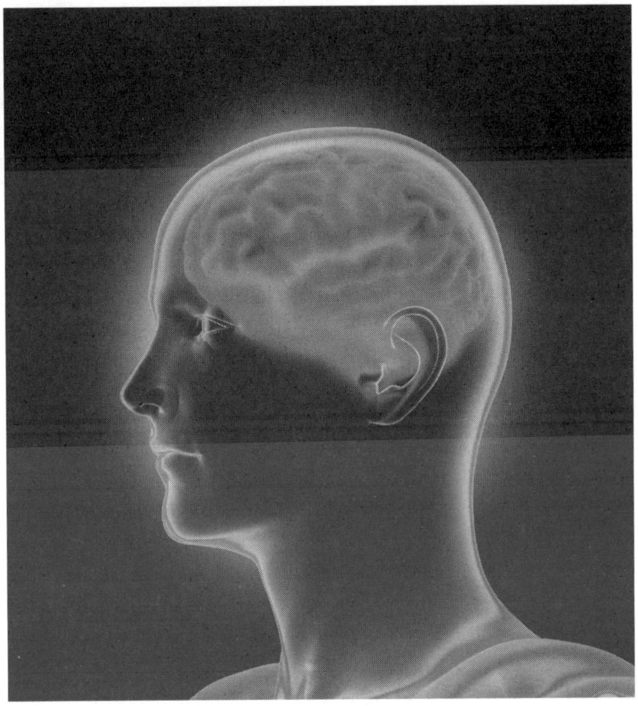

2 What would you prefer?

A Write questions with *would rather* or *would prefer* using the cues.

1. take a science class / an art class
   Would you rather take a science class or an art class? OR
   Would you prefer to take a science class or an art class?
2. study part time / full time
   ____
3. have a boring job that pays well / an exciting job that pays less
   ____
4. take a long vacation once a year / several short vacations each year
   ____

B Write answers to the questions in part A.

1. ____________________
2. ____________________
3. ____________________
4. ____________________

3 Love it or leave it

A First, complete speaker A's questions with four things you would not like to do. Use ideas in the box or your own ideas.

learn to play the accordion learn clothing design learn how to repair watches study sociology take a class in personal finance take a cooking class

1. **A:** Do you want to learn to play the accordion?
   B: I'd rather not. I'd prefer to learn to play the piano. OR
   I'd prefer not to. I'd rather learn to play the piano.
2. **A:** Do you want to ______________________?
   B: ______________________
3. **A:** Would you like to ______________________?
   B: ______________________
4. **A:** Do you want to ______________________?
   B: ______________________
5. **A:** Would you like to ______________________?
   B: ______________________

B Now write responses for speaker B. Use the short answers *I'd rather not* or *I'd prefer not to* and say what you would prefer to do.

4 Answer these questions and give reasons.

1. On your day off, would you rather stay home or go out?
   I'd rather stay home than go out because
2. Would you prefer to have a cat or a bird?
   ____
3. Would you rather live in the city or the country?
   ____
4. When you entertain friends, would you rather invite them over for dinner or take them out to a restaurant?
   ____
5. Would you prefer to see a new movie at the theater or download it and watch it at home?
   ____

5 Online learning, the schools of the future?

A Have you taken an online class? Would you like to? Would you prefer to study online rather than at school? Write your answers.

____

____

B Read the online newspaper article. Underline the sentences that contain the answers to these questions.

1. What is a MOOC?
2. Why do so few students complete a MOOC?
3. Do professors who teach MOOCs think that they are as difficult as courses taken in a classroom?
4. What are critics of MOOCs afraid of?

FREE COLLEGE FOR EVERYONE?

posted 21st of August

A revolution in education is going to happen. Massive Online Open Courses (MOOCs for short) are designed for students who cannot afford, cannot get to, or simply don't want to attend classes in a university classroom. MOOCs are going to be of great importance to economically disadvantaged people, as well as people who live far from a university campus. The only requirement to attend a MOOC is access to a computer with an Internet connection, which is becoming more common each day.

Many MOOCs are created by top professors in their fields who teach at prestigious universities in the U.S., like Princeton, Harvard, and Stanford. These professors may teach online courses at their universities, but with a MOOC they can reach students all over the world. At the moment, not all universities accept academic credit for a MOOC. However, almost half of the professors who have taught a MOOC believe that the coursework is as demanding as the work done in a traditional university class. Many of these professors are not paid for teaching MOOCs by their universities; they do it because they want to make education available to everyone, they love teaching, and they enjoy being able to communicate with so many students online.

MOOC students do not pay tuition, which is perhaps the greatest appeal of these courses. Most professors do not even require students to buy textbooks, which can be very expensive as well. This further reduces the cost of education. On the other hand, despite the affordability of MOOCs, MOOC students do not receive diplomas, which may lessen their appeal. Students may receive certification if they pass the course, but of the 33,000 students enrolled in MOOCs today, the completion rate is strikingly low, at only 10%. Because a MOOC doesn't cost anything, students don't have to worry about losing money if they decide to drop the class. And many of them ultimately do.

So while there are upsides to MOOCs, they are not without their critics. Some professors fear that in the future there may be two kinds of university courses: expensive and superior courses at a traditional university where small groups of students meet in classes with their professors, and inexpensive and inferior massive online courses where students will never meet their professors nor even their fellow students. These critics also point out that students must be disciplined self-starters to be successful in a MOOC and that students often develop the skills of perseverance, time-management, and self-discipline by learning together with other students in a traditional university classroom.

C Write answers to these questions.

1. Do you think MOOCs are going to be the courses of the future? Why or why not?

____

____

2. What do you see as the main advantage of MOOCs? The main disadvantage?

____

____

D What would you prefer to take as a MOOC: a humanities course (such as literature, art, or history) or a science course (such as biology, chemistry, or engineering)? Why did you choose that course?

6 Complete the sentences with *by* + gerund. Use *not* if needed. Use the ideas in the box or your own information.

cook at home	eat out	go out more often	study dance
eat good food	exercise regularly	stay home	use social media

1. A good way to enjoy the weekend is _not by staying home but by going out with friends._
2. A good way to keep in touch with old friends is ______
3. You can make new friends ______
4. The best way to save money is ______
5. You could stay in shape ______
6. I stay healthy ______
7. One way to learn self-confidence is ______

7 Choose the correct words or phrases.

1. Robin shows her ______ by volunteering to help people with cancer. (competitiveness / communication skills / concern for others)
2. When I was young, I didn't understand the importance of ______. But when I started paying my own bills, I realized it's an important skill. (money management / cooperation / perseverance)
3. I learned ______ from my parents. They taught me the importance of using my imagination and making art. (creativity / courtesy / self-confidence)
4. Gina always gets upset with people who disagree with her. I wish she would show more ______. (perseverance / self-confidence / tolerance)
5. I recently joined a choir, and I love it. But you need a lot of ______, because you have to practice the same piece of music for weeks before you're ready to perform it! (cooperation / perseverance / time management)

8 Personal qualities

A Read about each student in these descriptions and choose a suitable quality for each one.

☐ competitiveness	☐ creativity	☐ self-confidence	☐ time management
☐ cooperation	☐ perseverance	☐ self-discipline	☐ tolerance

1

2

3

4

1. Alex is always on time for everything. He's never even five minutes late. He keeps track of everything on his calendar. I wish I were as good at ____________________ as Alex is.
2. Frank finds school very hard, but no one tries harder than he does. He always spends the whole weekend at the library trying to keep up with his studies. He shows great ____________________.
3. Melissa always wants to do better than everyone else. In school, she always tries to get the best grades. Her favorite sport is field hockey because she's the best player in the school. No one needs to teach Melissa ____________________.
4. Jennifer has more ____________________ than any of her classmates. She writes fascinating stories that show she has a wonderful imagination. She's also very artistic and does very interesting paintings.

B Write two similar descriptions of people you know. Either use two of the qualities you didn't use in part A or choose other qualities.

1. ____

____

____

____

2. ____

____

____

____

9 My way

A List two methods of learning each of these skills.

1. become a good guitarist
   by teaching myself
   by taking lessons
2. improve my writing ability in English
   ______
   ______
3. become a more confident public speaker
   ______
   ______
4. learn more about personal finance
   ______
   ______
5. become skilled at auto repair
   ______
   ______
6. learn a new computer program
   ______
   ______

my first guitar

15 years later

B Which of the two methods in part A would you prefer to use to develop each skill? Write sentences using *would rather (not)* or *would prefer (not)*. Give reasons.

1. I'd rather learn guitar by teaching myself than by taking lessons.
   I'd prefer not to take lessons because they're expensive.
2. ______
3. ______
4. ______
5. ______
6. ______

9 Getting things done

1 Which service does each person need? Choose the correct word or phrase.

☐ computer repair	☐ house painting
☐ dry cleaning	☐ language tutoring
☐ home repairs	☑ lawn mowing

1. lawn mowing

Ken: I have a new home and don't have much time for yard work. I mowed the lawn two weeks ago, and I need to cut it again. I'd like to save money, but perhaps I'll just have to pay someone to do it for me.

2. ______________________

Akiko: I don't like the flowered wallpaper in my bedroom or the dark color of the walls in my living room. I want to have the wallpaper removed so the whole place looks bigger and brighter with fun, modern colors everywhere.

3. ______________________

Margaret: Now that it's getting colder, I need to take my winter clothes out of storage. Some things I can wash in the washing machine, but I should take my wool coat to that new place around the corner.

4. ______________________

Steven: I have a lot of work to do this week, but my laptop stopped working! I tried to fix it, but I don't know how. I can't afford to buy a new laptop.

5. ______________________

Eric: I'm so excited! I'm finally going to Quebec this summer. I studied French in high school, but I'm not sure how much I remember now. Do you know anyone who can help me improve my French?

6. ______________________

Karen: I really want to move into that studio apartment I found downtown. The only problem is that there are a lot of little things that need to be repaired. Where can I get a leaky faucet and a broken lock repaired?

home repairs

language tutoring

lawn mowing

2 Where can I get . . . ?

A Match the verbs in column A with the nouns in column B.

A	B	
cut	a stain	**1.** cut my hair
check	my blood pressure	**2.** ______
do	my computer	**3.** ______
fix	my hair	**4.** ______
print	my nails	**5.** ______
remove	my pants	**6.** ______
shorten	my photos	**7.** ______

B First, use the items in part A to write *Where can I get . . . ?* or *Where can I have . . . ?* questions for speaker A. Then write responses for speaker B using your own ideas.

1. **A:** Where can I get my hair cut?
   B: You can get it cut at May's Salon.
2. **A:** ______
   B: ______
3. **A:** ______
   B: ______

4. **A:** ______
   B: ______
5. **A:** ______
   B: ______
6. **A:** ______
   B: ______
7. **A:** ______
   B: ______

3 Where can you have these services done? Write sentences with *You can have . . . .*

1. You can have your hair cut at Salon 21.

At KWIK FIX
we repair all kinds
of shoes.

2. ____________________

We dry-clean

3. ____________________

CARPET
WORLD
We'll clean your
carpets so they're
as good as new.

4. ____________________

We do nails (and only nails)
at Nail File.

5. ____________________

car wash in town!

6. ____________________

Service your

to keep it running

Call Hal's Repairs
at 555-1838

7. ____________________

At EYE to EYE,
we can examine your eyes
in 30 minutes.

8. ____________________

4 Less could be better

A Look at the two pictures. Where have you dreamed about living, in an apartment in the city or in a house in the suburbs? Why? Where would your parents like to live? Why?

DOWNSIZING

Do you want your parents' furniture, family photos, old toys, and sports equipment? If you're a millennial, the answer is likely to be "no."

Millennials are people who became adults at the beginning of the 21st century, and they are not necessarily interested in collecting things. And boomers, Americans born in the years after World War II, are finding out that their children have very different ideas about how to live "the good life."

Millennials do not feel the need to have a lot of *things*. They would rather have *experiences*, like tourism, art, and sports activities. This preference for "less is better" – or downsizing – is partly a result of the world economic crisis and the student debt that many young adults have. The lack of jobs has made millennials want to lower their expenses. And they feel that they must pay off their student loans before they can get married and have children of their own.

Because millennials are waiting to start families, they tend to prefer to live in apartments rather than large houses like their parents. First, they simply don't need that much space. Second, houses are expensive. Third, houses are often located in the suburbs, farther away from the culture and diversity that cities have to offer and that many millennials want.

But, in the latest twist of generational clashes, millennials are finding it more and more difficult to afford city living. Boomers, who generally have more money to spend than millennials, are finally ready to sell their houses now that their children have moved out. When they do, many then use that money to buy an apartment in the city where they can start a new life with all the amenities cities have to offer to people with money.

With this increase in demand, the prices of apartments have gone up, and millennials are discovering that it is very difficult to compete economically with their boomer parents. One option is for millennials to live together. Today some of them are renting houses or large apartments that several people can share. More than a few people think that this kind of downsizing, besides being good for the pocketbook, is good for the planet.

B Read the article about downsizing. Check (✓) the true statements. For statements that are false, write the true information.

1. ☐ Adult children still enjoy receiving furniture from their parents.

   ____

2. ☐ Boomers are Americans born before World War II.

   ____

3. ☐ Downsizing is the philosophy that "less is better."

   ____

4. ☐ The competition between boomers and millennials has a lot to do with money.

   ____

5. ☐ The next step in downsizing could be for boomers and millennials to share houses and large apartments.

   ____

5 Write two suggestions for each of these problems.

1. **A:** I never have any energy, so I can never do anything except work. I sleep all weekend, so don't tell me to get more rest!
   B: Have you thought about *taking an aerobics class?*
   Another option is to improve your diet.

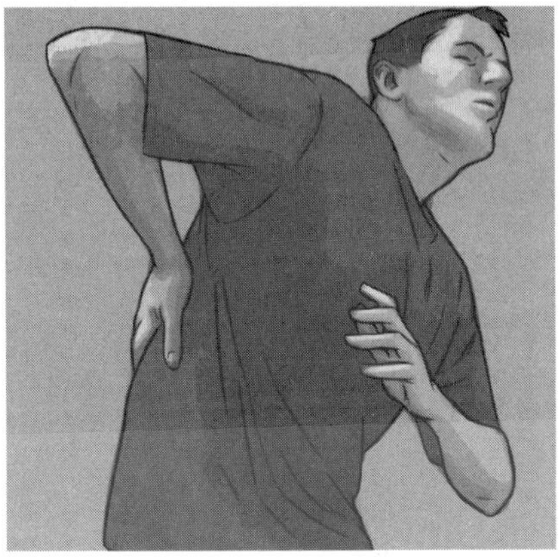

2. **A:** My problem is a constant backache. I just don't know what to do to get rid of it. I had someone give me a massage, but it didn't really help.
   B: Maybe you could ______________________
   ____

3. **A:** My doctor told me to get more exercise. She strongly recommended swimming, but I find swimming so boring! In fact, aren't all sports boring?
   B: Why don't you ______________________
   ____

4. **A:** I'm very sociable, and I have great difficulty saying no. I end up doing things every night of the week – going to parties, clubs, the movies. I'm so tired all the time!
   B: It might be a good idea ______________________
   ____

5. **A:** I like to be a good neighbor, but the woman next door drives me crazy. She's always knocking on my door to chat. And whenever I go out into the yard, she goes into her yard – and talks for hours!
   B: What about ______________________
   ____

6 Choose the correct three-word phrasal verb for each sentence.

1. I don't know how my grandmother ______________________ all the new technology. She's better at understanding new gadgets than I am! (comes up with / cuts down on / keeps up with)
2. My cousin didn't know what to do for her mother's 60th birthday, but she finally ______________________ the idea of a surprise picnic with the whole family. (came up with / got along with / looked forward to)
3. Ilene has done it again! She only met Chris two months ago, and already she has ______________________ him. Why doesn't she try to work out any problems? (broken up with / gotten along with / kept up with)
4. After Michelle saw her doctor, she decided to ______________________ eating fast food. She wants to lose some weight and start exercising again in order to keep fit. (cut down on / look forward to / take care of)
5. We're really lucky in my family because we all ______________________ each other very well. (come up with / get along with / look forward to)
6. I've done pretty badly in my classes this semester, so I'm not really ______________________ receiving my grades. (getting along with / looking forward to / taking care of)
7. I can't ______________________ that loud music anymore! I can't stand hip-hop, and I'm going to tell my neighbor right now. (cut down on / put up with / take care of)
8. I've been getting sick a lot lately, and I often feel tired. I really need to start ______________________ my health. (cutting down on / keeping up with / taking care of)

10 A matter of time

1 Circle the correct word that describes each sentence.

1. Events in December 2010 led to the peaceful removal of Tunisia's prime minister in January 2011. (natural disaster / epidemic / revolution)
2. In 2014, a new species of insect was found in Vietnam. It has a body over 30 centimeters long and is the second longest insect in the world. (discovery / invention / epidemic)
3. On June 12, 2016, a gunman entered a nightclub in Florida where he killed 49 people and injured more than 50. (invention / terrorist act / achievement)
4. Advances in robot technology have come a long way in recent years. Scientists like Japan's Hiroshi Ishiguro have created human-like robots that can have conversations with each other and with humans. (achievement / disaster / terrorist act)
5. Prime Minister Benazir Bhutto of Pakistan was killed after leaving a campaign rally in December 2007. (assassination / election / revolution)
6. In 2010, a series of floods in Australia affected over 200,000 people and caused nearly a billion Australian dollars in damage. (discovery / natural disaster / epidemic)

2 Complete the sentences. Use words from the box.

ago for from in since to

1. Jazz first became popular ____in____ the 1920s.
2. The cell phone was invented about 45 years ________.
3. Brasília has been the capital city of Brazil ________ 1960.
4. The first laptop was produced ________ 1981.
5. Mexico has been independent ________ more than 200 years.
6. World War II lasted ________ 1939 ________ 1945.
7. Vietnam was separated into two parts ________ about 20 years.
8. East and West Germany have been united ________ 1990.

jazz

Brasília

3 Nouns and verbs

A Complete this chart. Then check your answers in a dictionary.

Noun	Verb	Noun	Verb
achievement	achieve	existence	______
assassination	______	exploration	______
demonstration	______	explosion	______
discovery	______	invention	______
discrimination	______	transformation	______
election	______	vaccination	______

B Choose verbs from the chart in part A to complete these sentences. Use the correct verb tense.

Bangalore, a high-tech center

a research station in Antarctica

1. Over the past several decades, the Indian city of Bangalore has transformed itself into a high-tech center.
2. In World War I, many soldiers were ______ against typhoid, a deadly bacterial disease.
3. Aung San, the man who led Myanmar to independence, was ______ in 1947. No one is certain who killed him.
4. The European Union has ______ since 1957.
5. Until the 1960s, there were many laws that ______ against African Americans in certain regions of the United States.
6. In 1885, Louis Pasteur ______ a cure for rabies when he treated a young boy who was bitten by a dog.
7. In recent years, teams of experts in countries such as Cambodia and Angola have been safely ______ land mines in order to rid those countries of these dangerous weapons.
8. One of the few parts of the world that has not been ______ much is Antarctica. The extreme climate makes it dangerous to travel far from research centers.

4 Vaccines past, present, and future

A What are vaccinations? If necessary, scan the article to find out.

VACCINATIONS

For well over a thousand years, smallpox was a disease that everyone feared. The disease killed much of the native population in South America when the Spanish arrived there in the early sixteenth century. By the end of the eighteenth century, smallpox was responsible for the deaths of about one in ten people around the world. Those who survived the disease were left with ugly scars on their skin.

It had long been well known among farmers that people who worked with cows rarely caught smallpox; instead, they often caught a similar but much milder disease called cowpox. A British doctor named Edward Jenner was fascinated by this, and so he studied cowpox. He became convinced that, by injecting people with cowpox, he could protect them against the much worse disease smallpox. In 1796, he vaccinated a boy with cowpox and, two months later, with smallpox. The boy did not get smallpox. In the next two years, Jenner vaccinated several children in the same way, and none of them got the disease.

News of Jenner's success soon spread. In 1800, the Royal Vaccine Institution was founded in Berlin, Germany. In the following year, Napoleon opened a similar institute in Paris, France. It took nearly two centuries to achieve Jenner's dream of ridding the world of smallpox. In 1967, the World Health Organization (WHO) started an ambitious vaccination program, and the last known case of smallpox was recorded in Somalia in 1977.

The future of vaccinations aims at the eradication of three diseases that can be caused by mosquito bites: malaria, Zika virus, and dengue. Malaria is an infectious disease that is still a problem, in part because the virus that causes the disease hides in the cells away from the immune system. Zika virus has recently been discovered in various places all over the world, and it is particularly dangerous for pregnant women. At this time there is no vaccine for Zika virus, although scientists are working on one. Dengue is a disease that has multiplied alarmingly in recent years, but in the last two years a vaccine has been successfully developed for people between 9 and 45 years old.

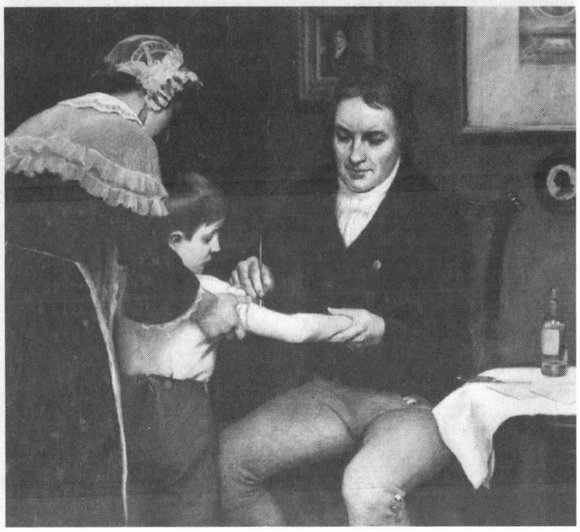

B Read the article about vaccinations. Complete the chart with the history of events in the story of vaccinations.

Date	Event
1. Early 16th century	Smallpox killed much of the native population in South America.
2. End of the 18th century	
3. 1796	
4. 1800	
5. 1801	
6. 1967	
7. 1977	
8. Future challenge	

5 Life in 2050

A Complete these predictions about life in 2050. Use the future continuous of the verb given. Then add two more predictions of your own.

Life on the moon?

By 2050, . . .

1. some people ___will be living___ in cities on the moon. (live)
2. many people ______________ temperature-controlled body suits. (wear)
3. most people ______________ cars that run on fuel from garbage. (drive)
4. people ______________ in a new Olympic event – mind reading. (compete)
5. ______________
6. ______________

B Complete these predictions about what will have happened by 2050. Use the future perfect. Then add two more predictions of your own.

By 2050, . . .

1. computers ___will have replaced___ people as translators. (replace)
2. ties for men ______________ out of fashion. (go)
3. scientists ______________ a cheap way of getting drinking water from seawater. (discover)
4. medical researchers ______________ a cure for cancer. (find)
5. ______________
6. ______________

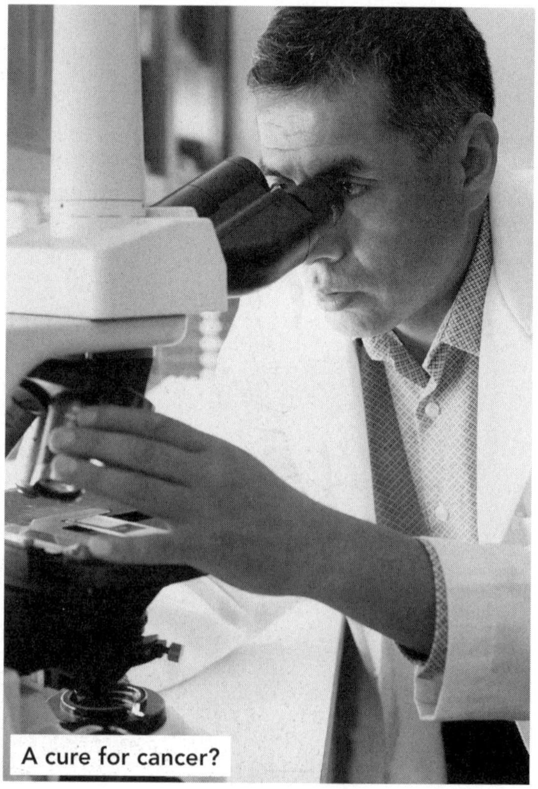

A cure for cancer?

6 Write two responses to each question.

1. What will or won't you be doing in ten years? (Use the future continuous.)

   I won't be living with my parents.

2. How will cities of the future be different? (Use *will*.)

   Cities won't allow cars downtown.

3. How will life in small villages in your country have changed in the next 20 years? (Use the future perfect.)

   More people will have moved back from cities to small villages.

4. How do you think the world's weather will change during this century? (Use *will*.)

   The weather will be warmer, and the summers will be longer.

5. What advances will scientists have made by 2050? (Use the future perfect.)

   Scientists will have found a way to grow enough food for everyone.

7 Think of four more ways that technology will affect how we live and work in the next 20 years.

1. Robots will be cleaning our homes.
2. ______________________
3. ______________________
4. ______________________
5. ______________________

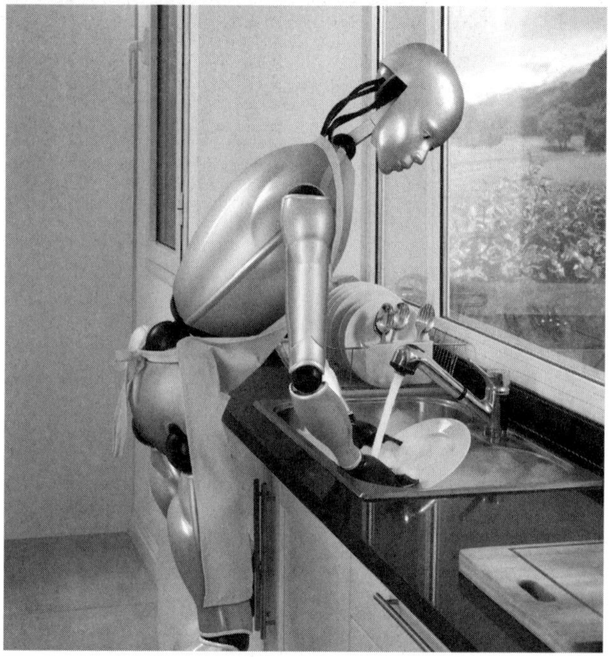

8 Write two paragraphs about one of these topics or a topic of your choice. In the first paragraph, describe the past. In the second paragraph, describe how you think the future will be.

a music group	changes within a country	health
space exploration	changes within a region	technology

Eyeglasses were invented in the 13th century in Italy. These early glasses didn't include earpieces to keep the glasses on the wearer's face. Instead, they had to be held in front of the eyes or placed on the nose. In the 1700s, eyeglasses were designed with earpieces, making them easier to use. In the 20th century, contacts became common, making it even easier and more convenient for people to use corrective lenses.

Technological advances have continued to make vision correction more practical and convenient. In recent years, doctors have developed laser surgery techniques, which can make corrective lenses unnecessary for people with certain types of vision problems. In the future, computer technology will probably replace eyeglasses, contact lenses, and laser surgery. It may even make it possible for blind people to see.

11 Rites of passage

1 Milestones

A Read these statements. Check (✓) the ones that are true for you. For statements that are false, write the true information.

Example: As soon as I got my first cell phone, I called all my friends.

The moment I got a cell phone, I called my parents OR
I've never had a cell phone.

1. ☐ By the time I was three years old, I had already learned two languages.
   ______
2. ☐ Before I started school, I was carefree – I used to watch TV all day.
   ______
3. ☐ After I started taking the bus by myself, I became more independent.
   ______
4. ☐ As soon as I got my driver's license, my parents let me drive everywhere.
   ______
5. ☐ The moment I earned my own money, I opened a bank account.
   ______
6. ☐ Once I started learning English, I quit studying other languages.
   ______
7. ☐ Until I graduated from high school, I was very unsophisticated.
   ______
8. ☐ Before I became more independent, I thought I knew more than my parents.
   ______

B Write three true statements about how things have changed over time for you, your family, or your friends. Use time clauses.

1. ______
   ______
2. ______
   ______
3. ______
   ______

2 Complete these descriptions. Use words from the box.

☐ ambitious	☐ carefree	☐ rebellious
☐ argumentative	☐ naive	☑ sophisticated

1. Sandra is so ___sophisticated___. She always dresses well, she knows lots of intelligent people, and she never says anything silly.
2. I just spent a horrible evening with Patricia. She questioned and criticized everything I said. I wish she weren't so ________________.
3. My sister is very ________________. She trusts everyone and thinks everyone is good.
4. Once I turned 16, I became less ________________, and my parents started to let me do what I wanted.
5. Eric is really ________________. He wants to own his own business by the time he's 25.
6. I wish I could be like Susie. She's so ________________ and never seems to worry about anything.

3 Do you have a friend who is special to you? Write about him or her. In the first paragraph, describe the person. In the second paragraph, describe a particular time when the person helped you.

One of my best friends is Jennifer. She's very mature and conscientious, and she always gives me good advice. Until I met her, I had been making some bad decisions . . . .

Jennifer is also very generous. She always helps her friends when they need it. For example, the moment she found out I was sick last winter, she came over and visited me.

____

____

____

____

____

____

____

____

4 Turning points

A Scan the article from a sports magazine about Usain Bolt. What lesson did he learn as a child?

LEARNING FAST

Usain Bolt is called "Lightning" Bolt because he is considered the fastest man in the world. The Jamaican runner is an Olympic champion in the 100- and 200-meter **sprint**, as well as in the 4x100 relay, a race in which four runners each sprint 100 meters and then pass the baton to the next runner. He is the first man in the modern Olympic Games to win nine gold medals in the sprint. He is also the first athlete to win gold medals in the 100- and 200-meter races as well as in the 4x100 relay race in three Olympic Games, in 2008, 2012, and 2016.

In his autobiography, *Faster than Lightning*, Bolt writes that sports interested him most as a child. He also says that in school he learned something important about himself: he is ambitious because he loves to compete and to win.

He doesn't want to be one of the **runners-up**. This desire to be the best, plus his natural physical speed, brought him to the attention of Pablo McNeil, the former Olympic sprinter who was teaching athletics at Bolt's high school. Pablo McNeil convinced him to concentrate on sprinting and trained him in that sport.

When he was 15, Bolt **launched himself into** world-class athletics in the 2002 World Junior Championships in Jamaica's capital, Kingston. He was so nervous that he put his shoes on the wrong feet! But that was another important lesson: he would never allow stress to affect him again before a race. In spite of his nervousness, he became the youngest World Junior athlete to win the **prestigious** gold medal when he ran in the 200-meter sprint.

At the 2008 Olympic Games, Bolt learned another lesson: he should never stop learning. He broke two records at those games, becoming the fastest sprinter in the 100- and 200-meter race. At the end of the 100-meter race, he shocked everyone when he slowed down before the finish line. He was **ecstatic** because he already knew he was the winner. Some people felt he was too carefree. They thought he should have sprinted all the way. In the following 200-meter race, he didn't slow down. He ran all the way in **record time**, like the fastest man in the world.

B Read the article. Look at the words and phrases in bold in the article. Write definitions or synonyms for each word or phrase.

1. sprint ____________________
2. runners-up ____________________
3. launched himself into ____________________
4. prestigious ____________________
5. ecstatic ____________________
6. record time ____________________

C What factors mentioned in the article do you think have helped Usain Bolt to become a successful athlete?

____

5 Write sentences about your regrets. Use *should (not) have.*

1. I spent all my money on clothes. Now I can't afford to take a vacation.
   I shouldn't have spent all my money on clothes.
2. I was very argumentative with my boss, so she fired me.
   ____
3. I changed jobs. Now I work in a bank. My job isn't very interesting.
   ____
4. I bought a new TV with my credit card. Now I can't afford the payments.
   ____
5. I studied music in school, but I'm much better at computer science.
   ____
6. I was completely rebellious when I was a student, so I got very bad grades.
   ____
7. My friend asked to copy my homework, so I let him. The teacher found out and gave us both Fs.
   ____
8. My cousin invited me to a party. I accepted but didn't put the date in my calendar. I forgot all about it.
   ____
9. I was very naive when I was younger. I lent money to people, but they hardly ever paid me back.
   ____
10. My friend asked for my opinion on her new hairstyle. I told her I didn't like it. Now she's not talking to me.
   ____

6 If . . .

A Rewrite the sentences as hypothetical situations. Use the words given.

1. I should have studied English sooner. (get a better job)
   If I'd studied English sooner, I would have gotten a better job.
2. We should have made a reservation. (eat already)
   ____
3. I should have put on sunscreen. (not get a sunburn)
   ____
4. You should have let me drive. (arrive by now)
   ____
5. I should have ignored your text in class. (not get in trouble)
   ____

B Write sentences describing hypothetical situations. Use the words given and your own ideas.

Can I borrow the car?
No, you haven't cleaned your room yet.

1. dependable *If I had been more dependable as a teenager, my parents would have let me borrow the car more often.*
2. ambitious ______________________
3. pragmatic ______________________
4. naive ______________________
5. rebellious ______________________
6. wise ______________________

7 Complete the conversation. Circle the correct time expressions and use the correct tense of the verbs given.

Hector: I've made such a mess of my life!

Scott: What do you mean?

Hector: If I ___hadn't accepted___ (not accept) a job (as soon as / before / until) I graduated, I ______________ (travel) around South America all summer – just like you did. You were so carefree.

Scott: You know, I should ______________ (not go) to South America. I should ______________ (take) the great job I was offered. (After / Before / Until) I returned from South America, it was too late.

Hector: But my job is so depressing! (Before / The moment / Until) I started it, I hated it – on the very first day! That was five years ago, and nothing's changed. I should ______________ (look) for another job right away.

Scott: Well, start looking now. I posted my résumé online last month, and five companies contacted me right away. If I ______________ (not post) my résumé, no one ______________ (contact) me. I accepted one of the job offers.

Hector: Really? What's the job?

Scott: It's working as a landscape gardener. (Before / The moment / Until) I saw it, I knew it was right for me.

Hector: But for me right now, the problem is that I get a very good salary and I just bought a house. If I ______________ (not buy) the house, I ______________ (be able to) take a lower paying job.

Scott: Well, I guess you can't have everything. If I ______________ (have) a better salary, I ______________ (buy) a house, too.

12 Keys to success

1 Complete these sentences with *In order for* or *In order to.*

1. In order for __________ a restaurant to be popular, it has to have attractive decor.
2. ____________________ a movie to be entertaining, it has to have good actors and an interesting story.
3. ____________________ succeed in business, you often have to work long hours.
4. ____________________ attract new members, a sports club needs to offer inexpensive memberships.
5. ____________________ speak a foreign language well, it's a good idea to use the language as often as possible.
6. ____________________ a clothing store to succeed, it has to be able to find the latest fashions.

2 Write sentences. Use the information in the box.

☐ have talented salespeople	☐ work extremely long hours
☑ keep up with your studies	☐ provide excellent customer service
☐ be clever and entertaining	☐ have drama and interesting characters

1. be a successful student
   In order to be a successful student, you have to keep up with your studies.
2. a clothes store to be profitable
   For a clothes store to be profitable, ____________________
3. manage your own business
   ____
4. an advertisement to be persuasive
   ____
5. run a successful automobile company
   ____
6. a reality TV show to be successful
   ____

3 Choose the correct word or phrase.

1. I didn't enjoy this book on how to succeed in business. It wasn't very well written. (affordable / well paid / well written)
2. I learned a lot about how to run a successful bookstore from taking that class. I found it very ________. (attractive / informative / knowledgeable)
3. Annie has so many interesting ideas, and she's always thinking of new projects. She's very ________. (clever / entertaining / tough)
4. Debra is a salesperson, and she's good at her job. She's so ________ that she sells three times as much as her co-workers. (unfriendly / affordable / persuasive)
5. Matthew is one of the top models in Milan. He goes to the gym every day, so he looks really ________. (clever / charming / muscular)
6. Before opening a new store, it's important to think through all of your ideas and have ________. (competitive salaries / a clear business plan / a reliable job)
7. My new job has great benefits. We have unlimited time off, excellent health insurance, and ________. (a good product / flexible working hours / a crowdfunding platform)

4 Read this information about journalists. Then write a paragraph about one of the people in the box or another person of your choice.

To be a successful journalist, you need to be both talented and dynamic. You have to write well and write quickly. In order to report the news, a journalist needs to have a good knowledge of world and current events. In addition, you must be able to report a story accurately.

an artist   a boss   a homemaker   a parent   a teacher

____

____

____

____

____

____

____

____

5 I like it because . . .

A For each pair of pictures, write one sentence about what you like and one sentence about what you dislike. Give reasons using the words given.

1. *I like this park because it's clean and there are a lot of trees.* (because)

I don't like this park since ________ (since)

2. ________ (since)

________ (the reason)

3. ________ (because of)

________ (due to)

B Think of an example in your city of each of these places: a restaurant, a hotel, and a shopping center. Write a sentence about why you like or dislike each one.

Example: *The reason I don't like Cho Dang Gol Restaurant in my hometown is its noisy location right by the freeway.*

1. ________

2. ________

3. ________

6 A new business with an ancient product

A Scan the article about Andean Grain. What is the secret that the company is selling?

SELLING SECRETS OF THE PAST

The Argentinian company Andean Grain is contributing to a **comeback** of highly nutritious foods that were unknown to many people during the last few hundred years. Andean Grain sells foods made from **indigenous** Latin American plants, like chia seeds, amaranth, and quinoa. These plants are coming **to prominence** today because knowledgeable people have discovered that chia seeds, amaranth, and quinoa are **superfoods**, incredibly rich in vitamins and proteins.

Chia seeds were grown by the Aztecs as an energy food. In order to travel long distances without having to stop, they drank a beverage consisting of chia seeds, lemon juice, and water. The Aztecs also cultivated amaranth, which they believed was a superfood, as do scientists today. Quinoa was grown in the mountains of the Andes by the Incas. All three of these foods **went out of favor** after the conquest of Latin America in the 16th century. Wheat was preferred over these native plants, and they were almost unknown outside the countries that grew them. Nevertheless, these foods have become popular once more due to the health benefits that they are supposed to provide. They appear to be of optimal benefit for the heart and brain, and **rumor has it** that they may help prevent cancer. They're also gluten-free. Because many people today have problems digesting the gluten in wheat, gluten-free foods have become very fashionable.

As a result, there is a great demand by the public for these superfoods. Andean Grain sells its products all over the world, but it is especially active in Europe, where it has a main office in the United Kingdom. From its base in Argentina, Andean Grain sends most of its native plants to Europe to be made into affordable breads, breakfast cereals, and today's popular trail mixes, which are combinations of dried fruits, nuts, and seeds.

The secret is out, and what was hidden from the world for so many centuries has today become an important discovery of foods for our health. Did you know about these superfoods before the rest of the world discovered them just a few years ago?

B Read the article. Look at the words and phrases in bold in the article. Write definitions or synonyms for each word or phrase.

1. comeback ______
2. indigenous ______
3. to prominence ______
4. superfood ______
5. went out of favor ______
6. rumor has it ______

7 Look at these advertisements and write two sentences about each one. Describe the features and give reasons why you like or dislike the advertisements.

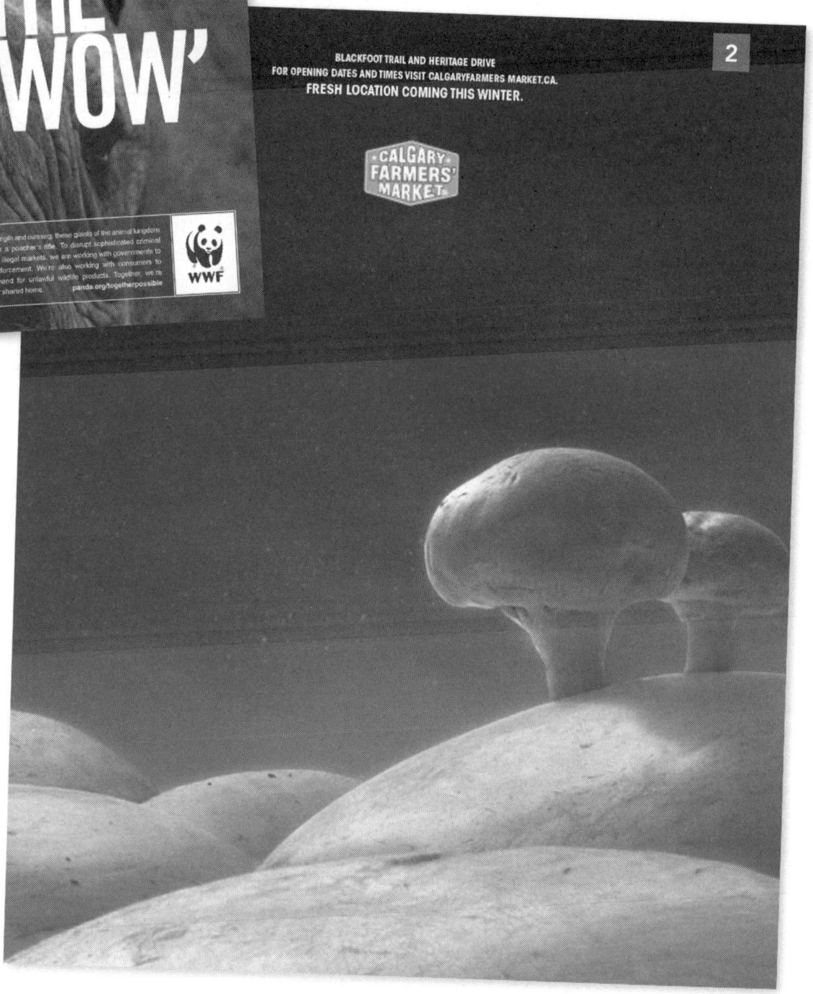

Example: I like the first ad because it attracts your attention.
I like the second ad because it has a simple and clean design.

1. ______________________________
____
____
____

2. ______________________________
____
____
____

8 Do you have the right qualities?

A Complete the sentences with the words from the box.

affordable	athletic	clever	entertaining	informative	knowledgeable	muscular	salesperson

1. I'm not ______________ enough about tools to be a successful salesperson in a hardware store. I'm familiar with some common tools, but I don't know how to use most tools.
2. To be successful, personal trainers need to be fit and ______________.
3. *Weekend Talk* ran for only three months because it was so boring. For a TV show to be successful on Saturday evenings, it really has to be ______________.
4. I wouldn't be a good ______________ because I'm not very persuasive.
5. I found a fantastic news website this morning. It's really ______________. It has very detailed stories about local and international news.
6. For a salesperson to be persuasive, he or she has to be ______________ with words.
7. Kate is so ______________. She plays soccer, tennis, and basketball, and she's excellent at all three sports.
8. I like this store, but it's not very ______________. Even the small items are expensive.

B Write sentences using the words below and infinitive clauses with *to* or *for*.

1. apply for a job / write a good résumé

   ____

2. be an effective personal trainer / listen to your clients' needs

   ____

3. a restaurant / be successful / delicious food at good prices

   ____

4. students / get good grades / study hard and do their best

   ____

5. learn a new language / practice every day

   ____

13 What might have been

1 What do you think happened? Write an explanation for each event using past modals.

1

2
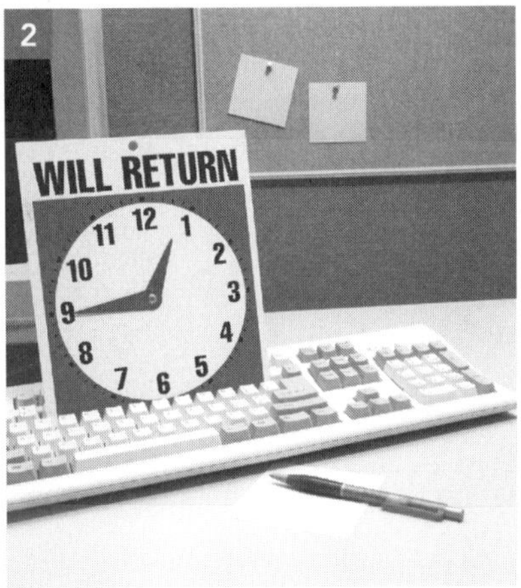

3

1. She may have lost her car key.

2.

3.

4.

5.

6.

4

5

6

2 Write two paragraphs about something strange that has happened to you. In the first paragraph, describe the situation. In the second paragraph, give two or three explanations for what happened.

I invited six friends to a barbecue on the beach. I suggested we meet at eight o'clock. They all said they would come and bring some food.

On the day of the barbecue, only two of my friends showed up. I guess my other friends could have overslept, or they might have decided to do something else. Another possibility is that they may have thought I meant 8 P.M. instead of 8 A.M. I'm not sure what happened!

____

____

____

____

____

____

____

____

3 Answer these questions. Write two explanations using past modals.

Why do you think the ancient Britons built Stonehenge?

1. They might have _built it to use as a church._
____
2. ____
____

How do you think early explorers communicated with people in the places they visited?

3. They could have ______________________________
____
4. ____
____

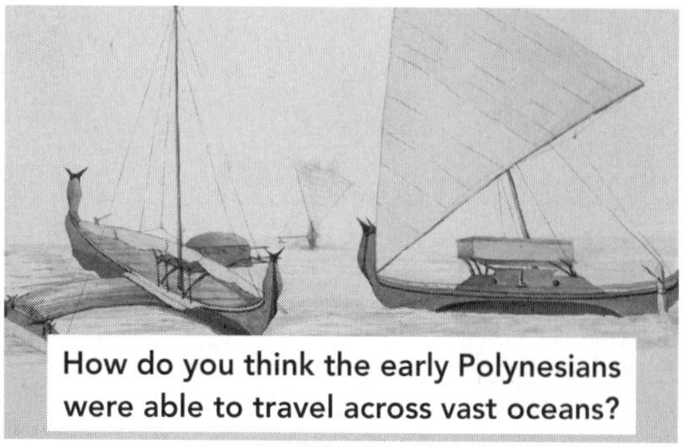

How do you think the early Polynesians were able to travel across vast oceans?

5. They may have ______________________________
____
6. ____
____

4 Strange creatures

A Skim the online article about a world-famous legend. Where does the legend come from?

HOME NEWS SPOTLIGHT LOCATIONS COMMUNITY

BIGFOOT

He has been described as a gigantic, hairy, mysterious man-like creature that lives in the forests of the Pacific Northwest of the U.S. and avoids people. He is called Bigfoot because of the big footprints people have found in the earth.

Scientists who seriously consider the possibility of Bigfoot's existence offer the explanation of ancient man-like apes that might have survived in small groups. The most popular possibility is Gigantopithecus, an ape that lived until about 100,000 years ago, was three meters (9.8 feet) tall, and weighed more than 500 kilos (1,102 pounds). Unfortunately, there are two problems with this possibility. Most scientists believe that Gigantopithecus would have walked on its hands and legs because its weight would have been too much for its legs and ankles to support. Also, the bones of this ape have only been found in Asia. It's more likely that people saw a large black bear that walks on its two legs, common in the Pacific Northwest, and they thought it was Bigfoot.

Another explanation for this mystery is that it's a hoax, a false story that some people invent as a joke. And of course they can make money by selling their story to television shows and newspapers. There have been quite a few hoaxes in the last few years. Some were very convincing, but all were proved false. If it seems quite certain that Bigfoot couldn't have existed, why do people continue to believe in creatures like this? British anthropologist Jane Goodall may have come up with the best explanation: "Well, I'm a romantic, so I always wanted them to exist."

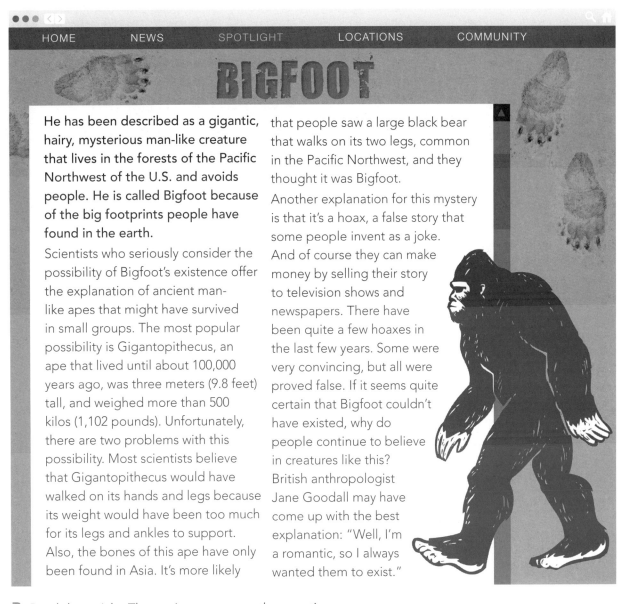

B Read the article. Then write answers to the questions.

1. How might someone describe Bigfoot?

____

2. Imagine that you have seen a creature resembling Bigfoot. Do you think you would have believed it was Bigfoot? Why or why not?

____

3. What is the most popular possible explanation for Bigfoot from scientists?

____

4. What is one problem with this popular explanation?

____

5. What do you think people might have seen when they thought they saw Bigfoot?

____

5 Should have, could have, would have

A What should or shouldn't these people have done? Read each situation and check (✓) the best suggestion.

1. Mrs. King wouldn't let her children watch TV for a month because they broke a window playing baseball.
   - [ ] She could have made them pay for the window.
   - [ ] She shouldn't have done anything. It was an accident.
   - [ ] She shouldn't have let them play baseball for a month.
2. Steve's old car broke down on the highway late one night, and his cell phone battery was dead. He left the car on the side of the road and walked home.
   - [ ] He should have stopped a stranger's car to ask for a ride.
   - [ ] He could have slept in his car till morning.
   - [ ] He should have walked to the nearest pay phone and called a tow truck.
3. Sarah was in a park. She saw some people leave all their trash after they had finished their picnic. She did nothing.
   - [ ] She did the right thing.
   - [ ] She should have asked them to throw away their trash.
   - [ ] She could have thrown away the trash herself.
4. Edward's neighbors were renovating their kitchen. They made a lot of noise every day until midnight. Edward called the police.
   - [ ] He shouldn't have called the police.
   - [ ] He should have realized that they were trying to finish the job quickly.
   - [ ] He could have asked them not to make any noise in the evenings.
5. Barbara's boss borrowed $20 from her a month ago, but he forgot to pay her back. Barbara never said anything about it.
   - [ ] She should have demanded her money back.
   - [ ] She shouldn't have loaned it to him.
   - [ ] She could have written him a nice email asking for the money.

B What would you have done in the situations in part A? Write suggestions or comments using past modals.

1. I would have made them pay for the window.
2. ______________________________
3. ______________________________
4. ______________________________
5. ______________________________

6 Nouns and verbs

A Complete the chart.

Noun	Verb	Noun	Verb
assumption	assume	________	predict
criticism	________	suggestion	________
demand	________	suspect	________
excuse	________	warning	________

B Complete the sentences using words from the chart in part A. For the verbs, use *shouldn't have* + past participle. For the nouns, use the appropriate singular or plural form.

1. Last year some economists said that food and gas prices wouldn't increase. Those ____predictions____ were wrong! Both food and gas are more expensive now.
2. Christopher ________________ having a beach party. It was so dark, I stepped in a hole and hurt my ankle.
3. Andy bought an expensive ring and gave it to Millie for her birthday. A year later, he asked her to marry him. When she said no, he made an outrageous ________________. He said he wanted his ring back!
4. I ________________ my co-worker not to be late for work so often. It was really none of my business.
5. Lori said she was late because she got caught in traffic. Hmm. I've heard that ________________ before.
6. Kevin ________________ I would still be awake at midnight. I was asleep when he called.
7. I thought that my roommate had taken my wallet, but I found it at the bottom of my bag. I ________________ that my roommate took it. He would never do something like that.
8. James ________________ me for wearing jeans and a T-shirt to a friend's party. He always has negative things to say.

7 Complete these conversations. Use the past modals in the box and the verbs given. (More than one modal is possible.)

could have	may have	might have	must have	should have

1. **A:** Where's Luke? He's late.

   B: He ___may have gotten___ (get) stuck in rush-hour traffic.

   A: He's always late! You know, he ___should have taken___ (take) the subway.

2. **A:** Judy never responded to my invitation.

   B: She ______________ (not receive) it. You ______________ (call) her.

3. **A:** Matt hasn't answered his phone for a week.

   B: He ______________ (go) on vacation. He ______________ (tell) you, though – sometimes he's very inconsiderate.

4. **A:** I can never get in touch with Kathy. She never returns phone calls or answers texts!

   B: Yeah, I have the same problem with her. Her voice mail ______________ (run out) of space. She ______________ (get) a new phone service by now.

5. **A:** Thomas is strange. Sometimes he works really hard, but sometimes he seems pretty lazy. Last week, he hardly did any work.

   B: Well, you know, he ______________ (not feel) well. Still, he ______________ (tell) you that he was sick.

6. **A:** I ordered a book online a month ago, but it still hasn't arrived.

   B: They ______________ (have) a problem with the warehouse, but they ______________ (let) you know.

14 Creative careers

1 Complete the conversation. Use the passive form of the verbs given.

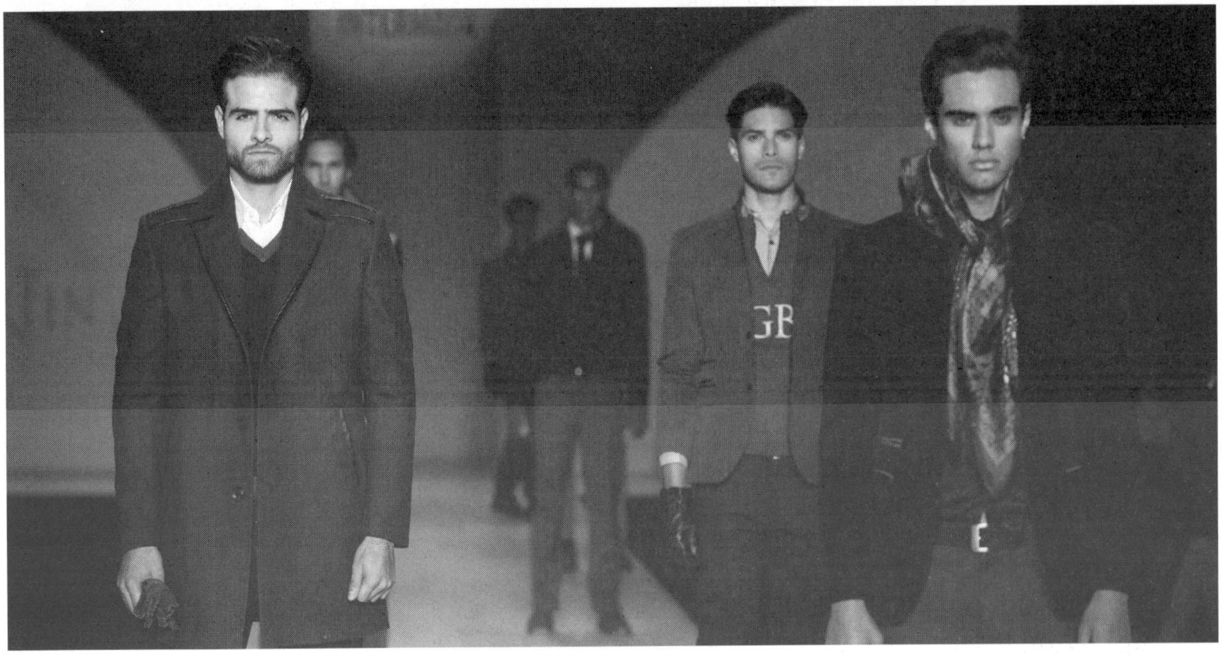

Anna: Putting on a fashion show must be really fun!

Marcus: Yeah, but it's also challenging. All the clothes have to ___be numbered___ (number) so that the models wear them in the right sequence. And they also have to ________________ (mark) with the name of the right model.

Anna: What happens if something ________________ (wear) by the wrong model?

Marcus: Well, if it doesn't fit, it looks terrible! First impressions are very important. A lot of clothes ________________ (sell) because they look good at the show.

Anna: Do you have to rehearse for a fashion show?

Marcus: Of course! There's more involved than just models and clothes. Special lighting ________________ (use), and music ________________ (play) during the show.

Anna: It sounds complicated.

Marcus: Oh, it is. And at some fashion shows, a commentary may ________________ (give).

Anna: A commentary? What do you mean?

Marcus: Well, someone talks about the clothes as they ________________ (show) on the runway by the models.

Anna: It sounds like timing is really important.

Marcus: Exactly. Everything has to ________________ (time) perfectly! Otherwise, the show may ________________ (ruin).

2 Choose the correct words or phrases.

1. Often, special music has to be ____________________ for a film.
   (written / designed / hired)

2. A play may be ____________________ for several weeks before it is shown to the public.
   (shot / taken / rehearsed)

3. Designing ____________________ for actors to wear requires a lot of creativity.
   (scripts / movies / clothes)

4. Newspapers are ____________________ to stores after they are printed.
   (written / delivered / reported)

5. ____________________ are added after the film has been put together.
   (Scenes / Sound effects / Actors)

3 Complete this passage. Use the passive form of the verbs given.

1. Nowadays, all sorts of things *are produced* (produce) in factories, including lettuce! At one food factory, fresh green lettuce ____________________ (grow) without sunlight or soil. Here is how it ____________________ (do).
2. Lettuce seedlings ____________________ (place) at one end of a long production line. Conveyor belts ____________________ (use) to move the seedlings slowly along. The tiny plants ____________________ (expose) to light from fluorescent lamps.
3. They have to ____________________ (feed) through the roots with plant food and water that ____________________ (control) by a computer.
4. Thirty days later, the plants ____________________ (collect) at the other end of the conveyor belts.
5. They may ____________________ (deliver) to the vegetable market the same day.

4 Professional fashion blogger

A Scan the article and use the past participle form of the words in the box to complete the sentences with the passive voice.

concern	**create**	**inspire**	**interest**	**interview**	**notice**

A Passion for Fashion

In just the last ten years, a new job category has been [1]______________: professional fashion blogger. The story of one of the very first professional bloggers is an inspiration to young people everywhere who are [2]______________ with how to make a good living while also doing something that is important to them.

In 2007, Imran Amed, a young Canadian-British citizen who had recently moved to London, decided to take advantage of some free time he had while he wasn't busy working at his job. He sat down in his living room and began to write about something he was passionately [3]______________ in: fashion. Sitting on his sofa, he created a blog that allowed him to communicate with readers who shared his fascination with the fashion industry. Naturally, at the beginning, his readers were mainly his friends and family. But because of his ability to tell interesting and perceptive stories that made readers want to keep on reading, his blog was soon [4]______________ by many people, and by professionals in the industry.

In time, advertisers began to pay Amed's blog, *The Business of Fashion*, for the opportunity to connect with all those readers and potential clients. Amed was also an excellent interviewer. His interviews with Karl Lagerfeld, Natalie Massenet, Nick Knight, and other giants in the fashion industry became another great attraction to his blog. Designers were willing to be [5]______________ by him because his questions and comments were relevant, intelligent, and [6]______________ by his passion for fashion.

Imran Amed, accepting the Business of Fashion Media Award at the 2016 CFDA Fashion Awards

Today, professionals in 200 countries consider *The Business of Fashion* to be required reading in order to keep up with the latest developments in fashion. Thirty employees now fill the demand for information on fashion. More recent fashion blogs like Chiara Ferragni's *The Blonde Salad* in Italy and Sabina Hernandez's blog *Te lo dije nena (I told you, girl)* in Argentina are now also very successful.

Potential professional bloggers, take note: passionate interest is fundamental to success. If you can discover your passion, then the power of that energy will be the magnet that captures and holds your readers' attention. That is exactly what happened one day when Imran Amed sat down and began to write a blog on his sofa.

B Read the article. Check (✓) the true statements according to the article. For the statements that are false, write the true information.

1. ☐ Imran Amed has always lived in London.

____

2. ☐ His family and friends are not interested in fashion and do not read about it.

____

3. ☐ Because Imran Amed knows how to tell an interesting story, many people began to read his blog.

____

4. ☐ Designers enjoy giving interviews to Imran Amed because his questions are intelligent and show that he is interested in fashion.

____

5. ☐ Chiara Ferragni's and Sabina Hernandez's blogs were started before *The Business of Fashion*.

____

6. ☐ If you want to be a professional blogger, the most important thing you will need for success is money.

____

5 Join these sentences with *who* or *that*. Add a comma wherever one is needed.

broadcast presenter

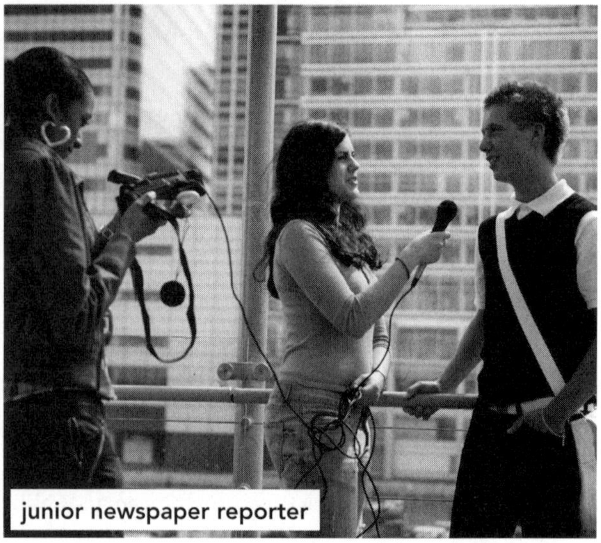
junior newspaper reporter

Examples:

Broadcast presenters are journalists.

They report the news on television.

Broadcast presenters are journalists who report the news on television.

A junior newspaper reporter should be curious.

He or she is often new to journalism.

A junior newspaper reporter, who is often new to journalism, should be curious.

1. An editorial director chooses only the most interesting stories.

   He or she tells the reporters what news stories to cover.

2. A game animator is a skilled artist.

   He or she creates detailed graphics for computer games.

3. A storyboard artist is a creative person.

   He or she illustrates plans for individual scenes for a movie.

4. Stunt people perform dangerous moves in films and TV shows.

   The films and shows have a lot of action scenes.

5. TV sitcoms include actors and actresses.

   They are recognized by television viewers around the world.

6 Match the definitions with the jobs.

1. a cinematographer __g__
2. a film editor _____
3. a gossip columnist _____
4. a graphic designer _____
5. a club DJ _____
6. a band manager _____
7. a web content manager _____
8. a talk show host _____

a. a journalist who specializes in reporting on the personal lives of famous people
b. someone who plays music in a dance club
c. someone that helps a movie director put together the best "takes"
d. a person who is in charge of choosing the text and pictures on a website
e. a TV personality who invites guests to come on his or her program
f. a person who takes care of business for a band
g. a person who operates the main camera during shooting
h. someone that creates the design for a printed work

7 Choose a job from Exercise 6 or another job you're interested in. In the first paragraph, describe the job. In the second paragraph, explain why the job interests you. Use relative clauses in some of your descriptions.

I'd like to be a band manager for a rock or pop band. Band managers are the people who schedule concerts and shows for bands. They also help bands make creative decisions about things like CD covers, magazine interviews, and even music. In addition, band managers who know people in the music business can help a band become successful.

This job interests me because I love music, and I enjoy being around people who sing and play instruments. Also, I'm organized and reliable, and I think that I have the skills that a good band manager needs.

____

____

____

____

____

____

8 Describe six steps in the process of renovating a restaurant. Use the passive form of the verbs given below.

1

2

3

4

5

6

1. First, a renovation plan is approved. (a renovation plan / approve)
2. Next, ______________________________ (new walls / build)
3. Then ______________________________ (the walls / paint)
4. After that, ______________________________ (new lighting / install)
5. Then ______________________________ (new furniture / deliver)
6. Finally, ______________________________ (the restaurant / reopen)

15 A law must be passed!

1 **What should be done about each situation? Write sentences about these pictures, giving your opinion. Use the passive form with *should, shouldn't,* or *ought to.***

1

Leaving large items on the sidewalk

2
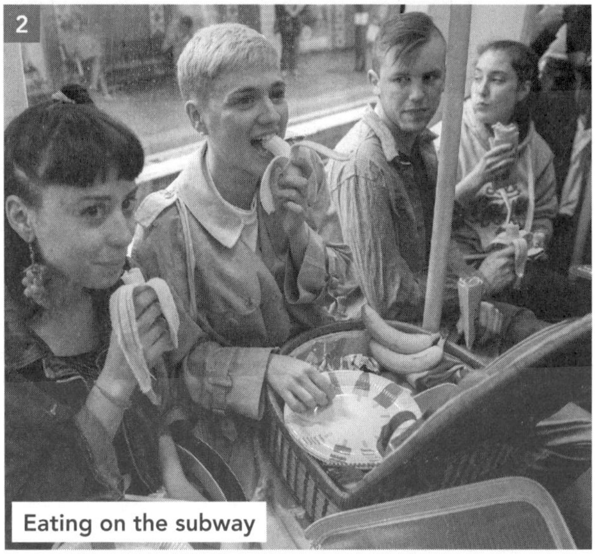
Eating on the subway

3

Playing loud music in your apartment

4

Letting dogs run without leashes

1. *People shouldn't be allowed to leave large items on the sidewalk.* OR
   People ought to be required to take large items to designated dumps.
2. ______________________________
3. ______________________________
4. ______________________________

2 Make recommendations about the situations in these pictures. Use the passive form with *has to, has got to, must,* or *mustn't*.

1

2

3

4

1. A law has to be passed to prevent people from losing their homes. OR
Something must be done to repair abandoned homes.

2. ______________________________

3. ______________________________

4. ______________________________

3 Think of four things that you have strong opinions about. Write your opinions and explain your reasons for them. Use passive modals.

Example: In my opinion, cell phones shouldn't be allowed in class. They distract students from the lesson.

1. I feel that ______________________________

2. I think that ______________________________

3. In my opinion, ______________________________

4. I don't think that ______________________________

4 Respond to these opinions by giving a different one of your own. Use expressions from the box.

That's interesting, but I think . . .
That's not a bad idea. On the other hand, I feel . . .
You may have a point. However, I think . . .
Do you? I'm not sure . . .

1. **A:** Everyone should be required to study Chinese.
   B: You may have a point. However, I think that English is more useful for traveling.
2. **A:** People mustn't be allowed to write unkind things about others on social networking sites.
   B: ______________________________
3. **A:** Public transportation should be provided free of charge.
   B: ______________________________
4. **A:** I think people ought to be required to buy hybrid cars.
   B: ______________________________
5. **A:** In my opinion, all plastic containers should be banned.
   B: ______________________________

5 Getting revenge

A Skim the web posts. What is a revenge story? Why is each of these stories a revenge story?

DO YOU HAVE A REVENGE STORY? SHARE IT!

1. Marcy: I used to have a friend who was a lot of fun. She always loved to go out to eat. There was just one small problem: Every time the server brought the check, she would say, "Uh-oh! I don't have enough money with me. Can I pay you back later?" This was OK the first and second time it happened, but these excuses happened again and again.

I finally got my revenge. The next time we went out for dinner, I said that I had forgotten my wallet. She was shocked, but she paid the check. However, she has never called me to go out again. I guess she was a moocher – a person who always tries to get someone else to pay.

2. Jonathan: My neighbors used to keep rabbits in their yard, but they treated them very badly. Rabbit pens should be cleaned regularly, but these rabbits were dirty, and the smell was really terrible. Worse, I noticed that the rabbits didn't have enough to eat or drink. When I complained to my neighbors, they said, "It's not your problem."

When I called the animal protection society, they said they would investigate. I waited a week, but nothing happened. One night, I stole the rabbits and took them home. The next day I gave them to a local pet store.

3. Chad: I was having problems sleeping because of a dripping noise coming from my air conditioner. I thought the air conditioner needed to be repaired, so I called a technician. She couldn't find anything wrong with it, but she said the dripping was coming from the apartment above me. I asked my neighbor to have his air conditioner checked, but he said, "If you can't sleep, that's your problem!"

The following day I climbed a ladder and turned off the electricity inside the air conditioner. My neighbor had to call the technician to turn it on, and when she did, she also fixed the dripping. It cost him a few dollars, but it was worth it!

B Read the comments. Do you agree or disagree? Write *A* (agree) or *D* (disagree).

_____ **1.** Marcy shouldn't have pretended to lose her wallet. She should have spoken with her friend and told her it was time she paid for a meal.

_____ **2.** I think Marcy did exactly what she ought to have done. Moochers must be taught a lesson!

_____ **3.** People mustn't be permitted to steal. Jonathan made a big mistake, didn't he?

_____ **4.** If people don't take care of their animals, something has got to be done. However, I don't think he should have stolen the rabbits.

_____ **5.** Sometimes neighbors must be taught a lesson. Chad didn't hurt anybody, so I think his nasty neighbor got what he deserved.

_____ **6.** You may have a point about some neighbors, but I think Chad should have called the manager of his building.

C Do you think getting revenge – doing something mean to someone in return – is acceptable behavior? Why or why not?

____

____

____

6 Add tag questions to these statements.

1. Bullying is a serious problem, ___isn't it___?
2. The city doesn't provide enough services for elderly people, ___does it___?
3. You can easily spend all your money on food and rent, ______________?
4. Some unemployed people don't really want to work, ______________?
5. Health care is getting more and more expensive, ______________?
6. There are a lot of homeless people downtown, ______________?
7. Some schools have overcrowded classrooms, ______________?
8. Laws should be passed to reduce street crime, ______________?

7 Nouns and verbs

A Complete the chart.

Noun	Verb	Noun	Verb
advertisement	advertise	______	pollute
______	bully	prohibition	______
______	improve	provision	______
offense	______	______	require
permission	______	______	vandalize

B Write sentences with tag questions using words from the chart. Use four of the nouns and four of the verbs.

1. Bicyclists should be required to wear helmets, shouldn't they?
2. ______________
3. ______________
4. ______________
5. ______________
6. ______________

7. ______________
8. ______________
9. ______________

8 Give one reason for and one reason against these opinions.

1. Children should be made to study a foreign language in primary school.
   For: It would help children understand other cultures.
   Against: I don't think it would be easy to find enough teachers.
2. Schools should punish students who bully other children.
   For: ______________________
   Against: ______________________
3. More tax money ought to be spent on cleaning up vandalism.
   For: ______________________
   Against: ______________________
4. Stray animals should be cared for in animal shelters.
   For: ______________________
   Against: ______________________

9 Complete the conversation. Use passive modals and tag questions.

Gina: You know, I just moved into this new apartment building, and I thought everything would be really great now.

Alec: What's the problem?

Gina: Well, yesterday, the manager gave me a copy of the house rules. I found out that I can't park my moped on the sidewalk in front of the building anymore.

Alec: But people shouldn't ______________________ (permit) to park their bikes or mopeds there.

Gina: Why not? There isn't any other place to park, ______________________? I guess I'll have to park on the street now.

Alec: I'm sorry that parking somewhere else will be inconvenient, but don't you agree that people shouldn't ______________________ (allow) to block the sidewalk or the entrance to the building?

Gina: Well, you may have a point, but parking spaces for all types of cycles need ______________________ (provide) for renters here. All renters with a car have a parking space, ______________________?

Alec: Well, yes, you're right. You should go to the next renters' meeting and discuss the issue with everyone else.

Gina: That's not a bad idea. My voice ought ______________________ (hear) as much as anyone else's – I think I will!

16 Reaching your goals

1 Match each profession with the correct achievement.

☐ actor	☐ student	☐ volunteer
☐ parent	☐ nurse	☑ high school counselor

1. I've managed to help hundreds of students get into college. high school counselor
2. I was able to clean litter from dozens of beaches over the last three years. ____________
3. I managed to maintain an A average during my last four years of school. ____________
4. I've been able to work with many of my favorite movie stars. ____________
5. I've managed to teach my children how to be responsible citizens. ____________
6. I've been able to help sick people feel better. ____________

2 Choosing a job

A Complete the chart with your own ideas.

Job	Goals of people with this profession	
1. social worker	help people	
2. university professor	educate people	
3. small-business owner		
4. emergency-room nurse		

B Complete these sentences with your ideas from part A. Try to add more details.

1. As a social worker, Jane hopes she'll have helped poor and elderly people in her community.
   She'd also like to have ____________
2. As a university professor three years from now, Paul hopes he'll have ____________
   ____
   He'd also like to have ____________
   ____
3. By this time next year, Jake, a small business owner, would like to have ____________
   ____
   In addition, he hopes he'll have ____________
   ____
4. In the next five years, Amy, an emergency-room nurse, hopes she'll have ____________
   ____
   In addition, she'd like to have ____________

3 **Write two paragraphs about an issue that is important to you. In the first paragraph, describe a past achievement related to that issue. In the second paragraph, describe a goal.**

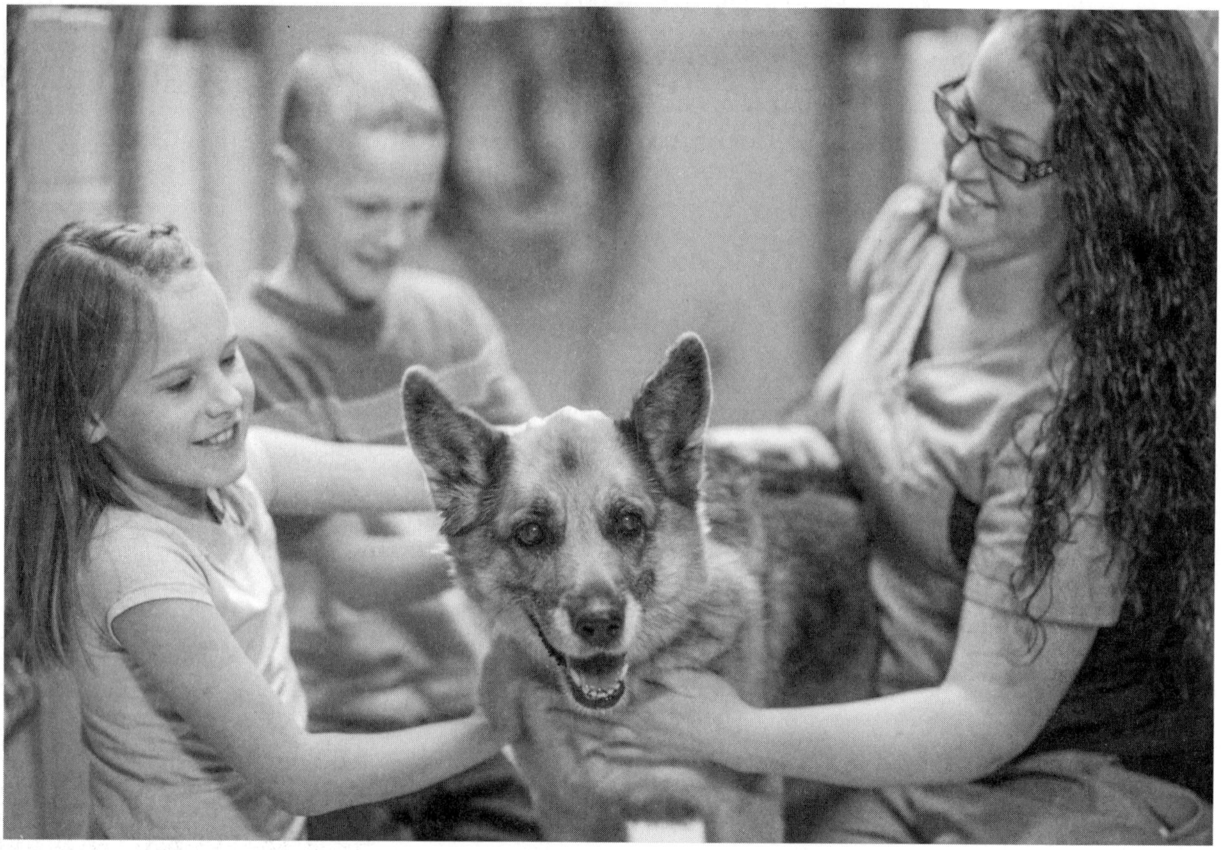

Last year, I began volunteering at a local animal shelter. I managed to help find homes for over twenty cats and dogs in one year. It was an incredibly rewarding experience.

In the next few years, I hope to help more animals find homes. I'd like to have placed a hundred pets in homes over the next four years.

4 The challenge of a lifetime

A Scan the first paragraph of the article. Where is Rupert Isaacson from? Where are his parents from? Where did he go?

RUPERT ISAACSON

Rupert Isaacson is a man who has faced a major challenge in his life. The son of parents who were born in Africa, he grew up in London and in the English countryside, where he discovered his love of horses. Because he grew up hearing so many fascinating memories about Africa from his parents, he went there and lived with nomadic people called the Bushmen of the Kalahari Desert. He then wrote a book, *The Healing Land*, about his experiences with the Bushmen and the problems of survival they face in the twenty-first century.

By the year 2000, Rupert was already managing to make a living as a journalist, writing articles and guidebooks about Africa and India. It was in India that he met his wife, Kristin. Today, they live with their son, Rowan, just outside of Austin, Texas, in the U.S. But Rupert faced the greatest challenge of his life when, at the age of two, Rowan was diagnosed with autism, a condition that affects people's ability to communicate and interact socially with others.

Rupert discovered that spending time with horses and riding them was helping Rowan. The presence of the horses was very calming to the boy. Rupert also knew that the Bushmen of the Kalahari possessed great knowledge about healing. He thought that if he could find a group of people with healing powers and a great knowledge of horses, there could be a possibility of helping his son. Unfortunately, the Bushmen of the Kalahari do not have horses.

So the family set off for Mongolia, where horses have been important for thousands of years. Rupert has written about this journey dedicated to helping his son in *Horse Boy*, and he has produced a documentary of the same name. In the film, viewers have the opportunity to see the family traveling in Mongolia, riding horses, and meeting healers in order to help Rowan.

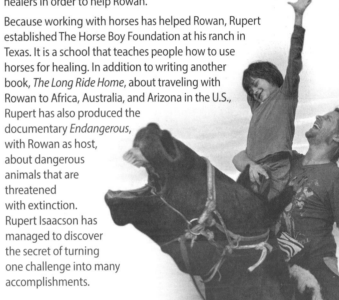

Because working with horses has helped Rowan, Rupert established The Horse Boy Foundation at his ranch in Texas. It is a school that teaches people how to use horses for healing. In addition to writing another book, *The Long Ride Home*, about traveling with Rowan to Africa, Australia, and Arizona in the U.S., Rupert has also produced the documentary *Endangerous*, with Rowan as host, about dangerous animals that are threatened with extinction. Rupert Isaacson has managed to discover the secret of turning one challenge into many accomplishments.

B Read the article. What is the challenge that Rupert Isaacson faced? What was one of the solutions to this challenge that Rupert found?

Challenge: ______________________________

Solution: ______________________________

C Answer the questions.

1. How does autism affect people?

____

2. Why did Rupert's family go to Mongolia?

____

3. What is the purpose of The Horse Boy Foundation?

____

4. What does Rowan do in *Endangerous*?

____

5. List three accomplishments of Rupert Isaacson.

____

5 Choose the correct word.

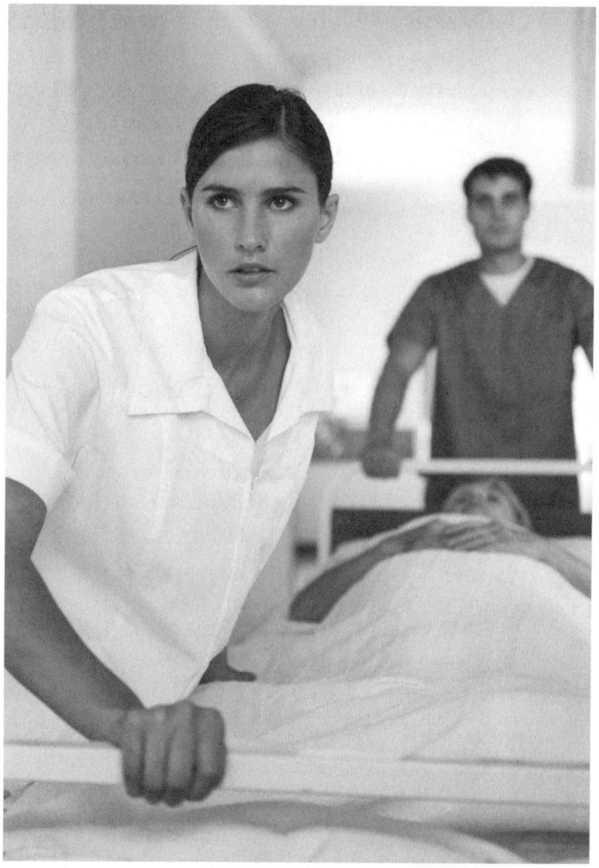

1. It's not good to be ______________________ if you're an emergency-room nurse. (courageous / timid / upbeat)
2. If teachers are going to be successful, they have to be ______________________. (dependent / rigid / resourceful)
3. You have to be ______________________ if you work as a volunteer. (adaptable / cynical / unimaginative)
4. If you take a job far from your family and friends, you have to be ______________________. (compassionate / dependent / self-sufficient)
5. One of the most important things about working with children is being positive and not ______________________. (adaptable / cynical / resourceful)
6. Being a role model for troubled youths requires someone who is strong and ______________________. (compassionate / insensitive / timid)

6 Read each sentence. Write *A* for achievement or *G* for goal.

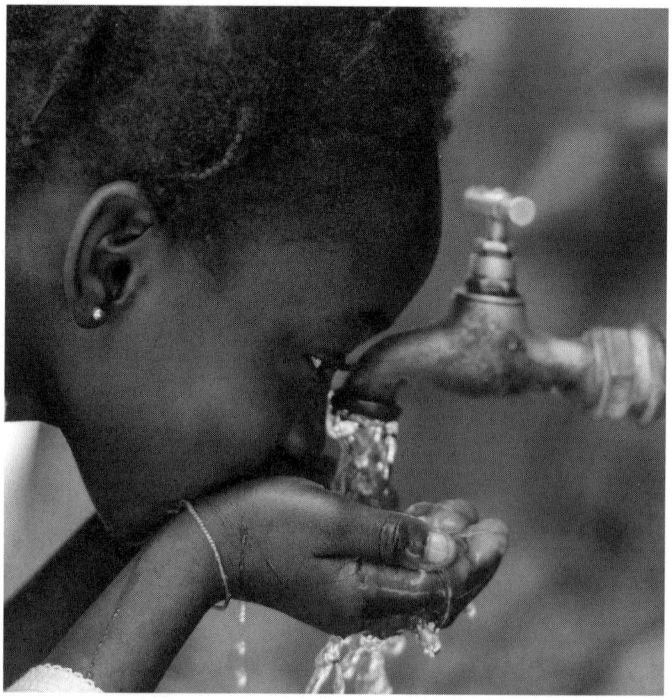

1. I've been able to provide clean water to three villages during my time as a Peace Corps volunteer. _____
2. By the time I'm 35, I'd like to have lived in a culture that's very different from my own. _____
3. While I was working abroad in Tokyo, I managed to learn to speak Japanese fluently. _____
4. After my time with Habitat for Humanity, I hope to have made a significant and positive difference in people's lives. _____
5. I'd like to have gotten another degree in two years. _____
6. I hope I'll have gotten married by the time I'm 30. _____

7 Accomplishments and goals

A Match the verbs with the nouns. Write the collocations. (More than one answer may be possible.)

Verb	Noun	
buy	a change	1. buy a house
get	debts	2. ______
learn	a house	3. ______
make	a promotion	4. ______
meet	new skills	5. ______
pay off	someone special	6. ______

B Write one sentence about an accomplishment and another sentence about a goal. Use the words in part A and your own ideas.

1. My sister and her husband have managed to save enough money to buy a house. I expect to have bought a house within five years.
2. ______
3. ______
4. ______
5. ______
6. ______

8 Personal portraits

A Write three sentences about the accomplishments of someone you know very well. Use the present perfect or simple past.

By investing his money carefully, my neighbor Enrico was able to retire at 40. Since then, he has managed to set up an organization that helps find jobs for people who are homeless. In addition, he has volunteered his time at a homeless shelter in the city.

____

____

____

____

B Write three sentences about things the same person would like to have achieved in ten years. Use the future perfect or *would like to have* + past participle.

Enrico would like to have started an organization to provide scholarships for needy college students by the time he's 50. He hopes to travel a lot, too. In fact, he hopes he'll have traveled all through Southeast Asia.

____

____

____

____

____